Robert Florey,
The French Expressionist

by Brian Taves

WITH A FOREWORD BY
Lloyd Nolan

BEARMANOR MEDIA
2014

Robert Florey, The French Expressionist
© 2014 Brian Taves. All Rights Reserved.

No part of this book may be reproduced in any form or by any means, electronic, mechanical, digital, photocopying or recording, except for the inclusion in a review, without permission in writing from the publisher.

Published in the USA by:
BearManor Media
PO Box 1129
Duncan, Oklahoma 73534-1129
www.bearmanormedia.com

ISBN 978-1-59393-762-1

Printed in the United States of America.
Book reconstruction by Brian Pearce | Red Jacket Press.

Library of Congress Cataloging-in-Publication Data

Taves, Brian, 1959-
Robert Florey, the French expressionist / by Brian Taves ; with a foreword by Lloyd Nolan.
    pages cm
Originally published: Metuchen, New Jersey : The Scarecrow Press, 1987.
Includes bibliographical references, filmographies and index.
ISBN 978-1-59393-762-1 (pbk.)
1. Florey, Robert, 1900-1979. 2. Motion picture producers and directors--United States--Biography. 3. Motion picture producers and directors--France--Biography. 4. Expressionism. I. Title.
PN1998.3.F625T38 2014
791.4302'33092--dc23
[B]

2014010736

To

VIRGINIA FLOREY

for her kindness and encouragement

During almost a half-century in the movies, from 1916 to 1963, Robert Florey directed 65 features and 220 television films at most of the major studios. His greatest success came in thrillers, scripting the original *Frankenstein* and directing such horror classics as *Murders in the Rue Morgue* and *The Beast with Five Fingers*.

Displaying skill in many genres, Florey also co-directed two renowned comedies, *The Cocoanuts* and *Monsieur Verdoux*. He was always known as an artist, gaining fame first through his experimental shorts, beginning with *The Life and Death of 9413 —A Hollywood Extra*, and his features remained distinctive for integrating European filmmaking styles into the Hollywood studio system.

Author Brian Taves takes advantage of numerous primary sources, including studio archives, interviews with associates, and access to all of Florey's papers. Taves thoroughly analyzes and locates Florey's films within the context of the times, relating them to such topics as the influence of expressionism and other techniques, the realm of the "B" film, the position of the contract director in the studio system, and the transition of movie talent to television.

This new edition of a book out of print since 1995 may permit many more cinephiles to learn of Florey's remarkable career.

"A book on Florey is long overdue... Now the job has been done, and done magnificently... I've already used the book in one of my film history courses, and I hope it'll find is way on to a lot of university shelves. And for the film history enthusiast, it's a must... Worth every penny..."

William K. Everson, *Films in Review*

"One of the most ambitious studies of a director who worked largely in B filmmaking..."

Kristin Thompson, University of Wisconsin-Madison

"Essential... An epic work that every horror fan should own... The depth of interpretation of Florey's style, his background, his detailed film career as recreated by Taves is simply gripping in its detail."

Gary J. Svehla, *Midnight Marquee*

CONTENTS

Preface to The New Edition	vii
Acknowledgments	ix
Foreword, by Lloyd Nolan	xi
Introduction	xv
I. An Artist in the Studio System	1
II. 1900-1928: Early Years	65
III. 1928-1932: First Major Commercial Films	104
IV. 1932-1939: Long-Term Contract Director	160
V. 1940-1950: Short-Term Contracts and Independent	230
VI. 1951-1963: Television Pioneer	315
VII. 1964-1979: Retirement	336
Conclusion	342
Bibliography	345
Appendix A: Books by Robert Florey	351
Appendix B: Filmography	353
Appendix C: Television Filmography	383
Appendix D: Charles Chaplin's Tirade Between Takes of Monsieur Verdoux (transcribed by Robert Florey)	393
Index	397

PREFACE TO THE NEW EDITION

Back in 1981, when I began this book as a Master's thesis at the University of Southern California, Florey had passed away a mere two years earlier. Only for his direction of <u>The Cocoanuts</u> and <u>Murders in the Rue Morgue</u>, and his writing of <u>Frankenstein</u>, had he been recognized. Even Florey's avant-garde films were better remembered for the brief collaboration with Slavko Vorkapich.

More than thirty years later, all this has changed. Florey's films have become more accessible, restored by archives, and preserved, screened, and released on video. Such channels as Turner Classic Movies have had entire days devoted to Florey, and his output continues to be shown not only in this country, but overseas as well. His contributions to such television series as <u>Twilight Zone</u>, <u>Alfred Hitchcock Presents</u>, <u>Thriller</u> with Boris Karloff, and <u>Outer Limits</u> remain perennials in re-runs.

Florey's avant-garde films made from 1927 to 1929 have emerged and are now far more widely seen than in their own time. The last surviving print of <u>Skyscraper Symphony</u> was located at Gosfilmofond to receive acclaim at Le Giornate del Cinema Muto in Italy, followed by DVD release in a National Film Preservation Board collection. <u>The Love of Zero</u>, preserved but largely unseen in archival vaults, also received DVD release, and both are now viewed alongside <u>The Life and Death of 9413 -- A Hollywood Extra</u>, a staple of film study for decades. There is no longer any question of Florey's contribution to the emergence of American experimental filmmaking.

Florey's films have now been the subject of countless articles and highlighted in numerous books. The contribution of my own first biography is for others to say; at the time I began, it was difficult to even find a complete filmography of Florey's feature films. And I vividly recall the challenging task of compiling the initial list of his television credits, from sources as diverse as Florey's own script collection to photos in his albums.

Over the years since writing this book, I authored a number of articles and chapters in anthologies, filling in various gaps in the pages of <u>Robert Florey, the French Expressionist</u>. A movie would become accessible, or I was able to offer in print information that was not possible to include in the book, or sometimes I could address topics in a broader context. A list of these essays is included on the final two pages of this new edition.

I had the pleasure of growing up as a friend of Robert and Virginia Florey; his wife, and my mother, had become friends in 1950, and remained so until Virginia Florey's passing fifty years later, in 2000. Robert Florey was a mentor who encouraged all of my historical and literary interests, but he preferred to talk about others rather than himself. I hope this book will make up for his reticence and allow his story to be fully told; this new edition of a book out of print since 1995 may permit many more cinephiles to learn of Florey's remarkable career.

ACKNOWLEDGMENTS

My deepest appreciation goes to Virginia Florey, whose patience, kindness, and graciousness over the years has been boundless. I am honored that Lloyd Nolan agreed to write a Foreword, as well as grant me an interview; other friends and professional associates of Florey supplied me with valuable reminiscences, including Irving Rapper, Willard Sheldon, Leon Ames, George Folsey, and Robert Buckner.

To Evelyn Copeland, who generously spent countless hours translating French into English and corrected my manuscript, I am deeply grateful. This book had its origins as a project towards a Master's degree in Cinema History and Criticism at the University of Southern California, and I was fortunate to have the guidance of Dr. Richard Jewell, a wise mentor whose revisions and encouragement made enormous contributions.

A number of others were exceptionally helpful as I gathered the necessary resources for this critical biography. Jack Spears, author of the pioneering 1960 Films in Review article on Robert Florey, graciously shared his memories of Florey and further information. Mr. Spears, along with James Curtis, Carlos Clarens, Ray Cabana and Anthony Slide, generously gave me copies of their correspondence with Florey. Kit Parker Films allowed me to examine their print of Meet Boston Blackie, David Bradley screened his print of The Hole in the Wall, and Ray Cabana and John Foster made a videotape of Those We Love, all important films I would not have been able to see otherwise. Christine Colgan loaned me copies of Dangerously They Live and National Archives documents relating to The Desert Song from her own Warner Bros. research. Ned Comstock's archival skills made it possible for me to make the fullest possible use of the cinema and television collections at the University of Southern California. The recent revival of Florey films at the University of California, Los Angeles, was of timely assistance, and Robert Gitt helped me to view films at the UCLA Film Archives.

Finally, I am most grateful to my mother, who not only inspired me, but has assisted with this project over the years and endured its tribulations. Nothing would have been possible without her concern, care and never-ending understanding.

FOREWORD

I'm delighted to be asked to write a foreword to this book on Robert Florey. I am especially indebted for the information it supplied me on Bob's youth in Paris and Switzerland and the early days in Hollywood. In spite of my lengthy friendship with Bob and the four pictures we had done together, I had no inkling of the wealth of American film experience, between 1921 and 1936, that he had already gathered. Although he was only two years my senior, he had been a professional at least ten years longer than I.

I had done roughly eleven pictures under contract to Paramount before I was assigned to <u>King of Gamblers</u> in March 1937, with Florey in the director's chair. He put on a deliberate little act for the cast, with a "Well, what do we do today?" attitude. I soon found out he knew the script backwards; he also knew the cuts and additions to be made--and just about how many days he expected to come in under schedule. He knew what sets could be converted, in a matter of minutes, by adding a ship's lifeboat, an arbor, park benches, a reversible doorway, etc., to the background with, of course, an artist's change of lighting. Bob had handled many types of cameras, good or bad, in his early days, and that knowledge gained him the respect and cooperation of all his technicians. He had that instinctive ability of a cameraman to create a mood in lighting, sets, and so forth. On the whole, he was better equipped in terms of talent than most of the other directors, despite not having the resources of big budgets and numerous stars that many of his colleagues were given.

Most of the time he would try to finish a "B" in three six-day weeks, with only a half-hour for lunch. Studio policy was to work you on Saturday until midnight, then give you a twelve o'clock call Monday. By the time you got home

Lloyd Nolan, Akim Tamiroff, and Claire Trevor in Robert Florey's King of Gamblers (Paramount, 1937).

and got to sleep you probably slept all day Sunday, too, and then started again Monday. They were long, hard-working hours.

A review of the acting talent used by Paramount in these films adds unexpected luster: Akim Tamiroff, from the Russian theater and one of the greatest character actors in American cinema; Robert Preston, whose first appearance on film foretold the tremendous career that would follow; Claire Trevor, brilliant actress and just as brilliant a painter; Tony Quinn, a young and eager novice at that time, whose subsequent career needs no embellishing; and Gail Patrick. J. Carrol Naish, an Irishman who made his career as a dark Italian and who was also a great punster and mischief-maker, played a gangster hiding in the garb of an elderly lady for King of Alcatraz--and walked around the lot, unrecognized in his costume, mumbling the most obscene language! Others, veterans

Foreword

of both theater and screen, who deserve mention were Mary Boland, Evelyn Brent, Anna May Wong, Russell Hicks, Robert Gleckler and, in one of her last appearances as an actress, Hedda Hopper. These are all artists (and I'm sorry if I missed some of them) whose names would add to any cast.

Paramount had a pool of truly excellent actors, and we formed a kind of rotating stock company of players for the studio to draw upon, each of us reappearing often in similar roles. Akim Tamiroff, Porter Hall, Harvey Stephens, Barlowe Borland, and I starred in King of Gamblers, and later that same year were reunited in Dangerous to Know, joined by Anthony Quinn and Gail Patrick. The next year Patrick, Quinn, Hall, and I were together again in King of Alcatraz. Finally, I was with Tamiroff under Florey's direction one last time in The Magnificent Fraud at the beginning of 1939, a movie that was a favorite of everyone involved.

Those four with Florey directing were all solid pictures, exciting and great fun in the making. I look back upon them with great fondness and gratitude to Bob. He, too, enjoyed them. I cite one instance. In King of Alcatraz Florey dubbed me "Big Beast" and Robert Preston "Little Beast." (Why? We had no idea--and it takes his Gallic accent to make it funny.) At the end of a long scene and seven or eight takes he would yell, "Print it!" open his director's desk, and throw a large rubber fish at our feet! That was our reward for being "good beasts"; the scene was done and he was throwing the fish to the trained seals. That was good for several laughs until I stole the rubber fish. He had a lovely sense of humor.

I think we had only one or two arguments. He was so amazingly fast that at times I thought he was neglecting important points. I remember one time he said, "If you want to direct the scene, do it," and, to his surprise, I did. "Stand out of the way," I said. It was a simple thing, easy to do, but he let me do it. He said, "Are you happy?" and I said "Yes, now I'll feel better." He was, to my way of thinking, brushing off the scene, where I thought it needed a bit more emphasis. But it was nothing bitter.

Years later Bob urged that I become involved in Four Star Playhouse. For some reason I didn't listen, although I wish I had, since it became such a successful series under his direction. I've always been sorry that I was never able to read any of his many interesting books on Hollywood, since they were all written in French; it's too bad they have not been translated. Bob Florey and I were close friends for over forty years. I used to come over and see his French historical museum, and still remember vividly just how fascinating it was during each visit. It is good to know that at last his life and films are receiving the recognition so long overdue.

Lloyd Nolan

INTRODUCTION

Consider this combination of credits:

- screenwriter of the original Frankenstein and eight other films;

- co-director of two of the most famous comedies of all time--The Cocoanuts, in which the Marx Brothers made their debut in the cinema, and Monsieur Verdoux, with Charlie Chaplin;

- creator of the first American avant-garde movies, including The Life and Death of 9413--a Hollywood Extra;

- pioneer in television, leading major motion picture directors into the new medium of filmed anthology drama in the early 1950s;

- director of three classic horror movies, Murders in the Rue Morgue, The Face Behind the Mask, and The Beast with Five Fingers, along with many other superb thrillers;

- premier historian-director of Hollywood, authoring over a dozen books and countless articles chronicling the development of motion pictures.

Add to this that he directed in virtually every corner of the globe, from the Orient and the South Seas to Mexico; in England, France, and Germany; and in most of the major Hollywood studios. Even with all these impressive achievements, the man responsible for them, Robert Florey (1900-1979), is not so well known as one would expect. But as his credits prove, his was one of the most remarkable careers in

Hollywood, spanning sixty-five features, dozens of shorts, and over 250 television shows.

This record indicates that Florey deserves to be the subject of far more attention than he has received to date, and it is the aim of this book to clarify the position of this important figure in the landscape of cinema history.

Robert Florey has been recognized as one of the few avant-garde filmmakers who became a prominent director in the major studios, although these commercial years were anything but ordinary. While becoming a director of critically and popularly successful features, he managed to remain true to his artistic integrity and background. Even as he labored during the golden age of the studio system, he was always in rebellion against its restrictions, causing him to seldom stay more than a few years at any one company before switching to another. He struggled for a measure of independence that was usually denied, yet managed to turn out a distinctive product. These tendencies and his continued interest in experimentation often deprived him of the big budget movies merited by his talents, bringing about a long association with medium-to-low budget pictures. However, he turned this potential liability into an advantage, becoming one of the most proficient of the so-called "B" directors. Florey used such products as vehicles to practice the integration of European and artistic techniques into the mainstream of American filmmaking. Although primarily a visual stylist, he was also a screenwriter--usually in collaboration with others--performing both tasks on some of his most significant movies.

I was fortunate to be a friend of Robert Florey for the last dozen years of his life. However, the respect and affection I have for him as an individual has not interfered with my critical objectivity. This project was not conceived until after Florey's death, when I saw a number of his pictures and formed an intense admiration for them.

The personal knowledge I have of Florey has given me special insight into his life and work. For example, I knew him best, during our friendship, for his infectious love of history; I encountered firsthand his reluctance to talk about himself. Indeed, by his own request, on only one occasion--during my last visit to him, just months before he died--did we ever discuss his filmmaking career. Similarly, in all his

Introduction   xvii

books on the history of Hollywood, only two chapters ("Ma Carrière à Hollywood" and "En Travaillant avec Charlot") in <u>Hollywood D'Hier et D'Aujourd'Hui</u> are autobiographical, and even these tend to de-emphasize his own work.

   However, his widow, Virginia Florey, has, with infinite kindness and patience, answered endless questions during the last few years. She gave me complete access to all of Florey's private memorabilia, including photograph albums, scrapbooks, clippings, scripts, letters, stills, etc. An added perspective on Florey was provided by a number of his professional associates, to whom I am very grateful for granting me interviews and letters: actors Lloyd Nolan and Leon Ames, cameramen George Folsey and Paul Ivano, directors Irving Rapper, Henry King, and Willard Sheldon (also a production manager), and writers Robert Buckner (also a producer), Marguerite Roberts, and Malvin Wald. Inside details of Florey's relationship with the studios were provided by the Warner Bros., Universal, and Florey television script collections at the University of Southern California. (A smaller duplicate collection of Florey's television scripts exists at Columbia University.) Together with my viewing of Florey's movies, all of this has enabled the writing of a study based chiefly on primary resources.

   The principal effort here has been to discern the qualities Florey brought to his pictures, describing what makes them so typically his own while drawing attention to specific neglected works whose virtues deserve more notice. The films have not only been judged by their capacity to endure and affect audiences today, but also placed in their historical context to achieve a fair and thorough evaluation. Florey's artistic achievements and unique style stand out clearly, indicating his importance as an individual creator amid the studio system.

Brian Taves

Chapter I

AN ARTIST IN THE STUDIO SYSTEM

FLOREY AND THE "B" SYNDROME

Robert Florey is usually known as a director of "B" films. But is this a correct label--and just what is a "B" movie? Technically speaking, the bulk of his features were made on medium rather than high budgets; just over one half were of this variety. But "B" pictures are all too often thought of as minor efforts by definition, and this has sometimes caused Florey to be labeled unimportant, especially since he spent so long in the field. Such an argument is faulty for several reasons.

What does the term "B" mean? For the purposes of this study, it has been defined by a variety of possible character- istics: a shooting schedule of no more than five weeks, the absence of any big name stars, and exhibition planned for the lower half of a double bill. To define a "B" film on the basis of a budget of a certain size or smaller is problematic, because of the wide variations in standards set by the different stu- dios. For instance, the amount spent on an M-G-M "B" was about the same as what Universal might spend on one of its major features. Similarly, in the early 1930s, most Warner Bros. movies, even fairly significant ones such as <u>Smarty</u> or <u>I Sell Anything</u>, were shot in about three weeks, and this hardly reduced them to the "B" category. To judge by run- ning times can also be deceptive, because of the differences over the years and in studio pacing: a Warner Bros. "A" might run as long as a more leisurely paced Paramount "B." Therefore, drawing exact lines of demarcation is next to im- possible because many pictures straddled "A" and "B." Just

1

as quite a few "Bs" turned out better than, and were released as, "A" movies, many big-budget films could barely pass muster on the bottom of a double bill. Florey had his share of the former, including such unexpectedly successful movies as <u>The Pay-Off</u> and <u>Dangerously They Live</u>.

Sadly, the term "B" has been abused and overused. Surely, for instance, there is a difference between a Mascot production and a major studio low budget picture, between a film made in twelve days and one made in five weeks, or between one with a cast of unknowns and one offering quite recognizable names, if not of top-draw marquee value. "B" movies are not necessarily derived from Poverty Row studios. Each of the majors had a "B" unit to supply their theaters' demand for double bills. It was companies like Monogram, Grand National and (for a time) Republic that specialized in "B" movies, and their conception of what these pictures entailed was widely divergent from that held by the majors --usually to the extent of tens of thousands of dollars or more. Yet all of these are frequently lumped together under the umbrella term "B." This leads to a degree of inexactitude and misunderstanding that has yet to be adequately addressed in cinema studies.

Don Miller[1] attempts to overcome this difficulty by using the term "programmer," whose precise meaning has often itself been rather nebulous. Although some regard programmer as synonymous with "B," Miller uses it to describe those films which fall somewhere between "A" and "B." Characteristics of these "nervous As" or "gilt-edged Bs" include reasonably elaborate sets, one or two moderately well-paid performers, and running times of about seventy or eighty minutes. While they might play the top half of a double bill, programmers did not attain the aura of prestige and splendor usually associated with "A" movies. However, they could combine some of the best features of "B" films, such as the willingness to experiment with content and style, without any of the attendant drawbacks of low budgets. Most of the movies from the major studios aimed at the lower half of a double bill were in fact programmers, with true "B" films usually shunned and left to the minors and the miserliness of Poverty Row. If this tripartite scheme is utilized--and it has been adopted for this study--Florey is revealed, properly speaking, to have been more often employed in the realm of the programmer than the "B." For instance, such pictures as <u>Don't Bet on Blondes</u>

and <u>King of Gamblers</u> are programmers rather than "B" movies. Boosted by stars like Warren William and Claire Trevor, along with some elegant sets, they are only barred from "A" status by relatively short running times and the fact they do not have the typical gloss expected for such a position.

"B" films also have a temporal context sometimes ignored. The type arose in the early 1930s in an effort to fill up double bills cheaply, a gimmick instituted to bolster sagging attendance during the Depression. Double bills would pair an "A" with an inexpensive "B," or place two medium budget programmers side by side, each having one or two major stars. Studios wanted increasingly impoverished audiences to believe they were receiving twice their money's worth, when in actuality they were offered something more like one-and-a-half times what their money had previously obtained.

The heyday of the "B" movie was from the mid-1930s to the end of World War II. In the following years, as attendance fell again, so did the faith in the "B" as an antidote, and the reliance and need for such films diminished as the studios lost their theaters and movie houses closed. Pictures planned as only filler material became too risky when there was little guarantee of regular weekly attendance. Thus, for example, the last feature Florey directed, <u>The Vicious Years</u> in 1949, though made in twelve days on a low budget with minor players, was not planned as fare for a double bill. Envisaged as part of a new wave of artistic productions aimed at a specific, if limited, audience, it was sold as a high-quality special attraction.

To assume that Florey must be an unimportant director because he did many so-called "B" movies is doubly mistaken. This view is a result of a misconception of the studio system, as well as of his career. He was originally hired by the majors, after the success of his experimental pictures, in the hope that he would be able to introduce new and provocative types of filmmaking. Irving Rapper, one of his first assistants at Astoria, recalled that Florey was not originally thought of as a possible prestige director, and that he eventually achieved this position was a sign of the tremendous progress he made.[2] Florey did finally achieve promotion to purely big budget movies; every picture he made between 1942-1948 (from <u>The Desert Song</u> through <u>The Crooked Way</u>) was a major production. In fact, this timing has detracted from the critical attention he might have received in recent years if he had been more heavily involved in 1940s film noir. Instead, he had already investigated the themes and style of such movies in his 1930s thrillers. Not until he was directing television in the 1950s did he go on to explore the use of noir again.

Why was this graduation into the top ranks so long in coming? Certainly it was not for lack of competence or reliability. Florey was kept continually and busily employed at the major studios; most of his work was done at Paramount or Warner Bros. But one difficulty in being employed by the best companies was that there was always intense competition for the biggest projects. He was periodically successful, about one third of the time, when he won such important assignments as <u>The Woman in Red</u> or <u>Till We Meet Again</u>. But frequently he found himself pigeon-holed in the "B" unit, although always in its front rank.

Florey's personality also played a role in keeping him relegated so often to the "B" movies. He wanted to be able to work on his own and resented the authority and interference of producers, who were more likely to hold a tight rein where big money was concerned. Because of this, he may have preferred at times the greater liberty generally afforded "B" directors. A favorite saying of his came from the scene in <u>Cyrano de Bergerac</u> when the proud hero rejects the patronage of the Cardinal rather than compromise himself and his art to cater to those in power: "Ne pas monter bien haut peut-être ... mais tout seul!" ("I stand, not high it may be ... but alone!")[3]

While without the enormous ego so typical of many inhabitants of Hollywood, Florey did have a French pride, and habitually refused to flatter the studio moguls or play the games of corporate politics.

> Bob's single problem was always with the studio "brass." He was not a diplomat, or bothered to try very hard, and he did not "suffer fools gladly," and every studio had a good share of them. He often rubbed production managers the wrong way, and had often to be defended against them.... Bob was usually right in what he did, just a bit arbitrary and tactless at times, with an unfortunate

> gift for sarcasm on occasions, but these abrasions left a few scars with the production people: the word got around town that Bob was "difficult" and this hurt him, not personally so much as career-wise. Nothing else retarded his progress and deserved reputation as much as this unfortunate fact.[4]

This evaluation comes from writer-producer Robert Buckner, a man who respected Florey both professionally and as a friend from collaborating together on <u>The Desert Song</u>, <u>God Is My Co-Pilot</u>, and <u>Rogues' Regiment</u>. But even these characteristics did not keep Florey from being regarded as a highly desirable talent by other producers, such as Sam Bischoff, Harold Hurley, William Jacobs, and, in television, Bill Self, Dick Powell, and Walt Disney. As Irving Rapper recalled of his one-time mentor, "Bob would denigrate some people, but not to a point of alienation. He would be a little sarcastic or cryptic, but I thought he had a wholesome respect for people above him." Rapper believed that "Bob would have gotten further if he had fought the right people for better assignments."[5] Thus, Buckner's statement must not be over-generalized, although Florey was known on rare occasions to expel an interfering supervisor from his set.

Another factor contributing to his long period as primarily a "B" director was the nature of the studio system itself. Being under contract, he had to take whatever assignments were offered, regardless of what he thought of them. Not only were his pictures chosen for him--often on very short notice--but he usually had no say whatever in casting, crew, script revisions, or budget. There was little, if any, possibility for protest or appeal; a director's career was controlled by the studios, which could nourish or abuse it as they wished. Yet, as Florey learned, the position of an independent filmmaker was even more precarious than that of one legally bound to the dictates of one company. Using an apt metaphor, he explained it this way.

> When a contract director refused an assignment he was suspended for a number of weeks and had to direct the previously turned down story upon his return, it was as the French say the: marche ou creve--do or die--system.[6]

For one who, like Florey, was determined to be his

own man, this led to much friction and frustration, so that
he seldom stayed more than a few years with any company
before leaving to join another. His penchant for urging the
production of biographies of great historical and artistic figures, as well as literary classics, caused him to be looked
on as a cultural highbrow and impractical intellectual, at
least at Warners. His enthusiasm for such topics was not
understood, especially as he could overwhelm with his detailed knowledge of a subject, as when King Vidor, hiring
Florey as technical advisor on <u>La Boheme</u> in 1926, found
himself promptly presented with twenty books on Bohemian
life. This was not the sort of reputation likely to win quick
advancement in the corporate world, but Florey's priorities
were elsewhere.

> My friends have always told me I was too independ-
> ent ... that I didn't like studio politics and didn't
> cater to the bigwigs. Perhaps it's true. But I
> never liked to ask favors. And if I felt like going
> to Mukden, or Tangiers, or Cartagena or Hongkong
> [<u>sic</u>], I just went for a month, or even six months,
> even if it meant losing a job. I have always felt a
> director should see the world and learn--and feel
> free. So I have had my ups and downs.[7]

However, Florey always preferred to keep busy, even
if it meant accepting some less prestigious projects. He
never assumed the air of an aloof artist, and this allowed
him to be willing to try television at a time when many of
his colleagues still thought the medium beneath them. But
he did not take anything that came his way, as some have
suggested, instead judging a script by its quality rather
than its budget--as in the cases of <u>The Face Behind the
Mask</u> and <u>The Vicious Years</u>. He summed up his philosophy
in this respect as follows.

> If allowed to direct a film adapted from a story he
> believed in, with a cast of his choice and without
> interference from the front office, a director wouldn't
> need any particular studio to make it in. A sound
> stage is a sound stage, they all look alike. An ex-
> cellent picture could be shot in a stable.[8]

While sometimes, as Irving Rapper said, Florey "seemed

An Artist in the Studio System

to be resigned regretfully to doing films unworthy of him,"[9] he resisted any assignment either inferior or unsuited to his skills. Although he always urged better material on the studios and preferred "A" movies, Florey was a realist who knew what was likely to sell; the unproduced scripts he wrote were usually thrillers, although there were a few prestige items.

As a "free spirit who valued his personal liberty within the studio system," unfortunately Florey could never "make that system work for him"[10]--despite the frequent commercial success of his pictures. Even after making an enormously respected and popular film like <u>The House on 56th Street</u>, he would receive as his next project the second-rate <u>Bedside</u>. The same continued to happen in later years, when <u>Danger Signal</u> succeeded <u>God Is My Co-Pilot</u>. Unfortunate and ill-conceived assignments were all too often Florey's lot, particularly under Jack Warner. Thus, Florey was less of a "B" director than one who suffered long under the constraints inherent to contract personnel. Directors commanded little respect or freedom and were intended to serve as cogs in a corporate apparatus whose sole interest was in running prolifically, profitably, and smoothly, often despite--as much as with--the talents of its employees. The effect the studio system had on Florey's career was undoubtedly one of stagnation, slowing down the natural rate of promotion he should have received because of the artistry and commercial and critical success of his output.

But probably the most important reason Florey was so often deprived of the projects he deserved was because of a tendency commonly known to afflict performers: typecasting. Producers discovered that Florey was one of the best directors of "B" movies and simply kept a good thing going. "Florey seemed to be stuck with 'B' films not because of lack of talent, but simply because he did them so efficiently, on time and often under budget."[11] Said Theodore Huff, "Perhaps his genial charm, ability to handle people, knowledge of technique, and reputation for turning out films quickly and smoothly have been something of a handicap ...."[12] Lloyd Nolan, star of three Florey programmers--<u>King of Gamblers</u>, <u>Dangerous to Know</u> and <u>King of Alcatraz</u>--recalled: "None of the 'B' directors were very inspiring, whereas with Bob it was fast, it was fun, and he was talented."[13]

Florey's "B" period lasted from about 1933 to 1942, during which he turned out up to seven movies in a span of twelve months; few directors were ever so prolific. In retrospect, he labeled these "nine hard years."[14] A quick worker, he was able to finish assignments on schedule. He could function within the constraints of a tight budget and fashion a polished product that appeared to have cost more than it did. "That's probably why," said Nolan, the studios, "to Bob's detriment, loved him as a 'B' picture director--because he got it through on time and got a good product out of it."[15] It was precisely Florey's skill at this sort of filmmaking, and talent for overcoming the odds it entailed, that kept him so long from promotion.

Thus, despite the sometimes inherent faults in the narratives, by and large these pictures turned out to be more intriguing than one would expect, markedly above the average for their type. Anthony Slide described Florey in this period as "a man of intelligence and craftsmanship who was responsible for some of the American cinema's best second features...."[16] "Naturally, no matter what company is involved," said William K. Everson, if Florey "worked there they seem to be the best!"[17] Without doubt, he was one of the top, and possibly the very best, director of "B" films at the major studios in the 1930s.[18]

However, the quality that continues to make movies durable and exciting today, and that proves Florey was not a minor director, was the purpose to which he put this prodigious output. "B" movies, being sold on a flat-fee rather than a percentage basis and without having the reputations of major stars to risk, could handle less conventional themes in an innovative manner that would be shunned in the big budget arena (illustrated by <u>Dangerous to Know</u> and <u>The Face Behind the Mask</u>). Florey used his projects of this type as opportunities for experimentation, especially in the adaptation and integration of expressionist and avant-garde styles into the American feature. As such, these "B" films and programmers demonstrated over the years an increasingly sure and expert hand, as Florey manipulated novel techniques into the films ever more appropriately. At the same time it was his ability to stay within budget and schedule that kept him from committing the excesses of a Josef von Sternberg or Orson Welles, thus remaining at work in Hollywood despite sometimes adverse relations with producers. Florey was able

An Artist in the Studio System

to utilize the "B" movie as a form of artistic endeavor--as much, if not more so, than could be seen in most "major" pictures. This fact, along with the high standards he brought to this type of film, indicate Florey was far more than a director of double-bill movies, but was a significant innovator with a most worthwhile purpose.

GENRES

Like so many directors working in the golden age of the Hollywood studio system, Robert Florey was assigned to, and proved a talent for, films in virtually every genre. These ranged from musicals and comedies to war and women's pictures; he enjoyed success in all these disparate types. But the genre in which he was recognized as having the greatest skill was the thriller. These movies were not only the most influential of his output in their day but have best stood the test of time. The following pages will systematically examine his thrillers, as well as the other genres to which he contributed. Little attempt has been made to classify the nearly 250 television shows he directed.

The thriller was the genre in which Florey was most profitably and most prolifically employed. Most of these films were made in the 1930s, particularly at Paramount, where nearly every picture he made was of this type. Largely medium- to low-budget features, they were typically shot on schedules of two to five weeks. The screenplays were unpretentious and, though lacking originality in basic story conception and outline, typically managed to be effective, crisp, and fast moving. Within the extremely limited range of authority given him--he was not allowed to demand rewrites and had minimum preparation time--Florey had to overcome the script's defects as much as possible. He became adept at minimizing such disadvantages, concealing the movie's faults and shortcomings, frequently by application of the expressionist style. His efforts could make a conventional tale both unusual and worthwhile through visual creativity and experimentation, but he also had an interest in people and human emotion that made his thrillers more than mere exercises in style.

King of Gamblers, an unexpectedly virtuoso item that turned out as well as a programmer could, was the film that really started the cycle. The studio noticed the surprisingly good work he did, even when given such an unpromising assignment, and began to regularly hand Florey routine "B" projects with the virtual certainty that his talents would make them into far better dramas than there was any reason to expect. Sometimes he managed to pull off a miracle and repeat the King of Gamblers success, as in Dangerous to Know and King of Alcatraz, while others, such as Daughter of Shanghai and Parole Fixer, had their moments, and a few --Disbarred, Death of a Champion, Women Without Names-- were pictures that "even his considerable wit could brighten only sporadically."[19]

Florey became so proficient at these "B" and program thrillers that he found himself almost typecast, passed over for promotion even when he had proven that his skills merited better projects. He had originally enjoyed thrillers, but soon came to resent them for preventing him from having the opportunity to try other genres. Even in the 1940s and in television he returned again and again to the form; it could well be argued that it was his ability with this type that kept him so busily and consistently employed over such a long span of years.

To examine Florey's contributions to the thriller genre, it will be useful to divide them into several subtypes. The largest number were mysteries. He wrote some scripts of this type, A Study in Scarlet and the unproduced Wormwood Scrubs Murder Cases, along with the Nick Carter and Lone Wolf outlines. In the screenplays, he showed himself to be heavily influenced by the classical British murder mystery, with its dark, fog-bound streets, bevy of suspects, and highly intelligent detective. Florey received his baptism in mystery direction with Girl Missing at Warner Bros., making I Am a Thief and The Florentine Dagger there two years later. His expertise with camera work and recreation of intriguing atmospheres considerably enhanced the latter two, as well as The Preview Murder Mystery and Daughter of Shanghai at Paramount. However, Death of a Champion was too silly, and Danger Signal too muddled, to be much helped by his skills.

Florey also enjoyed spy movies and directed five of this type; most of them, unlike the other thrillers he made, were released as "A" films. Till We Meet Again, Hotel

An Artist in the Studio System

Imperial, Meet Boston Blackie, Dangerously They Live and Rogues' Regiment were all set against wartime backgrounds, and all used the motif of disguises and deception prominently. Each had a pair of innocent lovers who suffer misunderstandings as they become involved in espionage, although the activity eventually brings them together. Florey used expressionism when called for, the style being especially noticeable at first but diluted in the last two pictures.

Before proceeding to related genres, a few other movies in the suspense category should be mentioned. These are I Sell Anything, a comic caper about auction thieves, and The Magnificent Fraud, primarily though not wholly a political conspiracy thriller. Danger Signal and The Crooked Way are also frequently regarded as part of the film noir movement. Florey further labored in translating this style to television in a number of Four Star Playhouse shows, particularly those with Dick Powell, such as Welcome Home and the "Willie Dante" segments.

By the time Florey began to work in the gangster genre during the mid 1930s, its initial heyday was over and the form was in a transitional period. Only one of his gangster films, the semi-documentary Roger Touhy--Gangster, was perfectly tailored to the conventions of the type, while Parole Fixer was a story of the G-men and Women Without Names and Lady Gangster were prison dramas. Two others, King of Gamblers and Dangerous to Know, fell into the archetypal pattern of a criminal's fall from power. But most of Florey's gangster pictures did not fit neatly into the genre. This was especially true of the late 1930s pictures, King of Alcatraz and Disbarred, which may be more accurately described as gangster-thrillers.

Each of these used gangsters as prominent characters, but they had to either share center stage or occupied secondary roles. The gangsters make fatally flawed decisions, setting up a chain of events that will bring about their demise. Everyone, innocent and gangster alike, faced great odds and were vulnerable to sudden and violent death. The gangster often found a weaker character, operating without experience and outside the law, to be the direct cause of his downfall.[20]

The gangster movie seems to have been Florey's least favorite type of thriller, and, from 1939 to 1948, with one exception he avoided them altogether, only returning to the form with The Crooked Way and Johnny One-Eye when employment was becoming scarce. The only gangster film Florey truly liked was Roger Touhy--Gangster because he was able to infuse it with stark realism as a result of the location photography--an innovation for the time. Stylistically, the gangster films were the least expressionistic of all Florey's thrillers. The only one influenced by this style was King of Alcatraz, while King of Gamblers and Dangerous to Know revealed characteristic Paramount high-key gloss, and Parole Fixer foreshadowed the realist drift of the 1940s.

Florey's horror pictures belong to another genre closely related to the thriller. Doubtless his movies of this type are the most famous in his canon; many historians would claim they were also his best work, although no one would have dissented more vigorously from this statement than Florey himself, despite the pleasure he sometimes derived from them. Most (Frankenstein, The Face Behind the Mask, The Beast with Five Fingers) are widely acknowledged masterpieces of the genre, with one clear runner-up (Murders in the Rue Morgue) and another that struggled against the technological constraints of the time (The Hole in the Wall). One reason for their excellence may lie in the influence Florey had over the scripts of each, more than he had with his other genres--co-authoring Frankenstein and Rue Morgue, revising and writing the continuities of Hole in the Wall and Face Behind the Mask, and planning the hallucinatory sequences of Beast with Five Fingers (though much of what he added was awkwardly edited out). Three are pure horror stories (Frankenstein, Rue Morgue, Beast with Five Fingers), as are the unproduced Monsieur de Paris and the famous television show Thriller: The Incredible Doktor Markesan, with Boris Karloff, while two combine horror with elements from the gangster and love story genres (Hole in the Wall, Face Behind the Mask). All were quickly made, in a month or less, although only Face Behind the Mask is, properly speaking, a programmer. Beast with Five Fingers was the notable exception, shot in ten weeks, a schedule that no doubt helped to make possible the elaborate photography.

Florey's horror pictures were the most extreme examples of his application of expressionism to the thriller format. They also illustrate how he used that style in varying ways over the years. At first, his work displayed the overwhelming influence of The Cabinet of Dr. Caligari, with the emphasis on decor and heavily distorted set design. This was necessary in The Hole in the Wall because of the inhibitions sound had placed on the creative potential of the camera; these limitations still had some effect on Frankenstein and Murders in the Rue Morgue. While the expressionism Florey had written into Frankenstein and exhibited in his test was largely misused by James Whale, who directed the film, it came through clearly in Rue Morgue. The later horror movies (The Face Behind the Mask, The Beast with Five Fingers) placed a greater stress on extremely mobile, often angled camera work, as well as the superb characterizations provided by Peter Lorre. The expressionism in these two appears primarily through the photography rather than the decor.

Several other stylistic traits were evident throughout these films. Undoubtedly, the memory of the Grand Guignol plays Florey had known in his youth came to mind. The make-up of the performers was crucial, combining with dramatic lighting and close-ups to delineate character before a word was spoken. The sound effects, musical scores, and vocal intonation all played crucial roles in generating a feeling of dramatic intensity. He realized immediately the importance of the sound track to the horror genre, paying great attention to this element not only in filming but in the scripts as well.

All of the pure horror pictures have a period setting; the combined genre films take place in contemporary times. All are usually marked by some grisly occurrence, a type of mutilation which puts the plot in motion. However, any solemnity is usually relieved by a deliberate streak of frothy light-heartedness. This element was partly due to Florey's "very macabre sense of humor"--as one colleague said[21]--and because he never took horror movies too seriously. Each film has a romantic subplot on which the tale pivots, and when the villain endangers the heroine the drama reaches its high point of excitement.

Florey also directed many comedies and musical comedies. While none of the comedies was especially unique in its treatment, several of them, especially The Cocoanuts, Smarty, and Mountain Music, were extremely popular at the box office. In addition to the hits listed above, The Pusher-in-the-Face, Going Highbrow, Don't Bet on Blondes, and Two in a Taxi belong in this category, one in which Florey's humor was generally in a slapstick vein--although he also did well with 1930s dialogue comedy. While enjoying a few of these, particularly Pusher-in-the-Face, Smarty, and Mountain Music, he virtually abandoned the genre when he turned to television and had a greater say over what he would handle, making only a few comedies as opposed to hundreds of dramas.

However, two comedies remain that do not fit into the above formulas, Le Blanc et le Noir and Monsieur Verdoux, which were different to a large degree because of the dominance of his collaborators. Le Blanc et le Noir, based on the Sacha Guitry play, showed that Florey had a talent for sophisticated European humor; unfortunately this would never have passed American censors. As he wrote:

> Having directed a Sacha Guitry film and other Parisian comedies, I always hoped to be given a similar assignment, or perhaps a good French drama, but it never happened.[22]

Probably the closest Florey ever came to this goal while working in the United States was on Monsieur Verdoux, but it was so tightly controlled by Charlie Chaplin that the only traces of his collaborator's influence was the light-heartedness that occasionally showed through the picture's otherwise bleak view.

Florey had more interest in musicals than in comedy, although the studios never gave him the biographical or artistic musical he always wished to do (at least until he directed The Clara Schumann Story for The Loretta Young Show). While he did a burst of musicals at the beginning of his sound-film career, including many early one-reel talkies, they became rarer as the years went on. Some had dramatic stories, such as Night Club, The Battle of Paris, and the operetta The Desert Song, but most were comedies like the short travelogue Bonjour, New York!, The Cocoanuts, La Route est belle, L'Amour chante (and its Spanish and German versions, El Profesor de mi senora and Komm' Zu Mir Zum Rendez-Vous), Ship Cafe, and This Way Please. Several were "big" movies commercially in terms of budget and popularity, but none has been recognized as historically significant--except for Cocoanuts, with its inventive photography.

Like most directors in the 1940s, Florey found himself assigned to his share of war movies, eagerly proving his ability with several different types. Two were dramas of the homefront, one dealing with espionage (Dangerously They Live), the other with the struggle for increased productivity and the need to accept painful domestic sacrifices in the effort to reach victory (Man from Frisco). Another pair examined the war in the far regions of the world--the adventurous Desert Song, which he also co-authored and contemporized, and God Is My Co-Pilot--and were among Warner Bros. biggest hits of 1944-45. Even after the war, Florey was still interested in the issue of tracking down escaped Nazi war criminals, particularly when they were shielded by official French policy, as he exposed in Rogues' Regiment.

A common theme of all these pictures was that spiritual values do, in the end, triumph over war and its effects. Lovers, while often separated or alienated from each other by the conflict, are eventually brought closer together than ever before. Indeed, there is a gain, rather than a loss, of emotional intensity in combat situations that provides salvation for the fighting man. Florey habitually downplays the confrontations with the enemy, often limiting them to a few scenes, in favor of dwelling on the psychological and emotional--and sometimes political--elements of the story.

Florey dabbled in a few other genres as well. The Pay-Off was a tale of journalism and sports racketeers. Tarzan and the Mermaids was an adventure fantasy. Bedside, Registered Nurse, and Outcast formed a medical trilogy, the first dealing with a crooked but popular physician, while the last portrayed the reverse, an honest doctor who was almost lynched (Warren William played both roles). These, together with Monsieur Verdoux and The Vicious Years, were the closest Florey ever came to the social consciousness film, a type in which he was not interested.

The two genres Florey most wanted to work in were the historical movie and the love story. While he was unable to realize his ambitions with the former, he did make

a large number of "women's" films, at least in the 1930s.
He was attracted to this type because he was a warm-hearted
and sensitive individual who never forgot birthdays or anniversaries and who observed the French custom of Saint's Days
throughout his life in America. Possibly his lonely childhood,
and certainly his happy second marriage, contributed to his
enjoyment of the love story. His own scripts, That Model
From Paris, The Man Called Back, Hollywood Boulevard, and
the unproduced Times So Unsettled Are, were of this genre,
as were The Romantic Age, Face Value, Those We Love,
Ex-Lady, The House on 56th Street, The Woman in Red,
and most of the thirty-eight episodes of A Letter to Loretta
and The Loretta Young Show that he directed for television.
Of course, many of his other movies had romantic subplots.

His chief limitation in dealing with this type of tale
seemed to be his weakness with dialogue, though if there
was the chance to put any movement, atmosphere, or suspense into the scenes his visual ability could overcome the
dialogue problems. The performances were usually more
than adequate, although occasionally the scripts he received
were a bit melodramatic. Most were well-received, and Ex-Lady, The House on 56th Street, and The Woman in Red all
turned out to be strong, effective vehicles for stars Bette
Davis, Kay Francis, and Barbara Stanwyck, respectively;
Loretta Young twice received an Emmy nomination for Best
Actress while under his direction, in 1953 and 1954.

There are a number of motifs that appear in Florey's
"women's" films and in his other pictures containing romantic
subplots. Seldom was there much family presence; if there
were, as in The Woman in Red, the family members were unsympathetic types. The characters were usually alone, without relations--as in Till We Meet Again--and with few friends.
Strangers were generous, trusting, and humane to one another. The two lovers, finding each other, know at once
that what they share is precious and rare. Florey, without
doubt a romantic and a man of sentiment in the best sense
of the words, believed that love and devotion between two
people could exist and endure.

An unusual element in Florey's movies--particularly
considering they came from a Frenchman and a director who
worked mostly in the 1930s and 1940s--was the strength of
his female characters. If one looks at the films where women

play large roles, it becomes clear that in nearly all these pictures women prove to be intelligent, courageous, and seldom submissive to men; there are very few wholly subservient women. No consistently more commanding group of women appeared than those of his spy movies. Gertrude Michael, Isa Miranda, Nancy Coleman, and Marta Toren of Till We Meet Again, Hotel Imperial, Dangerously They Live, and Rogues' Regiment, respectively (and even, to a lesser extent, Rochelle Hudson in Meet Boston Blackie), were every bit as clever and often more forceful than their male counterparts. Even in his gangster and mystery thrillers, genres where women usually play insignificant or weak parts, his female characters were often the protagonists or almost equally important to them. Examples include Anna May Wong in A Study in Scarlet, Daughter of Shanghai, and Dangerous to Know; Ellen Drew in Women Without Names and The Crooked Way; and Gail Patrick in Dangerous to Know, King of Alcatraz, and Disbarred. For instance, Claire Trevor was actually the central character of King of Gamblers, motivating the attentions and rivalry of Lloyd Nolan and Akim Tamiroff, becoming the catalyst for their confrontation and, ultimately though unintentionally, causing Tamiroff's death.

Even the female characters of Florey's "women's" pictures were strong-minded. In the twenty-year span of The House on 56th Street, Kay Francis has four leading men, while Barbara Stanwyck in The Woman in Red refused to conform to the expectations of her high-society in-laws. There were of course many dependent women in Florey's oeuvre, such as in the horror movies--although not in the other thrillers. Principal cases of dominated women include Bette Davis in Ex-Lady and Patricia Morison in The Magnificent Fraud, but while their romantic lives were controlled by men, they periodically did show some independence--as in Ex-Lady--and were seldom completely subordinate.

Florey's experience as a technical director in the 1920s, and his wide-ranging knowledge of the past, would have served him well in historical pictures. His efforts to work in this type--Napoleon, Joan of Arc, Carnival--La Vie Parisienne --shed the greatest light on his own desires as well as the pressures under which he was forced to labor and conform his output.

> At first I was astonished and had to marvel at the
> technical facilities and equipment of the studios;
> however, they did not compensate for the filmmaker's
> ignorance of the life, customs, history, arts and
> habits of the foreign countries. They didn't seem
> to know what I was talking about when I mentioned
> the names of French musicians, authors, painters
> and politicians. Once when I remarked that "Ritch'-
> loo"--as they called Cardinal de Richelieu--would
> not have slept in an Empire bed, no one understood
> why.[23]

This serious interest in the historical field was so well known that it ultimately did him a disservice, preventing him from being assigned to projects in the genre, because the studios were afraid he would be too rigorous in demanding accurate reproductions of the past. At the same time, the reverse was also true--he was not about to be associated with a producer who had no concern for such details, turning down a job with Edward Small because of his reputation for historical distortion and error. The closest Florey came to historical pictures was in co-authoring <u>The Adventures of Don Juan</u> and directing <u>Outpost in Morocco</u>, both period adventure tales. However, a number of his television shows were set in the past and dealt with historical events; perhaps most notable was the Mata Hari story with Merle Oberon, <u>General Electric Theater: I Will Not Die</u>, which he co-scripted as well as directed.

Thus Florey exhibited a versatility with many different genres, and would likely have demonstrated an even greater range had the studios permitted him to do so. However, he was not a director who wished to try his hand at everything; he had his own special interests that remained fairly constant --and too often frustrated. While his thriller work is incontestably the most remarkable, it should not be forgotten that he contributed to many other genres, and that the most prominent trait of his style, the will to experiment, could be found to varying degrees in all the types he tried.

THEMES AND MOTIFS

In view of the times Florey was working in, there was a surprising degree of ambiguity in his stories and characters.

An Artist in the Studio System

He always had mixed feelings about Hollywood and the film industry, feelings which were apparent in his pictures set in movieland. The Magnificent Fraud revealed Florey's ambivalent attitude toward a different subject, analyzing a coup d'état that manages to salvage democracy and a needed foreign loan in a banana republic. While Florey did not denounce war in Till We Meet Again, he endorsed the action of a couple who fled patriotism and the conflict of World War I. Akim Tamiroff, as a gangster with a multifaceted personality in King of Gamblers and Dangerous to Know, had enough virtues so that his death was an event evoking not only relief but sorrow as well. Peter Lorre in The Face Behind the Mask found himself rejected by society and kept from employment because of his disfigurement; a life of crime was the only way to keep himself alive. Though Lorre found revenge satisfying, Isa Miranda discovered that the same emotion in Hotel Imperial led her to endanger the life of a guiltless and brave officer. In The Beast with Five Fingers, Lorre's own crimes drove him insane, but the audience had been forced to enter his mind and share his delusions and torment; as well, his adversaries were an avaricious lot.

Much of this complexity was not so apparent in the scripts and came through mostly in the performances and visual style. As a European, Florey always approached movie making with a continental sophistication and depth often lacking in his American counterparts. He was fully aware of a picture's sub-text and was able to infuse his films with a meaning beyond the surface entertainment, such as in his examination of the French Foreign Legion and colonialism in Rogues' Regiment. Indeed, perhaps it was this quality which led Chaplin to choose Florey as an appropriate collaborator for Monsieur Verdoux.

In Florey's universe, people were often not what they appeared to be. This motif manifested itself in several forms. The most extreme of these was the direct masquerade. This was seen most obviously in the four films dealing with facial mutilation (Face Value, The Florentine Dagger, The Preview Murder Mystery, The Face Behind the Mask) and its consequences on individuals, especially how they were treated by others.

There was a similar group of characters, who, though not literally masked in such a blatant way, deliberately sought to deceive others as to their true identity by pretending to be someone or something they were not--leading, in a sense, double lives. Examples of these masqueraders include the mad scientist of Murders in the Rue Morgue as a part of a carnival sideshow, the spies behind enemy lines in Till We Meet Again and Hotel Imperial, Akim Tamiroff going from actor to dictator in his dual role in The Magnificent Fraud, Arab rebel leader Dennis Morgan hiding either behind a bernouse or as a musician in The Desert Song. Others tried to change themselves in the course of the narrative to escape their past. Such characters included the Marx Brothers becoming real estate brokers in The Cocoanuts, Warren William in Outcast re-establishing his medical practice away from those who knew him, Anna May Wong turning chameleon to track down the smugglers in Daughter of Shanghai, Akim Tamiroff attempting to change from a man of crime to one accepted by society in King of Gamblers and Dangerous to Know, and Nazis Stephen McNally and Henry Rowland trying to hide in the French Foreign Legion in Rogues' Regiment.

While the plot of all these pictures hinged on the use of the masquerade, the same device appeared, though less significantly, in a number of Florey's other movies. Seldom was the use of a mask to achieve a false identity more than temporarily successful; the attempt to change a former self was always uncovered. This literal use of masks, impersonations, and double identities helped to give the characters an increased degree of ambiguity, complexity, uncertainty, and potential for deception. This concept was particularly useful for Florey in his thrillers, adding the element of unpredictability to the plots to help create tension and surprise.

Florey's films tended to center on downtrodden or underdog characters, who received sympathetic treatment. The examples are almost too numerous to mention: the aging actor and extras in Hollywood Boulevard and The Life and Death of 9413--A Hollywood Extra, respectively; the Arabs in The Desert Song, the Chinese of God Is My Co-Pilot, and the Vietnamese of Rogues' Regiment; the couple in Till We Meet Again, and the endangered innocents of Outcast and Women Without Names; Peter Lorre, scarred in The Face Behind the Mask and insane in The Beast with Five Fingers; the orphan of The Vicious Years. Florey seemed to be interested in exposing the plight of these victimized characters,

An Artist in the Studio System

not in a socially-conscious way, but simply and humanely. He presented these people as individuals, not members of collective groups; his interest in them was from an artistic, not political, viewpoint--with the exception of those subjugated by colonial rule, the Arabs, Chinese, and Vietnamese. Perhaps this view can be connected to his childhood, which, though lonely and unhappy because of the premature loss of his parents, was, thanks to his middle-class stepfather, never economically deprived--at least according to the standards of the contemporary French boarding schools.

Florey's characters tended to be unsophisticated, plain-spoken people (in contrast to his own witty and intellectual conversation). Their manner was direct, though never crude or uncouth, except for the most hardened criminals. As often embodied by "B" players, these people lacked much of the typical Hollywood gloss and fakery, making them appear more ordinary, believable, and human, no matter what situation they were thrust into. Gestures, poses, and movements were likely to be simple, perhaps because Florey's training was entirely in the cinema rather than the stage.

There is a strong distinction, of which these individuals were aware, between the powerful and the powerless. The weak were opposed to, and could never be part of, the established, controlling interests of society--whatever side of the law that group was on. The main characters of his pictures were unexceptional; when the powerful were present, it was because someone had been victimized and pushed into a corner from which he could do nothing but fight, regardless of the hopelessness of the outcome.

The life of the ordinary person seemed to be controlled by an arbitrary, incomprehensible fate which randomly forced individuals into positions where they were vulnerable and defenseless. The ironic and the fantastic, the unexpected and the incredible, were all operative forces in Florey's universe which could take over the lives of his characters at any moment. No movie more perfectly epitomizes all these elements than <u>The Face Behind the Mask</u>, but each statement is true to varying degrees in all of his films.

Florey was most proficient at pictures depicting characters on the edge of psychological breakdown, examining their reactions to various degrees of torment and stress.

His stylistic ability with lighting, close-ups, the subjective camera, and bizarre camera angles allowed the audience to share a tormented individual's experiences. Occasionally the trauma is survived, but more often it leads to a seemingly predetermined and unavoidable destiny. Certainly this is the central conflict in the quartet of Florey's most important thrillers, The Florentine Dagger, Dangerous to Know, The Face Behind the Mask, and The Beast with Five Fingers. It also appears in others, such as Danger Signal and The Crooked Way, along with many television films, like his first two Twilight Zone shows (Perchance to Dream and The Fever). The same motif can be found in some of his non-thrillers, including Registered Nurse and God Is My Co-Pilot, as well as many of the movies he wrote: Frankenstein, The Man Called Back, Hollywood Boulevard, Rogues' Regiment--even The Life and Death of 9413--A Hollywood Extra.

These tales of gradual mental disintegration have much in common with the German expressionist school from which Florey drew so much inspiration, except that his contain no trace of the Freudian influence. Some of his most memorable work was in conveying the anguish of wives abused by their husbands, as in The Man Called Back, The Florentine Dagger, Danger Signal and The Golden Opportunity and A Jury of Her Peers segments of Alfred Hitchcock Presents. There was even an unusual acceptance in some of these narratives for the ultimate necessity of murdering their spouse. Florey was also profoundly successful with stories involving characters who take their own life, such as Registered Nurse, The Pay-Off, Dangerous to Know, and The Face Behind the Mask. There was no judgment, certainly no condemnation, of these suicidal individuals on Florey's part. Instead, one finds only a compassionate effort to comprehend the pain that impelled their actions.

Florey's pictures, particularly the gangster thrillers, frequently dealt with an exposé of some contemporary criminal racket. However, "exposé" may be too strong a word for the extremely superficial treatment accorded such activities in these movies. Though they often claimed to be "ripped from the headlines," these topical problems usually were only the springboard for the tale and did not consist of any serious social criticism. Essentially, the studios would try to cloak a standard "B" thriller in the guise of respectability and relevance.

An Artist in the Studio System

The first such film was <u>Bedside</u>, the beginning of a trilogy which included <u>Registered Nurse</u> and <u>Outcast</u> (also an anti-lynching picture), dealing with medical malpractice. In quick order, the spotlight was turned on antique dealers (<u>I Sell Anything</u>), sports racketeers (<u>The Pay-Off</u>), gambling syndicates (<u>King of Gamblers</u>), the importation of illegal aliens (<u>Daughter of Shanghai</u>), political corruption (<u>Dangerous to Know</u>), crooked lawyers (<u>Disbarred</u>), Latin American political capers (<u>The Magnificent Fraud</u>), and abuse of the parole system (<u>Parole Fixer</u>). While these topical themes may have had their roots in the first Warner Bros. period, it was not until his return to Paramount that the cycle began to flourish. Although the genre tended to fade in the 1940s, Florey always remained very cognizant of contemporary events, and films like <u>Dangerously They Live</u>, <u>Desert Song</u>, <u>Man from Frisco</u>, <u>Rogues' Regiment</u>, and <u>The Vicious Years</u> reflect his awareness of what was happening around the world and his own views on the political situations of the time.

Among the films Florey both wrote and directed, he gave two topics thorough examination. The first, during the decade 1927-36, described the plight of the forgotten movie actor (and is discussed fully in the section on <u>Hollywood Boulevard</u>). The second series, made between 1939 and 1948, dealt with issues of international politics, particularly as they related to French colonialism. He directed a half-dozen pictures on foreign matters, enjoying all of them and even co-authoring some. However, all of these--on the surface at least--were action films; while not cautious, they did cloak their viewpoints, avoiding the didacticism of the "message" film. In this way Florey succeeded in placing anti-imperialist themes into the mainstream Hollywood feature.

Robert Florey usually avoided films with overt political content. Even when involved with such projects as <u>Outcast</u>, <u>Monsieur Verdoux</u>, and <u>The Vicious Years</u>, he tried to minimize the "message" elements. This was not because he was politically conservative; he was a registered, though nonpartisan, Democrat of moderate views who supported the New Deal. He showed a great sensitivity to the plight of unfortunate members of society in movies like <u>Face Value</u>, <u>The House on 56th Street</u>, <u>Registered Nurse</u>, <u>The Florentine Dagger</u>, <u>Hollywood Boulevard</u>, <u>Women Without Names</u>, and <u>The Face Behind the Mask</u>--although such characters were treated as individuals, not as members of a class or group demanding social justice.

Florey was not a man to flaunt his opinions or ever allow political views to interfere with a job. He had no sympathy for ideologues of any stripe; one of the few crews he did not get along with were the French leftists of Adventures of Captain Fabian. This practical attitude kept him from any involvement in the various upheavals experienced by Hollywood over the years, so that he was able to work amicably with individuals as politically diverse as Charlie Chaplin and Adolphe Menjou.

However, while no domestic social vision emerges from Florey's pictures (perhaps as an immigrant he was unwilling to criticize his adopted country), he was unique in another way, by clearly enunciating a foreign policy platform. The most opinionated of these films exposed the colonial practices of his native France, a topic he may have felt free to discuss because of its seemingly indirect relevance to America. The subject appeared to be a safe one to approach, although in retrospect these movies have acquired added interest for their prescience.

The first picture of the series was The Magnificent Fraud. It accurately reflected the dominance of the United States over Latin America, not only financially but also through the direct intervention into a banana republic's domestic troubles by an unofficial American adventurer. Although containing such generic elements as romance, suspense, and political intrigue, the plot could also be interpreted on a less obvious level as a multi-layered exposé of United States control in the area. The necessity of obtaining an American loan was the motivation for all the characters. While the local military wanted it for personal gain, others hoped to use it unselfishly to bring prosperity to their nation, and the latter aim was the purpose of the Lloyd Nolan/Akim Tamiroff charade that brought an idealist to power.

The unproduced scenario, Destination Unknown, told of the hostile treatment found throughout the Mediterranean by a boatload of Jewish refugees fleeing persecution. Although he wrote the scenario in 1939 and promoted it for the next ten years, Florey was not able to make this film, with its warning of the inhumanity of ignoring Fascism. But he was

An Artist in the Studio System

allowed to direct one of the Warner Bros. pre-Pearl Harbor dramas of domestic Nazi spy activity, Dangerously They Live, and turned out a strong piece of propaganda that urged a naive and complacent America to join its natural ally, Britain, in the conflict. Although his attitude toward World War I had been ambiguous, as evidenced by Till We Meet Again, Times So Unsettled Are, and Hotel Imperial, he approached the new war unhesitatingly and with determination, characteristics seen not only in Dangerously They Live, but also in The Desert Song, Man from Frisco, and God is My Co-Pilot.

The most intriguing of Florey's foreign policy movies expand on the core idea of The Magnificent Fraud, forming together a closely related tetralogy. These latter three-- The Desert Song, Rogues' Regiment, and Outpost in Morocco --all deal with the changing French empire in the twentieth century. Florey's interest in the theme is indicated by the fact that he co-authored as well as directed the middle two of the series.

In these two the same device is used, linking colonialism with Fascism. The French Army and Foreign Legion are shown to be corrupted and manipulated by Nazis for their own ends: the subjugation of colonial peoples makes possible the building of a German-sponsored railway (The Desert Song); determination to hold on to colonies, despite native resistance, causes a manpower shortage that leads to the induction of former German soldiers in the Legion (Rogues' Regiment). Thus, imperialism is denigrated when it perpetrates cruelties or leads to the Legion offering refuge to mankind's worst enemies. On seeing ex-Naxis in combat with the Vietnamese, whose cause has been explained and personalized by Philip Ahn, one cannot help but sympathize with the rebellion. In between these two pictures, Florey touched upon this issue again when he directed God Is My Co-Pilot, portraying the Flying Tigers as a group of courageous altruists battling Japan to keep China free from foreign domination.

Florey's last colonial project was one he did not write, Outpost in Morocco. Because this was a period story of the type he had so long wanted to direct, it may have aroused the French patriot in him. He did not regret its lack of concern with the contemporary issues that had permeated

The Desert Song and Rogues' Regiment. Denunciations of colonialism were saved for films set during the modern era of World War II and its aftermath, rather than imposing current morality on the past. However, Florey moderated considerably the ideology typical of the adventure genre, displaying an awareness that the values it embodied were becoming outmoded. As this last work illustrates, there was always a certain residual ambiguity in his attitude; he was an admirer of Charles DeGaulle for his role in the war, while disagreeing with his effort to maintain the empire. (For a time Florey was involved with an aborted DeGaulle movie at Warner Bros., and Jack Warner, needing a tall Frenchman, suggested that Florey consider playing the role--a notion which dismayed the director.)

In total, this trilogy illustrated the decline of French imperialism. Even in the earlier era depicted in Outpost in Morocco, managing the empire became more complex than one was accustomed to, for the audience as well as the characters. The Desert Song and Rogues' Regiment indulge in actual denunciations of colonialism, finding in it similarities to, and a home for, Fascism and its tendencies. The equation Florey was making was unmistakable as he brought out parallels between the two systems. His skill for visualizing the story and stating the theme through nuances of acting, camera work, and plot line, rather than simple dialogue explication, allowed him to get his stories past the censors and others who might have objected to the point of what he was doing, had they been able to understand it. But his private convictions without doubt confirm his intentions.[24] His French birth, far from blinding him to his homeland's policies, clarified his vision; in this area he showed evidence of a political sophistication astonishing for its day.

Florey's films were always notable for the skill and care with which he went about creating a very palpable feeling for atmosphere, the sense of locale of a story. He was able to summon effectively the proper lighting, camera work, acting, and set decoration needed to give the tale a sense of immediacy and authenticity, usually with little time and only meager resources. "The camerawork would be great and he had the art of cheating on scenery and making it look much better than it was," commented Lloyd Nolan. "Very few other directors could do that."[25]

This ability was primarily the result of two factors: his experience as a technical adviser in the 1920s, and the geographical and historical knowledge gathered from a lifetime of traveling and reading with the production of motion pictures always on his mind. This was evident in his unproduced historical scenarios, Joan of Arc, Carnival, and the episodes for an unrealized Four Star Playhouse series. He always preferred stories with a colorful background, those set in the Far East holding a special fascination for him. His travels in South America and the Orient, as well as his European background, clearly influenced and contributed to his movies set in those areas.

His pictures "stay in the mind through the obvious care Florey took in making us believe in and be part of their ... worlds."[26] Frequently he personally decorated a set, as in Till We Meet Again, Dangerous to Know, and The Desert Song, using various items he had collected, even furniture from his own home. During the television days, said one assistant,

> He could work with the set decorators on what he wanted on each set. He had those things at home, and he worked with them all his life, and it had a big influence on the pictures he did, and I'm sure it was the same thing with the features.[27]

At the same time, he knew when to let his imagination play a role in providing the intangible extra qualities needed to transmit vitality and mood to a scene. Not only do his horror films reflect these traits, but so do many of his "B" movies and television fantasies. This was another way in which he coped with modest budgets.

Although Florey was adept at reproducing an atmosphere from any corner of the world, whether it be Europe (a dozen features), Africa (The Desert Song and Outpost in Morocco), the Orient (God Is My Co-Pilot and Rogues' Regiment) or Latin America (Daughter of Shanghai and The Magnificent Fraud), the predominant setting in more than half his films was the contemporary American city. He turned into "an expert director of purely American subjects."[28] By dint of practice in many "B" thrillers, he became proficient at depicting working-class urban life, usually dominated by gangland activities and the violence of mobsters and racketeers.

Frequently this view was transmitted through the eyes of a recent immigrant who is trying to learn the ways of the United States, an experience Florey understood. Though some of this emphasis on the city, the immigrant, and underworld activities may have stemmed from Florey's boyhood image of America formed by Nick Carter detective stories, it was largely a result of the social milieu of the time and the predominating conventions of the crime genre in which he labored so intensively. Nonetheless, however unoriginal the atmosphere might be, his meticulous reconstructions always gave his movies a sense of realism and vitality.

Both in terms of style and content Florey had a special talent for stories containing elements of the unusual (especially the macabre), or, as he thought of it, material requiring imaginative treatment. This had been evident as early as his avant-garde films, with their fusing of romantic, fantastic, often bizarre themes and techniques. He displayed a special skill for finding the appropriate visual correlative to enhance the feeling and believability of a piece. For example, in The Beast with Five Fingers, Peter Lorre's behavior appears entirely logical during the running of the movie because of the way the camera adopts his viewpoint, though in retrospect his actions at times seem peculiar because of the excessive editing.

Florey's talent for handling offbeat plots was revealed in pictures like Dangerous to Know, The Magnificent Fraud, The Face Behind the Mask, Hollywood Boulevard, and Rogues' Regiment. The latter two, which he co-authored, as well as some of his unproduced projects (for example, Monsieur de Paris, Destination Unknown, The Broken Heart Cafe, and Carnival), reveal his inventive mind conjuring new variations on established genres, recombining them in novel ways to avoid the rigidity of formulas. He displayed a capacity to juggle the ingredients of a number of different genres at the same time and create an original and effective synthesis.

He preferred to deal with atypical personas, not pre-established types, so he could explore new situations and characters. This tendency would be of little value on routine projects, but if given a script allowing an opening for ingenuity

An Artist in the Studio System

and originality, he emphasized the most interesting and unique aspects of the narrative. This was one of the reasons he preferred some of his television work; although he did many formulaic shows, dozens of his anthology segments were not tied to genre conventions. Suspense and fantasy or history were mixed effectively in such shows as Favorite Story: The Gold Bug; in many of the Four Star Playhouse dramas, such as The Man on the Train and The Devil to Pay; A Letter to Loretta: The Bronte Story; General Electric Theater: I Will Not Die; Alfred Hitchcock Presents: A Jury of Her Peers; Alcoa Premier: It Takes a Thief; and Twilight Zone: The Long Morrow.

Probably the most bizarre motif to appear in Florey's films and television shows was that of bringing the apparently dead back to the realm of the living. While such a theme might be expected in horror stories and can be found in his movies of this type, it also is evident in other contexts as well, including a number of pictures that he wrote himself. Although this idea was certainly around before Florey's time, his script of Frankenstein did much to codify the concept, giving it parameters that are still influential today. The fact that Florey continued to have an interest in the theme even after Frankenstein is made clear by his unproduced treatments for The Monster Lives! and Monsieur de Paris. It can be found right through to the end of Florey's career, in television films such as Alfred Hitchcock Presents: The Changing Heart and Thriller: The Incredible Doktor Markesan. The notion of the dead returning to life is even present in as unlikely a place as Bedside, wherein Warren William utilizes a machine (invented by Donald Meek for reviving animals), to bring back a patient who has succumbed to his incompetent surgery.

This same idea, without the science-fiction element, can be found just as frequently in Florey's canon. Johann the Coffin Maker is based on the experiences of a carpenter who spends a night with the dead. In The Beast with Five Fingers, Four Star Playhouse: The Man on a Train and The Man Who Walked Out on Himself, and Outer Limits: Moonstone, to name a few, something apparently lifeless re-enters the world we know. There are also intriguing variations on this idea, such as that offered by The Florentine Dagger. Donald Woods believes that as the last of the Borgias he has inherited their murderous bent; instead, as he overcomes his own obsession of belonging to a half-dead world, he discovers individuals who do embody those characteristics he feared, such as Henry O'Neill. Woods even finds out that O'Neill's wife, thought to have been dead for many years, is in fact very much alive, an incident that recurs in The Preview Murder Mystery.

STYLE

Florey wrote, "A director is a man who tells a story with pictures, and as the French say, he is an 'imagier.'"29 He explained how this worked in his case.

> Each director has his own style, each director tells his stories, his own way. If a producer would give the same identical scenario to ten different directors, the story would, of course, have to remain the same, at least in its foundation. But the way of illustrating the story would be entirely different, each director seeing the illustrations, or pictures, with his own personality.30

In this area Florey achieved distinction, developing an assortment of visual techniques that he manipulated masterfully and with originality. He "tells a story in pictures ... superlatively and economically."31

No term appears more frequently in this study than expressionism, and that is because no style had more influence on, or is more readily apparent in, Florey's canon. Expressionism affected his work from almost the beginning, starting with The Life and Death of 9413--a Hollywood Extra, The Loves of Zero, and Johann the Coffin Maker, through such features as Murders in the Rue Morgue, The Florentine Dagger, The Preview Murder Mystery, and The Beast with Five Fingers, to television shows like A Letter to Loretta: The Mirror, Alcoa Theater: The Clock Struck Twelve, and Thriller: The Incredible Doktor Markesan. The influence of expressionism was strongest on Florey in the late 1920s through the 1930s; by the 1940s, it had begun to wane and appeared only periodically in his big-budget movies and television work.

Florey's expressionism consisted of a number of elements

An Artist in the Studio System

Tamara Shavrova and Joseph Marievsky in The Loves of Zero, created by Florey and William Cameron Menzies in 1928.

descended from the German cinema of the 1920s. Most prominent was a fondness for shadows and dark compositions, often emphasizing contrasts of light and shade. His frame compositions were frequently unusual and artistic, and he used the subjective camera often and effectively. Frequently, his decor was artificial, as in the avant-garde pictures, The Hole in the Wall and Murders in the Rue Morgue; this seemed especially compatible with his skill in creating an imaginative atmosphere of the unreal. Such visual techniques were often supportive of stories dealing with tortured souls, insanity, and the macabre, as in The Florentine Dagger and The Beast with Five Fingers.

However, just as generalizations labeling Florey as simply a "B" director are inaccurate, so too expressionism was not the only style he utilized. Like any good director, he had a repertoire of techniques and chose the one most appropriate to the content of the narrative. Never did he impose a style incompatible with his material, nor did he over-indulge his favorite techniques, generally avoiding the showy or self-conscious. In this respect many of his films, particularly those in the "women's" or comedy genres, are relatively indistinguishable from the efforts of other directors. But over one half of his movies were various types of thrillers, and in these expressionism was the dominant style.

The influence of the avant-garde was also ever-present in Florey's lifelong love of unusual camera angles. While odd angles were related to expressionism, they were not a prominent trait of the mainstream German expressionist features of the 1920s. Instead, the use of the tilted camera would become a mainstay of experimental films, appearing occasionally in 1930s features before becoming frequent, and even conventional, in movies of the 1940s and beyond.32

There was also a third distinctive stylistic strain, realism, that started to affect Florey's output in the 1940s. It had antecedents in some of his earlier work, such as the footage he shot on his trips to China, and Parole Fixer, as well as the concern for location accuracy in The Desert Song. The picture that heralded a break from the past was the topical Roger Touhy--Gangster, followed by Man from Frisco, God Is My Co-Pilot, and The Vicious Years, the last made in the style of Italian neorealism. The trend can be found through much of his television work, such as Wire Service: The Johnny Rath Story, a taut thriller of a journalist's role in a child's rescue. As indicated by the content of these films, the change was partly the result of world conditions, partly the adjustment he had to make in the 1940s to a position as director of bigger budget movies. In such productions, the use of expressionism was less accepted, nor was it appropriate to genres usually given class "A" treatment. (Nonetheless, he was able to apply expressionism to a few big-budget features, such as Till We Meet Again, Hotel Imperial, and The Beast with Five Fingers.) But even more, the interest in realism was a mark of his own maturing as a director, an outgrowth of his desire to make more serious pictures (he thought little of his thrillers). At the same time, his artistic tendencies would never allow him to become a strictly conventional director; for example, he always disliked the glossy M-G-M house style.

An Artist in the Studio System

Florey (holding megaphone, to right of camera) and Karl Freund (at left, with pipe) obtain one of their bizarre camera angles for Murders in the Rue Morgue, as Leon Ames (in the central foreground) hears the ape committing mayhem.

Florey was thus constantly in the forefront of change. "He was indeed bold with his unconventional use of the camera," said Irving Rapper, "his techniques a little too unorthodox."[33] "He idolized pictorial changes in Russia and Germany ... he felt he was doing the new thing and the right thing, and he was."[34] Expressionist techniques in both visual and narrative style were still fresh and novel to Hollywood when Florey set about integrating them into the feature. By the time expressionism began to be more common with the 1940s film noir movement, he had all but abandoned the style to try his hand at developing newer techniques, such as realism. The methods of the avant-garde were even more unusual to the studio system, and few directors have made such a successful transition from the avant-garde to feature movies while still preserving the integrity of their style. In fact, his combination of expressionistic and avant-garde techniques was one of his most unique qualities as a filmmaker and contributed greatly to the artistry and fascination of so many of his pictures, particularly the thrillers.

Unfortunately, he has been least recognized for his pioneering efforts in introducing a brand of newsreel-type location realism to the screen, years before Louis de Rochemont began his well-publicized cycle. Florey would again prove his adaptability when he became a television director in 1951. Speeding up his techniques and working methods, he made an easy transition to the faster schedules and demands of the small screen.

The main component, therefore, uniting the various strands of Florey's style was his willingness, even determination, to experiment. This lent to his movies a certain unforeseen, occasionally uneven, quality. "Certain incidents or scenes from his films remain vividly in the memory whilst the main work is [sometimes] dimmed...."[35] He typically experimented in characteristic ways, using expressionistic lighting or unusual compositions and angles. This distinctive directorial signature--what might be called the "Florey touch"--was thus primarily visual. He had the eye and mind of a cameraman and was especially concerned with the photographic and pictorial aspects of his movies. Without the commercial or studio power to have a strong influence over the substance of his films, he had to content himself with experiments in the medium. He seized upon the most promising

An Artist in the Studio System 35

Shadowy lighting, camera angle and depth combine to create a sense of tension in this Floreyesque composition from The Crooked Way, with John Payne and Sonny Tufts (bottom foreground).

moments for stylistic experimentation even in the unlikeliest projects, such as the musical comedies The Cocoanuts or Mountain Music. This inclination, as delineated below, was central to the sophistication not only of his thrillers, but of his work in other genres as well.

It is in this way that Florey may be regarded as an auteur. Although this author has been unable to discern any overriding theme that draws together all Florey's pictures, they are united by their inventive visual style. Whether through realism, or more frequently through avant-garde and expressionistic techniques, he constantly sought to develop new approaches to the medium of film and to refine the use of these methods into mainstream cinema. His personality impelled him toward artistry, particularly experimentation, and his movies taken as a whole seldom appear ordinary. There can be no question, when The Life and Death of 9413--a Hollywood Extra, The Beast with Five Fingers, and Alcoa Theatre: The Clock Struck Twelve are placed side by side, that, despite coming from three different media over a period of thirty years, they are the product of the same hand. Even such efforts as The Cocoanuts, Hollywood Boulevard, and The Desert Song on the one hand, and A Study in Scarlet, Dangerously They Live, and Rogues' Regiment on the other, show a great degree of consistency. At the same time they reflect variety and a rich imagination. They reveal the intellect, sensitivity, and visual craftsmanship of a single consciousness, whose firm goal had not altered since he made his own avant-garde shorts and wrote that "the ideal thing ... would be to combine artistic ideas, technique and treatment with the scenarios produced for the general public."[36]

TECHNIQUES

Careful attention to the creative possibilities of lighting was a consistent element of the Florey oeuvre. He preferred the medium of black and white as best suited to his cinema, since it offered the possibility for the dramatic use of chiaroscuro; his only color film was The Desert Song.

He showed, especially at the beginning of his career, a fondness for dark compositions and a heavy use of shadows. This low-key lighting often included an emphasis on contrasts

An Artist in the Studio System   37

Noir lighting and ambiance: the atmosphere of a Saigon street in Rogues' Regiment, with Victor Sen Young and Dick Powell.

between light and dark. His 1930s thrillers, like Murders in the Rue Morgue, The Florentine Dagger, and The Preview Murder Mystery, clearly reveal this; even as unlikely a vehicle as Ship Cafe could not escape such tendencies. But starting in the latter part of the decade, beginning with Outcast and its extensive location photography, the expressionism became tempered. He turned more often to characteristic Paramount high-key lighting, even for thrillers like King of Gamblers or Dangerous to Know.

By the end of the 1930s, Florey was moving toward a middle way with a naturalistic lighting style, doubtless partially spurred on by his growing interest in realism. Nonetheless, the legacy of expressionism still occasionally appeared, sometimes in isolated scenes, sometimes striving for dominance, as in Rogues' Regiment. But full-fledged examples

One of Florey's favorite compositional devices was to shoot through foreground objects, as visible above in the arrival of the coroner from The Florentine Dagger. Florey's style was marked by unmistakable consistency over the years, as the frame below, from the television show Thriller: The Incredible Doktor Markesan, with Boris Karloff, reveals when compared with The Florentine Dagger composition above, taken almost three decades earlier.

An Artist in the Studio System

of reversions to this previous style were increasingly rare, especially in television, despite such major exceptions as The Beast with Five Fingers and Alcoa Theatre: The Clock Struck Twelve.

One manifestation of the combined influence of expressionism and the avant-garde was Florey's preference for striking artistic compositions. Despite the pressures of the studio and editors, he became notably proficient in filling the frame in a distinctive manner, using such devices as close-ups, odd angles, dark lighting, and subjective points of view.

There were a number of reappearing compositions typical of Florey's oeuvre. He liked to shoot a scene from within a fireplace so that it frames a shot, the flames leaping high in the foreground; this device is noticeable in A Study in Scarlet, The Woman in Red, The Florentine Dagger, The Face Behind the Mask, and The Beast with Five Fingers. He usually found some unique way to introduce a character, often through forbidding or low-angled shots, as in Dangerously They Live. Another favorite was a view of a character through foreground objects that indicate his or her mental condition--for example, Peter Lorre is seen through a skeletal globe of the cosmos which his tortured mind is endeavoring to comprehend in The Beast with Five Fingers. Often performers were arranged so they could be perceived twice within the same shot by use of their reflection in a background mirror, as with Akim Tamiroff in Dangerous to Know.

Florey even tried to assemble his players in a three-dimensional manner, arranging them along planes, using both foreground and background, as when Lloyd Nolan and Akim Tamiroff meet in Claire Trevor's apartment (King of Gamblers). This attempt at depth showed Florey's inventive mind at its most creative, antedating the necessary technology to properly fulfill his aim as well as the well-publicized "innovations" of others, such as Jean Renoir and Orson Welles.

No aspect of Florey's compositions was more instantly arresting and pronounced than his choice of camera angles. It is probably safe to say that no other variable of film technique was more important to him; one constantly finds this mentioned most often in his interviews. He had an "eye" for unusual angles and perspectives, a trait apparent not only in his movies but even in the still photographs he took on his

Florey was fond of the use of mirrors to photograph scenes simultaneously from different camera angles, sometimes keeping one character partially concealed, as in this instance of Rod LaRocque being menaced by Ian Keith in <u>The Preview Murder Mystery</u>.

travels and elsewhere. Irving Rapper recalled, "Florey said, 'I don't care what angle I use, so long as it is not conventional.' Some went very radically off of any conventional angle. Bob had a great flair for that sort of thing, and he impressed a lot of people."[37]

The roots of this aspect of Florey's style derived not so much from the expressionist movement as from the influence of the avant-garde and French impressionism on his development, both in Europe and America. As with so many other elements in his repertoire of techniques, the use of odd angles first became noticeable in his experimental shorts, especially the last, <u>Skyscraper Symphony</u>, with its collage of striking perspectives documenting the New York skyline.

An Artist in the Studio System   41

One of Florey's numerous striking and artistic compositions for Hotel Imperial.

Just previously he had made his first feature exhibiting this tendency, The Cocoanuts.

   This emphasis on ingenious, rather than conventional, camera angles was part of Florey's imaginative approach to filmmaking. At every opportunity, when shooting from other than eye-level might be appropriate, he tried a wide variety of angles, creating many different compositions and moods. Not only did his musicals continue the innovative approach of The Cocoanuts, but also his thrillers.

   As Florey explored the potential of the tilted camera and oblique frame in his 1930s Paramount movies, a clear progression can be discerned. Usually such shots were not fleeting, lasting more than several seconds, though rarely over half a minute. At first such angles seem to be rather awkwardly inserted, in an overly disorienting way. For example, those contained in pictures like King of Gamblers and

Daughter of Shanghai appear a bit too abrupt, serving an aesthetic effect rather than an emotional one. But over the years he refined his techniques, choosing angles to better approximate the mood at more timely moments. Hotel Imperial was a sign of progress in this regard, though perhaps it contained an overabundance of stunning angles; in The Face Behind the Mask and Dangerously They Live, two of his last programmers, their integration was nearly perfect. During the 1940s, Florey's use of unusual angles was virtually always functional and seldom, if ever, gratuitous. But at the same time, as his output was increasingly dominated by "A" projects in non-thriller genres, his reliance on this device diminished greatly. However, the skill remained, and The Beast with Five Fingers stands as a triumph of the ideal blending of incredible camera angles in a manner that is completely integrated and practically "invisible" to the unsearching eye. In the 1950s and early 1960s, when tilted camera angles had become a fashion, often overused, he continued to practice them in his television work, though

Florey continued his unusual techniques and the noir style in many of his television films, as exemplified by this frame from Alcoa/Goodyear Theater--A Turn of Fate: The Clock Struck Twelve.

An Artist in the Studio System

more rarely, subtly, and ingeniously than ever, setting a standard of effectiveness with this device matched by few other directors.

Florey's choice of camera angles was, literally, eye-catching, and one of his greatest strengths as a director. In his oeuvre, the position of the camera spoke more loudly, and often with more eloquence, than either enactment or dialogue. He truly was a pioneer in the use of unusual angles to create tension, suspense, and uncertainty in the thriller, and beautiful compositions in the musical, long before better-known and better-remembered directors like Busby Berkeley and Carol Reed made a trademark of them. Florey's best claim to being an original contributor to the cinema was undoubtedly his early and imaginative use of striking camera angles.

Florey made a specialty of close-ups, much more so than many other movie directors of the 1920s, 1930s, and 1940s. This characteristic was noticeable as early as <u>The Life and Death of 9413--a Hollywood Extra</u> and would eventually ease his transition into television. He tended to reduce long shots to a minimum, using them only as a means of establishing the scene before leading into the frequent medium shots and close-ups. While medium shots were the predominating type (as would be almost unavoidable), close-ups were never far behind in quantity. Angled close-ups from various perspectives were one of his specialties in both dramas and comedies.

He used the close-up for many purposes, never hesitating to exploit it fully. As early as <u>Murders in the Rue Morgue</u>, Florey favored this device as a means of creating mood (in sharp contrast to James Whale's stagy direction of <u>Frankenstein</u>). Shadows frequently lined the face and etched in strange patterns, the contrasts accentuating the expressionistic qualities of the lighting. He usually opted for more complex designs than simply dividing a face between an illuminated and a dark half. In <u>The Preview Murder Mystery</u> and <u>The Face Behind the Mask</u>, the mutilated visages of Conway Tearle and Peter Lorre, respectively, were largely concealed by changing shadows from a variety of directions. The angles (in films as disparate as <u>Dangerously They Live</u> and <u>Twilight Zone: Perchance to Dream</u>) and lighting of the face (particularly in <u>The Beast with Five</u>

A trademark of Florey's style was the oblique close-up, as in this shot of Boris Karloff from Thriller: The Incredible Doktor Markesan.

Fingers) often said more about the characters than the dialogue.

Florey tended to favor having his performers express their emotions to the audience in vivid and immediate close-ups. Reviewing The Preview Murder Mystery, the Hollywood Spectator commented: "In this picture we have some extraordinary portraiture shots ... to build drama by registering in close-ups the reaction of the various characters to dramatic scenes in which they appear."38 He relied on close-ups not only to advertise a glamorous star like Herbert Marshall in Till We Meet Again, but also to capture the exotic mystery of a player like Anna May Wong in Daughter of Shanghai and Dangerous to Know, or the skillful facial acting of Peter Lorre in The Face Behind the Mask and The Beast with Five Fingers.

An Artist in the Studio System 45

Florey was fond of the subjective camera and managed to work it into a large number of his films in several different ways. There were short bits of dialogue spoken in close-up directly to the camera, as between Lloyd Nolan and Akim Tamiroff near the end of King of Gamblers or during the jumbled views of their subsequent fight. Then there were whole sequences, often lasting half a minute or more, frequently of the long-take variety, including Alan Dinehart's mystery visitor in A Study in Scarlet and Akim Tamiroff menacing Edward Pawley in Dangerous to Know. Such sequences were especially effective in engendering a mood of suspense and immediacy.

Florey's efforts in exploring this unique perspective were singularly successful to a large degree because of his ability to devise smooth transitions into and out of this point of view, and because of his appropriate choice of scenes for such treatment. He would have liked to use the subjective camera more extensively, but the studios frowned on such ideas. Columbia turned down his suggestion to shoot The Face Behind the Mask almost entirely in this manner, while Warner Bros. excised many such shots from The Beast with Five Fingers even though this created some confusion in the narrative. One of the scenes from Beast with Five Fingers which remains demonstrates Florey's use of this viewpoint at its most complex. He alternates between two subjective views at once--that of a lawyer on the night after Victor Francen's death, and the latter's apparently living hand that has come to commit mayhem. First, a close-up of the moving hand is seen emerging from around a door, then the lawyer's terrified expression as he gazes at what is attacking him and is apparently about to be strangled. Both vantage points are utilized twice, the second time from a medium shot. The next scene has the sound of the music Francen played when he was alive, rousing everyone in the mansion although no one is at the piano. The use of the subjective camera at this juncture effectively adds to the idea that the hand may have returned to life on its own.

The rapidity with which Florey directed most of his films was matched by their fast pacing. He was influenced less in this way by the Warner Bros. house style than by his experience assisting Louis Feuillade and making silent "quickies." Florey explained his technique this way:

> Some directors shoot a scene from many angles (Long shot, medium shot, close shot, close-ups, over the shoulder shots, side angles, reverse shots, and what have you), leaving the footage to the editor and hoping that he'll extract something good from all these angles. As a matter of fact, the studio bosses used to want all such shots, "for protection," they said, and if a director missed one he was often sent back to the stage in order to take it.
>
> I never understood the real necessity for this quantity of shots for the coverage of a single scene, and often when making a film for an independent, I would "cut in the camera" and not photograph angles that I knew would not be needed. If I felt like cutting from an extreme long shot to a very large close-up without an intermediary cut, I just did it my way and the result was effective.[39]

Yet on only a few occasions (such as The Florentine Dagger and The Magnificent Fraud), despite his own wishes, was he ever able to supervise the editing of his movies; more often he could not even win entrance to the cutting room. He explained that a

> handicap of the contract director was the fact that he had no part in the final cutting and editing of the film. The producer and studio boss would do as they pleased with editing, sometimes changing the order of sequences, suppressing favorite scenes. And the director could object and try to influence them, but they had the power and final word.[40]

Florey recounted what he once experienced on an "A" picture at Warner Bros. in the 1940s.

> Once the editor and the director had finished the first cut, they brought it to J.L. [Warner]'s home about eight p.m. for its first showing to the Boss. It was then that a new W.B. director realized how it had been to protect himself with medium close and long shots, reverse angles, "over the shoulder" shots, criss cross shots, dolly shots and others, because J.L. Warner started re-editing the film, a secretary taking down notes of what he wanted to

Even the standard shot-reverse shot sequence was treated imaginatively by Florey, as these two successive frames from Hotel Imperial, with Isa Miranda and Ray Milland, demonstrate.

be done. He would say: "Eliminate that straight on close-up, replace it by an over the shoulder; don't let this character exit on a full L.S., use the dolly shot and follow him to the door; cut out this entire sequence, it is too slow and I don't think it will be missed." All this was more or less expected....[41]

Nonetheless, Florey's pictures displayed a consistency in their rhythm, spanning various editors, studios, genres, and years. Generally speaking, his films move very quickly. He could impel a story and script along with a great economy of shots. Since most of his work was in the thriller or related genres and of the programmer or "B" variety, this should not be too surprising. A movie such as King of Alcatraz relied almost solely on its whirlwind pace to achieve distinction, as did a sparkling musical comedy like This Way Please. One reason the running times on so many of his films, even the "A" movies, were so short was because of his swift timing, his work averaging ten to twenty percent faster than that of most of his colleagues.

However, Florey was not confined to one mode; "he has a marvelous ability of varying the tempo to suit the matter."[42] For example, despite their similar storylines, King of Gamblers and Dangerous to Know were completely different in mood due largely to variations in rhythm. Although Dangerous to Know actually had a shorter running time than King of Gamblers, the former seemed the longer, not only because of its thoughtful script, but also resulting from the reflective pace. This contemplative mood was created through many lingering close-ups, some long-take style scenes, and a preference for camera movements over simple cutting. Florey was more interested in handling each sequence in an appropriate manner than in preserving an even rhythm; he would pause for humor, to create tension, or to allow time for collecting one's thoughts, rather than relentlessly drive forward. The Magnificent Fraud, with its often languid mood, demonstrated his commitment to varying the pace not only according to the subject of the picture, but also the content of the scenes.

His "B" thrillers of the 1930s tended to rely on quick cutting between scenes to give them their rapid pace. Shots were usually brief--rarely more than a few seconds--and

An Artist in the Studio System 49

followed one another very quickly. This may have been partly necessitated by the short shooting schedules, allowing little time for elaborate set-ups, and by the fact that Florey was then more interested in expressionistic lighting and angles than camera movement. By the 1940s, however, this had changed somewhat; he depended more on longer takes and camera mobility. One can only speculate as to how much of this was in response to the bigger budgets and longer schedules he received at that time and to what degree it was another indication of his growing interest in realism.

Tension, in most cases, was built through cutting from frame to frame, rather than utilizing activity within the shot. He sometimes relied on intercutting to create a mood, shifting back and forth between various angles and close-ups, as in Anna May Wong's suicide at the end of Dangerous to Know and the astronaut's return in Twilight Zone: The Long Morrow. To capture a crowd's terror, Florey would swiftly sample a number of faces in close-up, as in Murders in the Rue Morgue. Long takes were reserved as a special device to make a certain passage stand out, such as a subjective sequence, or the panning between Andrea King and Peter Lorre that reveals the latter's insanity in The Beast with Five Fingers, or Mary Astor's decision to stay with her family in Those We Love.

WORKING METHODS

In his working methods Florey managed to combine the seemingly conflicting traits of being both meticulous and relaxed. Despite sometimes strained relations with management, he was always on the best of terms with everyone else around him. He made a special effort to get to know those he labored with, no matter how minor their positions. "He had an interest in you, while so many people you work with, their interest was with the job at hand and that was it," said Willard Sheldon, a television associate of Florey.[43]

This inclination distinguished the Florey set for its warmth and lack of tension--traits seldom found, especially when schedules were tight. Leon Ames, star of Murders in the Rue Morgue, remembered:

> He was very much like the other European directors. They were all sort of a breed of people who were different. But Bob was a very kindly man, a very smart man, and a pleasure to work for. Some of them weren't. They could be kind of nasty, but Bob never was.... He didn't harp on the work.... Bob was an extremely talented man, a charming man to work for and with.44

Reginald Denny, a friend since the 1920s and star of The Preview Murder Mystery and several of Florey's television shows, wrote, "It is, and always has been, a real joy working for you."45 Lloyd Nolan echoed these sentiments.

> He was very easy to get along with. He was an expert director; he was a very fine cameraman also, which doesn't hurt, and fast, and very jovial, and we became very good friends after the first picture.... He never carried his troubles onto the set with him, which was good. I suppose that is one of the great values Bob had, an equable temperament, a lack of temper too. He did his job, he did it fast, and he did it well.46

Florey also knew how to have fun on the set. Irving Rapper, who began in movies as Florey's assistant, recalled: "Bob was easy to work with ... very amiable.... He was very amusing, liked to have jokes with people, and because of his French accent he was thoroughly amusing."47 Florey kept up a number of running gags over the years. One involved a long-standing wager with his friend and colleague Nick Grinde to see who could most often insert into their films a character who carried an electric fan around with him. (Examples include Charles Bickford in Daughter of Shanghai and Gene Lockhart--as "Père Fan-Fan"!--in The Desert Song.)48

There was a sensitivity to Florey as well; he never used his wit or humor to humiliate a fellow artist. For instance, on the set of one of his 1930s musicals, a practical joke was played on dance director LeRoy Prinz. A phony letter was written enclosing a medal from Florey's military collection, supposedly from a German air ace--Prinz having served in the Lafayette Escadrille. However, Prinz found the spurious tribute extremely touching, and rather than

An Artist in the Studio System

embarrass him by revealing how easily he had been fooled, Florey convinced everyone involved to keep it a secret. He was not about to see someone lose their dignity over an attempt at humor that had gone too far.[49]

Florey's relationship with performers was marked by patience and respect for their talent. "He took for granted that you knew what you were doing," said Leon Ames, who remembered the understanding with which Florey treated him as he made his movie debut in Murders in the Rue Morgue.

> I had to learn, while I was doing that picture, camera technique, which I knew nothing about.... That part of my learning was under Bob. He taught me everything.... And he was very kind about it.

Those who worked with Florey in various other capacities over the years shared similar recollections. Marguerite Roberts, co-author of Hollywood Boulevard wrote, "I found him to be a charming and talented man and very tolerant of a tyro screenwriter.... I considered it a prize assignment."[50]

Florey was known for treating his performers with an uncommon adroitness and concern for their egos, solving problems with subtle ingenuity rather than seeking to embarrass or demean anyone. While doing Wagon Train: The Ruth Owens Story with Shelley Winters, whom Willard Sheldon described as having gone out of control, overplaying and demanding retakes, Florey avoided confrontation. He did this by allowing his assistant to increase the already liberal doses of vodka she had already introduced into her morning orange juice. This sedated Winters sufficiently so she did not object as the bulk of the show was shot without her, using a double for all except close-ups, leaving the remainder of scenes to be photographed rapidly late the final afternoon before she could realize the situation and make a fuss.[51] Yet, despite this odd shooting method, the episode won Florey another nomination from the Directors Guild for Best Television Directing.

On the other hand, because of his foreign birth and late learning of English, Florey sometimes was uncertain with dialogue. Whenever writing a script, he would always have a collaborator, a Garrett Fort, Reginald Owen, or Robert

Buckner, to take care of this element in the screenplay. Leon Ames recalled, "He wouldn't be sure whether it would be this way or that way in English. I remember he used to say, 'Do you feel comfortable with this speech?'"[52] This, along with Florey's belief that movies should be primarily a visual medium, caused him to minimize dialogue and replace it wherever possible with action. "My aim was to illustrate the dialogues in a creative way with interesting images and to give movement to the cinema that too much talk had rendered static."[53]

Some have criticized Florey's canon as placing too little stress on the importance of acting. Irving Rapper was one who agreed with this assessment, believing the lack of an extensive theatrical background lessened Florey's ability. "He never showed any particular patience with dialogue."[54] "Bob did not embrace all the facets of making films.... He was much more interested in technical direction and camerawork than he was with actors. He would leave the actors alone, and they were helpless."[55] While this is a valid assessment--from an associate of Florey's at Astoria--of Florey's early years as a director, it is not equally true throughout his career.

During the 1930s, the many genre pieces and "B" movies to which he was assigned offered little potential for quality performances. Lloyd Nolan said:

> Bob was only given one or two stars, and maybe of a medium nature, to work with. I'd say that The Magnificent Fraud would be about the finest cast he had. In some of the other pictures, the casting was pretty bad, which made Bob's work a little tougher for him.[56]

Florey had to overcome many other obstacles, including rapid shooting schedules and second-rate scenarios full of melodramatic incidents. This led him to once defend his performers by saying, "Even if the actors were impassible-looking [sic] Japanese players, absolutely expressionless, the plots of these stories are such that the full cast would seem to be overacting."[57] Indeed, that so much quality acting can be found in films made under such conditions is a monument to his ability. Gradually, as the years went by, he was given better projects and performers. Movies such

An Artist in the Studio System

as The House on 56th Street, Registered Nurse, The Pay-Off, Outcast, Dangerous to Know, The Face Behind the Mask, God Is My Co-Pilot, and many of his television shows reveal a progressively steadier talent for directing performers. "His work ... with a variety of actors is of sufficiently high quality to place him very close to those in the front rank."[58]

Although his players were generally not top box-office stars, they were frequently more skilled and talented than those who were. Peter Lorre in The Face Behind the Mask and The Beast with Five Fingers, Akim Tamiroff in Dangerous to Know and The Magnificent Fraud, Martha Raye in Monsieur Verdoux, John Halliday in Hollywood Boulevard, and Anna May Wong in Dangerous to Know, all gave memorable performances. Florey had a special skill and compatibility with players who were fellow Europeans or of an ethnic extraction. Lorre, Tamiroff, Wong, J. Carrol Naish, Herbert Marshall, and Reginald Owen come to mind in this regard. When given good actors and actresses and a worthy script, Florey could do as well handling performers as almost any director. This was true even when under the pressing demands of the tight schedules given "Bs" or television shows; for example, note the intense, compelling performances of Anne Francis, Christopher Dark, and the entire supporting cast of The Untouchables: The Doreen Maney Story, a one-hour program shot in just over five days.

Florey had few illusions about working in Hollywood. He was always acutely aware and often reminded of the constraints imposed on the creative artist by the studio system. In spite of the frequent commercial success of his pictures, he usually had little, if any, say in selecting a cast and crew; at most he could make suggestions for supporting and bit players. He was one of the first directors to constantly urge shooting on authentic locations, but such notions were rejected until the 1940s, and he had to content himself with modest, incremental additions to the decor to render a more effective atmosphere. Projects were arbitrarily handed to him as assignments his contract obliged him to fulfill; as "a stock director I didn't have the privilege to choose the stories I filmed."[59]

A director under contract to a studio didn't have

the power to choose a scenario. I would never have
directed a picture if I had refused the ones assigned
to me. I did take a suspension several times, in
protest against a story that I disliked strongly.
Sometimes I had to do the picture when I returned
on salary. I suggested stories that I wanted to
bring to the screen. I received a firm "No." It
was disappointing when these were made years later
by producer-directors or independent ones.[60]

But he was not unduly disappointed by these conditions.
After his experience as Louis Feuillade's assistant, he said,
"Hollywood assembly line production shouldn't have dampened
whatever spirit I had."[61]

Florey "was as gifted as a raconteur as he was as a
director," said his friend and collaborator, producer-scenarist
Robert Buckner. His desire to write was second only to his
wish to direct. Not only do his scripts of Frankenstein and
A Study in Scarlet suggest the quality of which he was capable, but Buckner, with whom he co-authored The Desert
Song and Rogues' Regiment, believed that with their rare
combination of talents Florey and he could have had a very
profitable career simply writing original screenplays, had
Florey not proceeded into television directing. While most
of the projects Florey suggested to the studios were rejected, he nonetheless had a surprising degree of success
in working as a writer-director, especially considering that
his career took place at the height of the studio system's
impersonal, mass production era. Buckner suggests why
Florey was able to function in both capacities so often: "Of
all the directors I ever worked with his was the best all-
round mind, in story construction, camera-wise, in improvisation of sets and props, and the speed with which he
worked."[62]

On those assignments where he was presented with a
completed script, Florey hoped to have sufficient time--and
management permission--to allow him to make alterations and
improvements. Even when he was not given added pay, such
as on The Face Behind the Mask and Dangerously They Live,
he would make the extra effort to revise the script to make
it appropriate to his camera style. There is a clear relation
between those films where he collaborated on the script to
some degree, and his best pictures, particularly in effectively
utilizing his typical European techniques.

An Artist in the Studio System

Florey's process in preparing a script is indicated by his stress on the continuity, the final draft in which every sequence is broken down into numbered, individual shots. The value he placed on continuities reflected the influence of his decade in silent motion picture language and technique, when one had only individual shots, without dialogue, to direct from. Because of this training, Florey was primarily a visualist who seldom foregrounded the literary elements in his work.

A lifetime in filmmaking made him think as if a camera were permanently rolling in his consciousness. "When I read a novel or see a play I immediately transfer it in my mind into picture cuts," he explained, and this was the way he approached the script.[63] The story would be taken apart and dissected into scenes and shots. Often the staging and arrangement of performers would be sketched in the margin. Characteristics of each shot, such as the lighting, camera angle, lens, and movement, were elaborately described beside the appropriate dialogue. This was one reason a movie like A Study in Scarlet still revealed his style, even though he only wrote and did not direct it--everything had been planned in advance. Said Florey:

> Writers, never knowing which standing sets might be used in the making of a film, nor knowing which angle a director would decide to use--and which lens to photograph with, on which tripod or high hat--could not give indications regarding the shooting continuity of a motion picture. They mostly wrote or adapted a story and the dialogue, writing in, for convenience, here and there--"long shot," "medium shot" or "close up"--vague indications, disregarded by all directors, who traced their camera moves on pieces of paper and wrote their own continuity and indications of editing, given to the script girl and transmitted to the film editor, as they progressed in the making of the film.[64]

Adequate preparation time was usually at least a week or more for a "B," and much longer for a big-budget movie. Within this context, if Florey did not exceed the allotted budget, he was allowed a certain amount of artistic freedom. "As long as I remained on schedule, I could shoot all the angles and set ups I wanted, and move the camera whenever and wherever I wanted to, in the limited time I had."[65]

Florey would go through these same detailed, thorough preparations for every picture, large or small, never becoming sloppy even when the assignment was a minor one. The same was true of his television films. While shooting a movie, he would become totally absorbed in it. Said Lloyd Nolan:

> I believe he did his homework very well, because everything was planned out and ready and fast and frugal. He didn't take a lot of shots, whereas many of your ace directors wasted film like mad.[66]

It was necessary, Florey believed, for the director to be able to have an impact on the script, and he was frustrated when not allowed to have such input. This was most frequently the case during his first Warner Bros. period (1932-35). For instance, before starting Don't Bet on Blondes, he had written to Hal Wallis:

> Since you requested me to stay away from the writers and not to work on the script with them, I want you to know that from the time I get a final completed script I will require about six days to prepare for the shooting of the picture....
> It is impossible for me or anyone to make a good picture without any kind of preparation whatsoever. I am not asking for a few weeks as other directors get but only for five or six days of personal work and preparation after the reception and reading of the final script.[67]

But Wallis would only give Florey the weekend to look at the screenplay before shooting began. Nevertheless, Florey learned to overcome such adverse conditions and direct credibly on short notice, as on Mountain Music.

The attention to detail and thorough planning involved in writing the continuity, along with Florey's patient, accommodating personality on and off the set, made him a favorite of technical crews. "He could adapt himself to any problems that arose. He was a director that had respect for an assistant or a production manager that knew his business," said Willard Sheldon, who served Florey in both these positions on many television films at Universal-Revue.[68] The visual sense indicated by the manner in which he approached the screenplay made cameramen especially fond of Florey; he

An Artist in the Studio System

knew their concerns and jobs, often as well as they did. While he always had a strong idea of what he wanted in advance and took a strong role in determining the photography, he was always willing to take suggestions, even when on "B" or television schedules. "He'd tell them what he wanted; but if the cameraman said, 'Wouldn't it be better if we moved over here ...,' Bob would always listen."[69] Cinematographers, according to Lloyd Nolan,

> respected Bob because they knew that he himself was a very good cameraman.... His overall ability as a cameraman and director, and being artistically sensitive, made him a very desirable director to have.[70]

Because of this, regardless of who was director of photography, Florey's movies consistently have a "visual quality [that] has always been their strongest point."[71] His expressionist tendencies made him exceptionally compatible with European cameramen. Not only did he work with Karl Freund on Murders in the Rue Morgue, but with many others of a similar type, always with superb results--individuals such as Theodor Sparkhul, Rudolph Maté, Franz Planer, and Curt Courant. "My collaboration with these five artists is a happy memory," said Florey.[72]

INFLUENCES AND LEGACY

The primary influences on Robert Florey originated in his European background. His films always reflected a continental taste, a result of his European upbringing and early exposure to a variety of artistic movements. Frequent travels and a long stay in Switzerland may account for the fact that his style was not dominated by his French origin, but seemed to be more Germanic in nature. "Despite Franco-German hostilities, the German expressionist films were very popular with the French...."[73]

Along with expressionism, another movement that had a significant impact on his youth was his association with the avant-garde in the late 1920s, after he had come to the United States. Florey was a very intellectual man; in subsequent years he studied different types of art from all over the world. His pictorial compositions and style were influenced

by his study of the impressionist painters, on whom he collected hundreds of volumes. He also had "a sophisticated
knowledge and appreciation of contemporary European art,
particularly the Dada and Surrealist movements that were
little known in the Hollywood production establishment of the
day."74

However, Florey always maintained that his techniques
were never simply an imitation of continental filmmaking,
pointing to the differences in story, setting, and time frame
of his pictures.75 For instance, he would say, "If I was
ever influenced by [The Cabinet of Dr.] Caligari, it might
have been perhaps during the making of ... The Loves of
Zero.... Also during the making of Murders in the Rue
Morgue, but certainly not while preparing and shooting
The Hole in the Wall."76 Apparently he believed there was
a tendency to exaggerate the connection between expressionism and his movies. Although working in a tradition, Florey
did indeed carve out an individual path, as the Hollywood
Spectator pointed out:

> Robert Florey's direction of a picture gives me the
> impression he would like to break loose and go for
> eign directors one better in the application of the
> technique which distinguishes so many otherwise
> undistinguished pictures which come to us from
> Europe.77

His preference in stories was dominated by the love of
history so impressively reflected in his vast museum of artifacts from the Napoleonic era. He also collected thousands
of relics from the past of other countries, particularly European and Oriental. His literary interests were wide-ranging,
but mysteries and all types of fantasy were among his favorites and clearly had an impact on his films. Combined with
these was a vast knowledge of contemporary events. This
gave him a background to draw on to create an original
movie like Rogues' Regiment, with its elements of historical
tradition, suspense, and politics.

Just as his oeuvre reflected a number of artistic movements, so too the influence of a few individuals was apparent.
He was always fond of the creations of Georges Méliès, whom
he had observed as a child and who was one of his inspirations to enter the cinema. Despite the large number of

An Artist in the Studio System 59

directors Florey assisted, he said he was greatly disappointed with all except Henry King and Josef von Sternberg, from whom he claimed to have learned the most. Florey never worked for Ernst Lubitsch or René Clair, but he knew both well and admired their movies. He had the chance to observe Lubitsch directing Rosita while they were at Pickfair in 1922. Clair, a friend from the days in 1920 when both had labored together for Louis Feulliade, was respected for the French touch he was able to bring to his movies. It should not be surprising that Florey was a fan of Alfred Hitchcock, considering that both made so many suspense pictures, though Florey regarded him as only an entertainer. One director whose influence was directly traceable in Florey's style was F.W. Murnau. While writing Frankenstein, Florey had in mind Nosferatu far more than Dracula, which he believed was inferior to its predecessor. He even planned short strips of negative in his script, a device from Nosferatu he had already utilized in the credits of The Cocoanuts.

Because of Florey's extensive writings and the manner in which his collections have been preserved, one can pinpoint with certainty the greatest influences on his films. It is more difficult, however, to assert that he had an effect on others. For one thing, directors tend not to acknowledge any influences from an individual whose fame and importance has not been already established as greater than theirs.

Nonetheless, one movie that has won some recognition for at least prefiguring, if not also inspiring, the later work of two better-known directors was The Cocoanuts. Rouben Mamoulian was on the set at the time of the shooting, learning how to use the camera; he was especially interested in the innovations Florey was developing.[78] Also, Busby Berkeley's characteristic low- and high-angle and overhead shots of chorus girl formations were first visible here, though in less lavish routines.

Another important theatrical figure apprenticed to learn filmmaking from Florey at Astoria was Irving Rapper, who assisted on The Pusher-in-the-Face and The Hole in the Wall. The next year Marc Allegret would serve Florey on L'Amour Chante, then go on to finish Le Blanc et le Noir and commence his own feature career. One more talent Florey may have affected was Albert Lewin, with whom he collaborated on some unproduced scripts at M-G-M in the 1920s. Later, when both were at Paramount and Lewin was a producer, Florey presented him with a list of twenty great classics of literature. He "asked to be allowed to direct as many as possible. Lewin put him off, and later told Florey the properties were too expensive to produce. Yet, when Lewin became an independent producer-director a few years later, two of his first films were The Moon and Sixpence and The Private Life of Bel-Ami, both on Florey's list." The former had been labeled an "impossible idea" by Lewin when Florey suggested it.[79]

A strong case can also be made for Florey's impact during his months at K.B.S. on a lesser figure, Edwin L. Marin. Not only did Marin serve Florey twice as assistant director, but he was given the script and continuity of A Study in Scarlet that Florey had prepared. With this in hand, Marin proceeded to turn out a picture in the same style as Florey. In subsequent years, Marin showed a talent for quality "B" films and programmers, continuing to utilize similar techniques, such as odd camera angles and complex compositions.

Even more significant, but not previously acknowledged, was the effect Florey had on the series of Universal horror films of the 1930s. This extended far beyond the writing and directing of the cinematically advanced Murders in the Rue Morgue. His extensive collaboration with writer Garrett Fort and cameraman Karl Freund may have had an impact on the future efforts of both, particularly when Freund turned to directing and adapted his technique to suit American features.

More certain is the impact of Florey on the man regarded as the chief architect of the series, James Whale. Frankenstein was only the third film Whale directed, and it marked his baptism in the horror genre. He had not only Florey's detailed continuity to follow, but also his expressionistic set designs and the twenty-minute test. In later years Whale's mastery of mood would become pronounced, but not until he had the example of the Florey-created Murders in the Rue Morgue to observe.

In terms of more general influences, Florey's efforts (along with those of many others) to integrate and disseminate expressionist and avant-garde styles into American

An Artist in the Studio System

features of the 1930s were arguably most important, laying a foundation for the later development of film noir and a more artistic cinema. The realistic Roger Touhy--Gangster was made at the very studio, Twentieth Century-Fox, that in the late 1940s was most identified with this new technique. Florey's early entrance into television provided a lead for other directors to follow, and his many nominations for a variety of awards, especially the nearly annual recognition from the Directors Guild, indicated the esteem his pioneering efforts in this medium earned from his colleagues.

NOTES

1. Don Miller, "The American 'B' Film," Focus on Film, No. 5 (Winter 1970):31-32.
2. Irving Rapper, interview with the author, March 7, 1985.
3. Jack Spears, Hollywood: The Golden Era (New York: A.S. Barnes, 1971), p. 360.
4. Robert Buckner, letter to the author, July 19, 1984.
5. Rapper interview.
6. Robert Florey, letter to Henry Hart, June 12, 1959.
7. Spears, pp. 359-360.
8. Robert Florey, unidentified correspondence, Florey collection (private).
9. Irving Rapper, letter to the author, September 4, 1984.
10. Richard Kozarski, Hollywood Directors, 1914-1940 (New York: Oxford University Press, 1976), p. 117.
11. Don Miller, "B" Movies (New York: Curtis, 1973), p. 43.
12. Theodore Huff, "Book Reviews: 'Hollywood D'Hier et D'Aujourd'Hui,'" Films in Review, 3 (April 1950): 31-32.
13. Lloyd Nolan, interview with the author, August 5, 1983.
14. Florey, letter to Henry Hart.
15. Nolan interview.
16. Anthony Slide, "'Hollywood Boulevard,'" in Frank Magill, ed., Magill's Survey of Cinema, second series (Englewood Cliffs, N.J.: Salem Press, 1981), p. 1041.
17. William K. Everson, letter to Ray Cabana, n.d., Florey collection.
18. Jack Spears, letter to the author, November 15, 1982.
19. Kozarski, p. 117.

20. Lewis Jacobs, The Rise of the American Film (New York: Harcourt, Brace, 1939), p. 513.
21. Willard Sheldon, interview with the author, January 7, 1982.
22. Robert Florey, letter to Ray Cabana, January 16, 1979, Florey collection.
23. Robert Florey, unidentified correspondence, Florey collection.
24. Virginia Florey, interviews with the author, 1980-83.
25. Nolan interview.
26. Markku Salmi, "Robert Florey," Film Dope, No. 16 (February 1979):43.
27. Sheldon interview.
28. Eric H. Rideout, The American Film (London: Mitre Press, 1937), p. 59.
29. Leonard Maltin, "Directors on TV--Robert Florey," Film Fan Monthly, No. 126 (December 1971):22.
30. Robert Florey, unidentified correspondence, Florey collection.
31. Salmi, p. 43.
32. This is not to say that the tilted camera was not used in the German cinema of the 1920s, but it was certainly not an integral part of the expressionist style to the same degree as lighting effects, set design, and acting. However, some of the German avant-garde films of the 1920s contained oblique angles and doubtless influenced Florey. For example, his experimental short Skyscraper Symphony was of the same school as Walter Ruttmann's Berlin, the Symphony of a Great City (1927).
33. Rapper, letter to the author.
34. Rapper interview.
35. Rideout, p. 59.
36. Robert Florey in Robert Herring, "Art in the Cinema," Creative Art, 4 (May 1929):361.
37. Rapper interview.
38. "Interesting Murder Mystery," Hollywood Spectator, February 15, 1936.
39. Maltin, p. 22.
40. Robert Florey in Ella Smith, Starring Miss Barbara Stanwyck (New York: Crown, 1974), pp. 68-73.
41. Robert Florey, letter to Ray Cabana, February 16, 1979, Florey collection.
42. Rideout, p. 59.
43. Sheldon interview.

44. Leon Ames, interview with the author, June 22, 1982.
45. Reginald Denny, letter to Robert Florey, January 17, 1962, Florey collection.
46. Nolan interview.
47. Rapper interview.
48. Virginia Florey interviews.
49. Ibid.
50. Ames interview; Marguerite Roberts, letter to the author, March 18, 1986.
51. Sheldon interview.
52. Ames interview.
53. Florey, letter to Ray Cabana, January 16, 1979.
54. Rapper, letter to the author.
55. Rapper interview.
56. Nolan interview.
57. Florey, letter to Henry Hart.
58. Rideout, p. 59.
59. Robert Florey, unidentified correspondence, Florey collection.
60. Florey in Smith, pp. 68-73.
61. Robert Florey, unidentified correspondence, Florey collection.
62. Buckner, letter to the author, July 19, 1984.
63. Maltin, p. 22.
64. Robert Florey, letter to Carlos Clarens, December 13, 1976.
65. Robert Florey, unidentified correspondence, Florey collection.
66. Nolan interview.
67. Robert Florey to Hal Wallis, inter-office communication, April 16, 1935, Don't Bet on Blondes file, Warner Bros. collection, University of Southern California Special Collections Library.
68. Sheldon interview.
69. Ibid.
70. Nolan interview.
71. Salmi, p. 43.
72. Robert Florey, letter to John Baxter, September 15, 1976, Florey collection.
73. John J. Michalczyk, The French Literary Filmmakers (Philadelphia: Art Alliance Press, 1980), p. 3.
74. Gerald F. Noxon, "The European Influence on the Coming of Sound to the American Film, 1925-1940--A Survey," in Evan William Cameron, ed., Sound and the Cinema (Pleasantville, N.Y.: Redgrave, 1980), p. 149.

75. Jack Spears, letter to the author, September 6, 1982.
76. Robert Florey, letter to Ray Cabana, November 21, 1968.
77. "Interesting Murder Mystery."
78. Robert Florey, Hollywood D'Hier et D'Aujourd'Hui (Paris: Editions Prisma, 1948), pp. 155-156.
79. Spears, letter to the author, September 6, 1982; Jack Spears, "Robert Florey," Films in Review, 11 (April 1960):229.

Chapter II

1900-1928: EARLY YEARS

CHILDHOOD AND EDUCATION, 1900-1917

Robert Florey was born at 1 Rue du Helder, on the Boulevard des Italiens in the Chausée d'Antin, which Balzac called "not only the heart of Paris but also the center of the world."[1] The day was September 14, 1900.

Florey's father died not long after his son was born. His mother remarried, but she, too, died within a few years, leaving the boy with no relatives outside his stepfamily. Treasuring always the few memories he had of his mother, Florey was a lonely child, tender-hearted and serious, who matured early and disliked any feeling of dependency on others.

His young imagination was fired when living near Robert Houdin's Magician's Theatre, where Florey watched Georges Méliès put together his primitive motion picture fantasies. Florey's stepfather introduced the boy to the classical theater, and over the years took him traveling through much of Europe, including Austria (where he regularly spent summer vacations), Italy, Switzerland, and Spain.

His stepfather also arranged for his education, which, while typical for the French middle class, left Florey with many unpleasant memories. He attended a number of boys' boarding schools in the suburbs of Paris, saying:

> The name "College" is given to such French schools certainly by derision. I spent several unhappy

years in this "boîte," of which I have only kept a
confused remembrance of horse meat, indigestible
beans, bad smells, [weekly cold showers], bearded
teachers, kicks in the pants, algebra theorems and
the date of the Battle of Marignan.[2]

About one teacher, he recalled:

> He used to tell each one of us that we were "good
> for nothing" and that we would die "on the guillo-
> tine like murderers...." "Or like Kings ..." I
> answered him once.... I was severely reprimanded
> for my daring (dry bread and water for three days).[3]

But Florey's schooling did instill in him a life-long love
of French history, in which he was winning the first prize
by age eleven. His youthful taste in literature extended
from Nick Carter mysteries, horror stories, and westerns
(which his teachers punished him for reading) to the adventures of Jules Verne, whose works were awarded as
prizes to the best pupils.

Not long after, while walking through the Place de
l'Église with some friends, Florey came across a movie company in the process of filming.

> I had never seen such a thing, but in a few seconds
> the love of cinema was born in my heart. It is then
> that I decided what my vocation would be. I no
> longer dreamed of anything but stars and cinema.
> At the end of the school year we were asked the
> habitual question: what do you want to do in life,
> etc. and without hesitating I wrote, "I want to do
> films for the cinema." After having read this edify-
> ing response, our principal let fall on me a look
> full of scorn, while he murmured "Cinematographer?
> Magic Lantern?" he added, raising his voice,
> "Clown! You'll finish badly!"[4]

In July 1914, having passed his examinations, Florey
was scheduled to enter Engineering College. Although he
sought to join the French army at the beginning of World
War I, he was rejected as being too young and underweight.
His health, never strong, required a change of climate, and
he moved to Switzerland, starting at the École Professionelle

1900-1928: Early Years

of Geneva in 1915. When Florey was sixteen, his stepfather died, making it necessary for him to leave school.

APPRENTICESHIP, 1917-1928

Europe

Florey's first employment in the movies had actually been while on vacation in 1915, when he was paid fifty cents to walk through a few travelogue compositions. But it was not until leaving school two years later, at age sixteen, that he found his first steady job in the industry in March 1917. He worked as a patcher, cutting French titles into foreign pictures for the Select Film Company of Geneva. There he met Max Linder, whom he assisted briefly.

During the summer he joined the Kursaal Operetta Company, aiding the stage manager and performing small parts. Remaining active in theater and movies, he organized a road show of "Grand Guignol" horror plays during the winter. The next year journalism was added to his repertoire of activities, writing for several newspapers, covering sports, and serving as second editor on L'Auto-Sport. Joining summer stock again, he met the noted French humorist Willy, who engaged Florey as critic and editor of the theatrical paper Le Mondain. He even found time to act the part of the detective in Alfred Lindt's one-reel picture, Le Cirque de la Mort.

Movies were still in their infancy in Switzerland at this time, but Florey soon expanded his involvement with the medium. In December 1918 he joined with some friends, as the group's scenario writer, forming a motion picture company which began production the next year. With the backing of producer-cameraman-actor Leon Tombet, who had long experience in filming travelogues of the Swiss countryside, they amassed a little capital and bought an old Ernemian camera. Costs were kept low by buying the film stock in France, with Tombet doing the developing himself. Most of the photography was done out-of-doors because the only studio they could afford was a friend's attic, where lighting was always a problem. Many of the players were recruited from the Casino and from the Comédie de Geneva, or were

Robert Florey with Walter Gfeller, the "Swiss Chaplin," for whom he wrote and later directed Isidore shorts in 1919.

simply amateurs; even the crew took turns in front of the camera. However, this necessitated five or six rehearsals before each take so as not to waste film.

During World War I, the movies of Charlie Chaplin had been very scarce in Switzerland, but also very profitable, so for their initial venture Tombet Films-Geneva decided to try a picture imitating the style of Chaplin. Because he used the same costume and mannerisms, the lead role was given to the acrobat Walter Gfeller, who was known as the "Swiss Chaplin"; Victor Baumgarth and Jean Bades were also featured. Isidore a la Deveine ("Isidore is Out of Luck") was directed by Tombet in only a few days and had a length of some 1,300 feet. Florey supplied the scenario of the two-act burlesque, his first such task, and also assisted as an actor and cameraman.

1900-1928: Early Years

Florey shooting interiors for Une Heureuse Intervention, with producer-director Leon Tombet at the right and, in the center, leading man Frank Danchene and femme fatale Claudine.

After two months of careful preparation, in May 1919 Tombet Films turned out Une Heureuse Intervention ("A Happy Intervention"), probably the first feature-length Swiss movie. Despite its five-reel duration, the picture was completed in a mere eight days on a $350 budget. Florey again wrote the screenplay, a sentimental melodrama concerning a young sportsman (Tombet) who, rescuing a young girl (Molly Creighton) from a band of thieves, begins to win her heart from a cowardly fiancé (Frank Danchene)--especially after she discovers his compromising letters to a mistress. The six-act structure was designed episodically so that, depending on the success of Une Heureuse Intervention, new segments could be added and it could even be turned into a serial. Once more, Florey was a cameraman and actor--this time playing an elderly millionaire--but he also received his baptism as a director for a few scenes, although Tombet was given official credit.

The next month another bogus Chaplin film was made,

and this time Florey was allowed to direct his own scenario. *Isidore Sur le Lac* ("Isidore on the Lake"), a two-reeler, featured the same cast and was shot in the Parc des Eaux Vives of Geneva. However, since responsibilities were shared in the little company, with whomever was not acting in the scene becoming cameraman or even director, allocating absolute credit for any of the productions is problematical. Florey often neglected to mention these first efforts, made while he was still a teenager, when asked about his beginnings as a filmmaker.

Anxious to learn from a leader in the industry, early in 1920 he left Geneva, returning to France after an absence of more than five years. He found a job at the Gaumont studio in Nice with Louis Feuillade, who was directing *L'Orpheline* and *Saturnin*. "I had to do a little of everything," Florey recalled. "I was the assistant director, the set dresser, the casting director, the prop man, and once in a while an actor...."[5]

> At dawn I pedaled up to Feuillade hotel up the hills above Nice. After hearing my call he appeared at a window of the third floor throwing out a piece of paper containing a resume of what he intended to shoot that day--the product of his imagination during the night. His hieroglyphs deciphered I went to different districts awakening the needed actors, often out of temper, then would stop at several bistros to hire the requested extras, not always an easy task when character types were wanted. [Afterwards I] rushed to the studio ... to tell the propman-set dresser if the boss had changed his mind or we were going to keep on shooting on the same set or have to change it ... the flats (walls) remaining where they stood or to be quickly repainted and moved around. If the furnitures had to be changed at the last minutes and not available in the stock room it was also one of my duties to find them in a hurry, free of charge and if an actor or an extra was missing at the last minute, I took his place, I was IT.[6]

However, Florey and his associates (among them René Clair) found Feuillade's cinematic techniques archaic. They admired the American cinema much more, especially its acting, although knowing little of the Hollywood studio system, they thought that directors in the United States had complete artistic control over their product.

While working in the movies, Florey continued his journalistic career, joining the staff of Cinemagazine, the first truly popular French movie magazine.[7] Young Florey's knowledge and serious interest in the cinema impressed those he interviewed, including Max Linder, who urged Florey to try his luck in the United States. Promising to accept articles about Hollywood stars, his editor, Jean Pascal, helped to arrange financing for a trip to America. In return, Florey said he "was supposed to stay a few weeks, write a few articles and a book about the American movies." But "I would have come anyway," he asserted, "[I] loved the movies so much."[8]

Florey left Cherbourg aboard the Royal Mail Steam Packet S.S. Orbita in September 1921. Although the transAtlantic voyage lasted a mere ten days, it marked a daring move for the intrepid young Florey, for he knew scarcely a word of English.

United States

Following his landing in New York, Florey departed immediately for Hollywood. While crossing the continent he was heartbroken at meeting no Indians along the way. On his arrival he wandered about for hours, mistaking the Chinese and Mexican quarters of Los Angeles for movie sets.

Still carrying his suitcase, he was finally directed to the Fox studio, and, as there were no gatekeepers, simply ambled in. Pausing to watch the Monte Cristo company at work, he became so dismayed by the inaccuracy of the French atmosphere that, "obeying an irresistible force, I threw myself in front of the two cameras and stopped the takes. Pushing, shoving, questions--of which I didn't understand a word."[9] Fortunately, the cinematographer was another French émigré, Lucien Andriot (with whom Florey would collaborate over 25 years later on Outpost in Morocco and Johnny One-Eye). Andriot, realizing the legitimacy of the young man's protestations, managed to persuade the director, Emmett J. Flynn, that Florey should not be ejected from the set but rather hired as technical advisor.

The job lasted several weeks and began the process of turning Florey into a Hollywood insider. When Monte Cristo was done, he became a gagwriter for Al St. John's Sunshine Comedies. Because of his height (six feet, four inches), Florey was sometimes called on to do bits, such as the sheriff in Straight from the Farm. He quickly began to make the right connections, and the people he went to interview for Cinemagazine found him charming. He became the friend of many of the elite, such as Alla Nazimova, Renée Adorée and Charlie Chaplin, and was closest to fellow members of the French colony. Paul Ivano, a cameraman of the same age who had arrived from Europe two years earlier, recalled an example of the ingratiating Florey manner.

> I met him at a party in 1922. A copy of Cinemagazine had a fantastic article about Hollywood, and I didn't know who [the author] was. I said, "Who is the idiot that wrote all that stuff?" He said, "It's me!" and we became friends.[10]

In November, Florey was made director of foreign publicity for Mary Pickford and Douglas Fairbanks. In this position he handled such matters as fan mail and wrote the French titles for Robin Hood (1922); later he authored a book, Douglas Fairbanks, sa vie, ses films, ses aventures. Florey became a favorite of the famous couple, often joining them for breakfast at Pickfair, teaching French to Fairbanks, and learning English from Pickford. Nearly forty years later she would still recall, "Douglas and I were so fond of Bob. He was so charming and eager to please, and he had such a capacity for hard work."[11]

During this time Florey continued to send back articles to France and expand his circle of friends. He became a member of the select group who were regular companions of Rudolf Valentino. Together with Ivano, Jean de Limur, and actors Mario Carillo and Douglas Gerrard, they engaged in various types of sporting activities and indulged in huge feasts. The star did not object when Florey said Valentino was being miscast and that no authentic Arab would act as he had in The Sheik (1921).

The friendship, however, resulted in some of Florey's first troubles with the studio moguls. When Valentino attempted to hire him as an assistant for foreign publicity, the

1900-1928: Early Years

proposal was rudely rebuffed by the corporate management and Florey was temporarily banned from the lot; Valentino was not even allowed to invite him or any other friends to previews. Thus, when Valentino quit Famous Players-Lasky to publicize Mineralava Cold Cream, he naturally asked Florey to join him as press agent. Florey left Pickfair in May 1923 and was soon directing a "Screen Snapshot" short of Valentino at his Whitley Heights home. Florey managed the publicity for the subsequent tour, traveling around the United States and Europe, where he worked with extra effort to arouse interest in the Latin idol of America. While on the trip Florey even shot--mostly in England--enough footage of Valentino and his wife, Natacha Rambova, for several one-reel travelogues. All of Florey's activities were undertaken at the star's own expense, and although Valentino had hoped that Florey would assist in the direction of his future movies, the contractual difficulties that plagued his remaining years prevented this from transpiring.

By October, Florey was back in Hollywood. He had never lost sight of his goal of resuming the filmmaking career he had begun in Switzerland, and he and Paul Ivano often discussed the possibility of setting up an independent production company. Ivano was to be the cameraman and Florey the writer-director. Finally, the necessary backing was acquired through the investment of Ivano's friend Humphrey Birge, a dealer in Pierce-Arrow cars who wanted to enter the motion picture business.

Fifty-Fifty, written and directed by Florey in November 1923, was a two-reel vehicle for the French comedian Maurice de Canonge, who was depicted as going around the world in a battered old taxi. The plot required many varied exteriors, some of which proved troublesome. After shooting in Palm Springs, Florey hoped to film a Far Eastern episode in the Chinese quarter of Los Angeles--but he and his crew were chased out of the district, barely escaping the wrath of residents who disliked being photographed. (The Florence Vidor studio substituted instead.) On location in the village of Mexicali, Canonge disappeared for a day and had to be rescued from an all-too-successful attempt to find relief from Prohibition while across the border. The remaining interiors were photographed on a rented portion of the Universal lot and designed by Danny Hall.

Robert Florey directing his first American film, Fifty-Fifty (1923), with cameraman Paul Ivano at right.

Of those in the cast, many besides Canonge were personal friends of Florey, such as Gertrude Astor and Max Constant; others featured include Kathleen Bennett, Stella de Lanti, Bennie Stone, Lewis Williams, Richard Blaydon (doubling as assistant director), and assorted cowboys, policemen, and Orientals, used as extras. Unfortunately, this first production of the Florey-Ivano-Birge company, Imperial Pictures, had only a few showings in Los Angeles, although these were successful. Failing to find a distributor for Fifty-Fifty, Florey had to abandon, for the moment, his hope of becoming a freelance director.

By this time he had written two full-length books on Hollywood (Filmland--which sold some 15,000 copies--and Deux ans dans les studios américains), and soon began a

1900-1928: Early Years

series of biographies of such stars as Pola Negri, Charlie Chaplin, and Adolphe Menjou. All were in French and published in Paris. Florey then became an assistant director to Louis Gasnier on Wine for Universal.

In June 1924, Florey left for Canada with Charles de Rochefort (a French dramatic actor imported by Famous Players-Lasky in 1923 to replace Valentino) and others to produce short plays and sketches in French. One of these, the "pièce de résistance" (despite its one-act length), was a pantomime called L'Apache, written and directed by Florey. He recalled: "For three months we gave shows in Montreal, Quebec, Sorel, Trois Rivieres, and all over French Canada. We didn't make much but had a lot of fun."[12]

Returning to movies in October, he assisted Al Santell on Parisian Nights at F.B.O. There he made the acquaintance of another young assistant, Josef von Sternberg. A month later, at Nazimova's request, Florey spent a few days playing a Bohemian in The Redeeming Sin. For the next several years he served as an assistant director and technical advisor, frequently combining both capacities, steadily moving up to more prestigious pictures. His care and attention to detail in creating European atmospheres, particularly at Metro-Goldwyn-Mayer, won him much praise.

Meanwhile, von Sternberg had been hired by M-G-M to direct Escape and asked Florey to be his assistant; he continued with von Sternberg on The Masked Bride. Sadly, in each instance the studio disliked von Sternberg's approach; Escape was remade by another director, and Christy Cabanne completed Masked Bride. After his mentor left M-G-M, Florey continued at the studio on both these pictures. Undoubtedly, von Sternberg had a greater influence on Florey than any of the others he assisted; he later said, "I learned more from him than from any other Hollywood director."[13] Florey found von Sternberg's direction ahead of its time and full of humor, despite mediocre scenarios. His techniques were different from anything Florey had seen, offering an excellent lesson in photography, lighting, and the use of shadow. Florey was also one of the few to see von Sternberg's The Sea Gull in 1926 (before producer Charlie Chaplin impounded it), and worked again near him in 1930 while both were directing at the Ufa studio. "I really knew him well," remarked Florey, who remained a friend of von Sternberg's until his death.[14]

During the next eighteen months, Florey directed tests and served as technical advisor at M-G-M, designing costumes and sets on a number of productions. Among those he assisted were Christy Cabanne on Monte Carlo, Edmond Goulding on Paris, Robert Z. Leonard on Dance Madness and Time the Comedian, Phil Rosen on The Exquisite Sinner (the re-make of Escape), John M. Stahl on The Gay Deceiver, and King Vidor on The Big Parade, La Boheme, and Bardelys the Magnificent. Florey was particularly fond of Goulding and Leonard.

But of all the directors Florey was to serve in Europe and the United States, only two did not disappoint him, Josef von Sternberg and Henry King. His other experiences were not much more profitable than the months with Louis Feuillade had been. Florey had been especially anxious to meet Christy Cabanne, having admired his movies made with Douglas Fairbanks, but found he "was only a good technical commercial director." He rated Cabanne on a par with Emmett Flynn and Al Santell, but superior to Phil Rosen or Louis Gasnier, although all used the same techniques. Beginning each sequence with a long shot, they moved in for a medium shot, picked up some close-ups, and here and there an "over-the-shoulder"--then on to the next scene. There was little if any concern for atmosphere, and the stories were of little help; Florey commented that Monte Carlo was handled as if it were set in any city, from Santiago to Vladivostok. The actors had no text to learn and were told to say anything in keeping with the action--the film would simply cut to a title anyway (which was probably not yet written). This was the basic style of many directors, "and some, the lucky ones, became famous because they were given good stories and a cast of actors that the public wanted to see."[15] Ironically, by the late 1940s, many of those Florey assisted in the 1920s had worked their way down into the realm of low-budget pictures, directing for the Poverty Row studios Florey always shunned.

With his varied experience, Florey felt qualified to become a director of features, and in the spring of 1926 asked the M-G-M executives for a promotion. Proposing some scenarios and screening Fifty-Fifty, he was promised a few projects, none of which were ever made. Finally they suggested that Florey should begin with an independent production, securing him a position at Tiffany. Arriving there,

1900-1928: Early Years

he was told that what was most needed at the moment was not a director but a writer. He was given until the following evening to complete a scenario and continuity for which his collaborator, Houston Bill Branch, had only the vaguest plans. But after laboring well into the night, That Model from Paris was ready at the appointed time. Only three days later shooting began on this romantic comedy. During production, director Louis Gasnier became ill, and Florey was called upon to replace him. But he received no screen credit for his efforts in either of these respects.

One Hour of Love, one of the studio's top films of the season, soon followed. In this case Tiffany, well pleased with Florey's previous work, assigned him to help write the continuity, then gave him full direction of the movie. The story told of a romance in the modern, developing West as a spoiled society girl learns not to trifle with the affections of a tough-minded construction engineer with whom she unintentionally falls in love. Made in twelve days in July for $100,000, One Hour of Love starred the studio's most important players, as well as some outside stars who were brought in. During the course of filming, Florey was taught many of the tricks of the "quickie" trade, such as editing in the camera and never photographing a shot from more than one view, avoiding multiple coverage. In this way he only exposed some 30,000 feet of film, barely one-tenth what the majors would have utilized on a similar production. The picture received rather good reviews (especially for the efforts of a novice director saddled with a cliche-ridden scenario) and was commercially successful, especially for the product of a small company.

Proud of his first American feature, Florey looked forward to showing the result of his efforts at his old studio. He made an appointment with M-G-M executive Bernard Hyman and reserved a screening room. But when Florey arrived, he was told that Hyman was tied up in conference for the rest of the day and would be unable to see One Hour of Love. Disappointed, holding seven cans of film under his arm, he was standing dejectedly when hailed by John Gilbert. A friend from Monte Cristo and the months spent at M-G-M, Gilbert asked to see One Hour of Love, promising to tell Hyman about it. Florey was deeply touched that such a major star would be so considerate and, remembering the kindness, tried to help Gilbert years later when the silent star's career had declined.

The Tiffany program for the year being nearly complete, there were no more directorial jobs available at the studio. Not wishing to return to an assistant's job, Florey collaborated on a number of other scenarios before leaving to look for work elsewhere. But momentarily disgusted by the conditions on Poverty Row, he decided to accept a job at Fox helping Frank Borzage prepare the atmosphere of World War I Paris for 7th Heaven. In September, Florey joined the Samuel Goldwyn Company to become first assistant director to Henry King (whom he had met in 1923 on the Valentino tour) for The Magic Flame, and this kept him busy for eighteen weeks.

In early 1927 Florey spent a couple of months at United Artists preparing a scenario of John Kendrick Bang's 1895 novel, The Houseboat on the Styx; it involved a multitude of famous historical characters returning in the present to be played by all the top stars associated with the company. The performers were to play shades of themselves: Douglas Fairbanks as D'Artagnan; Mary Pickford, Mary Stuart; Charlie Chaplin, Hamlet; John Barrymore, François Villon; Gloria Swanson, Cleopatra; and Norma Talmadge was to be Madame du Barry. Florey even suggested Ernst Lubitsch portray Napoleon. The idea had been proposed by Florey at a Pickfair Christmas Party, where it was enthusiastically received; however it had to be abandoned when director Emmett Flynn, who owned the screen rights, demanded too high a price and the budget seemed prohibitive.

The Romantic Age, made in March for Columbia, marked Florey's return to directing on his own. He called this romance of a flapper who falls for an older man "a nice comedy drama...."[16] Although made even more speedily than the Tiffany pictures had been, it was rather well received.

Face Value was started two months later at Sterling Pictures, an independent company headed by Joe Rock and based at Universal. This film was a stark drama of a disfigured World War I veteran and the difficulties he and his fiancée encounter in trying to adjust to his condition. Florey disliked Face Value and only took it for the opportunity to direct. Some forty years later he saw the movie again and found his opinion unchanged. "I was very disappointed by Face Value, found it slow and poorly done--the actors were not very good. We made these features in about ten shooting days, locations included, and for extremely little money...."[17] (The budget was around $15,000.) Nonetheless, reviewers found many more redeeming qualities in Florey's effort than is indicated by his harsh self-critique.

He remained at Universal, becoming gagman and assistant in July to William Beaudine on The Cohens and the Kellys in Paris. He also headed the second unit on this comedy, shooting the climactic aerial sequences. Florey then decided to resume assisting Henry King, who was about to embark on production of The Woman Disputed in the winter of 1927-28. He explained the move this way:

> I couldn't afford to be director for the independent studios.... Columbia and Tiffany paid me $175-200 a picture--and that usually included editing it. A good first assistant at the majors got $250 a week, and was assured of months of employment.[18]

Florey found that making independent movies was not leading to a directorial contract with the majors. In fact, it would not be these initial features that would start him on the road to acclaim, but rather the experimental shorts he made in 1927 and 1928.

AVANT-GARDE FILMMAKER, 1927-29

The four experimental shorts Florey made between 1927 and 1929 marked the beginning of his career as a director with a distinctive stylistic signature. The influence of expressionism and the avant-garde, as well as the humanistic concern that would characterize some of his finest films, first became evident here. The best known of these, The Life and Death of 9413--a Hollywood Extra, and its three successors--The Loves of Zero, Johann the Coffin Maker, and Skyscraper Symphony--demonstrate a trait that would become a truism of Florey's canon: his best work was frequently done when he had only the most modest resources at his disposal. He had the ability to operate within a meager budget at a rapid pace, while still turning out a product that was inventive and of high quality.

Florey had been toying with making non-commercial films on his own for at least two years before he was ready

to exhibit a product. In fact, The Life and Death of 9413--
a Hollywood Extra was not his initial such effort, but only
the first he completed and allowed to be shown publicly.
Around 1925 he had shot short strips of film showing the
abstract appearance of a hand in motion and the bizarre
patterns of light and shade this produced. This "futuristic
study of a hand against a shadowy background with a glit-
tering shaft of light alongside," he explained, "was obtained
by placing a milk bottle beside the hand with a flashlight
and screens to direct the light just where it would do the
most good."[19]

The next year he developed the scenario for a horror
picture, to be titled The Mad Doctor, which he admitted distinctly revealed the influence of The Cabinet of Dr. Caligari
(Germany, 1919). Florey photographed tests with Michael
Visaroff in the title role, which is as far as the project
seems to have gone; only a few stills survive today. These
reveal Visaroff in a distinctively "Caligari-esque" costume,
pose, and lighting, similar to Bela Lugosi's appearance as
Doctor Mirakle in Murders in the Rue Morgue, six years
later. As well, some of the Bohemian tests Florey designed
and shot for Lillian Gish for La Boheme have an expressionist element; one resembled Caligari's encounter with inacces-
sible policemen perched atop unnaturally high stools.

The Life and Death of 9413--a Hollywood Extra was,
however, certainly Florey's first complete and important attempt to make a non-commercial film. It had a long gesta-
tion period in his mind. Within a few years of arriving in
Hollywood, he conceived of the idea of making a short picture based on the impressions of an "everyman" actor who
arrives in the movie capital, dreaming of becoming a star,
only to have his hopes crumble.[20] This concept was perhaps inspired by Florey's contact, while correspondent for
Cinemagazine, with many aspiring performers, both successful and not, who found their careers dependent on the whims
of public fancy and the vagaries of producers. But it was
not until late in 1927 that a delay in the shooting of The
Woman Disputed provided him the opportunity to bring his
idea to fruition.

The inspiration for the scenario came to Florey while
attending a performance of George Gershwin's "Rhapsody in
Blue." He explained:

1900-1928: Early Years

Michael Visaroff in a Caligari-esque costume and pose for a test as The Mad Doctor, directed by Florey in 1925.

This 1925 test (directed by Florey) of Lillian Gish for La Boheme again reveals the influence of The Cabinet of Dr. Caligari in the unnatural elevation of Henry Victor on a stool.

1900-1928: Early Years

> It was after having heard this extraordinary composition that I had written, under the influence of a sudden inspiration, the continuity in musical rhythm of the adventures of my extra in Hollywood, the movements and attitudes of which appeared to synchronize themselves with Gershwin's notes.[21]

The script was worked out in precise detail, shot by shot, until Florey knew exactly how much footage he would need.

> I sit down and write my scenario.... Then I figure out my scenes--so many scenes, so many feet. You see? Long shot--ten feet. Close-up, four feet. So. I want 1,200 feet and no waste.[22]

This planning was necessary because the cost of film stock would be one of the most expensive items involved in the production.[23]

> Negative $25.00
> 5-and-10-cent Store Props 3.00
> Developing and printing 55.00
> Transportation, odds and ends 14.00
> $97.00

The budget was always of concern because the finances were supplied by Florey's own modest salary.

The prices charged for negative film through the studio suppliers were prohibitively expensive, so he tried a different source.

> Fairbanks had just finished camera work on The Gaucho, and I knew that at the end of "shooting" on every big picture in Hollywood there is always much good scrap film left over in the cameras. I went over to the Fairbanks "lot" and succeeded in getting a thousand feet of negative in ten- and twenty-foot strips.[24]

He then spliced the strips together into a full reel of negative.

Another even greater potential obstacle had to be overcome: acquiring the use of a camera, the cost of which was unquestionably beyond Florey's resources. One evening in a restaurant he met Slavko Vorkapich, the Serbian artist later famous for his montages. Florey, discovering that Vorkapich owned a camera, recalled how they agreed to pool their resources:

> He has a little amateur camera--what they sell for "toy" cameras. It has one lens--a DeVry; I say to Slav, "Slav, I have an idea but not much money--you have a camera and you are a clever painter. Let's make the picture in collaboration and we will split the benefit."[25]

Vorkapich became responsible for the construction of the miniature sets, made mostly of paper cubes, cigar boxes, tin cans, children's toys, and other odds and ends. Days were spent on this task, Florey cutting the cardboard from laundered shirts and shaping them into squares, while Vorkapich painted them impressionistically to resemble buildings. The "effect of [a] golden pavement" in heaven was derived from the "skillful placement of some polished sardine cans."[26] Forty-five sets in all, none larger than about two feet square, were assembled; the most elaborate took three hours to build and the most expensive cost $1.67.

All the lighting in the picture was provided by a single 400-watt bulb. Vorkapich created some of the spectacular illumination on the miniatures, while the actors had to function as their own lighting men. When moving, they simply passed the light from one hand to the other. Thus, with players doubling as electricians, the set designed as photographer, and the director as actor, cameraman, author and editor, responsibilities were shared all around.

Most of the camera work was done by Florey himself, along with Vorkapich and Paul Ivano. Gregg Toland, then assistant to George Barnes, had use of a Mitchell camera, allowing some shots which would have been impossible with the single-lens DeVry. These scenes, taken in Toland's large white-walled garage, included some three hundred feet of close-ups and what Florey called "trick stuff ... four or five exposures on one plate."[27]

Only three professional performers appeared throughout the picture. The title role was played by Jules Raucourt,

Gregg Toland visits Florey two decades after The Life and Death of 9413--a Hollywood Extra, in 1948, just a few weeks before Toland's death.

formerly a leading man who, by 1927, was--appropriately for his part in A Hollywood Extra--unemployed and nearly forgotten. (He later wrote a novel using the movie's title.) The vapid star was portrayed by Voya George, a Rumanian friend of Vorkapich. The female part was played by Adriane Marsh, an authentic extra. A few others were seen momentarily, including Florey, whose disembodied mouth and pointing finger portrayed the casting director.

A Hollywood Extra was prepared and shot over a period of only three weeks. Six evenings and two Sundays--during which exterior scenes were taken around Hollywood and the major studios--were spent photographing the 150 scenes that comprise the short. Florey painted two walls of his apartment black to serve as sets and constantly played a record of Gershwin's rhapsody "so that both my players and even myself would become 'saturated' with the rhythm of the 'blues'"[28]--much to the discontent of his neighbors and landlord.

Together with Vorkapich, Florey edited A Hollywood Extra to a one-reel length of 1,200 feet, arranging all shots, moods, movement of players, and repetition of scenes to be synchronized with "Rhapsody in Blue." (This is no longer true of the shortened and mutilated versions still extant, which have lost most of the original rhythm and lyrical quality. Florey himself had no interest in seeing these distorted relics preserved.) Although Vorkapich's famous montage work in later years has caused some to ignore Florey's role in this aspect of the film, the "skillful understanding of editing"[29] shown in all four of his avant-garde pictures indicate the excellence achieved in this instance was hardly due exclusively to his collaborator.

Indeed, Florey began his movie career as an editor and often, on his features, "cut in the camera." His skill in editing on his own is exhibited in the surviving two reels of silent 16mm film he shot during his 1937 trip to the Orient. One sequence, of the embarkation of a steamer--beginning with Florey and Nick Grinde waving and ending on a child and their bouquet--provides a virtuoso demonstration of this ability. The mood of farewell is captured as it reaches a fever pitch, the crowd waving flags and thousands of light streamers connecting boat and dock. They flutter in the wind, with departure foretold by their decreasing density

1900-1928: Early Years

Florey made the camera his hobby as well as his profession, which his films shot in the Orient during the 1930s indicate. Here he is filming the flurry of activity surrounding the embarkation of a ship, later edited (on his own) into a remarkable sequence.

and buoyancy. In between these shots numerous changes of camera angle take place, first from one end of the ship, then the other, as Florey discovers the visual poetry inherent in this ritual. Isolated details are picked out from the mass of humanity: a girl choking back tears, dabbing them from her face; one man with his camera and another lighting his pipe; a mounted life preserver with the ship's name and home port; a saddened old man and a sleeping baby.

Although Vorkapich had no role in either the scenario or direction of A Hollywood Extra, his impact being limited to the set design and miniature lighting, Florey generously insisted on sharing equal credit for conceiving and realizing the picture (note the use of the French term for filmmaking). Vorkapich's name was later written into the contract by

Florey's own hand. While doing nothing to promote the film at the time, in subsequent years when it was recognized as a classic, Vorkapich tried to claim more and more responsibility. Later critics tended to grant him such credit, although contemporary accounts of the picture's production record Florey as the dominant artistic influence. In both subject matter (see especially the section on <u>Hollywood Boulevard</u>) and visual style, <u>A Hollywood Extra</u> reflects the later work of Florey, not Vorkapich. As Ivano recalled, "Vorkapich tries to get credit, but he didn't do much."[30]

Upon its completion, Florey showed his little film to Charlie Chaplin, who was so impressed that he watched it five times and then invited the elite of Hollywood to a screening at him home. The audience merely expected one of the comedian's gags. Florey, fearing a negative reaction from the guests because of his satire of Hollywood, hid in the projection booth and snipped his name from the credits. But to his surprise "the producers and stars present ... were vitally interested in this new technique and at the unexpected angles of the shots."[31] When Chaplin divulged the identity of the movie's creator, Florey was cheered. Douglas Fairbanks was moved to offer Florey his editing facility to prepare <u>A Hollywood Extra</u> for public exhibition. The enthusiasm was echoed even by such a traditional director as Henry King: "Everybody went wild over it.... It was way ahead of its time ... a stroke of genius ... it was the most original thought I ever saw."[32]

Also present was Joseph Schenck, who arranged for <u>A Hollywood Extra</u> to be shown at the new United Artists theater on Broadway, where it was given the presentation that usually accompanies a "big" picture. A special musical score, prepared by Dr. Hugo Riesenfeld and based on "Rhapsody in Blue," was played by a live orchestra. Eventually the film was released by F.B.O. to over 700 theaters in America alone.[33]

Critics heaped praise on the movie and its young director, giving it the coverage attending a major presentation. <u>Film Mercury</u> said, "If this production had been made in Europe and heralded as a hit, it would ... have been called a masterpiece."[34] There were literary comparisons: one called Florey the Eugene O'Neill of the cinema,[35] another claimed the film "ranks in cinema production somewhere about

1900-1928: Early Years

where Gertrude Stein ranks in poetry."[36] Other comments were even more laudatory. Anabel Lane predicted:

> Robert Florey will one day hold a position of one of the bigger film directors. It may take some time, he may have many rebuffs but eventually he will gain prominence.[37]

Hollywood Magazine went so far as to editorialize, "when his finances are such that he can turn out feature-length pictures, his fame will be spread around the world."[38] From the other side, Variety cynically announced "a suspicion this is an unannounced foreign-made short."[39]

It is ironic that a movie so well received by the established Hollywood filmmaking industry was also one of the earliest American avant-garde pictures, and the first to show the influence of German Expressionism, particularly The Cabinet of Dr. Caligari (Germany, 1919), according to Lewis Jacobs and David Curtis.[40]

> Expressionism not only appealed to the ideological temper of the time, but suited the technical resources of the motion picture novitiates as well. Lack of money and experience had to be offset by ingenuity and fearlessness. "Effects" became a chief goal. The camera and its devices, the setting, and any object at hand that could be manipulated for an effect were exploited toward achieving a striking impression.[41]

There is also some of the influence of Georges Méliès in the trickery and playfulness of some of the style and settings.

The story of The Life and Death of 9413--a Hollywood Extra "is a brilliant, biting and correct exposé of the experiences of an extra."[42] Florey described his plot this way:

> "It is not much. Just about a man who is a fine actor in Iowa or somewhere and who comes to Hollywood and expects to conquer it overnight. Pompous, all ego...." And he illustrated with a very Napoleonic pose.... "The would-be idol of Hollywood goes to studios.... The casting director--he is merely a hand that rejects or selects. [He inscribes a number,

9413, on the forehead of the actor (Raucourt), making him an extra.] And the rest just tells how he loses out all around."43

Other performers audition at the same time. One of these has a completely bland, expressionless face (George), contrasting with Raucourt's evident sincerity. George dons a series of masks, mimicking other well-known actors in an effort to compensate for his own lack of personality. His "blah-blahs" are greeted with enthusiasm by the studio chiefs and the public. When Raucourt appears in a scene opposite George, he is treated with disdain by the new star, Raucourt's own mask appearing dingy in comparison to that of the vapid celebrity. Success eludes Raucourt as he is daily faced with the haunting sign, "no casting today." (The generally overwrought, tormented style of the acting was another aspect of the debt to German expressionism.) Frantically he searches for a part, to no avail, finally dying of privation (represented by the cutting of a film strip). Although his burial is mocked by his fellow performers, Raucourt ascends to Heaven, where the offensive number is erased and he becomes an angel--a denouement intended as a satire on Hollywood's traditional happy endings.44

Florey uses shapes, angles, and disorientation to tell a melodramatic narrative. The compositions in A Hollywood Extra can be divided into roughly three varieties: newsreel-type scenes of Hollywood and the studios; close-ups with live actors; and miniatures, buildings, machines, and geometrical designs made of paper and metal and characterized by distortion and superimposition. These lively caricatures of the movie city quiver, reflecting light in a myriad of directions according to the mood of its inhabitants, embodying their impersonality.

As a contrast to the artificial scenes of the city are newsreel-type shots of the streets and local sights of Hollywood, along with the images of spotlights criss-crossing the night sky at movie previews. The studios are symbolized by scenes of moving cameras, reels, and dangling celluloid strips. Strangely, all these authentic, non-expressionistic scenes, naturalistic in content even if shot from a wildly moving or tilted camera and edited into rapid juxtapositions, are announced with the subtitle "dreams." Florey seems to be saying that this is the false surface of Hollywood: the city, the glitter, the ceremonies, all those things at which Raucourt marvels. This seemingly objective world--in terms of pictorial content--is the one labeled as the dream mode, while expressionism is used to tell the story of disillusionment. In A Hollywood Extra, seeing filmland as anything but a fantastic place is to see it as a dream; only when regarding the motion picture capital as an unreal "paradise" of cruelty and failure is one perceiving the truth behind the facade. Thus, Florey reverses conventional expectations of the visual style customarily used to tell the different parts of the story, handling the reality of Raucourt's experiences expressionistically, while portraying objectively the glamor and success that turn out to be only the material of dreams.

The third type of composition predominating in A Hollywood Extra was the heavy use of the close-up. Placed against a black background, the faces of the three performers are often kept partially in shadow--blocking off part of their features and depriving them of wholeness. This effect further reduces Raucourt's individualism, a point emphasized by the drawing of the number on his forehead and a star on that of the bland actor who succeeds. The casting director is mocked with an extreme close-up revealing only his mouth stuffed with a cigar, one hand holding a phone the other shaking a pointed finger.

This reliance on the close-up was due not only to the limited lighting available from the single 400-watt bulb, but was also deliberate, becoming a brand of Florey's style explored in his later features, especially Murders in the Rue Morgue, The Preview Murder Mystery, and The Beast with Five Fingers. Other ingredients of A Hollywood Extra reappeared in later Florey pictures. The scenes taken around Hollywood closely resemble those seen in the first reel of Hollywood Boulevard. The purely expressionist cemetery, with its distorted and angled tombstones, was used in almost equally bizarre fashion in Johann the Coffin Maker, Frankenstein, and Hotel Imperial. Superimpositions and split screen would be heavily employed in his next avant-garde short, The Loves of Zero, and even appear in The Hole in the Wall and The Cocoanuts. The overall style, and even portions of the story, such as Raucourt rising from his grave, were echoed in Florey's later horror films. As well, the actors who donated their time to help Florey discovered that he did not forget the favor, and such people as Joseph Marievsky and Agostino Borgato were frequently seen in bit parts in Florey's features over the next two decades.

A Hollywood Extra is a highly cinematic film, without subtitles; even the two captions are of moving cardboard cutouts with light flashing through and casting spreading shadows, making them a fully integrated and visual element. Sound is even approximated through the vigorous motions of a hand playing a trombone and close-ups looking into the horn of the instrument. Virtually every trick of the camera is employed, with special attention given to tempo, rhythm, and substitution, applying "innuendo in place of photographic realism."[45]

Many consider A Hollywood Extra the single best and most complete film Florey ever made; this may be because it was one of the very few efforts in which he had total control over all phases of production. Certainly it has received more praise and attention than his other pictures. It clearly demonstrates his indebtedness to the German school and The Cabinet of Dr. Caligari in particular. At the same time, A Hollywood Extra serves as a blueprint for Florey's future techniques, giving evidence of his interest in visual experimentation and use of the expressionistic style to tell stories that are both humanistic and yet have a tinge of the macabre. A Hollywood Extra was something new to America, both in style and substance; more than any other single American film it began the avant-garde in this country.

The Loves of Zero, Florey's second avant-garde short, was prompted by the success of A Hollywood Extra. This new film, made in March 1928, had a budget between $92 and $125 (according to various sources), with a 1,200-foot, ten-minute length. Production was under the auspices of United Artists. Two Russians, Joseph Marievsky, a dancer with Nikita Balieff's "Chauve-Souris," and Tamara Shavrova, were given the leads, with Anielka and Marco Elter and Arthur Hurni also featured.

On this effort Florey again had a collaborator. William Cameron Menzies, then thirty-one and set designer on The Woman Disputed, had seen A Hollywood Extra and was eager to work with its creator. Together they co-authored the scenario of The Loves of Zero; Florey directed (Nate Stein was the assistant) while Menzies designed the sets. (Notably

Menzies' own subsequent experimental pictures cost several thousand dollars apiece, indicating it was Florey's talent that kept the budget so low.)

Herman G. Weinberg provides one of the few complete outlines of the plot.

> The Loves of Zero tells the serio-comic story of an absurd Harlequin, who plays his trombone while courting Columbine. An ecstatic courtship follows and then Columbine is called away, much to her and his chagrin. Harlequin tries to console himself with another ravishing creature but she only laughs at him and goes away with two flaneurs. His despair lasts until news comes of Columbine's death. This is too much. He is haunted by evil, leering faces. A huge hand closes in on him and snuffs out his unhappy existence.[46]

The Loves of Zero did not provoke the universal critical acclaim that greeted A Hollywood Extra. Comparing Zero to its predecessor, reviewers found this new film less impressive and entertaining, some complaining that the theme and story were elusive. While not truly abstract, neither did it possess a strong narrative. One critic claimed the movie "proved that a sense of cinema was hampered by an uncinematic theme."[47] Another reviewer wrote:

> There are fragments of magic in The Loves of Zero .... But the fragments remain fragments, which, however fantastic or beautiful, do not succeed in generating emotion in the beholder.

However, he concluded, "Let's hope that they continue their experiments."[48]

The Loves of Zero did receive commendation for the imaginative techniques it utilized.

> Despite the thinness of its story and its occasional too-clever tricks, [Zero] is interesting for the simplicity of sets, formalized movement and general feeling for cinematic quality.[49]

Whereas Florey had only begun to experiment with superimpositions and the split screen in A Hollywood Extra, they

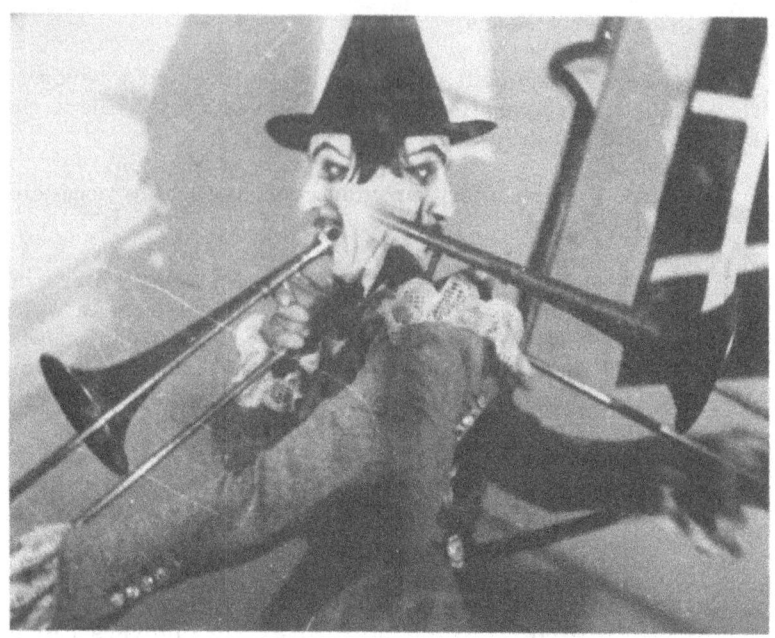

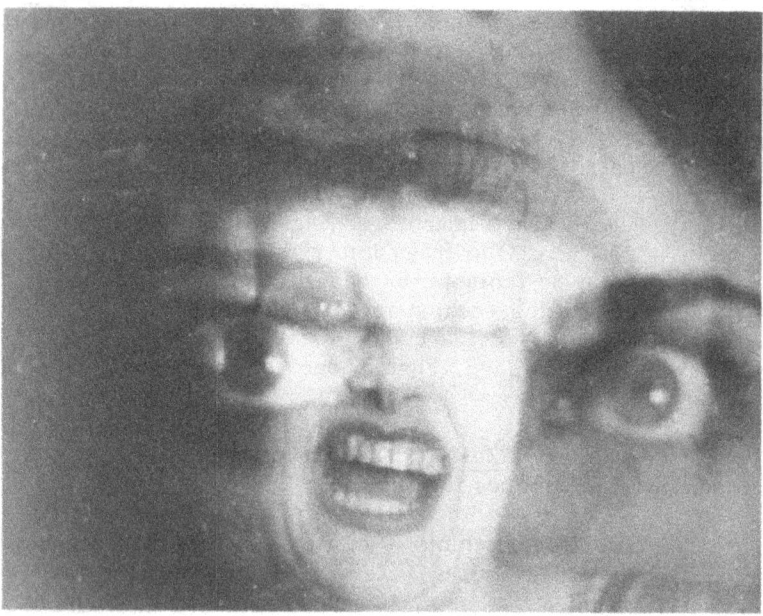

Trick shots in <u>The Loves of Zero</u>: Joseph Marievsky, above, and the introduction of the prostitute, Anielka Elter, below, with the use of double exposures.

1900-1928: Early Years

Joseph Marievsky, in the lower left corner, is overwhelmed during the machine street sequence of The Loves of Zero.

were pervasive in The Loves of Zero. "Psychological reactions are expressed by photographic devices such as the multiplication of faces in a revolving circle"[50] and large close-ups of characters split into many different size parts. Another instance was

> the remarkable Machine Street sequence, in which the upper portion of the scene is filled with multiple exposures of whirling machinery and the lower portion showing the tiny figure of the lonely hero walking home.[51]

Johann the Coffin Maker (sometimes simply known as The Coffin Maker) was made at the request of the Film Art Guild of New York upon completion of The Loves of Zero. This time Florey worked essentially without an active collaborator except for cameraman Edward Fitzgerald, who had also photographed Zero, and a few set designs prepared by

Menzies. Johann the Coffin Maker was the most ambitious effort so far, costing $200, lasting two and one half reels, and featuring a cast of over twenty. The title role was played by Agostino Borgato (a star of The Magic Flame who in later years could be frequently spotted doing bits in Florey's features), and the others included Tania Smirnova as the prostitute, Nina Ivanova, David Mir, Alexander Woloshin, E. Achron, Serge Tamoff, and Arthur Hurni. As in the previous pictures, actors and associates donated their time, judging that the resulting publicity would provide adequate compensation.

> The players were recruited from a mob of extras that had worked on the set earlier that day in [The Woman Disputed]. Florey had no written script, but only a rough idea of what he wanted. It was begun at six o'clock on Saturday night and finished early Sunday morning. Only a few "retakes" were necessary on Monday night.[52]

The plot concerns an old man whose trade is death and who had just received an order for a child's coffin. It is Christmas Eve, and Johann brings back a few of the dead from their graves--a murderous Apache, a soldier, and a prostitute--offering them a bottle of wine to tell how they met their deaths. There were only three sets: "the coffin maker's workshop, a lonely room of mourning, and a graveyard."[53]

> When they return to their homes beneath the sod the coffin maker hears a knocking at the door. It is his own bride--Death--come to wed him. Together they climb into a casket he built for himself. And he closes down the lid.[54]

Herman G. Weinberg described it as "a Poe-like scenario" with "a dash of Baudelaire and Heine at their bitterest."[55]

Johann the Coffin Maker was, like its predecessors, photographed in a very expressionistic style--though in a more straightforward manner, as was appropriate to the simple tale. It lacked the extensive effects, miniatures, and superimpositions of the first two. Perhaps because of this, as well as the relatively comprehensible narrative, Johann the Coffin Maker was warmly received by the press. The

1900-1928: Early Years

Agostino Borgato as Johann in Johann the Coffin Maker.

Los Angeles Herald commented that this "venture into futuristic symbolism ... betrays an unschooled imagination of some power."[56]

Skyscraper Symphony (sometimes simply called Skyscrapers) was Florey's last contribution to the avant-garde, made in the late spring of 1929, over a year after Johann the Coffin Maker. By this time he had become an established contract director at the Paramount Astoria studios in New York. His feature, The Battle of Paris, was being shot at night because the few sound stages were operating on a 24-hour schedule. When he arrived at his apartment in the morning, the noise of riveters at work on a new building on nearby Lexington Avenue kept him awake. So Florey decided to take advantage of the unusual hours and do another short picture on his own.

Only a few months before, he had filmed a travelogue, Bonjour, New York!, at a variety of metropolitan locations,

<u>Skyscraper Symphony</u> was a montage of the patterns made by New York buildings against the skyline from various bizarre camera angles.

and Florey's new experimental movie was to show the influence of the "city symphony" genre, then in vogue. During three mornings he photographed, with a hand-held DeVry, a montage of scenes emphasizing the geometrical patterns made by buildings when shot from low angles. Florey described his film as "an architectural study of the New York skyscrapers seen from way high or from down shooting up, with wide and sometimes distorted angles, 24mm shots, and quick pan shots with fast editing."[57] <u>Skyscraper Symphony</u> lasted a single reel in length and received more limited distribution than its three predecessors.

Prior to Florey's efforts, aspiring artists had regarded individual expression through the cinema as a goal that could not be realized. It seemed impossible for an original scenario to survive the standardizing pressures of producers, stars, and directors. To avoid conformity, one had not only to

1900-1928: Early Years

write, but also to make the film--and the costs of financing such a venture could be prohibitive. Even The Salvation Hunters, directed by Josef von Sternberg, which had appeared to go the limit for a low budget at only $5,000, was still well beyond the range of an ambitious single artist.

But the small cost of Florey's pictures, all financed out of his own pocket, placed the potential for independent filmmaking in the hands of almost anyone. Their success inspired a flood of experimental movies utilizing the expressionistic style. Admittedly, Florey possessed advantages from the outset that were unavailable to many others. He was already a member of the film community, with access to studios. He knew powerful people like Charlie Chaplin and Douglas Fairbanks who championed his cause.

Florey had decided to make these movies out of an urge to present unusual stories on the screen in an artistic manner. He explained, "As a protest against the stupidity of the scenarios of the pictures that I directed, here and there (1926-1927) I decided to re-act and to produce pictures of my own!"[58] He probably hoped they might advance his career, although he could never have guessed what a positive reception his efforts would have. He was not particularly wedded to the idea of participating in the avant-garde movement; his involvement with it was relatively short-lived, lasting less than three years. Twenty-five years later he would suggest some dialogue mocking the pretentions of self-conscious artistry for a Four Star Playhouse television drama, For Art's Sake. Nor did he place much value on his own experimental films, believing that they

> should be made only to throw away, after they have served their purpose of showing the amateur the flaws of his work. The real artist will someday make something that satisfies him--that will be the beginning of a beautiful picture later. No momentary disappointment will discourage him from pursuit of this ideal.[59]

Instead, his real goal from the very beginning seems to have been to mix expressionism and avant-garde methods into studio-made features, for in early 1929 he wrote "the ideal thing ... would be to combine artistic ideas, technique, and treatment with the scenarios produced for the general public."[60]

Thus, although Florey's actual association with the avant-garde was brief, its influence on his cinematic style was apparent throughout the remainder of his career. Certainly it was largely responsible for his long affection for oblique camera angles, a persistent trait in his movies, particularly during the years when such effects were less fashionable and discouraged by the studios as inimical to the classical seamless style. Indeed, Florey's connection with the avant-garde and his fondness for its style may have been partially responsible for his assignment in the 1930s to so many "B" productions.

This attitude was enunciated by one reviewer who, disenchanted with the unconventional style of Florey's experimental films, pinpointed the source of her frustration.

> At no time does he introduce his characters in equilibrium if he can pilot them on horizontally or at some grotesque diagonal angle. We find half of one man's face grafted on to half of another's, close-ups of ladies with eight or nine heads vibrating hydrawise around one forlorn body, Brobdingnagian beings condensing amid Lilliputian settings and then dissolving again.[61]

A more perceptive and eloquent critic summed up the technique and its purpose in the following words:

> M. Florey seems influenced by <u>Caligari</u>, but there is a freshness about his work, and an individuality, which show how the cinema can be used to express nothing more tangible than an idea. It is the effect he wants to bring out, his idea, that M. Florey relies on; the means are secondary and slight, but the greatest use is made of them and though striking, they remain subservient to the general plan. There is none of that piling up of material in the hope that it will impress by its size if not express by its significance.[62]

Ironically, despite unusually wide distribution in the United States and overseas, from England to Italy and even the Soviet Union, Florey never earned a cent from any of these films. In their French release, handled by Pierre Braunberger, Florey received no credit either on the screen or in publicity. Worse, the original negatives of all the movies were inadvertently destroyed while in storage in New York, and distributors lost or disposed of their prints, heedless of preservation efforts. Only A Hollywood Extra survives in battered form and is readily accessible for appraisal today--in a version assembled from some 700 fragments! A copy of The Loves of Zero reportedly survives in the British National Film Archives, although it is unavailable elsewhere, while Johann the Coffin Maker and Skyscraper Symphony have completely disappeared, leaving nothing but contemporary reports and stills by which to judge them.

NOTES

1. Robert Florey, photo album I: 1900-1931, Florey collection.
2. Ibid.
3. Ibid.
4. Robert Florey, Hollywood D'Hier et D'Aujourd'Hui (Paris: Editions Prisma, 1948), p. 209. All translations courtesy of Evelyn Copeland.
5. Florey, photo album I.
6. Robert Florey, unidentified correspondence, Florey collection.
7. Richard Abel, French Cinema: The First Wave, 1915-1930 (Princeton, N.J.: Princeton University Press, 1985), p. 247.
8. Florey, photo album I.
9. Florey, Hollywood D'Hier et D'Aujourd'Hui, p. 122.
10. Paul Ivano, interview with the author, November 13, 1981.
11. Jack Spears, Hollywood: The Golden Era (New York: A.S. Barnes, 1971), p. 338.
12. Florey, photo album I.
13. Ibid.
14. Robert Florey, letter to Jack Spears, January 2, 1970.
15. Robert Florey, unidentified correspondence, Florey collection.
16. Robert Florey, letter to Jack Spears, June 18, 1971.
17. Robert Florey, letter to Jack Spears, December 20, 1972.
18. Spears, p. 341.
19. "How a Big Lens and Lighting Specialist Gets His Effects," Washington Post, June 9, 1929.

20. "Young Director Here Describes His Impressionistic Film Drama," unidentified newspaper clipping (n.d.), scrapbook 1928-29, Florey collection.
21. Florey, Hollywood D'Hier et D'Aujourd'Hui, p. 145.
22. Kay Small, "He Made a Movie for $97!" Hollywood Magazine, March 23, 1928, p. 7.
23. A.L. Woolridge, "$97 Movie Made in Hollywood Kitchen," Modern Mechanics (n.d.), p. 152; scrapbook 1928-29, Florey collection.
24. "Young Director...."
25. Small, p. 7.
26. "How a Big Lens...."
27. Small, p. 29.
28. "Young Director...."
29. Anthony Slide, in Christopher Lyon and Susan Doll, eds., International Dictionary of Films and Filmmakers, Volume 2 (Chicago: Macmillan, 1984), p. 191.
30. Ivano interview.
31. Florey, Hollywood D'Hier et D'Aujourd'Hui, p. 145.
32. Henry King, interview with the author, July 28, 1981.
33. "As Is," Close Up, 2 (June 1928):5.
34. Anabel Lane, "Short Dramas Should Be Encouraged," Film Mercury, July 27, 1928.
35. Small, p. 7.
36. E.M.K., "Unusual Film From Hollywood," unidentified newspaper clipping (n.d.), scrapbook 1928-29, Florey collection.
37. Anabel Lane, Film Mercury, August 17, 1928.
38. Hollywood Magazine, June 8, 1928.
39. Weekly Variety, June 20, 1928.
40. Lewis Jacobs, "Experimental Cinema in America" in The Rise of the American Film (New York: Teachers College Press, 1965), p. 547. Cf., David Curtis, Experimental Cinema (New York: Universe Books, 1977), p. 39.
41. Jacobs, p. 547.
42. Lane, "Short Dramas...."
43. Small, p. 7.
44. Spears, p. 342.
45. Herman G. Weinberg, "A Paradox of the Photoplay," Movie Makers, 4 (January 1929):867.
46. Herman G. Weinberg, "A Trio of Thrillers," unidentified newspaper clipping (n.d.), scrapbook 1928-29, Florey collection.
47. Robert Herring, "Art in the Cinema," Creative Art, 4 (May 1929):361.

1900-1928: Early Years

48. Gilbert Brown, "Filmarte," Los Angeles Express (n.d.), Scrapbook 1928-29, Florey collection.
49. C. Adolph Glassgold, unidentified magazine clipping (n.d.), scrapbook 1928-29, Florey collection.
50. National Film Archive, Part III: Silent Fiction Films, 1895-1930 (London: British Film Institute, 1966), p. 268.
51. Spears, p. 344.
52. Weinberg, "A Trio of Thrillers."
53. Ibid.
54. Irene Thirer, "Fifth Avenue Playhouse's Fine Program," unidentified newspaper clipping (n.d.), scrapbook 1928-29, Florey collection.
55. Weinberg, "A Trio of Thrillers."
56. "Filmarte," Los Angeles Herald, June 29, 1929.
57. Robert Florey, letter to Anthony Slide (n.d.).
58. Florey, photo album I.
59. Marguerite Tazelaar, "Amateurs Point the Way," Movie Makers, 4 (September 1929):599.
60. Herring, p. 361.
61. Katherine Zimmerman, "Fifth Avenue Playhouse Offers Impressionistic Photoplay Program," New York Telegraph, October 11, 1928.
62. Herring, p. 360.

Chapter III

1928-1932: FIRST MAJOR
COMMERCIAL FILMS

PARAMOUNT (ASTORIA), 1928-29

The success of Florey's avant-garde pictures brought him to the attention of the managers of Paramount-Famous-Lasky, then looking for new talent as they embarked on the production of their first talking pictures. As part of this move, the old Astoria studio on Long Island was being reopened to facilitate filming with the stars of the New York stage. The man supervising these operations,[1] Monta Bell, had been one of those present at the dinner party where Charlie Chaplin presented The Life and Death of 9413--a Hollywood Extra. Bell, having known Florey for years and admiring his skills, arranged to obtain him a contract within weeks of taking over at Astoria. Since virtually no one had experience with the new medium of sound movies, Florey was suddenly as qualified a director as many more senior men in the industry.

The novelty of the techniques displayed in Florey's avant-garde films made him seem a promising talent in the midst of the transition to sound. As Irving Rapper, shortly to become his associate, recalled, "Florey had distinguished himself doing shorts with trick photography ... Bob was recruited by people like Bell because of his differences, camera angles so revolutionary they were totally un-American and very interesting. He would take a bit from the Russians and Germans, and was regarded as quite a newcomer."[2] Despite having seen only a half-dozen talkies, Florey was signed in June 1928 and dispatched to the East Coast the same night. (Earlier that month he had become an American citizen.)

When Florey arrived at Astoria, the most minimal resources were scarcely in place. Only one stage had been crudely soundproofed, a small basement that was broiling in the summer and freezing in the winter. While a larger stage was readied, Bell needed a young director who could quickly film dozens of tests, from eight in the morning until midnight, each usually lasting around 2,500 feet including close-ups. The purpose of this frantic activity was, as quickly as possible, "to find some photogenic faces with good recording voices to replace the Hollywood silent actors no longer 'usable.'"[3] Almost everyone of note, from performers to explorers, were recorded to discover if their voices were suitable for talking pictures; among those who received their baptism before Florey's camera were Ethel Barrymore, Walter Huston, Edward G. Robinson, Donald Meek, and Preston Foster. "They all came anxious to see and listen to how they sounded on the screen," Florey would recall, sadly remembering the many who gave up hope of movie careers upon hearing their test.[4]

The next step was to try out some of those whose tests had been successful in one or even two reel shorts. Florey filmed some two dozen of these humorous and musical skits; most were vehicles for well-known singers, comedians, and celebrities. As George Folsey, chief cinematographer for all the pictures at Astoria, recalled, "Anything that moved and talked in those days was a novelty, and we got people ... that played and sang, doing their numbers."[5] Often working on Sundays, these shorts were turned out at a prodigious rate, sometimes as many as three in a single day. Despite this, Florey managed to distinguish himself, as Irving Rapper observed.[6] Many of these one-reelers were made with black backdrops or other devices to integrate an expressionist or avant-garde flavor.

The popularity of the shorts was such that they were rushed into circulation so rapidly that Paramount usually did not even bother to copyright them; thus it is no longer possible to name more than a fraction of the titles. Those that are known provide a sampling: <u>Songs of Alice Boulden</u>; Eddie Cantor in <u>Back in Your Own Back Yard</u> and <u>Eddie Cantor</u>; <u>Two Sketches with Elinor Glyn</u> and <u>What Is "It"?</u>; <u>Borah Minnevitch and His Harmonica Rascals</u>; <u>Lillian Roth and Her Band</u>, <u>Lillian Roth and Her Piano Boys</u> and <u>Songs</u>

and Dances of Lillian Roth. Some of Florey's shorts, including one with Cantor and another with Helen Morgan, were saved and later added to the feature, Glorifying the American Girl, credited to Millard Webb. Florey felt expecially honored when Admiral Richard E. Byrd, fresh from a triumphal ticker-tape parade, stopped by Astoria to be directed in a ten-minute interview that became the prologue to the Academy Award-winning documentary feature, With Byrd at the South Pole. The next year Florey did more shorts, such as Tito Schipa and Alice Boulden, with Joseph Santley handling the staging.[7]

Night Club, a dramatic semi-feature and Astoria's first major musical, was entrusted to Florey in August 1928. The film resembled what he had been doing in the shorts, with a cast of over twenty Broadway stars performing musical routines. Others enacted brief vignettes of the activities going on in the main lounge and ladies' room, including risqué dialogue, adultery, prostitution, drug addiction, and suicide. Among the performers who appeared were Fannie Brice, Ann Pennington, Tamara Geva, Bobbe Arnst, Minnie Dupree, Pat Rooney and Pat Rooney, Jr., and Jimmie Carr and his Silver Slipper Orchestra. Based on a Katherine Brush story, Florey's creation of the atmosphere of Night Club was masterful. He would memorably vivify this milieu many times, most often as a cacophonous, animated environment full of bizarre behavior, in such movies as Hollywood Boulevard, Daughter of Shanghai, and The Desert Song.

Florey managed to summon the title setting of Night Club despite having to make the picture in a basement of the studio, the only space available. Sound quality presented a continuous problem. Up to 200 people were crowded into the makeshift set, during the worst heat of the summer, with many of them collapsing as the recording engineers demanded as many as ten takes of each scene. Nonetheless, some of the voices still "cackle like a yard full of perturbed hens,"[8] and Paramount waited a full year before putting Night Club into general release. By then they had taken advantage of its episodic structure and many revues to edit it substantially, until barely twenty-eight minutes of the film were left. Only a twelve-minute prologue by Donald Ogden Stewart kept Night Club from having been turned into, at forty minutes, a lengthy short. (The Pusher-in-the-Face was frequently thrown in to round out the program.) Later,

1928-1932: First Major Commercial Films   107

Night Club was abridged even further to one-reel. This version was re-titled Broadway Nights and preserved only a few of the specialty numbers; Florey's name did not even appear on the credits.

The Pusher-in-the-Face, based on F. Scott Fitzgerald's humorous short story, was Florey's next picture, and one of an entirely different nature. A three-reeler (edited down from four), it was started in September and also shot on the small stage in the basement. Neither of the unpredictable stars, Lester Allen and Raymond Hitchcock, felt the need to learn their script, instead relying on improvisation, much to everyone's amusement (and co-star Estelle Taylor's confusion); Florey felt they improved on their lines. Part of the narrative involved a play within the movie, which the scenarist (Pierre Collings) did not have time to write. So this was left to the director, and he decided to develop a parody of detective dramas--entitled "The Grey Seal from Scotland

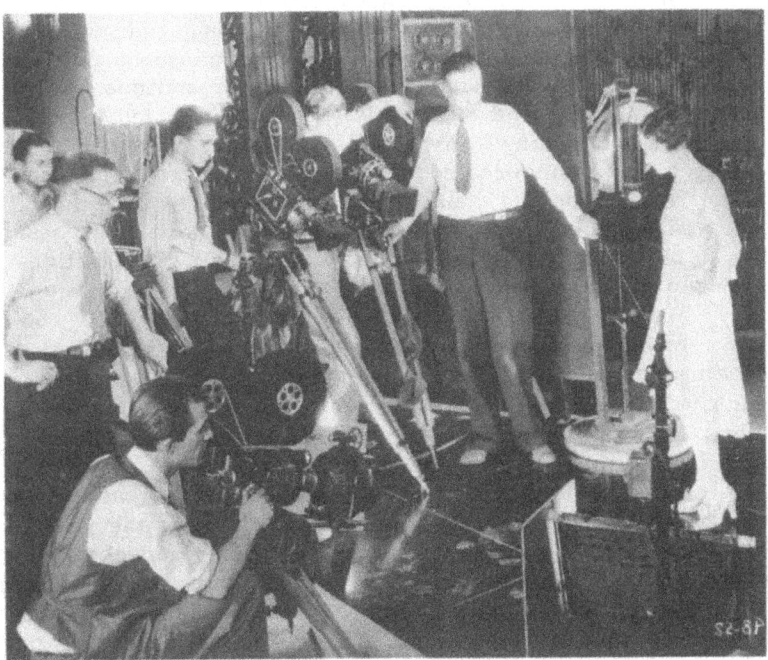

Astoria, late 1928: Florey (center) directing an insert of tap-dancing for Night Club.

Yard"--with cast member Reginald Owen writing the dialogue. (Florey and Owen would later collaborate on the script of A Study in Scarlet.) Enjoying the contributions he was able to make, Florey felt The Pusher-in-the-Face was a worthwhile effort and a more than ordinarily amusing comedy.

Conditions were difficult in the making of all these pictures because of the primitive equipment, and the results seem crude and archaic today. For instance, in filming a short with Elinor Glyn, she demanded a park atmosphere with real doves flying about as she recited poetry. Although the soundman noticed no interfering noise while recording, a machine-gun-like sound could be heard when the 900 feet were projected; only after two more tries was it realized that this resulted from the flapping of the birds' wings! Another year or two would pass before the sound medium began to be mastered with more advanced technology--by which time Florey was in France, where the state-of-the-art in recording lagged behind what was available in America. In 1928 the sound-on-disc system was in use at Astoria, meaning scenes had to be staged in such a way as to shoot nearly 1,000 feet--the amount contained in a film magazine--in a single take. Three to five cameras would operate simultaneously, one for the long shot, others for multiple medium and close shots. And all of this without pans, dolly shots, or camera movement of any kind, since the camera had to be enclosed in a soundproofed booth lest the noise of the mechanism register on the soundtrack. However, by getting as much as eight or nine minutes of film per take it was possible to obtain an easily edited hour-and-a-half movie within only ten or eleven days.

In his frequent discussions with Bell, Florey urged "the making of drama, action or mystery pictures, with a minimum of dialogue simply replacing the subtitles of the silent films--but now he ... wanted 'talk' only."[9] The managers determined to film successful plays, using, if possible, the original cast--since the studio was so near Broadway--as the public demanded "100% talkies." If this was the goal, suggested Florey, it could be achieved faster and cheaper by simply sending four cameras and a sound crew to the theater. During a special morning performance they could film directly off the stage in ten minute intervals to allow for time to change reels; a motion picture director would be practically unnecessary. After considering the idea, Bell decided that better quality could be obtained at the studio. Nonetheless, the idea showed the inventiveness of Florey's mind, anticipating contemporary methods even if they were beyond the technical facilities of the day. George Folsey judged that Florey "had a kind of new approach ... a desire to change things [which, although] awkward to do because of the sound situation ... was one of the things in his favor."[10]

Bonjour, New York! was Maurice Chevalier's first talking picture. Near the end of October 1928, Florey was informed that Chevalier would be arriving in New York from France two days later. Although the film was not included in the actor's contract, Paramount wanted something to satisfy French exhibitors for a few months until his first feature, to be made in Hollywood, would be ready. The suggestion of a three-reel travelogue fit in with what was needed, leaving Florey with barely forty-eight hours to plan a scenario.

Shooting began at seven the very morning after Chevalier disembarked. Four days were spent on a tour of the sights of the city, including skyscrapers, the Statue of Liberty, Wall Street, the Bowery, Fifth Avenue, Greenwich Village, and the Astoria studio itself. Photographing all of the newcomer's impressions, cinematographer Al Wetzel used mostly silent cameras for the extra mobility they allowed; the soundtrack was recorded later at the studio, Chevalier providing a commentary by singing and telling stories in French. (No English-language version was made.) Shooting went very rapidly, at virtually the rate of a television show; thirty-five scenes alone were completed in the first five hours. While Chevalier worried whether all Paramount movies were made so quickly, he was delighted with the technicians' proficiency and became a lifelong friend of Florey. However, Chevalier was displeased when Paramount reneged on their promise to distribute Bonjour, New York! free of charge to French-speaking countries; instead the company found the almost accidental venture to be very profitable when it was released overseas.

The Hole in the Wall[11] was Florey's first sound feature and a film that offered him a respite from the spate of musicals and comedies that had so far occupied all his time at Astoria. A remake of a 1921 silent film based on a Broadway play, The Hole in the Wall involved gangsters and spiritualism;

its title referred to mediums who serve as portals to communicate between the world of the dead and living. Work on the continuity and exteriors began in November, with principal photography taking place the next month. Cameraman George Folsey noted that with this project (similar to Johann the Coffin Maker) Florey seemed at last "in his element" to a degree he had not in his work to date.[12]

However, Florey's style in The Hole in the Wall is not always consistent with his later work, since he was constantly running up against the technological limitations of early sound equipment. For example, there was little use of lighting effects, and the camera tended to be stationary, relying on long and medium shots with few close-ups. But there were a few novel camera angles, in the morgue and of the line of dancing chorus girls, as well as a number of superimpositions as had been used in his recent avant-garde movies.

Florey experimented with the use of sound in many scenes with varied results. Those involving the creation of the supernatural mood, as in the spiritualistic scenes, were most successful. Some difficult and probably unprecedented challenges were presented by the exterior work, such as in Central Park; many of these were eliminated, with the scenes along the Hudson, New York street corners, and a moving "el" train among the few to be retained. About three fourths of the shots following the simulated crash of this elevated train were censored as too brutal for public consumption, many having been taken at a wreck which happened to occur during shooting.

The shortcomings caused by the extensive editing and technological problems may partially account for one of the more disappointing aspects of The Hole in the Wall--the lack of integration between the camera style and the expressionist settings. Their combination in The Hole in the Wall does not enhance the mood nearly as effectively as in Murders in the Rue Morgue. Most striking in The Hole in the Wall are the looming specters in the medium's waiting room, before a swami-type figure leads visitors into a chamber with bizarre statues and strange architecture. (Many shots featuring twisted Caligari-like windows were edited from the picture.) The plain decor of the morgue, more suggested than actually reconstructed, provides an interesting counterpoint that nevertheless maintains some of the expressionist flavor. Florey seems to have been eager for more such set design, but apparently the promised embellishments were not forthcoming. The art director, Ernst Fegté, recalled: "Florey wanted a sketch of some ghosts. I was too busy with other things, but he pestered me daily: 'Where are my ghosts?'"[13] Another interesting set-piece was the gangster's headquarters behind the medium's chamber, filled with skulls, masks, imitation spooks, and the assorted bric-a-brac necessary to produce the illusions of the spiritualist's trade. The decor here strongly resembles that of the maskmaker's shop in The Florentine Dagger.

The Hole in the Wall is perhaps most widely remembered today for launching the motion picture careers of Claudette Colbert and Edward G. Robinson. Both were stage stars for whom this was their first talkie, having only made one silent film apiece several years earlier. In The Hole in the Wall Robinson began the gangster persona--the criminal who despises and lives in defiance of the law--he would make famous and continue for many years, although he was a more sympathetic character in this case. Florey remembered the challenges of directing him.

> Eddie always wanted to know which enclosed booth contained his close-up camera. And being an actor, I noticed that he would have the tendency not only to constantly face such camera but approach it little by little, closer and closer, never looking at the actor or actress to whom he was supposed to speak. Having to protect my final cutting, I had to remedy his behavior, and from this point on always told him that his close-up camera was placed either on the right or on the left, almost back of the other actors whom he was then obliged to face.... After Hole was completed he was greatly amused when I told him of my deception.[14]

Colbert, on the other hand, is scarcely recognizable; she plays a dramatic role far different from her later comedienne image. Her capable work, in conjunction with Robinson's, did much to aid the picture.

To assist in the theatrical dimensions of The Hole in the Wall, Florey had another director for the dialogue staging,

Irving Rapper. "This was my first introduction to the Astoria studios," Rapper recalled. "I had directed plays in New York ... Monta Bell met me, and thought what a great combination Florey and I would make (?)."[15] Observing Night Club and The Pusher-in-the-Face, he commented with awe, "It was all fantasy to me--Bob knew a great deal and I knew so little about pictures."[16] On his next movie, The Cocoanuts, Florey would again be paired with a stage director, Joseph Santley.

Probably the weakest point of The Hole in the Wall is the improbable plot; Florey reported the reaction of Colbert as similar to his own. "After having become familiar with the scenario, Claudette made a grimace. She was not wrong."[17] Rapper termed the tale "silly ... Monta Bell gave us a very poor story."[18] From the first, an unnaturally slow pace is noticeable (particularly in the delivery of dialogue); it becomes especially bothersome as the gangsters grow fond of a child they have kidnapped. Not until the suspenseful conclusion does the narrative finally come to life. In an amazingly convincing scene, Colbert discovers she has true spiritual powers and serves as the medium for a dead man to assist in locating the imperiled child. Another interesting touch is that of a mad carnival escapee held prisoner by the gangsters, his banshee wails used to accompany their seances. Given the chance, he turns on his "masters," allowing for the gang leader to be caught. Here was clearly a foreshadowing of, if not the inspiration for, Florey's addition of Dr. Frankenstein's assistant Fritz when he came to write the script of Frankenstein some two years hence.

Perhaps a director content with conventional results could have made a smoother film of The Hole in the Wall, but it would also have been a less significant achievement. The movie was a daring, ambitious effort for its day, marking "an encouraging move in the direction of a more flexible use of sound."[19] Apparently Paramount was well satisfied, shortly signing Florey to a three-year contract with six-month options. The Hole in the Wall came during a transitional time when sound movies did not remain in circulation long because advancing technology made them seem quickly outdated. According to William K. Everson, while "unknown today, [The Hole in the Wall] may eventually establish itself as one of the most interesting and certainly one of the most curious films of that uneven period."[20]

1928-1932: First Major Commercial Films 113

The Cocoanuts has turned out to be one of the most important movies of Florey's career. Despite its age, it is widely seen today since it launched the Marx Brothers into motion pictures. Although the comedians had been successful on the stage, putting them on the screen was considered a risky venture by producers Bell and Walter Wanger, who wanted Cocoanuts to be made quickly and inexpensively. Because Florey had been hired for his skill in making the most of modest budgets, this was an obvious project to give him. On first hearing of his new assignment, he recalled having been amused by the play two years earlier; before starting the film, he attended their latest presentation, Animal Crackers.

But Florey was disappointed, having understood from Bell when signing with Paramount that he would work mostly on dramas. Instead, he had been given musicals, comedies, and a thriller. Even so, Florey had been considerably more comfortable with the slapstick of The Pusher-in-the-Face and the opportunity for cinematic ingenuity contained in the musicals and The Hole in the Wall, despite the latter's stage origins. But he had considerably more reservations about this latest project. Over forty years later he stated, "I never cared too much for Cocoanuts";[21] it "was not exactly what I had always dreamed of directing."[22] Florey knew that since the producers wanted to faithfully film a recent stage hit, the result would be rather static, especially because of the immobile sound cameras. In an effort to compensate, "I suggested that perhaps we should go on location for a couple weeks in Florida to photograph some of the exteriors and give the film a little fresh air and movement-- but the idea was rejected."[23] However, the Marx Brothers could not interrupt their regular schedule of New York stage appearances, and Bell was unable to understand Florey's point: "Why are you so concerned with having real backgrounds when one of the leading characters wears an obviously fake moustache?" Replied Florey, "With that kind of logic, what could I say?"[24] Instead, the Florida scenery was painted on shaky canvas and hung in the windy soundstage, so that the backdrop trembled whenever someone opened a door.

Production began as soon as Florey finished his continuity in January 1929 and lasted a mere twenty days. Events soon proved that the studio was not the only obstacle to "opening up" the production. The Marx Brothers themselves could not be convinced to adjust their methods and routines for the new medium. "What was there to rehearse with the Marx Brothers? They had performed the show a thousand times!" Florey observed. "You couldn't direct the Marx Brothers any more than you could a Chaplin or a clown who had been doing the same number for many years. They did what they did and that was it."[25] Because of the necessity to capture on primitive sound equipment the verbal barrage of the foursome's humor, delivered in its original theatrical style, camera movement had to be minimized. As well, Groucho, Harpo, and Chico never became accustomed to remaining in the limited space being photographed and were constantly walking out of the field of vision. Since the bulky, enclosed sound cameras could not pan to follow the moving actor, he would seem to disappear and then re-enter the frame or be cut in half inexplicably. Naturally, this necessitated frequent retakes, and Florey had to fashion a cinematic style to suit the Marx Brothers' behavior. The result, at least in the portions in which the foursome participated, were extended long shots of the comedians' repartee--essentially a filmed play. However, during the scenes with the other, more cooperative, players, Florey was able to intersperse more frequent cuts and angle changes.

The Marx Brothers were no treat to direct, and their antics continued even when the cameras were not running. "Nobody could be at ease with the Marx Brothers," said Folsey.[26] They arrived late and then had to leave early to return to New York City every evening for their regular Broadway performance of Animal Crackers, while on Wednesday and Saturday they could only come in for three hours in order to get back in time to do their matinees. Florey wrote:

> The Marx Brothers gave me a great deal of trouble. You could never catch them all together. Harpo ... spent his time making gags and running after the girls. We found Chico on the roof of the studio or in the basement and cellars. Zeppo ... came late, and Groucho delivered interminable speeches.[27]

At other times, if forgetting or becoming confused in their lines, the four "would start to talk about things that didn't

1928-1932: First Major Commercial Films   115

make any sense and couldn't be edited off--on account of
the recording on disc." So the scene would have to be
stopped and all cameras reloaded before starting another
take. "This picture gave me a pain in the--neck," said
Florey. "I'd rather do a tough western or a war film any-
time."[28]

Despite the difficulties, Florey enjoyed working with
the brothers. "Harpo was my favorite," he said.[29] "I
would have loved to have done a picture with just him."[30]
He found the task of inventing visual gags for the silent
member of the quartet particularly challenging. Among
Florey's contributions were the chocolate telephone Harpo
devoured and his sudden game of darts. "After all, as
long as the thing was crazy anyway," Florey asserted,
"one might as well add to it!"[31]

Although The Cocoanuts today is viewed almost exclusively because of the Marx Brothers, equally important
in 1929 were the musical sequences accompanying several
Irving Berlin melodies. Because of this element, Florey had
to share directorial credit for the only time in his career.
But the so-called co-director was hardly that; he was forty-
year-old Joseph Santley, formerly "America's Greatest Boy
Actor," and member of a famous dance team with his wife
Ivy Sawyer. Santley was one of the many talents from the
theater signed by the studios to work in talkies during the
transition to sound. He was new to movies, and Wanger
wanted Florey to train him as a director. The general idea
was for Santley to help out, if needed, with the staging--
but not the photography--of the musical numbers, which
was his speciality. However, there was little for him to do
here, as these scenes constituted only a portion of the
script and had already been choreographed by Chester Hale
and Maria Gambarelli. Florey, not looking forward to Cocoanuts anyway, had even suggested that Santley be allowed to
direct it himself. But the two cooperated amicably, with
Santley operating in a secondary capacity. As Folsey said,
"Every one of us had the feeling that Florey was the important man; Santley was an additional aid to him, that's all."[32]

Restrained as Florey was from creative cinematic treatment of the comedy scenes, he turned his innovative mind to
the musical numbers, with auspicious results. "It was at
least an attempt," he said, "to make the play a film and it

added some imagination to what was happening."33 He took this as far as he could; the avant-garde influence is apparent from the very first frames of Cocoanuts. The credits were projected against a dancing chorus line shown in negative form, revealing a definite debt to F.W. Murnau's Nosferatu (Germany, 1921) that would reappear elsewhere in Florey's canon. The opening shot of the movie appears as a circular spoked wheel, through which the outline of a girl's face is seen, before being revealed as a twirling parasol. A virtual split-screen effect was obtained in the scene of a bungled robbery. This takes place entirely in two adjoining hotel rooms, the characters running from one to the other, seen together in a long shot with a thin wall dividing them. The camerawork here takes "on almost a mathematical precision and the rhythm of a drumbeat."34

Florey rehearsed "the dance numbers for certain camera angles I was anxious to get and that I shot silently"35 for the greater mobility this permitted. For example, portions of the first dance of the usherettes in Groucho's hotel are photographed from the floor, giving the line's motions a geometrical, slightly abstract quality. Later on, Mary Eaton's solo dance (the "Monkey Doodle-doo") is shot from multiple directions, foreground and background, high and low angles, even pulling out during the routine from long shot to extreme long shot in one take. "The Camera seems to float through a wide arc to pick fresh points of view."36 These different heights were achieved by placing three cameras in their soundproofed booths on top of each other, all filming simultaneously.

Florey took the necessary time to obtain the interesting angles he desired for the dances, in one case, for the opening shot of the wedding banquet, "spending a full morning hanging a silent camera [from a scaffolding] above a set under the stage ceiling." He used this overhead view to shoot at a formation that resembled, he said, "a flower opening and closing its petals"37 (an effect enhanced by the billowy appearance of the dancers' skirts)--a vision enjoyed by Cocoanuts' audiences.38

> A group of shadows within a circle opens up like a six-pointed star--just as you might see by gazing through a kaleidoscope. It turns out to be a ring of beautiful girls extending their arms with hands clasped together.39

Florey's creativity was not only innovative and something his cinematographer, George Folsey, had never seen before, but was also a very appropriate introduction to the exotic flavor of the costume dinner that follows. Folsey has commented:

> My association with Florey was pleasant, interesting and involved because of the various things he wanted, he had an eye.... He was an artist, with a good sense of balance and composition and very productive ideas. He knew how to handle a chorus line from below, he knew it was interesting to shoot down on a bunch of chorus girls unfolding like flowers--we hadn't done that before.[40]

All this was noticed by the press at the time, with the London Sunday Pictorial writing that "Cocoanuts is excellent evidence of what talking pictures can achieve when they have the courage to disregard the limitations of stage conventions. There is in this picture a sense of space, and of a spreading of wings."[41]

Thus, many of the innovations in the photography of musical sequences, traditionally credited to Rouben Mamoulian and Busby Berkeley, can be found in Florey's Cocoanuts. But these musical passages are usually ignored by film historians who only comment on the Marx Brothers' debut in the cinema. With Mamoulian, at least, there is a direct connection. Paramount had given Florey the responsibility of revealing all the latest in camera techniques to Mamoulian before the latter began to direct Applause, and he spent a number of days with Florey on the set of Cocoanuts. In the case of Berkeley, while the basic ideas for the routines and overhead shots of formations which he made famous are also to be found in Cocoanuts, they are admittedly in a simplified form. Florey had none of the extensive background of Mamoulian in the theater or Berkeley in staging and dance. Florey acknowledged this, saying

> Busby was much more elaborate and more rich in his production. What I shot, I did very quickly. Busby would rehearse a number for weeks. I would do a quick rehearsal on one day and shoot in half-a-day on the next.[42]

Cocoanuts was only the beginning of these devices--but a

beginning it certainly was, and one long overdue for proper recognition.

Cocoanuts is very much a movie of its time, belonging in spirit to the optimistic 1920s, with its flappers and get-rich-quick schemes of the days just before the crash of the stock market. Nonetheless, the comic style is still enjoyable; all that dates it is the obviously early sound technology. Because of this primitive appearance--by today's standards-- Cocoanuts has acquired an undeservedly low critical reputation. But in 1929 it was a huge commercial success, grossing almost $2 million and launching the Marx Brothers on their prolific film career.

The Battle of Paris, also called The Gay Lady, was the only picture with a French background to which Florey wished he had never been assigned. Walter Wanger had signed Gertrude Lawrence, the famous actress and singer of the English stage, in hopes of turning her into a movie star. Her vehicle was to be made within a limited number of weeks, as she had to return to England by a specific date. Monta Bell, not having sufficient time to look further for any better material, purchased a distinctly mediocre property. Florey, just returned from a vacation to Cuba in May 1929, was asked to prepare the continuity and was alarmed to read such an "afflicted scenario ... ridiculous ... stupid...."[43] "The Battle of Paris was not a good picture. Gene Markey must have needed the money badly, his script--hastily written--was awful. I told Monta Bell that I didn't want to do it...."[44]

The story was set in Paris, August 1914; Florey felt Lawrence and Charles Ruggles were miscast as Montmartre street gamins, and his suggestion to co-star a French performer such as Maurice Chevalier was rejected. Anxious to know what Lawrence thought of the screenplay, Florey was disheartened to find she had paid little attention, being delighted with the score and period costumes.

Florey anticipated that the project would be helmed by John Meehan, a screenwriter and stage director who was new to the cinema. But three days after shooting started, Meehan gave up, staying on for only a short time in the reduced position of dialogue director. All other directors on the lot being occupied for the duration of the June-July production

1928-1932: First Major Commercial Films

schedule, The Battle of Paris was handed over to Florey, who "made the film the best I knew how but without any particular enthusiasm."[45]

The Battle of Paris was doomed from the start by a poor script. Despite being a musical, it contained many ingredients incongruous with the genre, having little comedy and emphasizing a dramatic story. This did, however, offer the opportunity for more fluid and creative camerawork than The Cocoanuts, and some telling moments were achieved --such as the frequent use of shadow effects and a dissolve from dancing feet to a marching parade as the army mobilizes. The highlights of the picture were the four Cole Porter songs, carried by Lawrence with great flair in a lively and attractive manner (Florey called her "a great performer and a real trooper"[46]), demonstrating she deserved a better showcase for her talents in the movies.

In August, Florey left for a month-long working vacation in Bermuda, taking along an Eddie Cantor screenplay to prepare. On his return, Metro-Goldwyn-Mayer hired Florey to photograph backgrounds for their upcoming production of Anna Christie. A week was spent shooting, with doubles, some 10,000 feet of film along the East River and the Hudson, with Jackson J. Rose as cameraman. Because three versions of this movie were made, in Swedish, German and English, it is unclear how much of Florey's footage was eventually used.

Florey was unhappy at Astoria, despite being able to work on the final continuity draft of most of his screenplays (nearly all written by his good friend Pierre Collings). He had hoped for different assignments, having suggested the plays R.U.R. and Outward Bound, along with some stories of Guy de Maupassant; even when promised The Letter he was switched to The Cocoanuts to make room for his compatriot Jean de Limur. When Monta Bell mentioned more musicals in collaboration with stage directors, Florey willingly allowed his contract to expire--more promising offers having come from France. George Folsey summed up the Astoria period in Florey's career as follows:

> He was young, he was new.... We have to think of him at that time as a beginner, a person who filled a little niche, who did certain things and got

himself started. So he had to be a minor factor among the directors; it was an opportunity, and he made the most of it and did well. Then he went on to bigger things and became a well-established director.47

RETURN TO EUROPE, 1929-31

While vacationing in Bermuda, Florey had received a wire from Pierre Braunberger, a young, independent French producer whom he had met several years before. Braunberger asked Florey to come and work in Europe. "I had for a long time desired to take a tour on the old continent," Florey recalled, "and now that the occasion presented itself, I accepted the offer."48

After a year's diet of sound films in various languages, French audiences were demanding movies in their own tongue, and producers were hastening to supply the demand. Braunberger had made arrangements to film the first French all-talking and singing feature in England, as no suitable facilities were then available in France. Directors with experience and multilingual skills were needed, so Braunberger lured Florey with a powerful incentive: five percent of the profits of the pictures he directed. If French talkies were as successful as their American counterparts, this promised to be a sizable payment indeed. Florey left for Europe in October 1929.

La Route Est Belle ("The Beautiful Road") was the title of the first film Braunberger handed Florey. After a short stay in Paris to meet with his producer and shoot some silent exteriors with cameraman Georges Perinal, Florey was able to read the scenario and write the continuity on the way to London. The movie attempted to follow the pattern of The Jazz Singer (1927), telling of a Parisian street singer who rises to fame, never losing his innocence and charm; it starred Andre Bauge, the premier French baritone of the time.

While the story seemed simplistic to Florey, he was even more concerned with the conditions under which the movie was to be made, for Braunberger had allotted less than $100,000 to the production. He had rented one of the sets of the British International Studios at Elstree, but for only twelve days. All the scenes had to be shot on a single stage with only furniture and accessories changed. Three days were wasted in a futile attempt to synchronize several primitive sound cameras, and finally only one could be used. Cinematographer Charles Rosher "had never worked with such pitiable technical means," and together he and Florey fondly remembered Tess of the Storm Country (1922) with Mary Pickford, when production lasted for months.[49]

On top of these problems, the presence of a thick fog on the set limited the shooting to only half the normal hours per day. Nonetheless, the picture was finished within the remaining time, by the first part of December. The speed of their work was all the more amazing, considering that two separate versions of La Route Est Belle were made, one with a French soundtrack and another silent, to be post-synchronized with music and sound effects for foreign distribution or for titles to be inserted for theaters not yet equipped for sound. Then, while still in Britain, Florey directed what he called "a lovely short," Trees of England; the next five months were spent traveling throughout most of Europe.[50]

Upon its release in February 1930, La Route Est Belle proved tremendously popular, grossing close to one million dollars--nearly six times its cost. The film was seen in several European countries, remaining in circulation for many months. But this did not mean a windfall for Florey because Braunberger, instead of paying him, took his earnings and decided to buy a studio, promising Florey the direction of his next movie.

L'Amour Chante ("Love Sings") was Braunberger's second talkie, a co-production with Harmonie Films to be made at Ufa's sound-equipped Neubabelsberg studio outside Berlin. Because European audiences were displaying increasing discrimination in their enthusiasm for talking pictures, preferring movies in their own language (dubbing was not yet technically feasible nor popularly accepted), the project was done in trilingual form. Three separate versions were made simultaneously with a French, German and Spanish cast and an international crew. This made conditions almost as hectic as they had been at Elstree, despite the technical superiority of the German facilities. Florey described the situation this way: "It was a new experience to have a cameraman from Prague, a British soundman, a German production man, two French assistants, and actors speaking different languages."[51]

Florey began preparing his continuities in May 1930. L'Amour Chante was a musical comedy based on the humorous complications created by an adulterous young wife in the lives of everyone around her. While directing the original, he also supervised the Spanish version, El Profesor de mi Señora ("My Wife's Teacher"), although many of the details were left in the hands of a highly competent Spanish assistant. The directorial chores on the German version--titled Komm Zu Mir Zum Rendez-Vous ("Come with Me to the Rendezvous")--were handled by Carl Boese, who together with Florey had written the German adaptation. All three films were completed inside of a month.

Reviewed from Paris by Variety in November, L'Amour Chante was judged very favorably, "distinctly above the average French production," with good photography and excellent direction throughout.[52] Once again, however, Braunberger failed to honor his agreement with Florey, although the producers of Harmonie Films, Schwab and Rosenfeld, did make the promised payment. But having fulfilled his part of the contract, Florey decided to return to the United States and left Berlin in August.

Back in New York, he found Monta Bell still desirous of promoting collaborations with stage directors; Florey was unable to convince Paramount to invest in an idea for a picture to be made in the south of France. Thus a cable from Braunberger asking Florey to return in haste to direct a new movie found him receptive, and by November he was back in France.

Le Blanc et le Noir ("White and Black") was the title of Braunberger's new project. By now the producer had completed renovation of the Billancourt studio, but Florey noted with disappointment that the Western Electric sound system with which it had been equipped was already considerably dated from what he had just seen at Astoria. To assist in the expansion, Braunberger had been forced to accept a wealthy partner, Roger Richebe, the son of a major exhibitor in Marseilles. Jean Renoir, who would join the studio shortly, described Richebe by mentioning that his father was in the habit, whenever he thought a feature being screened became tedious, of interpolating some scenes from a bullfight--much "to the bewilderment of the audience."[53] Unfortunately, despite his lack of experience, young Richebe played an increasing role in the management of the studio and its productions.

Le Blanc et le Noir, based on the play by Sacha Guitry, marked the beginning of Guitry's association with talkies. The continuity was written in collaboration with Florey, using a style of "theatricalized film" and a four-act structure.[54] "The hours I spent in his company," Florey recalled, "while we prepared our scenario, were for me very precious."[55] Although Le Blanc et le Noir is one of the few Guitry pictures which he wrote but did not direct, Florey was very "impressed with Guitry's ideas on filmmaking."[56] The unusual story was presented as a satirical comedy-drama centering around a husband's discovery of his wife's infidelity when she gives birth to a black child and their eventual reconciliation when that baby is exchanged for a white orphan.

However, for Florey, the actual shooting of Le Blanc et le Noir was not such a pleasure as the writing had been. Richebe took an instant dislike to him and began to regularly interfere with the production. (Renoir would soon leave Billancourt after receiving similar treatment.) Simultaneously, Florey was irked by Braunberger's failure to pay him the many thousands of francs owed from the profits of La Route Est Belle. He withstood these twin pressures for weeks until finally, two days before finishing Le Blanc et le Noir, Florey refused to carry on any further without receiving at least a part of what he was owed.

Richebe's response was to bar Florey from the studio and ask his former assistant, Marc Allegret, to complete the movie. This move allowed Braunberger to attempt to give Allegret sole directorial credit and remove Florey's name entirely. Although Braunberger and Richebe finally settled on handing Allegret a separate listing for "artistic direction," many sources--even today--mistakenly perpetuate the producers' petulance by listing Florey and Allegret as co-directors of Le Blanc et le Noir.

Despite a subsequent lawsuit, the very substantial sum that Florey should have received was lost. Braunberger-Richebe were soon in grave financial difficulties from overexpansion and mismanagement, and their partnership was dissolved in 1933. Although pleased with his European pictures, the mistreatment that Florey received from these producers made him resolve never to work for an overseas company again. After leaving France in January 1931, he turned down a number of such offers and would not return to directing on the Continent until nearly two decades later.

UNIVERSAL, 1931-32

Frankenstein is one of the revered classics of the cinema, yet few cinephiles are aware of Robert Florey's crucial contributions because Universal removed his name from the American credits. Despite the legions of fans James Whale and Boris Karloff have acquired as a result of their participation in Frankenstein, Florey's role as principal author of the screenplay has been either ignored or minimized. Of the many books and articles that have recounted the complex saga of the making of this film, none has offered a complete and accurate account of its development; most repeat half-truths and misinformation. Now, for the first time, the complete story of Florey's association with Frankenstein will be told.

One day in March 1931 Florey, having recently returned to Hollywood from Europe, was lunching at the Musso and Frank Restaurant on Hollywood Boulevard. He was approached by an old acquaintance, Richard Schayer, head of the Universal story department. Schayer indicated that his studio was looking for ideas for a new horror film to star Bela Lugosi, one that would follow the enormous popularity of his previous vehicle, Dracula. At a later meeting, Florey and Schayer discussed several possibilities: The Invisible Man, Murders in the Rue Morgue, plays presented by the Théatre du Grand Guignol de Paris, and Frankenstein. Both agreed that Mary Shelley's tale held the most intriguing possibilities, but Schayer questioned whether it could be adapted into a movie, telling Florey that he would have to sell it on his own to the Universal management.

Not long afterwards, Florey met with Universal's

immature studio boss, twenty-two-year-old Carl Laemmle, Jr. Florey recalled his introduction to Laemmle this way:

> During the course of a singular interview, while Carl Laemmle, Jr. was delivering his fingers to a manicurist, his hair to a hairdresser, his thoughts to his secretaries, and his voice to a dictaphone, I explained to him the general plan of the film. He asked me to quickly type up my story and give it to the head of the scenario department.[57]

Before the end of the month, Florey wrote a five-page outline of the story, which Universal believed fit their needs perfectly. He was then able to demand and receive (in April) a contract to both adapt and direct a movie for them, although he failed to notice at the time that nowhere did it specify that the picture was to be Frankenstein.

Before beginning, there was a delay of over a month as Universal temporarily closed down due to financial difficulties. When the studio reopened and Florey began writing the screenplay, he was assigned to collaborate with Garrett Fort, who had assisted in preparing Dracula for the screen. Fort was chiefly responsible for the dialogue, with Florey only suggesting what the characters would say.

Beginning work on May 15, they were nearly finished by June 20, and Florey was putting the last touched on his director's continuity. It contained more than six hundred shots, with every composition, set-up, camera angle, lens, and sound and special effect described in detail. The only uncertainty remaining was whether Henry Frankenstein was to be killed at the end along with his monster. Over the objections of Fort and Schayer, Florey was holding out to keep him alive, believing strongly from the first that the film would be sufficiently successful to demand a sequel--although even Florey never imagined that the scientist's creation would have so many incarnations in the cinema.

However, young Laemmle was uncertain about Frankenstein and asked Florey to direct a test. The front office had decided that Lugosi would not play the part of Dr. Frankenstein, as Florey had suggested, but that of the monster. The star was enraged at being asked to enact a role that called for no speech and would require him to

Robert Florey and Garrett Fort, co-authors of the original Frankenstein, posed for a gag photo during an apparently pessimistic moment while writing their script.

spend hours each day having uncomfortable make-up applied. Despite Lugosi's protests, he, Edward Van Sloan, Dwight Frye, and a couple of extras were gathered by Florey on the old Dracula castle set. There, with Paul Ivano as cameraman, they filmed over 1,000 feet on two-and-a-half reels, shooting in continuity on June 16 and 17 after a day of rehearsals.

Unfortunately, this test has disappeared, permitting much absurd speculation to be made about it--particularly based on statements by those not present at the time. As indicated in Florey's continuity, the test covered the visit of Victor Moritz to Dr. Waldman and the birth of the monster. Ivano--who retained a few frames of the test until the 1940s--stated that Whale followed the photographic style of the test footage.[58] Despite a story told by Van Sloan (thirty years after the fact) that Lugosi's make-up resembled that of Paul Wegener in The Golem (Germany, 1920), the appearance and acting of Lugosi were virtually identical to Boris Karloff's, according to both Florey and Ivano. (The "Golem" comparison had been a shorthand approximation used by all concerned at the time, as there had been no prior movie creature to compare with the one in Frankenstein.) The memorable touch of the bolts on the monster's neck ("which Lugosi kept pulling off")[59] was Florey's contribution, added to the script in his own handwriting; all his life he derived simple pleasure from drawing and embellishing monsters.

After editing the test material down to some twenty minutes, into a form suitable for theatrical-style presentation, Florey showed it to Laemmle. Ivano recalled that it had "numerous bizarre angles creating a nightmare atmosphere ... a rather rare thing for that time." In one scene, as "Dr. Frankenstein and his assistant descended the staircase, our Mitchell camera had been placed in the center and was taking 360° panoramic shots of the decor, stopping in front of the table where the monster was stretched out lifeless." The set resembled the interior of a well, so that all of the lighting had to come from above. Wrote Ivano: "These trials were so successful, so beautiful from the artistic and photographic point of view, that all the directors of the studio wanted to make the film."[60]

Laemmle was well satisfied, believing that Frankenstein held out important commercial possibilities. Even Lugosi was impressed, handing Ivano a five-dollar cigar and saying, "My profile looked magnificent!"[61] But the star was not long reconciled to a role he felt any extra could play and requested to be relieved of the assignment.

About the same time, one of Universal's new prestige directors from the stage, James Whale, arrived at the studio with a generous contract and the absolute support of young Laemmle. Whale obtained the Frankenstein script and thought it the best available on the lot. He probably also saw the test and must have seen promise in it, for he seized the opportunity to demand for himself the direction of Frankenstein. In fact, he refused to do anything else. Laemmle, often inconstant in dealing with his employees, readily acceded; as his confidence in the project's importance grew, he was eager to hand it to a big-name director.

Meanwhile, Florey, unaware of the actions of Whale and Laemmle, was asked by Schayer to help out on Murders in the Rue Morgue, being told that he was the one who could succeed in putting it into movie form. The other writers laboring on the Edgar Allan Poe story had been having difficulty in adapting it to the screen. Florey wondered what had become of Frankenstein, having been under the impression that the cast was set and shooting would begin the next month; it appeared that production had been delayed while plans for Murders in the Rue Morgue were moved ahead. Then he heard, in mid-July, that both he and Lugosi had been taken off Frankenstein and switched to Rue Morgue. Enraged, he went to check his contract and found it had indeed promised him the opportunity to both write and direct one picture. But the studio then informed him of a loophole--the agreement had not specified the film, and they could determine which it would be. Lugosi was the only one pleased with the change. Schayer advised Florey that there was no chance of successfully opposing Whale's clout with Laemmle. Angrily, Florey took home his copies of the directorial continuity he had prepared and kept them among his personal papers.

This original, hand-emended script is now available to be examined. For the first time, it is possible to delineate accurately and precisely Florey's contributions to Frankenstein. As his screenplay is in continuity form and as the movie has been published as a book,[62] shot by shot and line by line, using the dialogue with over one thousand frame blow-ups, Florey's continuity can be readily compared with the final version. While of course a screenplay and a finished film are not entirely comparable, the nature of Florey's continuity does legitimize the attempt to imagine how a Frankenstein he directed would have appeared and to examine how it would have differed from Whale's product in specific terms.

Despite two months of additional work on the script by Fort and Francis Edwards Faragoh, whom Whale brought in to make revisions, very little was changed. The screenplay was revamped only slightly, just enough for a pretense of justification in removing Florey's name from the credits. The order of a few scenes was altered, a change which may in fact have taken place during editing. The introduction of Victor and Elizabeth, with their concern over Frankenstein's disappearance, followed the scene at the gallows (in Florey's script) rather than the theft of the brain (in the film); the first scene of the monster in the dungeon comes immediately after he is brought to life, not after the confrontation between Victor, Elizabeth, the Baron, and the Burgomeister; and the death of Waldman does not precede, but is subsequent to, the tranquil interlude between Elizabeth and Frankenstein.

Only a few scenes were substantially rewritten, two of which unquestionably suffered as a result. Florey had provided a stronger motivation for Victor's loyalty to Frankenstein, explaining in the introductory scene with Elizabeth that they had been lifelong friends (an element preserved from the novel). This also had the effect of diffusing the clichéd concept of the romantic triangle involving Victor, Elizabeth, and Frankenstein. The principal importance of this rivalry had been lost anyway when the decision was made to keep Frankenstein alive and not unite Victor and Elizabeth on his death--as Fort had desired.

Florey had planned to intercut the theft of the brain and the meeting of Waldman and Victor. At the lecture, Waldman was to display only one brain--that of a criminal-- not two, as in the Whale version. The introduction of a second, normal brain by Whale or his writers tends to contradict the pathos with which Karloff invested the monster. Frankenstein's ignorance of the criminal brain he had used, and the humor derived from it, were not in the Florey script but fit in well with Whale's approach to horror. Ironically, some critics, eager to demean Florey's contributions, have seized on this very passage that Whale embellished.

The dialogue between Victor and Waldman was rewritten and is much less logical and realistic than what Florey had prepared. (Some glaring grammatical errors indicate that he must have authored this entire sequence, including dialogue, without assistance from Fort.) There were a couple of clever Florey touches that should have been retained: Waldman is seen subjectively when he says Frankenstein was only interested in creating human life; and the cranial operation Frankenstein will use is demonstrated by analogy when Waldman flips off, like a coffee-pot, the top of a human skull which he uses as a tobacco container in his office.

The deletions were extensive. The cemetery locale was much more fully exploited in the Florey script; most of its expressionistic camerawork, such as shooting an upward angle from inside a grave, was eliminated. Whale's version of the funeral compares unfavorably not only with Florey's original continuity, but with the direction of a similar sequence in Florey's Hotel Imperial. The same happened with the scene at the gallows; Whale handled it in a very stage-like manner, whereas Florey intended to convey a sense of dimension by photographing it from a variety of perspectives.

The sequence in which the monster is brought to life--to be the stylistic highlight of the film--was planned by Florey in an extremely expressionistic manner, even containing a touch of surrealism. The lab was originally set in an old mill inspired by a Van de Kamp bakery (whose logo was and remains a windmill) across from Florey's Ivar Street apartment. This brought the story full circle by its conclusion; but before Florey's transfer, the lab had been moved to an old watchtower. Four pages of Florey's continuity were spent describing the setting, whose source was made clear: "It is more impressionistic than scientific, and designed to create a feeling of modern scientific 'magic'--something suggestive of the laboratory in Metropolis [Germany, 1927]."63 Florey enjoyed this science-fiction aspect of the story, which Whale would not fully exploit until The Bride of Frankenstein (1935).

Most of the bizarre touches Florey included were left out, a trait Whale would correct in his later movies. For instance, Florey had the untimely arrival of Victor and Waldman (Elizabeth is not present) heralded by several huge close-ups of the professor's hand rapping with supernatural loudness. There were to be double-exposures, such as Frankenstein's face over the electrical machinery during the storm, and, at its height, several twelve-frame negative strips of flash close-ups of the characters. The monster's chalky face had actually been seen by the audience before the storm, and his coming to life was indicated not only by the movement of his arm, but also by the hand slowly changing in color from black to white in front of the viewer, while he emits "a whimper, like that of an animal in pain."[64] (This last effect was included in The Bride of Frankenstein.)

Perhaps Whale's main fault was his inability to create the proper atmosphere. This was always one of Florey's greatest strengths, and he had written numerous touches to convey the forbidding presence of the central European locale. The best Whale could do was to give it the appearance of an English country village whose inhabitants dress in Tyrolean suits and play "patty-cake," destroying the mood of many scenes, particularly those surrounding the wedding and the carrying of the drowned girl into the town.

Emblematic of this was Whale's transformation of the Baron into a buffoon. Florey had imagined the character quite differently, even allowing him to observe the monster. The change in the Baron's persona eliminated the subtext theme of fatherhood written into the original Frankenstein screenplay. In a number of instances the idea of the monster as an unnatural creation had been conveyed by Florey through nuances of dialogue and short scenes, such as cutting from a peasant mother gently rocking her cradle to Frankenstein savagely whipping the monster into submission in the dungeon. And the Baron, despite seeing the transgressions of his son, did not turn on his offspring as Frankenstein had.

There was even a loss of suspense in a few sequences, particularly in the elimination of many unusual angles and expressionistic, mobile camera work. For example, Florey's build-up of shots to the monster's murder of Waldman, climaxing in an upside-down close-up of his face being strangled, was much more effective (and was used in the flashback sequence at the beginning of The Bride of Frankenstein).

On the other hand, of those elements absent from the Florey script but present in the picture, few made any substantive contribution; some are even harmful to the mood of the whole. Falling into the latter category were the inappropriate atmosphere, the extended, talky wedding, and the tacked-on postscript with the Baron. The curtain opener of Waldman's warning and the introduction of the monster to sunlight in the tower, were also new. There were, however, a couple of intriguing additions: Elizabeth is menaced by the monster on her wedding day (an incident inspired by the novel), and a sympathetic element is introduced to the monster's persona--though it should be remembered that this aspect of the monster's character did not take on central importance until <u>The Bride of Frankenstein</u>.

In fact, one of the few correct ideas in existence regarding Florey's conception of <u>Frankenstein</u> is that he imagined it as a much more grim spectacle than the film Whale gave us. In the Florey version, the monster is shown as having no redeeming traits (though he is treated cruelly by Frankenstein and Fritz), and is doomed from the start because of his criminal brain. (However, anyone claiming that Florey was incapable of introducing an element of pathos in his horrific characters is obviously unfamiliar with Peter Lorre's roles in <u>The Face Behind the Mask</u> and <u>The Beast with Five Fingers</u>.) After killing Waldman, the monster comes across an amorous young peasant couple in their cabin and, spying through a window, breaks in and brutally murders them. The attack on Elizabeth can be regarded as a subdued version of this scene. The encounter between the monster and the little girl by the lake was considerably shorter, simply showing him as if about to strangle her; the business of floating flowers and her drowning were later additions. It was Whale who sought to actually show the monster kill her, in shots that were finally excised before release. Thus, it is clear that Whale's changes were hardly consistent but seem often contradictory as he was groping to find a style and approach to the theme: adding sympathy for the monster, alternately inserting and subtracting incidents of his violence, and creating the contrast between the criminal and normal brains.

Not only was Florey's continuity left behind for Whale to follow, as was the twenty-minute test, but so were a series of about fifty drawings for set designs which Florey had prepared with his long-time friend Danny Hall. These included decor and the placement of shadows to evoke the proper ambiance. Thus there was a complete blueprint already in place which, generally speaking, Whale copied.

The most significant changes came in Florey's plans for the camera work. While some of his ideas were adopted, Whale usually preferred to photograph scenes as if they were taking place in the theater and often allowed the pace to become

Two autographed sketches by art director Danny Hall for Murders in the Rue Morgue, revealing how carefully they influenced the sets, decor, and camera positions. Florey collaborated with Hall on these drawings just as he had on similar ones in preparing Frankenstein: in this way, James Whale's style in directing the latter film was influenced by Florey.

wearisome. He kept Florey's decor, even when changing the photography so that the two elements were no longer compatible.

> [Whale's] direction is primitive at best. The film is really shot as a stage play.... His work does not exhibit a good knowledge of screen direction or film technique.... One need only examine Florey's work on The Cocoanuts, shot in 1929, to recognize Whale's deficiencies ... in spite of James Whale Frankenstein is a classic....65

This would have been different had Florey directed, as demonstrated by both his continuity and later efforts on Murders in the Rue Morgue. In fact, his cameraman on Frankenstein was to be Karl Freund, with whom he eventually collaborated on Rue Morgue. The most notable cinematic difference between Florey's Frankenstein continuity and Whale's movie was the emphasis Florey put on the moving camera as an expressionist device; Whale was seemingly oblivious to the developments Freund and F.W. Murnau had brought to the Germanic style since The Cabinet of Dr. Caligari and The Golem. Florey also described dozens of shots composed in depth, using both foreground and background. The unusual angles, compositions, and expressionist lighting characteristic of Florey were to be present in profusion. While some of the latter devices were retained, nearly all those using the moving camera--particularly to develop a long-take--and techniques to give dimension to shots were eliminated. On the other hand, nearly every one of the creative or expressionistic touches Whale finally used had already been described in the Florey continuity. "Murders in the Rue Morgue showed ten times as much imagination as Mr. Whale's pedestrian picture,"66 wrote Jack Spears; "Whale's stage training may have been responsible for some of his limitations as a director."67

All of this can only fuel the belief of some film scholars that Florey could have directed a better Frankenstein than did Whale. "There is a growing opinion that Florey's version would have been superior to Whale's,"68 and the comparison now possible between Florey's continuity and the final movie increases this belief. Such an analysis can only serve to highlight the excellence of the manner in which Florey visualized Frankenstein and draw attention to Whale's shortcomings.

Strange as it may seem, losing the direction of Frankenstein was not the most appalling part of the treatment Universal gave Florey. As the preceding analysis has proven, not only was he principally responsible for the plot and script of Frankenstein, but he even had a role in the preparation of its direction, through his continuity, test, and set designs. But Universal tried to erase, as much as possible, all evidence of Florey's participation on Frankenstein. His name was purged from the files, his role in initiating the sequel was suppressed, and the Lugosi test was conveniently lost. On the film's release, every writer except Florey--from Shelley to Fort and Faragoh and even Schayer--received screen credit. This action was not corrected in any of the subsequent releases. The combination of losing the direction and authorship credit made Florey justifiably angry. "Had Florey been allowed to keep the assignment, he would doubtless have become a major Hollywood director," wrote Anthony Slide.[69]

However, Florey won some consolation when, in the European release of Frankenstein, he received proper credit with Fort (Faragoh was deleted); in some advertising Florey was the sole writer listed. As a Universal memo from the Paris to Hollywood offices indicates, this was how the credits should have read in the first place:

> We beg to acknowledge receipt of your letter, dated 4th of December, with regard to Robert Florey whose name was omitted on the main title of Frankenstein.... We have taken good note of your instructions and we will give Mr. Florey the proper place on the main title as well as in our publicity.[70]

Once the film achieved its popularity, the studio heavily publicized Florey's involvement during the few remaining months he remained under contract. Their estimation of the quality of his services as a writer is shown by the fact that he continued to be employed in this capacity throughout his time at Universal. Ironically, almost thirty years later, Junior Laemmle, hoping to revive his own career, contacted Florey about a collaboration on a new horror movie; after listening politely, Florey refused the offer, tactfully but truthfully saying that he was too busy with his many television commitments.

Frankenstein has proven to be one of the most popular,

In the French posters for Frankenstein Florey finally received a share of the screenplay credits.

1928-1932: First Major Commercial Films

durable, and legendary movies ever made. In Europe, Robert Florey is known to be its main screenwriter. Is it not time that he received the same recognition in America?

Murders in the Rue Morgue came to Florey as the assignment to compensate for the loss of Frankenstein and to fulfill the contractual obligation to both adapt and direct a film for Universal. While hardly pleased with the switch, Florey explained, "I had been away from Hollywood for a long time, making pictures in New York, Germany, England, and France, and was so anxious to establish myself again in the old place that I accepted...." The Edgar Allan Poe story had been among the original suggestions he had given to Richard Schayer back in March, before being assigned to develop Frankenstein. Now, as the second horror movie put into production to capitalize on the success of Dracula, Murders in the Rue Morgue was to be made for $100,000 less than Frankenstein; "they wanted to produce Morgue quickly and cheaply." Florey had just over one week in which to write a five-page adaptation, for which he did receive separate screen credit--at last. Several other authors then collaborated on the screenplay and wrote the dialogue before Florey joined them to rapidly complete a continuity.[71]

Shooting lasted twenty-three days in October and November, going five days over schedule but remaining under budget. Frankenstein went into release just as Murders in the Rue Morgue was finished, and the enormous grosses the former immediately brought in convinced the studio to spend another $23,000 for seven days of retakes and added scenes in December, bringing the total budget to $189,000. Leon Ames, playing the hero, was making his screen debut and remembered his first director vividly.

> Bob wasn't happy on the picture, but he never talked about it.... He did the best he could; I thought he did a good job.... He didn't like the script. He wanted to fix it and they wouldn't let him.... He was always under pressure from the front office which bugged him.... He wasn't a powerful director in those days; that's what frustrated him.... He didn't care too much for the executives.[72]

Little remained of Poe's tale in the Florey adaptation.

(In 1952, he would direct a television version of Poe's "The Gold Bug" for the series Favorite Story.) Only two of the short story's incidents were used in the picture: the discovery of a corpse stuffed feet-first up a chimney, and the amusing argument over what language the murderer (an ape) spoke. But like Poe, Florey maintained the period setting in a dark, unfamiliar Paris of the nineteenth century. The film also follows Poe in combining elements of horror and detection, with the former predominating in the first half, and the latter in the second half. Unfortunately, this causes a distinct letdown in the movie's suspense, since the audience has already seen what the on-screen hero must deduce for himself. The frustration of waiting for him to catch up with what is already known is compounded by a certain unevenness in the picture, with some scenes far more effective than the film as a whole.

In terms of plot, however, there was almost no similarity between the Poe and Florey works. "I had to strengthen and lengthen the Poe short story," he wrote. "I added numerous characters...."[73] The major reason for the drastic changes was the need to turn Murders in the Rue Morgue into a vehicle for Bela Lugosi; there was no personality in the original tale which he was suited to play. Florey was not especially pleased to discover that he was once again scheduled to work with the same actor he had directed in the Frankenstein test. "I do not know what happened between Lugosi and Whale, but Karloff got the part of the monster [in Frankenstein] and I was back with Lugosi."[74] To make Murders in the Rue Morgue his vehicle, a completely new persona had to be invented--Doctor Mirakle-- with a horrific dimension added. "I had to write an adaptation to star Lugosi as a demented charlatan," Florey commented.[75]

Mirakle is a crazed scientist, a fanatical pre-Darwinian evolutionist who desires to prove mankind's kinship with the

---

[Opposite:] One of the few scenes retained from Edgar Allan Poe in Murders in the Rue Morgue was the discovery of a corpse stuffed feet first up a chimney. Note Florey's use of depth and the fireplace as a framing device. To the right of the gendarmes are Leon Ames and Herman Bing (clean-shaven and without hats).

ape by transfusions of blood between his pet orangutan and various women. Florey's choice of theme showed his tendency toward topical issues of the day, even when the story had a period setting; audience reaction was probably accurately predicted when a listener rises to accuse Lugosi of "heresy!" Poe's own character, Dupin (Leon Ames), was altered from a detective presaging Sherlock Holmes to a romantic young medical student. Lugosi represents in many ways the darker side of Ames's work (the two scientists are frequently paralleled in both plot and visuals),[76] as his friends and fiancée worry about all the time he spends around the morgue.

Because of this restructuring of the movie's plot to accommodate Lugosi's presence, there are other recognizable influences at least as strong as Poe which seem to have affected Florey and his script collaborators. One, clearly, was Frankenstein. This should not be surprising; Florey had been preparing the screenplay of Frankenstein for months and, suddenly given days in which to come up with a new scenario, it would be unusual if the two stories did not contain some elements in common. There are a number of obvious similarities between Frankenstein and Murders in the Rue Morgue: the scientist's peculiar assistant who symbolically bridges the gap between the doctor and his creature;[77] the lab in an abandoned hovel; the creature's superhuman strength; and the climax, when the monster attacks its master and is pursued by a raging mob. Florey candidly admitted the resemblance.

> The Universal people, not being particularly bright, didn't realize that I again used the same plot, using an ape instead of a monster and this time giving the Doctor's part to Lugosi. I called him Doktor [sic] Mirakle instead of Dr. Frankenstein, and I had him looking for human blood for his ape instead of a brain for a monster![78]

Both Lugosi as Mirakle and Henry Frankenstein are prototypical "mad scientists," trying to recombine existing species in violation of the laws of nature, creating monsters that are half men and half beasts. In fact, there is even more resemblance between Florey's version of Murders in the Rue Morgue and H.G. Wells's novel The Island of Dr. Moreau than to Poe's story.

1928-1932: First Major Commercial Films   141

The plot of Murders in the Rue Morgue is also indebted to The Cabinet of Dr. Caligari. (Already, around 1925, Florey had shot tests for a "Caligari-esque" avant-garde picture to be called The Mad Doctor.) Murders in the Rue Morgue is perhaps the German classic's most direct descendant in the United States. William K. Everson has called Rue Morgue "if not a re-make, then certainly a more than casual parallel ..." which proves Caligari to be "a constant source of design- or character-inspiration in Hollywood films."79 But Rue Morgue is also far more than that: it is a popularization and Americanization of Caligari. Florey was concerned with integrating the artistry of the motion picture into the feature enjoyed by the mass public; this was the reason he had not continued with the avant-garde. Pressed for time in coming up with a scenario for Rue Morgue, he took the entire framed story of Caligari prior to the asylum, eliminated the themes of political oppression and mental illness, and with deceptive simplicity transformed it all into a horror film. Within this new context, the narrative of Caligari was made palatable to a mass audience.

A plot outline indicates the similarity between the two. Both open in a carnival, attended (in Murders in the Rue Morgue) by Ames, his fiancée (Sidney Fox), and a friend (Bert Roach). Among the exotic exhibits is one more serious, a tent where Lugosi lectures on his bizarre theories. He displays an orangutan, Erik, who, he claims, is semi-human, a relative of man that experiences human emotions. Lugosi has learned Erik's language, and by this power of communication he controls the ape. Soon, corpses of women are found in the river and taken to the morgue. Though he suspects Lugosi, Ames can prove nothing. Lugosi then sends Erik to kidnap Fox for one of his deadly experiments. But Erik does not behave as Lugosi had planned, and the climax comes when the ape, pursued by Ames and an angry crowd, carries off the girl. In these scenes, when Erik is finally shot from a rooftop, Rue Morgue clearly presages King Kong (1933).

The resemblance of the narrative of Murders in the Rue Morgue and The Cabinet of Dr. Caligari is thus readily apparent. It is even more striking when one realizes the correspondence among the main characters in the two movies: Lugosi as Mirakle = Dr. Caligari; Ames as Dupin = Francis (both innocent protagonists who suspect the scientist of

evil); Fox as Camille = Jane (romantically involved with Dupin/Francis); Roach as Paul = Alan (friends of Dupin/Francis). There is less difference between Erik the orangutan and Conrad Veidt as Cesare, the somnambulist, than there might seem. They are creatures controlled in a hypnotic state; while the somnambulist is subhuman, Erik has all the emotions of a man.

Not only is Murders in the Rue Morgue a Caligari-like story, but it also has similar set design. Florey effectively combined expressionism with the art styles of the picture's period, lighting and composing shots and painting the sets "black and white like the style of the prints of 1845 ... trying to obtain the ambiance of mystery and horror necessary to this type of film."[80] Leon Ames remembered that whenever Florey and his cameraman had any trouble with their lighting, they didn't waste time: "If he couldn't get the right shadow, he's have 'em paint it"[81]--a typical procedure for early German expressionist movies. Thus, in one respect he achieved authenticity in the costumes and interiors of the Paris of 1845. "Desirous of having all the details exact," he said, "I dressed the actors ... according to the sketches of Daumier."[82] Ames recalled, "We were all very mindful of the setting, the time, and costumes we were wearing. It was not modern, but a period thing, and kind of farfetched."[83]

On the other hand, given the small budget, Florey could scarcely strive for a complete historical recreation in the decor. This, coupled with the need to create a proper mood, led him to use expressionism to cheaply evoke the Paris of the Boulevard du Crime, a shadowy underworld of temptations, evil, and mysterious events. Particularly notable is the architecture of the houses, which grow outward over the street as they rise higher, jagged and angular chimneys piercing the skyline. Together with Art Director Danny Hall, with whom he had already collaborated in planning the visual design of Frankenstein, Florey surveyed the existing sets on the lot to see what could be used.

[Opposite:] A scene from Murders in the Rue Morgue revealing its debt to The Cabinet of Dr. Caligari and the expressionist style, as Leon Ames (right) visits Bela Lugosi and his ape in their carnival tent.

> We walked on the many dusty stages searching for
> and selecting the most appropriate standing units
> that Hall could redeem and change by adding flats,
> canvas ceilings, slightly bent walls, with misshaped
> doors and windows made of cardboard and painted
> chalking light effects around bracketed lamps. Old
> canvas left over from Eddie Polo's serials was em-
> ployed as frontage for the barracks of the Paris
> Street Fair, entirely photographed on a stage. The
> inevitable Wally Worsley's medieval Hunchback streets
> and rooftops were used for the final chase and other
> exteriors.[84]

Florey used these expressionist devices with great effect in creating the desired mood and atmosphere. Even backgrounds that are apparently normal, such as the carnival or the empty streets, are suffused with foreboding. Characters appear and are devoured by fog and shadows. Two men murder one another by a river, their indistinct movements half concealed by a fast-blowing mist, while the prostitute who started the quarrel watches hysterically nearby. The camera achieves a great mobility: following Fox's movements back and forth on a swing; panning from Lugosi hiding in the street up to Ames and Fox embracing on a balcony and back down again; crossing Lugosi's laboratory as a scene is first glimpsed in shadow before being fully revealed.

From narrative to set design to photography, no feature film of Florey's was so dominated by the Germanic style in both conception and treatment as was <u>Murders in the Rue Morgue</u>. There were several reasons for this. Most of his earlier movies were musicals or comedies or were hindered by the constraints imposed on the camera by early sound equipment; it would be years before he would again have a picture that so lent itself to this technique. Also significant was Florey's collaboration on <u>Rue Morgue</u> with cameraman Karl Freund. They proved a compatible team; their artistic ambitions were similar and the tendency toward expressionism was shared. Said Florey, "Freund, understanding what I wanted, was a great help in getting it on the screen"[85]--although he could also be "exacting and overparticular and unreasonable...."[86] Freund took advantage of Florey's fluent German, and Ames could seldom understand what they said to each other: "I never knew whether

One of the ingenious camera set-ups in <u>Murders in the Rue Morgue</u>, to observe Sidney Fox and Leon Ames (left) on a swing during the park sequence. Florey and Karl Freund (with pipe) are on the right.

they were speaking German or French!"[87] However, too often Freund has been given sole credit for the expressionism of Murders in the Rue Morgue. Because of the thoroughness of the Caligari style in all aspects of the picture, from plot to set design in addition to photography--along with the frequent use of Germanic techniques in Florey's other films berfore and after--there can be little doubt the writer-director, not Freund, was the dominating influence.

Murders in the Rue Morgue was, from a cinematic standpoint, a tremendous improvement on Frankenstein. While both movies were made only weeks apart--the Rue Morgue crew following the Frankenstein unit onto some of the same sets--Florey's direction reveals that James Whale's visualization of the Florey-Fort Frankenstein script was primitive and awkward by comparison. Florey's work was especially advanced over Whale's in terms of camera movement and the effective use of sound (such as the sarcastic treatment of the students' romances in the park or the cut from Arlene Francis' hysterical laughter to her screams in Lugosi's laboratory). In fact, later Universal horror pictures probably owe more to the example of Murders in the Rue Morgue than Frankenstein for their visual style.

Florey was satisfied with the result of his efforts but did not regard the picture as any great artistic achievement. As usual, he underestimated the value of his work. Upon its opening in February 1932, Murders in the Rue Morgue did modest business; its box office performance was nothing like Dracula or Frankenstein. But Rue Morgue frequently reappeared in later years on double-bills with other Universal horror films, going into re-release at least as late as 1949. Rue Morgue's ability to stand on its own alongside subsequent pictures indicates its technical and artistic advancement over other movies made in 1931.

The New Adventures of Frankenstein: The Monster Lives! (published in a French translation in L'Ecran Fantastique, #10 [1979]:62-63), written in December 1931, was Florey's seven-page outline for a sequel to Frankenstein. He had first proposed such a film while still preparing Frankenstein during the summer, and at Richard Schayer's suggestion Florey formalized his ideas for a follow-up in the hope that they might win for him the opportunity to direct it. However, a month later the outline was returned after

1928-1932: First Major Commercial Films   147

having been read and copied by the scenario department; plans for a sequel to Frankenstein had been temporarily halted because of the studio's poor financial condition.

Florey continued to work for Universal for a couple of months, collaborating on a number of horror scripts with Garrett Fort, from an adaptation of Robert Louis Stevenson's The Suicide Club to Cagliostro and a "were-wolf" story. Florey was announced to adapt and direct Boris Karloff in The Invisible Man, and even began the screenplay, but the deal fell through after he found he could not obtain an ironclad contract to protect himself from a repeat of his Frankenstein experience.

However, despite the fact that Florey was never to receive credit, portions of The Monster Lives! appeared in Universal's various Frankenstein sequels, especially The Bride of Frankenstein. Several sequences from The Monster Lives! were closely followed in Bride: the monster emerging from the charred ruins of the mill, the encounter with the old blind man and his family (abbreviated for the movie), and the monster learning to talk. Returning to Henry Frankenstein, the monster demands a mate and commits mayhem until his progenitor is ready to cooperate. They travel to the north of Scandinavia, there to resume grave-robbing and construct the new creature.

The remainder of The Monster Lives! parallels the latter part of the novel. Frankenstein flees before completing the mate, is arrested and acquitted of murder, then pursues the monster to the polar regions before expiring. Florey preserves the ruthlessness of Mary Shelley's creation, though allowing him some moments of sensitivity, such as at Frankenstein's death. Finally, Florey has the monster set fire to his boat in the middle of the Arctic Sea, presumably ending his life at last.

K.B.S., 1932

In early 1932, Florey gladly accepted an invitation to leave Universal, the site of so much frustration over the past year. The call came from producer Sam Bischoff, the new head of Tiffany, where Florey had last worked in 1926. Although since renamed K.B.S., the studio was still struggling financially, and conditions steadily worsened over the succeeding months even after it was bought out by World Wide. However, Florey was scarcely deterred by these obstacles, and in an association lasting less than a year he was active in writing and/or directing three admirable films.

The Man Called Back was the first of these projects. While originally hired for a gangster movie, Florey managed to convince Bischoff to replace the assignment with a suggestion of his own. This was to adapt, in collaboration with screenwriter Robert Presnell, Andrew Soutar's novel Silent Thunder (London: Hutchinson, 1932), a melodrama of redemption and tribulation as outside forces threaten an innocent love. Within a few weeks their preparations were ready and an excellent cast was assembled, including Conrad Nagel and such Florey regulars as John Halliday and Reginald Owen-- all of whom won praise for their performances. The Man Called Back was shot in April and May on a budget of a mere $68,000. With splendid atmosphere, photography, and production values, it appeared to have been made by a major studio for four times that amount. (One advantage was the crew's access to an elaborate jungle set recently constructed at Pathé for King Vidor's Bird of Paradise, which doubled for the South Seas in the opening reels of Man Called Back.)

Generally, the film won a favorable reception from critics, with a few endorsing it enthusiastically. The greatest complaint was that the narrative lacked originality, although most agreed that it was skillfully presented. But Florey's selection of material had shown his preference for tales of romantic attachment, especially when placed in the context of a dramatic and suspenseful plot. The movie won audience favor when it was released on the Warner Bros. circuit and was eventually seen in theaters usually reserved only for more prestigious fare. Twenty years later one of his early Four Star Playhouse telefilms, The Island, was a virtual remake, with David Niven and George Macready in the Nagel and Halliday roles respectively.

Those We Love, one of K.B.S.'s top productions, is a sentimental story of family love, one of the very few occasions when Florey was called upon to depict a domestic milieu. Unfortunately, the property from which it was adapted was rather poor and lacking in originality, although F. Hugh

1928-1932: First Major Commercial Films 149

Herbert's screenplay contributed many improvements. While well-handled by the filmmakers in nearly all respects, Those We Love is very old-fashioned in the treatment of the theme, based upon a tired mixture of the romantic triangle, the "vamped" husband, and alas, "the tie that binds."

Despite the movie's origins on the stage, Florey managed to create a smoothly cinematic motion picture which has nothing in common with the stilted, unimaginative techniques often applied to such projects during the early years of sound. Those We Love is a well-mounted presentation, fast yet evenly paced, and cleverly photographed to minimize the script's reliance on dialogue rather than visuals to create the plot. There is basically a two-act narrative structure, beginning with the meeting of the couple on Armistice Day, their courtship, and the early months of their marriage. It then skips ahead a dozen years, by which time they have a teenage son and their union will be tried by temptation. Despite the most minimal resources and only a few sets (at least one restaurant backdrop appears to have been left over from The Man Called Back), the mood of both these different eras was effectively captured, especially in the opening scenes of post-World War I celebration.

The picture has the advantage throughout of an excellent performance by Mary Astor as the wife who must decide, uncertain of her husband's fidelity, whether to try and continue their marriage. She is well supported, especially by Lilyan Tashman (in a sprightly role as the temptress, although she was gravely ill and had only a few months to live), Hale Hamilton, and many of the others in smaller roles and bits. Regrettably, it is true that the scenes with Astor are far superior to the ones in which she does not appear. The primary disadvantage of the movie is the periodic overplaying of Kenneth MacKenna, only sometimes credible in his role as Astor's husband, although he does improve considerably toward the end. Child actor Tommy Conlon, while sincere, seems almost a caricature by today's standards--despite the universal praise his acting received from critics at the time.

Even with these drawbacks, Those We Love is a generally better-acted film than most produced on a similar budget at K.B.S. or studios of its level. The primary distinguishing asset of the movie is the tension-filled and rather more honest than usual climax, as the female rivals, Astor and Tashman, confront one another. Tashman turns out not to be the stereotypical "home-wrecker" or libertine, but the victim of an unhappy marriage and a cruel and philandering husband who is waiting for an indiscretion on her part as an excuse for divorce; she is under constant surveillance and MacKenna is to be used as co-respondent. Although Astor still condemns Tashman, the viewer's reaction is one of understanding, if hardly moral acquittal. This sympathetic treatment of a woman who victimizes others as she has been herself victimized adds an extra level of depth and complexity to the characters and emotional drama of Those We Love. Thus, while following the general expectations of the genre, the picture offers a few original touches (along with some satirical injections of humor) that maintain interest throughout and allow for more universal audience appeal. After completing the project film in June, Florey left for a month-long vacation in Mexico.

A Study in Scarlet, begun in August, was Florey's third and best-remembered project at K.B.S. At the time, Sherlock Holmes tales were appearing regularly on the screen, seven having been made since the start of sound films. Producer Bischoff purchased the motion picture rights to the title of Conan Doyle's first Holmes novel for very little, but "for some reason known only in the cinema business," said Florey, "couldn't film the story."[88] This deal is perhaps not so surprising considering that in more than half the novel Holmes does not appear, the solution to the crime being told in a lengthy flashback (full of anti-Mormon rhetoric that might cause distribution problems in the United States). Only three other versions have been produced: two in 1914, an English feature and an American short, and a fifty-minute BBC television presentation in 1968.

Instead, Florey was told to compose an original narrative to fit the title and serve as a vehicle for Anna May Wong --as well as the character Holmes. The detective was to be played by Reginald Owen, recently arrived in Hollywood, who a few months previously had portrayed Dr. Watson in Fox's Sherlock Holmes--becoming the only man to act both parts of the famous team on celluloid. Florey and Owen had become close friends and, given a week off to come up with a scenario for A Study in Scarlet, they went down to Owen's Palm Springs home (which they frequently visited in the company of Frank Morgan and Edmund Goulding). Together they completed the screenplay in the allotted time, with Owen responsible for the clever, properly British dialogue. Owen and Florey collaborated on the continuity in consultation with the art director so as to utilize as many standing sets as possible. Florey was about to begin direction when circumstances arose to separate him from the project.

As had happened with Frankenstein, Florey's script was to end up in the hands of another director--though this time it was Florey himself, not the studio, who made the change. K.B.S. had been in unsteady financial shape for some time and in mid-1932 had been taken over by World Wide, which would not last much longer itself. The popularity of The Man Called Back and Those We Love, especially their success on the Warner's circuit, had turned the attention of that company to securing Florey's services for themselves. When they approached him in September, it was on the condition that he immediately take over their project Girl Missing.

The opportunity to rejoin a major studio, especially with K.B.S. going under, was too good to refuse. Florey's willingness to abandon K.B.S. is readily understandable when one realizes that he and Owen had to split screen credit and a $1,000 payment for their A Study in Scarlet script, while Warner Bros. was offering $5,500 alone to collaborate on the script and direct Girl Missing, with the option for a long-term contract on a weekly salary. Bischoff was understanding and released Florey from his K.B.S. commitment; both agreed that the assistant on his last two productions, Edwin L. Marin, "who had been waiting for such a break," should be given the chance to direct the movie.[89] Within a year, Bischoff would also join Warner Bros., where he supervised five of Florey's pictures in the next few years.

Although the plot demonstrated a familiarity with the world Conan Doyle created for Sherlock Holmes, Florey and Owen developed an entirely original script with no similarities to the novel. The screenplay, however, did contain many elements from other Holmes stories, especially The Sign of Four, "The Five Orange Pips," and "The Red-Headed League," and is complete with all the typical clues,

The creators of A Study in Scarlet: co-scenarists Reginald Owen (also the star, as Sherlock Holmes) and Robert Florey, with director Edwin L. Marin between them.

devices, and mannerisms. Unlike so many original film scenarios for Holmes, A Study in Scarlet has the feel of an actual adaptation of one of the Conan Doyle tales. The picture's title refers to a very exclusive organization called the Scarlet Ring, a group of eccentric and highly ambiguous characters who are so suspicious of one another that they are frightened to walk together. Upon the death of any member, his property is divided among the remaining survivors; suddenly they begin to die off at an alarming pace, under strange circumstances.

Some critics have pointed out the movie's similarity to And Then There Were None/Ten Little Indians, with suspects killed one by one, each murder announced by a nursery rhyme. But if anything the influence was the other way around because Agatha Christie's novel was not published until 1939. Not aware of the similarity until he saw his friend René Clair's 1944 screen rendering, Florey doubted that Agatha Christie had seen A Study in Scarlet, but he regarded it as a compliment if it had helped to inspire her.

The script of A Study in Scarlet is extremely well-constructed and polished, developing at just the right pace while carefully building the appropriate mood and environment. Florey seemed comfortable in the fog-bound streets of the Limehouse section of London, breathing life into the classically eerie atmosphere of the British mystery (as he was to do again twelve years later in an unproduced script, The Wormwood Scrubs Murder Cases). "Flavor of England has been particularly well imparted via the sets," wrote Variety, "and in the characterizations of the players."[90] One of the ways of conveying the sense of locale was by the use of a nearly all-British cast, unusual for a Hollywood version of a Holmes tale. Owen, having impressed Bischoff earlier in The Man Called Back, seems to have been given the necessary latitude to offer a different interpretation of the Holmes personality. Owen portrays a much more human, less remote man, not the misanthropic cocaine addict of the Sidney Paget illustration. The Holmes of A Study in Scarlet is more akin to the later Conan Doyle stories and is closest to the personification offered by William Gillette, to whom Owen even bore a physical resemblance. This was in contrast to the more prevalent screen archetype--these were the Arthur Wontner years--and Owen's "conception of the character is fresh and relieving."[91] The actor obviously enjoyed the role, although some purists criticized his work as being outside the true canon.

Despite Florey's absence during production, the stamp of his visual style is nonetheless present. A very appropriate sense of mood and atmosphere, with a pervasive feeling of fear, is created. Strange gatherings arranged by a secret code take place in abandoned, out-of-the-way buildings; dark and oppressive dead-end streets are places of isolation and terror; fog and shadows hide murderers and their victims. One of Florey's favorite devices for showing a character's terror--shooting a scene from the back of a fireplace, with flames dancing in the foreground--is used when the newly-widowed Anna May Wong invites an uncertain J.M. Kerrigan to her country house for the weekend.

Suspense is heightened by keeping the murderer unseen, while at the same time that individual's presence is suggested by having the crimes seen through the murderer's eyes using a subjective camera. The silhouette of a giant shadow appears on the wall as the victim stares and screams, "It can't be you," followed by a close-up of a hand checking off the name of one more member who has been killed. The climax of this technique comes in a long-take sequence with the still unknown murderer visiting the office of the criminal lawyer, Alan Dinehart. The camera adopts the viewpoint of the killer as Dinehart opens the door and the individual is offered a cigarette, puffs of smoke ascending in front of the lens.

This consistency in technique between a film Florey wrote but did not direct and the many pictures he made from scripts authored by others was a result of the manner in which he prepared his screenplays. As in the case of Frankenstein, each shot and sequence would be described in meticulous detail, including camera set-ups, so that the finished continuity could be directed by almost anyone and still reflect Florey's style. Such an elaborately prepared script is exactly what Florey bequeathed to Marin--along with its co-author as star of the movie (Owen could of course make any necessary last-minute revisions in the spirit of the original). Although Marin had only directed one picture on his own before, A Study in Scarlet launched him on a long directorial career, and Florey commented "that Edwin did rather well, he was a fine director."[92] However, George Folsey, who served as cameraman many times for both men, was less charitable: "I would not say Eddie Marin had one-tenth the quality of Florey, that's my impression.... He would have been guided by what's in the script. I don't see him as having anything to substitute."[93]

By the time A Study in Scarlet was released, in mid-1933, K.B.S. had folded and Fox handled the distribution. It opened to an excellent critical reception, and recently Anthony Slide labeled it one of the studio's best productions.[94] Had Florey completed the film, it would certainly have enhanced his reputation. But by then he had already completed two movies for Warner Bros. and was well into another period of his career--where, as a long-term contract director, he had to accept whatever assignment was handed him, with few opportunities to write, suggest, or even modify the screenplays of his projects.

1928-1932: First Major Commercial Films

Florey's first years as a director of features for major studios established the pattern of difficulties he was to have throughout the remainder of his career. He was never able to gain a position of power or authority in the corporate hierarchy despite huge commercial successes: The Cocoanuts, La Route Est Belle, and Frankenstein. The instability of his relations with the studios was compounded by two factors: his tendency to abandon a good position when he had one (such as leaving Paramount in 1929) if the urge to travel or a curious, though short-term, opportunity arouse (in this case, going to Paris to join Pierre Braunberger Productions); and his suspicion and mistrust of producers acquired through the loss of Frankenstein and Braunberger's violation of contractual obligations. "Unfortunately," said Irving Rapper, Florey "skipped from one studio to another."[95]

Associated with four companies in as many years, Florey turned out thirteen features and numerous shorts (including several of the three- to four-reel length) between 1928-1932. They were usually made in under a month, as were most of the films he made throughout the 1930s. One anomaly of these first years was that in no other comparable span of time was he called upon to author so many screenplays. Even on those movies to which he was assigned a script, he was almost always permitted to write the continuity.

As Anthony Slide wrote of Florey at this time, he "was not only totally cognizant of developments in the sound film, but also was able to bring ingenuity and fluidity to the medium."[96] Florey had no difficulty in making the transfer from silents, despite having had no training for the task. His natural inclination to experiment whenever possible served him well in motion pictures as diverse as The Cocoanuts and Murders in the Rue Morgue, helping him to avoid the staginess that afflicted so many during this period.

At the same time he displayed an ability with various kinds of movies, moving with ease from musicals to comedies to thrillers to dramatic love stories. Yet these years also reflect the beginning of the tendency to typecast Florey as a specialist in a specific genre. Unlike later years, when his output was usually dominated by the thriller, during this period he most frequently handled musicals. Indeed, the bulk of his films of this type were made between 1928-1930. Nonetheless, he was never more heavily influenced by expressionism than in this period, as his three horror projects (The Hole in the Wall, Frankenstein and Murders in the Rue Morgue) clearly reveal.

NOTES

1. Some sources mistakenly credit Florey with holding this management position at Astoria, which is wholly incorrect; he never worked in a supervisory capacity at any time in his career.
2. Irving Rapper, interview with the author, March 7, 1985.
3. Robert Florey, letter to Anthony Slide, May 31, 1975.
4. Robert Florey, unidentified correspondence regarding Astoria, Florey collection.
5. George Folsey, interview with the author, February 8, 1983.
6. Irving Rapper, letter to the author, September 4, 1984.
7. Others known to have starred in Florey's Astoria shorts were Maria Gambarelli, George Gershwin, the Giersdorf sisters, Photoplay editor James R. Quirk, Smith and Dale, and G.D. Washington.
8. Weekly Variety, August 14, 1929.
9. Florey, unidentified correspondence.
10. Folsey interview.
11. The 1931 film, Un Trou dans le Mur ("A Hole in the Wall"), Paramount's first feature made at their Joinville studios in France, was unrelated to The Hole in the Wall, although curiously it did incorporate musical numbers from The Cocoanuts.
12. Folsey interview.
13. Ernst Fegté, letter to Ray Cabana, November 8, 1968, Florey collection.
14. Robert Florey, letter to Ray Cabana, November 21, 1967.
15. Rapper, letter to the author.
16. Rapper interview.
17. Robert Florey, Hollywood D'Hier et D'Aujourd'Hui (Paris: Editions Prisma, 1948), p. 154.
18. Rapper interview.
19. New York Evening Post, unidentified magazine reprint of The Hole in the Wall reviews, scrapbook 1925-32, Florey collection.
20. William K. Everson, Claudette Colbert (New York: Pyramid, 1976), p. 42.

1928-1932: First Major Commercial Films 157

21. Florey, letter to Anthony Slide.
22. Robert Florey, in Groucho Marx and Richard J. Anobile, The Marx Brothers Scrapbook (New York: Crown, 1973), p. 116.
23. Florey, unidentified correspondence.
24. Florey in Marx and Anobile, p. 116.
25. Ibid.
26. Folsey interview.
27. Florey, Hollywood D'Hier et D'Aujourd'Hui, p. 156.
28. Florey, unidentified correspondence.
29. Florey, Hollywood D'Hier et D'Aujourd'Hui, p. 157.
30. Florey in Marx and Anobile, p. 117.
31. Ibid., p. 116.
32. Folsey interview.
33. Florey in Marx and Anobile, p. 116.
34. "How a Big Lens and Lighting Specialist Gets His Effects," Washington Post, June 9, 1929.
35. Florey, letter to Anthony Slide.
36. "How a Big Lens...."
37. Florey, unidentified correspondence.
38. Weekly Variety, May 29, 1929.
39. "How a Big Lens...."
40. Folsey interview.
41. The London Sunday Pictorial, quoted in typed notes on The Cocoanuts, Florey collection.
42. Florey in Marx and Anobile, p. 116.
43. Florey, Hollywood D'Hier et D'Aujourd'Hui, pp. 158-159.
44. Robert Florey, letter to Jack Spears, March 16, 1966.
45. Florey, unidentified correspondence.
46. Florey, letter to Anthony Slide.
47. Folsey interview.
48. Florey, Hollywood D'Hier et D'Aujourd'Hui, p. 160.
49. Ibid., p. 161.
50. Robert Florey, photo album I: 1900-1931, Florey collection. Another title for this film is Forests of England.
51. Florey, letter to Anthony Slide.
52. Weekly Variety, December 3, 1930.
53. Jean Renoir, My Life and My Films (New York: Atheneum, 1974), p. 105.
54. Gilbert Adair, "Sacha: An Introduction to Guitry," in Mary Lea Bandy, ed., Rediscovering French Film (New York: Museum of Modern Art, 1983), p. 96.
55. Florey, Hollywood D'Hier et D'Aujourd'Hui, p. 163.
56. Jack Spears, Hollywood: The Golden Era (New York: A.S. Barnes, 1971), p. 347.

57. Florey, <u>Hollywood D'Hier et D'Aujourd'Hui</u>, p. 164.
58. Paul Ivano, interview with the author, November 13, 1981.
59. Robert Florey, letter to Al Taylor (n.d.), Florey collection.
60. Paul Ivano in René Predal, <u>Le Cinéma Fantastique</u> (Paris: Editions Seghers, 1970), p. 34.
61. Ivano interview.
62. Richard J. Anobile, ed., <u>Frankenstein</u> (New York: Universe Books, 1974).
63. Robert Florey and Garrett Fort, <u>Frankenstein</u>, continuity screenplay, May 15-June 20, 1931, shot D-4, Florey collection.
64. Ibid., shot D-94.
65. Anobile, p. 6.
66. Jack Spears, letter to Robert Florey, March 24, 1961, Florey collection.
67. Jack Spears, letter to Robert Florey, August 26, 1968, Florey collection.
68. John Brosman, <u>The Horror People</u> (New York: St. Martin's, 1976), p. 270. Cf. Jack Spears, "Robert Florey," <u>Films In Review</u>, 11 (April 1960):220.
69. Anthony Slide, in Christopher Lyon and Susan Doll, eds., <u>International Dictionary of Films and Filmmakers</u>, Volume 2 (Chicago: Macmillan, 1984), p. 191.
70. Max Laemmle (Universal Film S.A, Paris), letter to Carl Laemmle, Jr. (Universal City), January 5, 1932, Florey collection. This evidence contradicts a recent theory put forth that all drafts of the screenplay of <u>Frankenstein</u> were based on a 1927 stage adaptation of the Shelley novel by Peggy Webling and revised by John L. Balderston, who were given screen credit. Florey always maintained that he never saw or read these plays; indeed, his outline for the film was written in March, well before Universal bought the rights to the Webling-Balderston versions.

    The plot parallels between the script and the plays offer less than convincing evidence to support the influence of the playwrights on Florey and Fort, since there are just as many differences as similarities between the stage and screen adaptations. Moreover, the Webling piece was hardly original, but was based on many previous stage adaptations developed over the previous century.

1928-1932: First Major Commercial Films 159

This readily explains any similarities that may exist between the Webling/Balderston and Florey versions. With his long interest in the macabre, Florey had doubtless seen Frankenstein, perhaps many times, in the theater. He may have even participated in such productions during his youth in Europe. Possibly also Fort and Richard Schayer became aware of Balderston's work, making suggestions in line with it without mentioning the source to Florey. At any rate, it would be unlike Florey to appropriate credit to himself where it was not due; he tended to be self-effacing. For example, he readily acknowledged the influence of the German silent cinema and the Grand Guignol theater on his preparations for Frankenstein.

71. Robert Florey, letter to Jack Spears, August 28, 1968.
72. Leon Ames, interview with the author, June 22, 1982.
73. Florey, Hollywood D'Hier et D'Aujourd'Hui, p. 165.
74. Robert Florey, letter to Jack Spears, April 11, 1975.
75. Florey, letter to Al Taylor.
76. Robin Wood, "American Horror Film," in Barry K. Grant, ed., Planks of Reason (Metuchen, N.J.: Scarecrow, 1985), p. 180.
77. Ibid., p. 179.
78. Florey, letter to Jack Spears, April 11, 1975.
79. William K. Everson, "The Influence of German Expressionism on American Cinema," Film Reader (1979-80):107.
80. Florey, Hollywood D'Hier et D'Aujourd'Hui, pp. 164-165.
81. Ames interview.
82. Florey, Hollywood D'Hier et D'Aujourd'Hui, p. 165.
83. Ames interview.
84. Robert Florey, letter to Carlos Clarens, June 5, 1978.
85. Ibid.
86. Robert Florey, letter to Jack Spears, August 28, 1969.
87. Ames interview.
88. Robert Florey, letter to Ray Cabana, January 16, 1979, Florey collection.
89. Florey, letter to Jack Spears, April 11, 1975.
90. Weekly Variety, June 6, 1933.
91. Ibid.
92. Robert Florey, letter to Anthony Slide, May 19, 1975.
93. Folsey interview.
94. Anthony Slide, letter to Robert Florey, May 26, 1975, Florey collection.
95. Rapper interview.
96. Slide in Lyon and Doll, p. 191.

Chapter IV

1932-1939: LONG-TERM CONTRACT DIRECTOR

WARNER BROS. (FIRST PERIOD),
1932-1935

Girl Missing (initially titled The Blue Moon Murder Case) began Florey's tenure at Warner Bros. rather uncertainly, despite the haste to sign him on as director. Negotiations had begun on September 27, 1932, with an agreement reached that he would also collaborate on the continuity, and Florey reported to work on October 3. But only twelve days later the contract was postponed, the studio promising another film.

Nonetheless, he returned to Warners on November 25, beginning direction of Girl Missing. Fourteen days later this humorous mystery, with a large cast of well-known house players, was completed on a budget of $200,000. Production chief Daryl F. Zanuck congratulated Florey on "a very fine job ... in record time," adding, "I am certain that the picture will cut up into a fast moving melodrama with a lot of swell comedy and a lot of unusual angles."[1]

On October 8 Florey unsuccessfully submitted a three-page outline of Monsieur de Paris, an original idea, to producer Henry Blanke, supervisor of Girl Missing. A horror tale, Monsieur de Paris leaves a gruesome impression not because of what is shown, but because of the subject: the domestic life of a state executioner (the title was a euphemism for the man who operates the guillotine). His son, described as a Preston Foster type, argues with his father over inheriting the "business," one the family has been engaged in for over a century that has driven mad two previous generations. Becoming involved with a prostitute, the boy joins a gang of apaches, kills a policeman during a robbery, and is sentenced and dies at the hands of the executioner--his father.

Until this point in the story, the father--a part suggested for Edward G. Robinson--has been characterized by the care and kindliness displayed both toward his family and the prisoners he must deal with; the only sign of his mental imbalance is the imperturbable calm with which he goes about all of his contrasting activities. But now desperate, he seeks out a pair of scientists who have been begging him for a freshly-killed corpse, claiming they can bring it back to life electrically. The executioner offers them his son, but the boy only revives for a few minutes, just long enough to revenge himself on the prostitute, before dying a second time. Her murder is pinned on the father, who goes insane from all he has seen; the doctors realize no one will believe their accomplishment.

With Monsieur de Paris Florey succeeds in creating a profoundly disturbing narrative, highlighting what the mind simply prefers not to contemplate: those who take care of society's unpleasant tasks and the psychological effect this has on them. There are memorable and tension-charged scenes, as when the father slices bread with infinite care or cultivates his garden with a variety of tools from spades to knives. Florey offers a very spare story with none of the conventional appeals of the genre, such as romanticism, black humor, or atmosphere. Admittedly, he does recycle some ideas from Frankenstein, although in a different context; he probably felt that, considering Universal's conduct towards him, he had every right to try and improve on what he had done before. But it is hard to see what commercial prospects so grim a story as Monsieur de Paris could have held for the company. Warner Bros. knew of Florey's multiple talents (a memo during initial contract negotiations mentions "he is as good a writer as a director"), but despite this, he was given almost no opportunity to prove it during his initial term at the Burbank studio.[2]

Ex-Lady, Florey's next task, was received within days of finishing Girl Missing. At three o'clock on the morning of December 13, he was phoned by Zanuck and told to be at the studio in a few hours, ready to begin shooting. An hour later, the movie's production manager called to say, "You'll start in the kitchen, scene twenty-four with Bodil Rosing and Alphonse Ethier." Florey responded that he "wanted to know if it was a comedy or drama--who was the star of the film--and if perhaps I could get the script ... or was it too much to ask?"[3] But Zanuck had ordered most of the script rewritten after taking two directors, Howard Bretherton and William Keighley, off the picture the previous day. When Florey arrived for work at dawn, only an old draft and a few pages of the new script were ready, and it was with these that he had to discuss the project with Zanuck and determine the mood of the first scenes.

Despite the sudden beginning, the movie was finished only sixteen days later. Ex-Lady gave Bette Davis--who had been tested and proposed by Florey for the Sidney Fox part in Murders in the Rue Morgue--"her first starring role."[4] The story, of a female artist with "modern" ideas who must learn that marriage still has value, was considered very spicy. Although Davis and her director disliked the picture, it received good reviews: "Florey ... put some 'Lubitsch' touches in treating some of the very risque and hot situations...."[5] Zanuck was sufficiently impressed to sign Florey to a long-term contract on January 5, 1933.

Good-bye Again offered the task of adapting a popular play (by George Haight and Alan Scott) to the screen. Florey was dispatched to New York, together with writer Ben Markson, to observe the stage version. The next day they began to prepare a cinematic continuity. But Florey was not enthusiastic about the project, disagreeing with Zanuck on how best to approach it. As the date arrived to commence shooting, direction was given to Michael Curtiz, and Florey's role in authoring the screenplay was not publicized, Markson receiving sole credit.

Soon thereafter, the proclamation of the bank holiday having caused a lull in studio activity, Florey was given a three-month vacation. He spent this time traveling through Cuba and Central America.

Napoleon Bonaparte was a lifelong hobby of Florey's, and over many years he gathered a huge private museum of

1932-1939: Long-Term Contract Director

artifacts from his reign. More than anything else in Florey's career, he wanted to direct a film about the French Emperor. Returning to the studio on May 31, Florey learned that Warners was considering a motion picture biography of Napoleon, and he wrote to Jack Warner.

> I have for the past twenty years made an extensive study of Napoleon's life. I have visited places all over Europe and outside of Europe associated with Napoleon--battlefields, palaces, etc., etc. I could make a picture of Napoleon that would be really authentic, yet at the same time present not a history book character but a live, human, honest to God real man.... Now that you propose to film Napoleon, I believe that I am better qualified than any director you have on the lot to make this picture.[6]

Florey's letter could not be considered presumptuous by anyone who knew the depth and scope of his knowledge of the subject, about whom he had almost a thousand books in his library.

Emil Ludwig, whose biography of Napoleon had been very popular, was brought in from Switzerland to rewrite Ernest Pascal's script. As Ludwig's knowledge of English was slight, Florey was assigned to guide him around the studio. Together they proposed to Jack Warner that the movie be made in Europe rather than on the backlot, a suggestion that was rebuffed.

While Napoleon was still being discussed at the studio, Florey was assigned to direct a number of other features. At the end of October, he filmed Ludwig in a series of trailers in different languages to advertise the forthcoming production. A month later, Ludwig returned to Switzerland, and the planning of the picture dragged on a year. Finally it was decided that Napoleon would be too costly, and the movie was postponed indefinitely.

A couple of years later, Florey would be influential in dissuading Charlie Chaplin from attempting the role, describing the comedian's test in the part as "pathetic."[7] (Edward G. Robinson had been suggested for the role at Warner Bros.) The closest Florey would come to his dream of directing

One of Robert Florey's greatest desires was to direct a film about Napoleon. However, the closest he ever came to having this wish fulfilled was in a scene with Akim Tamiroff, at right, from The Magnificent Fraud.

1932-1939: Long-Term Contract Director

Napoleon was a short scene with Akim Tamiroff, inserted in The Magnificent Fraud.

Jeanne d'Arc was another French patriot whose story Florey was long eager, but never able, to film. He began with a ten-page portion of a treatment--covering less than half the saga--from 1400 to 1429, when Jeanne first met the Dauphin. Apparently Florey, unlike so many other authors and filmmakers handling this subject, was primarily interested in the influences on Jeanne's childhood and the historical forces that made France ready to respond to her appeal, rather than concentrating on her trial and execution.

Florey carefully humanized the motivations for the conflicts, not only among the contending royal factions but between Jeanne and her family as well. Although generally her life was told in a straightforward way, with her visions illustrated by the usual spiritual soft-focus, he did add a psychological dimension, suggesting she may have been inspired by watching a play. (This is the "Legend of Lorraine," re-enacted with puppets by her uncle, in which a little girl from the district is chosen to be the savior of France.)

Wherever possible, Florey noted existing sites and buildings from the time that could be exactly reproduced, carefully mapping out the various localities where Jeanne's story took place. His detailed knowledge of French history allowed him to include many little-known facts so as to enhance viewer interest; he used one of these to suggest a clever visual touch.

> Playing cards were invented at that time ... to entertain mad King Charles VI. This gives a great opening to the picture because [the cards had been drawn] using the faces of all the historical characters of the period. By getting close-ups of the cards as this new game is explained to Charles VI we can introduce the characters of the picture to the audience ... we can even dissolve from a close-up of the face of Charles VI's wife Isabeau de Baviere to her real face as we see her talking to Philippe le Bon.[8]

Jack Spears has speculated that Florey "could have done

much better than the ponderous film Victor Fleming made about Joan with Ingrid Bergman" in 1948.[9]

The House on 56th Street was Florey's perennial favorite among his 1930s Warner Bros. films and, commercially speaking, the most important. A vehicle for star Kay Francis, this big-budget "women's" picture was shot in twenty-eight days (four over schedule) in July and August of 1933. The result was an excellent movie that received ovations at previews, convincing the studio to hold it for release over the Christmas-New Year season.[10] Performances were excellent: Kay Francis, Ricardo Cortez, and Margaret Lindsay were ideal, and John Halliday managed an improbable role; only a lackluster Gene Raymond and William "Stage" Boyd (appearing a few months before his death) fell below par.

Florey was enthusiastic about the assignment because of the story's period setting, during the early part of the century and later in Prohibition days.

> The first part of the film, based on the life of the girls of the famous "Floradora Sextette," pleased me particularly. This retrospective of the New York of 1905, which took place in the cafés, theaters and restaurants of the period, interested me a great deal.[11]

Warners spared no expense, with ornate decor and elaborate costumes all enhanced by an effective use of the music and songs of the time. Critics praised the quality of the historical recreation, citing a "good ... eye and ear for atmosphere ... [the movie] rings quite true as to the people written of and the locales brought up."[12] Unfortunately, Florey's attention to and success with such matters collided with the priorities of the new production chief, Hal Wallis, who had little concern for costuming Francis in the manner of the day. "Let's not overdo the wardrobe just because we are in a period," he said.[13] Florey's penchant for such accuracy would, in future years, usually preclude him from being assigned period films.

Florey's style was perfectly modulated to the tone of such a love story as **The House on 56th Street**. For instance, the early idyll of Francis' romance with Raymond is captured when their goodnight kiss is staged off screen, seen from behind through a half-open doorway. The honeymoon sequence is another that was masterfully done: in a whirlwind they are shown at the Moulin Rouge, in a Venice gondola, and at the gaming tables of Monte Carlo, each locale given a distinct atmosphere despite the extreme brevity of the scenes. As one reviewer wrote, "There is a mellow charm, not unlike the fragrance of lavender, about the early sequences of it."[14] Francis' prison stretch is shown in a montage as she plays solitaire, a pendulum swings overhead, and a long series of headlines flash by. Upon her release after twenty years, her emotion is effectively captured as she sees how New York City has changed; she is overwhelmed by a sudden rush of sound and a series of swaying skyscraper shots that affect the audience in the same manner.

The Hollywood Spectator elaborated on the effectiveness of Florey's technique as he opens on a series of close-ups of the Floradora dancers.

> [This] sequence of The House on 56th Street is a brilliant example of the correct employment of sound-cinema as a medium. Mr. Robert Florey's direction of it succeeds in conveying the complete flavor of a Floradora period musical comedy--not only the swing and color of the stage performance, but the atmosphere of a responsive New York audience as well; one has a sense of being in the theatre with them .... It was obtained here through capturing a sense of depth for the scene by cutting away from the members of a sextette chorus to various sections of the audience; and as the cutting was done in camera rhythm with a sprightly song, the muscular reflex which this process induces completed the illusion of reality.[15]

Unfortunately, there appears to have been some unnecessary editing between the previews and the movie's release. The picture suffers from Warners accelerated pace between scenes, which were directed in a slightly more relaxed manner, so that the tale is needlessly compressed and the extended plot line moves along at too fast a clip.

Reunited with Florey four years after The Cocoanuts, Francis had "a powerful part"[16] that follows a quarter of a

century in the life of a Floradora girl. Her character is that of a survivor who accommodates herself to whatever circumstances are offered, outliving her three leading men in the story and apparently taking up with a fourth as it closes. Francis handled the role superbly despite the changes in age and personality she was required to make, moving "from happiness to the most poignant misery, and finally a sort of triumph."[17]

The narrative is structured around Francis' two sacrifices, one involuntary and the other deliberate. Accepting the proposal of Raymond, she abandons Halliday, whose mistress she had been, but later accidentally kills him when he threatens suicide. While she is jailed as a murderess, Raymond is killed in World War I and their little girl grows to maturity not knowing her mother. On her release, Francis, the daughter of a professional gambler, uses her gambling skill to join Cortez in a speakeasy--located in the very same house Raymond had bought her as a new bride. One night the daughter runs up enormous debts and kills Cortez; to allow her to escape, Francis conceals the crime and accepts Boyd as her new partner in order to secure his assistance.

It is these two moments of high melodrama which are the weakness of The House on 56th Street. Yet, because these incidents are underplayed, they do not seem too sensational; the coincidences "have the advantage of being logical --in fact, inevitable."[18] The intervening events are most believable, with an intelligent, ordered build-up to each of the climaxes. There is a feeling of fate hanging over Francis' saga; she has let her cards decide her actions and, she says, marriage to Raymond was not in them. But she overrides their dictates, beginning the series of events that will end, ironically, with her keeping her promise to Raymond to remain forever in their house on 56th street--although not as she could ever have expected.

Bedside and Registered Nurse, Florey's next two assignments, were a pair of fairly significant films depicting

---

[Opposite:] The Floradora sextette of the period sequence in The House on 56th Street, with Florey and Kay Francis (in the center, to his left).

the seamy underside of the medical world. Bedside began
at the end of September 1933 and finished in the record
time[19] of seventeen days for $135,000. Although this initial
effort was actually the more elaborate and prestigious of the
two, Registered Nurse cost substantially more, $210,000.
The difference was due largely to the enormous advance required to obtain the services of Bebe Daniels for what would
ironically turn out to be one of her last starring roles.
Florey subsequently pushed Registered Nurse through in a
mere thirteen days, three ahead of schedule, during December. In between these two dramas he spent several days on
second unit labors for Ray Enright's comedy, I've Got Your
Number, starring Joan Blondell and Pat O'Brien.

Although made in the midst of a cycle of movies exalt-
ing the medical profession, Bedside and Registered Nurse
diverged from most of their counterparts by reacting against
the more prevalent portrayals of medical personnel as practi-
tioners of saintly rectitude. But despite this similarity in
basic attitudes, the two stories were entirely different.
While Bedside depicts the corrupt career of a quack physician in an almost socially conscious way, Registered Nurse
looked askance at the behind-the-scenes melodrama of life
at an urban hospital.

Similarly, the two films offer differing but complemen-
tary views of their milieu. Bedside is solemn, depicting the
rise of a suave roué, Warren William, a former X-ray operator whose only skill is his bedside manner that proves to be
enough to win him wealthy clients and a noted reputation.
A medical school dropout who gambled away the tuition money
saved by his demure nurse and occasional mistress, Jean
Muir, he has kept the truth from her by procuring the certificate of another doctor. The latter, having become a drug
addict, is more than willing to trade his credentials for a
supply of morphine.

Bedside provides some remarkable moments of highly-
charged drama. Becoming a renowned doctor (in name only),
we accompany William and Muir as he makes a typical round
of patients, giving them his nonchalant, perfunctory attention in knee-jerk examinations and following the findings
left for him by his qualified but unsuspecting associate,
Donald Meek. Eventually William comes to believe in his
own publicity, operating on and almost killing a patient as

1932-1939: Long-Term Contract Director

Muir tries to correct him and finally realizes that he is incompetent to practice. Most impressive is the tension-filled sequence as William's world tumbles down around him when he is asked to operate on Muir, the victim of an auto accident. Half-drunk, realizing that no one will help him as he pleads for a real surgeon, he is confronted by the sudden appearance of the drug-addicted M.D. whose certificate he has been using--seen in close-up through a distorted lens and resembling, in the words of the script, "an avenging conscience."[20]

Registered Nurse, on the other hand, is more light-hearted, taking an irreverent look at the social life of a hospital staff. Everyone's habit of lighting their cigarette by striking a match on a convenient "no smoking" sign provides a preview of the picture's debunking approach. There are many humorous touches, such as the incessant gossip of the nurses and their overt "gold-digging" among some of the patients.

But Registered Nurse offers convincing tragedy as well. For instance, when Bebe Daniels' husband--after years in an asylum--learns that his wife has built her own, separate life, he kills himself rather than try to be cured-- an exceptionally positive treatment of suicide for an American film. Daniels had become the object of the attentions of two resident doctors, John Halliday and Lyle Talbot, putting both off before agreeing to the latter's proposal of an illicit relationship. The two suitors had seemed equally worthy until the reappearance of her husband, whereupon Talbot reveals himself to be a cad. Daniels has just enough time to realize that it was the honest marriage proposal of Halliday she should listen to, and finally she accepts him. There is a positive feeling of relief at the exposure of the shallowness of Talbot's glamor and the triumph of the unassuming and charmingly unlikely Halliday; he is so unusual as a romantic lead that it gives the story an added dimension of novelty and authenticity.

Registered Nurse fulfills many of the larger conventions of "women's" melodrama within the format of the hospital tale. Daniels is called upon for a variety of emotions: to be dedicated, sacrificial, and manipulated, finally overcoming sorrow to begin life and love anew. The movie seems to have been designed around Daniels' needs, a decision which was a reasonable investment in her future as a star; she was given control over her dialogue and a say in the selection of top cameraman Sid Hickox. Florey had known Daniels since 1921 as one of the Hollywoodians who frequented Crystal Pier in Santa Monica.

Although Registered Nurse contains a large gallery of talented players, many of whom offer finely-etched vignettes, the stark confrontations of Bedside remain rather more memorable despite a less convincing plot line. Warren William makes Bedside credible with a striking, appropriately flamboyant performance that allowed him to display a variety of facets. He is established immediately as dissolute and disreputable, waking up on his sofa at mid-day, hair and tie wildly askew, a cigarette hanging out of his mouth. Staggering to his feet, he tries to remember the night before, but the only evidence he finds is an empty pocket and an unknown woman's high-heeled shoe. In the office, however, he is self-confident and assured, complimenting his patients flirtatiously, pleasing them as well as Jean Muir, who trusts him completely. Only occasionally can one recognize his periodic self-doubts as the sign of a troubled conscience about to break. The support in Bedside is effective as well; "above all there stands out the terrifying vision of the drug-sodden David Landau, on whose qualifications the doctor traded."[21]

Neither Bedside nor Registered Nurse won much critical praise in their time, arriving when the medical-film cycle was nearing exhaustion and only the most prestigious or original exponent might secure a favorable review. But despite the fact that Bedside received the better notices, Registered Nurse holds its own far more capably today. This is not because of any superiority in the script but rather due to the expert and highly visual way in which it was handled. Indeed, if done by another director, Registered Nurse might have turned out a much less involving picture--merely routine rather than exemplary soap opera.

The stamp of Florey's technique is evident in the pace and some of the clever camerawork in Registered Nurse. For instance, the ailing Sidney Toler ambiguously wheels himself from background to foreground after planting the idea of sacrificing himself for his wife's sake in the mind of Daniels' husband. Some subjective shots follow, making the subsequent suicide all the more unnerving as the audience is disbelievingly drawn into the portrayal of a taboo on the screen. Florey was also experimenting, in this and his next film, Smarty, with the appropriate use of close-ups. Not only did they serve to isolate dialogue one-liners, but he wanted to discover to what extent they could be relied upon to carry a scene, especially by isolating a single player facing toward the camera. He did this despite studio displeasure and the lack of understanding of his purpose on the part of production chief Hal Wallis.

Smarty, adapted for the screen by F. Hugh Herbert from his play Hit Me Again (a title the film retained in England), was enjoyed by Florey as "an amusing little comedy."[22] In this A-class production he directed yet another of the studio's top female stars, Joan Blondell, alongside Warren William and Edward Everett Horton. Florey described Horton, a friend from their silent days at M-G-M, as one of the best and most pleasant actors he ever worked with, a "conscientious artist and full of talent."[23] Shooting lasted eighteen days in January and February 1934, with the resulting picture becoming a "Box Office Champion" for June.[24]

Part of the reason for the popularity of Smarty may have been Herbert's free-spirited treatment of contemporary mores, telling of a woman who goes in and out of the divorce courts, apparently believing--as William remarks sarcastically--that she can "commute between husbands." The original stage title derived from the fact that Blondell drives two husbands to distraction: first the rather melancholy William, then the effeminate Horton. Eventually each of them slaps her and she switches allegiance between the two. Finally she returns to William after he tells her he has changed his apologetic ways, having seen women in the movies who receive a grapefruit in the face. As this outline indicates, Smarty is a rather patronizing, misogynistic film--as William enunciates the theme, "love is the illusion that one woman differs from another"--which would arouse more indignation than laughter if revived today.

Despite these drawbacks, Smarty is still refreshingly vibrant by comparison to many of the artificially romantic comedies of the 1930s, particularly those that adhered more closely to Hays Office norms. For instance, Smarty offers a range of characters without virtue, as would be expected

from a much more modern picture. Most notable is Claire
Dodd, who observes events throughout with a knowing
smirk and whose preference, we are told, for strange beds
led to her own divorce. A similar individual (although still
married) is Joan Wheeler, who takes up with a lonely William
but plays the part of the seductress against type, having
neither sultry looks nor a heart of gold.

Unfortunately, Blondell plays in a shameless and silly
vein which robs the drama of motivation; Florey seems to
have desired a more irritating actress (he suggested Genevieve Tobin) who could justify a more appropriate response
from her husbands. Otherwise, beyond keeping the movie's
stage origins well-concealed, Florey added little beyond a
few characteristic camera touches. He found himself the recipient of regular, detailed instructions from Hal Wallis, dictating compositions, gestures, and bits of business exactly
as he wanted them.

Florey left the studio for three months, beginning in
April 1934, to make a tour of the Far East. He visited Japan,
Hong Kong, Macao, and the Philippines, developing a feeling
for Oriental atmosphere that would contribute to such later
films as God Is My Co-Pilot and Rogues' Regiment. At Hal
Wallis' request, he spent three weeks in China shooting backgrounds for a number of projects set in that region, only
one of which, Oil for the Lamps of China (1935), ever came to
fruition. The production chief, noting the difficulties George
Hill had in getting location footage for The Good Earth
(1937), even with government sanction, advised Florey and
his cameramen, Fred Jackman and George Krainukov, to work
illegally. This brought them into many harrowing situations;
they would have been jailed if caught photographing without
a permit. To avoid detection, they went from city to city
hiding their equipment, sometimes shooting from inside a
hired taxi or with their portable "DeVry" wrapped in a newspaper. Evading police and escaping threatening crowds,
they managed to smuggle out of China 20,000 feet of film,
without ever submitting it for censorship or having to pay
official fees or bribes. Ironically, for all the risks he took,
Florey was paid nothing for his efforts; the footage was regarded as too realistic to be used in the studio-photographed
Oil for the Lamps of China.

I Sell Anything was Florey's first assignment following

his return to the studio on June 21, 1934. He took over, from Roy Del Ruth, a project which had been in production for a long time as various writers sought an appropriate story to deal with the topic of antiques racketeering. Earlier, before leaving for the Orient, Florey had spent a month collaborating on one of the unproduced variations on this idea, Beware of Imitations.

Finally Warners opted for a comedic exposé, a vehicle for Pat O'Brien to star as a crooked but charming auctioneer. The film was finished in July, after only seventeen days (three ahead of schedule), on a budget of $125,000. While enjoying the opportunity to work with O'Brien, Florey regarded the picture as mediocre; with self-deprecating humor he proclaimed that he should adopt as his slogan, "I direct anything."[25] Typically, Florey's personal evaluation was too harsh: reviewers described I Sell Anything as an amusing and enjoyable movie.

I Am a Thief was a "B" mystery, modest in nearly every respect. Recounting the train-bound pursuit of a valuable set of diamonds, first one suspect, then another, becomes involved in abortive efforts to steal the gems until nearly all the key characters turn out to be guilty in some sense. Florey capitalizes on every opportunity to emphasize the underhanded looks of the numerous criminals, picking them out initially among the crowd attending an auction and then later as they warily watch each other board the Paris-to-Constantinople train on which much of the plot will occur.

Unfortunately, the script, although satisfactory, was none too logical, partially because of harsh editing. The performers, especially Mary Astor and Ricardo Cortez as the slick thief she romances, must sometimes strain to achieve credibility. Nor was the story very original except for the idea of Astor as a female sleuth of the French Sûreté. Adding to these problems was the extremely wordy script that kept action confined to a minimum and made it difficult to sustain the suspense.

Made during August and September in sixteen days, two over schedule, for $120,000, Florey rather enjoyed I Am a Thief because of the technical challenges it posed. In this instance, he said, the job of director required him to be a magician, recreating the illusion of a traveling express without ever leaving the studio.[26] Convincing miniatures provided the necessary establishing shots. Full-size duplicates of Orient Express-type dining and sleeping cars were constructed on railroad tracks, with sliding partitions to enable the cameras to photograph any necessary angle. This authenticity was most effective in the cramped and oppressively close corridors as suspects brush past one another menacingly.

However, in other ways Florey was severely limited in his attempt to give I Am a Thief a creative treatment. He carefully selected background footage from the studio library for the sequences using rear projection, and eagerly anticipated recreating the atmospheres of the various European locales he knew so well. But attention to such details as costumes, make-up, and bit players was not appreciated by Wallis. "I don't want you to get too many screwy make-ups on the people just because it is being played in a foreign locale," he told Florey.[27] The result is that there is little to distinguish the various depots from each other, with pauses chiefly punctuated by a single oblique shot of a conductor blowing his whistle.

Because of the constraints imposed by Wallis and the script, Florey's cinematographic style in this instance tended to be rather typical for the genre. I Am a Thief contains frequent low-key lighting, and although evident shadows were few, with some judiciously selected unusual camera angles, the most striking shot is one of the convincingly villainous Robert Barrat in moustache and pince-nez, turning to gaze directly into the lens at the audience. A mildly diverting entertainment, I Am a Thief was received with rather surprising warmth despite its routine nature and was highly rated among the double-bill fare of the season.

The Woman in Red proved Florey's ability with a high-caliber star vehicle, in this case a domestic melodrama containing both romance and suspense, tailored to the talents of Barbara Stanwyck. (In the 1950s, he would direct her again in four television shows, labeling Stanwyck one of his favorite actresses for her consistent professionalism.) On The Woman in Red, he had three weeks to prepare, a budget of $230,000, and twenty-four shooting days (three over schedule) in November, so that for once he had the time and resources to mount an important film in the proper

1932-1939: Long-Term Contract Director 177

manner. Although Florey was not comfortable with the assignment, given to him because of the success of I Am a Thief, Jack Warner was most satisfied with his director's efforts, which were also singled out for praise by critics.[28] The final picture, while fast-paced, was also steady and orderly in its development, without any lapses or false moments. The choice of camera angles was effective throughout, mostly naturalistic although occasionally openly creative, typified by the introduction of Stanwyck's in-laws by shooting through a fireplace that closely resembled a picture frame except for the flames in the lower foreground.

On the other hand, there was nothing exceptional about The Woman in Red. Gene Raymond, scion of an elite but penniless family, is sent to form an alliance with a wealthy widow, the overbearing Genevieve Tobin; instead he falls for her stable-girl, Stanwyck, a professional rider. They elope and she is snubbed by his family, but she manages to transform Raymond from a corny, helpless, but proud aristocrat to a practical partner.

However, Tobin follows him, soon spreading rumors when Stanwyck innocently becomes involved in the scandal of a business associate. Much tension is built in the final reels as Stanwyck must decide whether to remain silent or risk her reputation and marriage to give evidence that would clear her friend. The camera makes effective swish cuts from a fox-hunting party to the courtroom as Stanwyck weighs her options, until she makes a dramatic decision to testify and is soon supported by her husband and the socialite in-laws she thought would abandon her.

The New York Times commented:

> Trite? Unquestionably. But Robert Florey's swift direction, the script writer's refusal to follow the set formula for such a situation and the earnestness of a competent cast prevent the picture from sloughing off into nothingness. Not first-rate entertainment, of course, but a generally interesting and well-acted picture.[29]

The Woman in Red was very popular, becoming the third best grossing movie for February 1935.[30]

The Florentine Dagger, Florey's best mystery at Warner Bros., was a noir-type thriller prefiguring some of his most notable later efforts such as The Beast with Five Fingers, The Crooked Way, and Alcoa Theater: The Clock Struck Twelve. As was so often the case at Warners, Florey was given many disadvantages to overcome on The Florentine Dagger. Assigned to two projects following completion of The Woman in Red, he had barely a week in which to write his continuity for The Florentine Dagger and make preparations. Much of Tom Reed's script, completed only days prior to the commencement of shooting, was rewritten during production; many scenes were excised and the entire ending was changed, all for the better. Despite intending the film as a high-quality item, a mere eighteen days and $135,000 were allotted to the production, and Florey went only two days over schedule. Together with supervising producer Harry Joe Brown, he had pleaded for an increase in budget and a replacement of the young lead, Donald Woods--in a difficult, ill-defined role--but both requests went unheeded. On the first day of shooting the concern over Woods seemed justified when he became so nervous that he lost his voice. But instead of becoming angry with him, Florey responded with patience, taking Woods to lunch at the hot-dog stand of a former gag writer for silent comedian Larry Semon, until Woods began to relax.

In The Florentine Dagger Florey had a complex script operating on multiple levels simultaneously. Despite being a mystery on the surface, it offered more than suspense without quite passing into the domain of horror--although certain overtones of the fantastic are evident, especially the influence of the apparently dead past on the present. Taking considerable liberties with Ben Hecht's novel, the movie actually surpassed its source while remaining faithful to its spirit. Both novel and film explore the psyche of a young man (Woods), a descendant of the Borgias who becomes so fascinated by the legends of his ancestors that he reaches the brink of suicide in the belief he has inherited their criminal tendencies.

From this point the book and the picture diverge, the latter concentrating on the unusual characters and motivations Hecht only hinted at or used as background. Admittedly, the film opens with an improbable set of coincidences, but out of this situation evolves a bizarre, almost other-worldly tale of the ungovernable passions which control many of its individuals. Woods is supposedly cured of his obsession by writing a play on the Borgias. But the uncertainty as to whether this prescription--suggested by a psychiatrist--actually provides a solution, along with the concern that whoever portrays Lucretia will become like her, spreads deliberate doubt about the viability of such a cure.

As the narrative unfolds, Woods discovers that he is hardly alone in his deep psychological turmoil. Nearly everyone around him behaves in a consistently strange and unnatural way, from the principals through the henpecked police inspector and the misogynistic old psychiatrist. In uncovering the murderer of his prospective father-in-law, a theatrical producer (Henry O'Neill), Woods stumbles on a maelstrom of revenge and viciousness stretching back over two decades. The death turns out to be a case of justifiable homicide when the depths of the victim's depravity are revealed. O'Neill had once tried to kill his wife by setting her dress afire; miraculously, she survived, forever concealing her now-hideous visage behind a lifelike mask. For the next twenty years O'Neill continues to make her life a hell, trying to separate her from her daughter (Margaret Lindsay) by a previous marriage. Having fallen perversely in love with the girl, forcing his attentions on her and disrupting her romance with Woods, O'Neill is finally killed by his wife. Overhearing her confession, the police inspector allows Woods to take Lindsay and his future mother-in-law away to the safety of his native country--a reversal of the script's original ending, which called for the latter's compensatory suicide according to the traditional Hays Office policy. Florey handles the denouement with considerable compassion, treating Lindsay and her mother sensitively, avoiding the temptation of a gruesome and exploitive unmasking that many directors would have found irresistable.

The Florentine Dagger is startling, and was even more so in the era of the Production Code, for the frankness with which it presented emotionally unsettled characters. The disturbing motivations of O'Neill and hints of his possible suicide; the morbid melancholia of Woods; the suspicion that Lindsay may be guilty of patricide, along with the lack of retribution visited on her mother, were all elements hardly to be expected in a period of censorship. In these respects, The Florentine Dagger is at least a decade, and arguably more, ahead of its time.

Florey directs Donald Woods, Eily Malyon, and C. Aubrey Smith in the mask shop climax during which the secret of The Florentine Dagger is exposed.

Fortunately, the cast was more than equal to the demands of their off-beat roles. Despite the early concern of the filmmakers, Woods gave his part the necessary neurotic touch, hovering on the edge of insanity; only Lindsay seemed too calm and distant for a young woman under such extraordinary stress. Robert Barratt memorably added needed humor as a vain and apparently lecherous chief of police. Pompous yet clever, constantly smoothing his moustache, he receives amorous telephone calls--no matter where he happens to be--from an apparently jealous mistress. In the end, she turns out to be the temperamental wife he dotes on. These supercilious pauses contribute much amusement, appropriately providing relief from the tension (as was Florey's custom). The effectiveness of the varied cast was actually enhanced by the absence of any real stars with pre-established personas, allowing each to be perfectly molded to the needs of their part. Only C. Aubrey Smith, as the doctor who diagnoses Woods' mania and goes on to assist him as an amateur sleuth, was clearly recognizable among the players.

Each of the expressionistic and avant-garde techniques that contribute so magnificently to Florey's thrillers were utilized to the fullest, perfect degree in The Florentine Dagger. Florey had realized, in the words of producer Brown, that the movie "must be done with some care, must be photographed beautifully and every set-up a picture."[31] The result was one of the finest examples of Florey's versatility and the manner in which he could skillfully adapt and integrate these styles to the requirements of the Hollywood feature. The Florentine Dagger was especially appropriate for such treatment not only because it belonged to the thriller genre, but especially because of the psychological overtones and the origins of Woods' initial dual personality. The motifs of Florey's technique appear everywhere: in the bizarre, oblique camerawork and overhead shots, heightening and revealing moments of drama; the reliance on expressionist lighting and shadow effects; the frequent use of composition in depth, often with an emphasis on foreground and background objects and the distortion created by their positioning. There are moments of superb creative effect, as when a drunken Woods lifts a large wine glass that misshapes his face, moving to a close-up of his eyes as he dreams of Lindsay, her father, and the latter's Florentine daggers.

What is perhaps most impressive about Florey's virtuoso direction of The Florentine Dagger is that it was done within such tight time and budgetary constraints. Yet, as was so often the case, these pressures seemingly served to bring out Florey's artistry at its best. His summoning of an authentic and properly eerie atmosphere for the semi-Gothic central European setting was excellent, and even more of an achievement considering the picture's financial limitations. Among his personal touches were the Oriental items--collected on his 1933 trip to the Far East--that decorate the walls of the theatrical shop where the secret of Lindsay's mother is revealed. Such elements as the clever interpolation of stock footage and the use of proper costumes and signs in the region's language all made palpable contributions, while the fog and cobwebs of the Borgia castle lend a chilling mood to the opening reel that persists appropriately throughout. Most of these embellishments appeared during the filming and were scarcely mentioned in the script, which was unquestionably enhanced by Florey's cinematic style.

The studio's indulgence of these various aesthetic effects demonstrates their apparent hope that The Florentine Dagger would achieve a certain prestige status, knowing that it could only succeed by the richness of its presentation. But the bizarre aspect is also retained because Florey had the rare opportunity to supervise the editing while directing retakes and added scenes for the Al Jolson/Ruby Keeler musical, Go into Your Dance. (Later Florey described Jolson as "a man practically unapproachable because [he was] constantly surrounded by a dozen hangers-on, yesmen and racetrack touts talking incessantly. Thank God Ruby Keeler was such a quiet and sweet person!")[32] Florey assembled The Florentine Dagger footage into an incredibly suspenseful, absorbing product whose rapid yet even pace never relented, proceeding flawlessly. The result is a glossy, ornate movie far above the "B" level, one Florey seems to have been proud of. Had The Florentine Dagger received more of a push from the studio at the time of release (in the "Clue Club" series), it might have won more serious critical accolades, but the movie has well withstood the test of time to achieve an enviable, if still insufficient, reputation.

Going Highbrow was the first of a pair of comedies Florey sandwiched in between two trips to New York to see the latest musical and dramatic presentations of Broadway. After watching these, returning to direct a movie like Going Highbrow must have been a disappointment; this was a minor film from truly minor material without sufficient plot or humor to justify its programmer pretensions. A picture cast with all support and no leads, it was completed in nineteen days in March and April 1935.

Going Highbrow might have been far better as a short than a feature. The story, of a nouveau-riche Kansas couple who try to enter the social elite of New York, offered an insufficient premise on which to develop a full narrative, with the result that it becomes increasingly jumbled and trite, burdened with unbelievable romantic entanglements and even two dreadful songs. These only serve to point out the dull pace, and by the end unpleasant dramatic situations of a type inimicable to comedy become predominant.

Only in the opening reels is Going Highbrow fairly amusing, with Guy Kibbee as a rich husband whose only ambition is to live a plain life, unencumbered by the worries of wealth. However, he bows to the wishes of his social-climbing wife, ZaSu Pitts, with her rather irritating manner and almost painfully high-pitched voice. The other performers do little to help the movie along; Ross Alexander is particularly unctuous as a romantic lead, and only June Martel offers a bright, cheerful presence. Even Edward Everett Horton, scheming to unite the midwesterners with snooty but impoverished aristocrats, is of only middling assistance.

Don't Bet on Blondes was a considerably better comedy, a programmer that would have been a more important release had not Dolores Del Rio backed out the very day shooting was to begin. Her role as the daughter of a Kentucky colonel played by Guy Kibbee was filled the next day by Claire Dodd, taking the lead opposite Warren William. The $190,000 production was completed seventeen days later in April and May. Florey was frustrated, however, that Hal Wallis refused to allow him more than a weekend to examine the script before commencing photography; indeed, word of the assignment had only come to him accidentally from his assistant while making Going Highbrow. Despite these obstacles, credible performances were achieved with amusing results.

The Pay-Off was planned as an unpretentious item that in the hands of many directors would have turned into a standard programmer. But instead it became one of those rare instances when, on the basis of quality alone, a small film is promoted to the "A" ranks and released alongside films costing two or three times as much. The Pay-Off was made for $153,000 on a busy June schedule of seventeen days--which included the replacement of cameraman William Rees, after a week's work, for incompetence. For comparison, Broadway Bill, a similar movie of the previous year directed by Frank Capra and Ross Lederman, had spent the same amount for horse-racing footage alone--a fact of which Florey was very proud.

The plot of The Pay-Off, a yarn of honest journalists and racketeers who collide in the world of sports, hardly seemed a natural for Florey. In fact, when signing his original contract with Warner Bros., it was with the stipulation that he "not be called upon to direct pictures with football, baseball, or basketball backgrounds."[33] However, The Pay-Off did not fall under such a classification since it dealt with the racetrack and the focus was not on sporting activities themselves. Instead it offered, like so many of Florey's best films--King of Gamblers, Dangerous to Know, King of Alcatraz, The Face Behind the Mask--a combination of ingredients typical of a variety of genres: romance, gangsters, and suspense.

However, none of these predominate over the others, so The Pay-Off could just as accurately be grouped with that peculiarily 1930s breed, the newspaper movie. In this respect, The Pay-Off compares very favorably with the prototypical picture of this group, The Front Page (1931) and is arguably more than its equal. The plot of The Pay-Off is far more credible, and the view of a journalist's life and the personalities who surround him is realistic yet entertaining. James Dunn, in the lead role, displays a staunch moral fervor and determination to report the facts straight--"as he sees them"--regardless of threats and actual bodily harm. Only his wife's profligacy can blackmail him into becoming a tool of the gang he had tried to break. Tormented by the corruption he has fallen victim to, Dunn finally loses his job and goes on an extended binge. Finally, some loyal colleagues come to his rescue. These include a fellow reporter (Patricia Ellis), who re-ignites his self-respect and whose affection had gone unnoticed by the faithful husband, along with a young jockey who provides Dunn with the chance to redeem his honest reputation. (His nickname, "the Real McCoy," was the original title of the film and a far more appropriate one.)

The story's possibilities were enhanced by a considerable amount of human drama effectively portraying the anguish and degradation the hero must undergo. A set of fully-rounded, believable individuals are offered, centered around a dynamic, flawless performance by Dunn. From the opening shots a conflict is established between his hard-working, conscientious nature and that of his wife (Claire Dodd), who demands that he support her at a standard beyond his means. Dodd's only interest in their marriage is her husband's income and, finding his ethics standing in the way of easy money, she betrays him into the hands of racketeers, eventually becoming the mistress of one of them (Alan Dinehart). She enjoys humiliating Dunn, taking advantage of his trust and willingness to shoulder all blame for her unhappiness.

But several factors keep the story from becoming a sexist or misogynistic one, such as the redemptive understanding offered by Ellis. Dunn too bears some responsibility for the initial tensions in the relationship with his wife because his ebullient personality and joy in his work often cause him to absent-mindedly neglect her. We also come to realize that Dodd's actions are the result of a disturbed mind: after being discarded by the "friends" who have manipulated her materialism, she kills Dinehart, then commits suicide. Florey wisely treats her as a self-destructive figure to be pitied rather than condemned.

While The Pay-Off could have been simple melodrama, it was handled in such a sincere, underplayed manner, with every sequence properly done, as to become not only plausible but affecting as well. There is a sharpness in the situations and a depth to the characterizations that is remarkable for a Hollywood movie, especially one planned as a programmer. The intelligent script was well acted to form a thoroughly engrossing, even memorable entertainment. The entire picture is rendered with great dramatic skill to create a model of perfect symmetry and balance in narrative development. Daily Variety commented:

> Robert Florey's direction is an excellent piece of craftsmanship. He swings the action along at fine pace, without sloughing character revelation and intense heart interest.[34]

At this time, Florey and his friend Pierre Collings had finally convinced Jack Warner and Hal Wallis to film a biography of Louis Pasteur. The two Frenchmen hoped to collaborate on the script with Florey directing, employing the same method they had used at Astoria. But the project was given to William Dieterle, and Florey received the lesser task of

directing The Pay-Off. He determined to leave the studio
when his contract came up for renewal a few weeks later (he
had already tried to leave the previous April). Dissatisfied
with the great majority of his Warners projects over the past
thirty-three months, he hoped to do better under different
conditions. Florey departed the company on July 6, 1935,
and immediately left for Arrowhead, writing, "Hurrah! I
have finished at Warners!" in his scrapbook beneath a photo
of him diving into the cool waters of the lake.[35] Six years
would pass before he would return to the Burbank studio,
and that was only when World War II had disrupted the
normal conditions of filmmaking.

    Florey wanted to achieve independence by working
outside of the studio system.

> It is obviously very interesting for a director to
> be attached to a studio by a contract which guaran-
> tees him a minimum of forty weeks of regular salary,
> but I thought after three years of efforts at the
> same studio it would be preferable for me to fly
> with my own wings and to become a free-lancer,
> that is to say an independent director working all
> over.[36]

But over the next few weeks he received a lesson in the
difficulties of being an independent, and it was not until
the 1940s that he truly achieved this goal.

    He signed on at Fox to direct a John Boles vehicle
and began to prepare the continuity. But only two days
later Florey was released when a management change dis-
banded the existing staff and discarded the project on
which he was engaged. Fortunately, he quickly found his
services in demand. Ernst Lubitsch, now production chief
at Paramount, was among those who heard that he was free.
As they were friends from Pickfair days and Lubitsch's producer Harold Hurley needed a director for the new Carl
Brisson feature, Ship Cafe, Florey returned to his old
studio in August 1935.

PARAMOUNT (HOLLYWOOD), 1935-39

    Ship Cafe, a modestly-budgeted sea front musical, was ready

to go into production as soon as Florey finished the continuity in collaboration with the screenwriters. The best that could be done with the routine script was to cover its lack of wit with snappy direction. Despite being a musical comedy, Ship Cafe does contain a few "Florey touches" more typical of his thrillers. One of the first scenes, set in a ship's dirty stokehold, presents a breathless fight between two stokers armed with shovels. The heat of the furnaces, the soot covering the duelists, and the dull, heavy clanging of the shovels lend to the fracas all the drama of medieval knightly combat. Florey was also able to insert a fine sense of mood and atmosphere in some places, as when the hero, lonely and out of work, wanders amid the fog and abandoned hulks of the docks, finally finding consolation in a cup of warm soup at an open-air cafe. And, despite the budgetary restrictions, the musical numbers managed to be diverting. Completed in September after some three weeks' shooting Ship Cafe was not an auspicious beginning at Paramount, although the fault was in the material. As Daily Variety commented, Florey's "direction has overcome what might otherwise have been mediocre screen fare."37

One month after the completion of Ship Cafe, producer William LeBaron asked Florey to film some three weeks of additional episodes for Rose of the Rancho, a musical western set in early California. The efforts of the original director, Marion Gering, despite costing almost a million dollars, had not edited well or pleased LeBaron. He turned to Florey, hoping he could salvage the screen debut of opera singer Gladys Swarthout with a minimum of time and expenses. Entire sequences had to be re-shot, including some action footage out at the Paramount Ranch, two musical numbers, and many other new scenes. Together, these formed a large part of the picture--although Florey did the work as a favor and was given no screen credit.

The Preview Murder Mystery, made at the end of 1935, was far more typical of the type of film Florey would make at Paramount than Ship Cafe had been. Preview, as the movie was originally titled, was a tale of murder set against the background of a motion picture studio. Despite its modest pretensions, Florey enjoyed the assignment, turning out a clever and sophisticated thriller with all the polish of a high-class feature--a "zesty little B effort ... well-acted and finely made...."38

The denouement of The Preview Murder Mystery--with Conway Tearle and Reginald Denny--exhibits the style typical of the film, with suspense maintained by concealing the face of the murderer in dim light.

With a story that is little more than a modernized version of The Phantom of the Opera (in France, Preview was titled The Man Without a Face), "this picture gets beyond its class in spite of a trite central idea."[39] This is due largely to the fact that Florey "created more suspense with the camera than is in the story."[40] Preview managed to catch and hold the audience's interest with fast-moving direction and a visualization that takes every opportunity to create mystery through unusual, sometimes angled compositions and dark lighting. The Hollywood Spectator wrote:

Florey has not relinquished the notion that screen

1932-1939: Long-Term Contract Director 189

art is a pictorial art, that the camera can set the mood of scenes and light and shade can be used to accentuate drama.... The composition and lighting of scores of scenes in this picture are gems of the photographic art.[41]

The camera denies the viewer access to menacing situations, which take place off-screen with the suspect's back turned, frustratingly far away, or in dim light. This prevents, for example, the face of the murderer, scarred by fire, from being clearly seen.

The studio atmosphere is accentuated from the opening credits, superimposed on a lively montage of preview and filmmaking scenes which delineate the world within a world that is the studio. Unstaged activities and settings around the Paramount lot and the presence of a number of silent stars on the sidelines are interspersed throughout the picture, adding to the feeling of authenticity.

The impact of expressionist set design is clearly evident in this scene from a horror film glimpsed during The Preview Murder Mystery, with Harry [Kleinbach] Brandon and John George.

The studio and its personalities are evenly caricatured to the proper degree, including an autocratic director, romantic publicity man, and an ineffectual studio boss, clearly an unflattering parody of Adolph Zukor and his type. There are also ironic situations in the course of the story: the murders on the lot cause the police to lock everyone in the studio, making all of them prisoners, a view of studio life with which Florey was thoroughly familiar. The wittiest moment is a look at the shooting of a horror film, whose sets are straight out of The Cabinet of Doctor Caligari and whose somnambulist star, the nightmare terror of thousands of moviegoers, turns out to be a vegetarian. Considering Florey's tongue-in-cheek attitude toward horror films, this seems to be a scene he conceived himself.

Till We Meet Again (originally titled Reunion and not to be confused with two later films having the same title) was Paramount's reward to Florey after his laudable efforts on the two low-budget movies, Ship Cafe and The Preview Murder Mystery. Made in six weeks in the winter of 1936, Till We Meet Again was not only an "A" class production, but also gave him a European period setting, something for which he was well qualified not only by birth, but by the depth and extent of his historical knowledge. For once he had an assignment both worthy of and suited to his talents.

Though set against a background of espionage in the first World War, Till We Meet Again was primarily a romance, a type of story Florey especially enjoyed. The quality of the film is apparent in a number of ways. The production values are high, and Florey's hand in supervising the set design with an eye for authenticity is noticeable; many objects from his own collection decorate a number of scenes. Even more important, Till We Meet Again offered direction of one of the biggest stars on the lot: Herbert Marshall, whose performance was a minor tour de force. Marshall's star presence allowed Florey to indulge his penchant for close-ups, playing many scenes, particularly in the beginning, in portraits and profiled two-shots. However, the later, more suspenseful portions of the narrative--most notably, an escape aboard a train--enabled him to create a mood of mystery and suspense with dark, expressionist photography. "Robert Florey's direction is a joy in its portrait lightings and highly resourceful in its scenes of action," commented The Hollywood Reporter.[42]

One especially memorable sequence was the loading of a giant cannon aimed at the heart of Paris. Florey depicts the placing of the shell into the cannon with amazing detail so that the audience becomes slowly aware that something is wrong--the gun has been sabotaged. An almost nightmarish quality is achieved by cutting between the mechanical loading and operating of machinery, close-ups of the unsuspecting faces of the soldiers, and tremendous long shots of the cannon being raised and aimed against the blackness of the night. This leads inevitably to the shocking explosion of the gun and the death of all those who handled it.

Though not a pacifist film, Till We Meet Again does make a subtle statement about the futility of war. The story concerns two lovers, Marshall and Austrian Gertrude Michael, stage performers who are separated on the eve of their wedding by the outbreak of war. Heartbroken, both later use their acting abilities to work as secret agents for their native countries. The similarity of the activities of each is made apparent in a series of parallel sequences in which the two are shown being inducted and trained. Each country's spies meet in basements and learn to sing the enemy's national anthem, and they use coded cigarettes to convey messages to their associates. The comparison is made more effective by intercutting between Marshall and Michael, engaged in nearly identical actions, each operating against the other without ever knowing it. For instance, a traitor to his country is seen for once in a favorable light: Marshall tells German Rod LaRocque of a giant cannon being used to shell Paris. "The choice is between French women and children, and German soldiers." LaRocque responds, "The choice is made." Ironically, it is Michael who will later trap LaRocque and cause his death. Thus, neither side gains any advantage from the efforts of Marshall and Michael; each only nullifies the work of the other.

Till We Meet Again explores the conflicting loyalties war forces upon the two lovers of different countries. They are swept up by the call to arms of their homelands, destroying the private world built between them. Before the war starts they comment on how their places of birth, so far apart on the map, could not keep them from finding one another; by the end of the movie, they have reunited and escaped together to a neutral country, leaving the conflict behind them. Florey eschewed the nationalism traditional in war pictures, and, despite his French birth, neither side

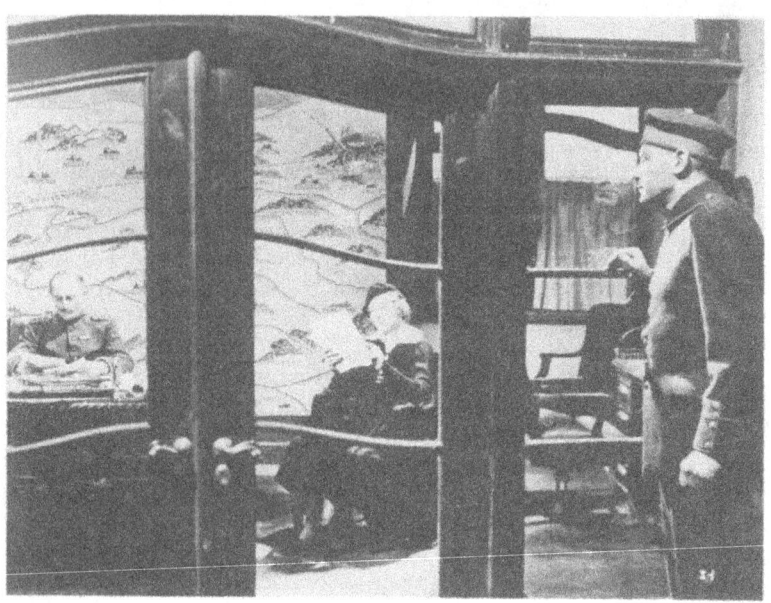

The use of composition in depth and photographing through foreground objects, such as these glass doors, were two of Florey's favorite stylistic devices, as shown by this shot of Frank Reicher, Gertrude Michael and Herbert Marshall in Till We Meet Again.

seems more virtuous than the other. Instead, he made a movie whose emphasis is on character, a trait that would recur in some of his later films with a wartime setting, such as Hotel Imperial and God Is My Co-Pilot.

Till We Meet Again turned out to be a good picture and one of Florey's best Paramount efforts, yet it was prevented from being outstanding by several factors. Though literate, well-edited, and directed with attention to detail, the final movie adds up to less than the sum of its parts, many individual sequences being superior to the film as a whole. The script relies on some improbable, though not impossible, events. Despite the skillful acting of Marshall, the support of Michael (in a role designed for Sylvia Sidney) and particularly of Lionel Atwill is second-rate. Nonetheless, the picture achieved artistry and sophistication, combining romance and suspense, and Florey was justly proud of his film.

Hollywood Boulevard returned Florey to one of the most deeply felt motifs to occur in his films: the plight of the struggling actor in the motion picture community. As in The Life and Death of 9413--A Hollywood Extra, made eight years previously, Florey now wrote (in collaboration) and directed another film centered on the tribulations of an actor amid the cruel splendors of movieland. However, since Hollywood Boulevard was a full-length feature, he had to embellish the concept and treat it in a manner suitable to attract mass audiences, an endeavor which had varying consequences.

Florey had a lifelong fascination and fondness for Hollywood. Stories using the motion picture capital as a background always appealed to him[43]; not only did he create A Hollywood Extra and Hollywood Boulevard, but he also directed The Preview Murder Mystery and two 1953 television shows for the Letter to Loretta [Young] series, The Hollywood Story and This Is a Love Story. Florey's interest in Hollywood's past did not end when he changed careers from journalist to filmmaker in the 1920s; he combined the two and became the community's resident director/historian.

This sense of the past prevented him from being blinded by the cinema's latest glories and newest celebrities. René Clair wrote:

> When I too was brought to California ... Florey, as soon as I arrived, insisted on showing me around --in his fashion, which is not everybody's. He didn't take me to ... the private swimming pools or the nightclubs in which the customers are seated according to their weekly paychecks. No ... he led me along nameless roads onto empty lots where a few sheds are all that remain of the Hollywood of the past, which the Hollywood of today is no more eager to remember than a rich courtesan is to talk about her adolescent years of love in a garret.[44]

This interest in preserving history led Florey to write a dozen books and hundreds of articles on Hollywood and its history.[45] These combined not only the reminiscences of the people he had known and the events he had seen, but also much historical research, so that his books have become basic primary resources, cited by countless scholars in many languages.[46]

Another aspect of this interest in Hollywood was the role Florey adopted as "unofficial French ambassador to the movie colony."[47] One of Hollywood's few intellectuals, he was a frequent host to visiting dignitaries from Europe, particularly Frenchmen. In the late 1930s and early 1940s he was especially busy helping European film artists seeking refuge from fascism to find a place in the American industry. Florey would take them to the studios or present foreign colleagues to the Directors Guild for membership, as he did with Clair, Jean Renoir, Julien Duvivier, Leonide Moguy, and others.[48] In the case of friends like Clair and Victor Francen, Florey helped them obtain contracts and find homes. If he had the opportunity, he would employ expatriates on his pictures, such as Eugéne Lourié, who was given his first job in Hollywood as technical advisor on Florey's Desert Song--after Julian Duvivier and Anatole Litvak had warned Lourié that he would never find work in the American studios. In later years, Florey frequently visited old friends at the Motion Picture Country Home; Leonard Maltin labeled him "one of the most generous and gracious men in Hollywood."[49]

Florey's interest in helping fellow emigrés find their way in Hollywood was doubtless stirred (in part) by the memory he had of those who helped him settle in 1921. He maintained a special sympathy not only for immigrants, but also for performers and the caprices of fate on which their careers often depended. During all his years as a director, he made a practice of giving parts--whenever he had the authority--to players who were no longer popular or could not find work. For example, in his first feature he cast Mildred Harris Chaplin (six years after her divorce from the comedian); old friends such as Herman Bing and Bert Roach appeared frequently in his films of the 1930s. For The Preview Murder Mystery, he tried to obtain the lead for John Gilbert and used a number of nearly forgotten silent stars in bit parts. Although seldom seen on the screen anymore, they were still recognized, enhancing the movie's atmosphere.

The warm reception accorded The Preview Murder Mystery caused producer A.M. Botsford to call on Florey for another story of filmland to be constructed around the title Hollywood Boulevard. After a few days he came up with a vague plot which was speedily approved. Florey's concept was to fashion an entire picture around the appearance of a host of old favorites seen in supporting cameo roles. Hollywood Boulevard would be a virtual Grand Hotel of stars of the silent days, twenty-three in all, more than any other film of its time.

Florey was assigned to work with Marguerite Roberts; "I dictated sequence after sequence ... and we went on to the shooting continuity, she writing the dialogue." Current Hollywood gossip and recent experiences provided plenty of inspiration. For instance, one scene satirized an independent project in which Walter Wanger had tried to interest Florey involving a Sheik taking an English girl to the desert. Florey even inserted a writer's complaint of having to "dish up a script for a monster we've got under contract"--a clear reference to his own experiences at Universal. But Florey "didn't like the story" that resulted from such quick work and was hardly anxious to receive credit; he suggested listing Roberts as sole author, which was done, although others were given credit for the story.[50]

Florey's intention was for each new sequence to open "on an exterior of a then well-known Hollywood spot, establishing the atmosphere...." "Before starting the film, I spent a week with a small crew, shooting Hollywood inserts and locations." Principal photography took place in June 1936, with a final running time of 83 minutes. He had hoped to delete some excessive dialogue during editing, while retaining the locations. But instead the production's supervisor, Eddie Cline (a Keystone relic), ordered the editor to remove all shots not absolutely essential to the plotline. Florey, sent away to Nevada to direct Outcast, could do nothing to prevent this change. Upon returning to the studio he was sickened by what had been done to Hollywood Boulevard. "More than eighteen extremely interesting exteriors vanished, and it became all plot and no more Hollywood," he said. Mae Marsh and Gary Cooper had their roles reduced, and Harold Lloyd's cameo was completely eliminated.[51]

However, enough location scenes were preserved in the first three reels for the viewer to gather a taste of what the original Hollywood Boulevard could have been. That the picture had been planned and executed by Florey as a self-conscious historical document is clear from both the cast and settings. He managed to capture the flavor of Hollywood, from nightclubs to the main thoroughfare itself, including authentic behind-the-scenes footage of the studio backlot in operation and some stunning vistas of Santa Barbara and Malibu resorts. These special features are the movie's chief virtues, giving Hollywood Boulevard a lasting value to cinephiles that makes it one of the most often revived of Florey's pictures.

Anthony Slide recently wrote:

> Hollywood Boulevard is unquestionably the best film ever made with a Hollywood filmmaking setting .... It provides fascinating glimpses of Hollywood in the 1930's.... More importantly, Hollywood Boulevard provides a useful social commentary on the Hollywood scene, its hypocrisy and its compromises.[52]

When placed in the context of its time, Hollywood Boulevard can be seen as the precursor of such later classics as Sunset Boulevard (1950)[53] and far superior to similar efforts like The Bad and the Beautiful (1953).

There are clear resonances between The Life and Death of 9413--a Hollywood Extra and Hollywood Boulevard. Both share an emphasis on the city and exterior scenes. Stylistically, Hollywood Boulevard is, on the surface, a departure from the low-key photography of A Hollywood Extra and The Preview Murder Mystery. Nonetheless, Hollywood Boulevard contains an unusual number of technical flourishes for a romantic melodrama, including split-screen effects and an extraordinary credit sequence, over a jazzy musical score, in the fashion of the avant-garde.

> It is interesting from the start of the first introductory title. Hollywood is planted in quick shots, then a comprehensive impression of the film capital is given, then back to a boulevard traffic signal as it changes to "Go," and the story begins. At the

1932-1939: Long-Term Contract Director   197

> end, there is a return to the signal as it changes
> to "Stop," and the story is over.54

The compositions are based on a preponderance of diagonals with frequent odd angles reflecting the disordered and askew nature of Hollywood life--described in the movie as "crazy, senseless, and exciting."

The basic plot of Hollywood Boulevard was an elaboration of A Hollywood Extra.

> It is a story of Hollywood heartaches, of the cruelty
> of Hollywood's neglect of players who have made it
> famous, and the cruelty of the sensational fan maga-
> zines which present as facts their fictional concep-
> tion of the private lives of screen players.55

Once again the central figure is an unemployed actor looking

Florey's bleak vision of the movie capital: the former idol (John Halliday, at right) exiled to waiting alongside the hopefuls and the extras to see an agent in Hollywood Boulevard.

for a job, fighting against the cold-heartedness of Hollywood. "That the story more than had its roots in reality was proved by its supporting cast."56 But in expanding his previous idea to feature length, several subplots had to be introduced that steadily diminish the importance of the central characterization, depriving Hollywood Boulevard of the singleness of purpose that made A Hollywood Extra so unforgettable. The severe editing served to heighten the unfortunate overemphasis on a disillusioned romance between the actor's daughter (Marsha Hunt) and an idealistic screenwriter, Robert Cummings, whose unctuous performance provides the only jarring note in a skillful and believable cast. Today the situations in which the people of Hollywood Boulevard find themselves seem to be extremely melodramatic, but this was apparently not so at the time. Variety said it has "one of the best scripts ever possessed by a behind-the-scenes-in-Hollywood picture."57

The use of cliches was not accidental, however. The characters of Hollywood Boulevard live out the very type of lives they portray on the screen. As the declining star (portrayed superbly58 by John Halliday in a difficult role) observes, "Does it occur to any of you that we're acting like the characters in a play--and a very bad play?" Just as he had in A Hollywood Extra, Florey was making light of, and simultaneously paying lip service to, the conventions of movieland self-portraits, mocking their excesses with an artificially contrived denouement.

Hollywood Boulevard shared a number of other motifs with A Hollywood Extra and, to a lesser degree, The Preview Murder Mystery and the two episodes of A Letter to Loretta. The city is a place of broken dreams and false pretenses, ready to exploit, consume, and discard all those who offer themselves to it. Hollywood demands total obedience, requiring those who desire success to be willing to sacrifice all compassion and self-respect. They must be prepared to destroy anyone who stands in their way, an act that carries with it the seeds of their own future destruction. Personifying the film capital's evil underside are uncaring figures like the casting directors and sensational publisher, each catering to Hollywood's mass desire to use and destroy people. Hollywood Boulevard thus expresses both a cynical and an affectionate view of the motion picture community. These were feelings Florey had for the city and his part in it, making Hollywood Boulevard a personal testament of his experiences.

The film, despite having no current big box-office names, had far more care and attention lavished on it than an ordinary programmer. "Hollywood Boulevard is an excellent piece of direction, away above what we find in 90% of the pictures made by the big directors.... Single bill houses rarely show a better one." On its release, it managed to appeal on the basis of its older stars, becoming popular among audiences and critics who regarded it as an unusual movie and an accurate glimpse of life in Hollywood. As the Hollywood Spectator commented, "There is no ... extravagance in the telling of the story, nothing but a plain recital of things which could happen, admirably acted and admirably directed."59

Times So Unsettled Are was the second of his own scripts which Florey was slated to direct in 1936; however, it was an assignment and not a project he initiated. In this case, unlike Hollywood Boulevard, he wrote the entire screenplay, adapted from a short story by Tess Slessinger and altered to reflect his personal concerns. The dialogue was by Marie Ann Chapin; Franz Schultz handled the portions in German. By mid-September, the 183-page continuity was ready. Besides the length, other factors indicate it would have been a big-budget movie: a period, foreign setting--with half the tale taking place in Europe--and a narrative requiring four principal performers. Possibly it was the problem of selecting appropriate stars, two of whom would have to be acceptable as Austrians, which caused the production to be postponed, ultimately indefinitely.

This was very unfortunate, for the picture would have moved Florey's career in a new direction. The screenplay of Times So Unsettled Are, along with similar sequences in other films such as the just-completed Till We Meet Again (with which Times So Unsettled Are shared a vaguely pacifist sentiment) reveal he had the potential to be a master of the romantic melodrama. A man of great sensitivty and sentiment, he could handle a "woman's" movie or "tearjerker" with great finesse and feeling (recall, for example, The Man Called Back and The House on 56th Street). Yet he also knew the necessity of keeping the narrative probable and injecting enough humor to prevent it from turning maudlin.

The story takes place primarily in Austria during the early summer of 1914. Florey portrayed the atmosphere, customs, and people of this country with as much affection as he had for his native France. However, a contrast is created between the warmth of the people and the cold bureaucracy (seen in the marriage sequence), suggesting he believed it was the state--not any inherently violent streak in the people themselves--which caused the forthcoming conflict. The romantic plot tells of a pair of Americans, Mollie and Dick, who, with the help of an Austrian couple, Mariedel and Heinrich, fall in love in Vienna. After a double wedding, all are about to leave for the United States when war breaks out. While Mollie and Dick return home, Heinrich must join his regiment. He is killed, and five years later his widow follows her friends to New York in search of a new life.

As the story's locale shifts from the Old to the New World, the mood of sincerity is replaced by one of cynicism. Though close-ups had predominated the first part, the camera would now have moved back, according to Florey's continuity, and taken a more distant, analytical view of the characters and the subsequent proceedings. A few days after her arrival, Mariedel discovers that her friends, in whom she hoped to rediscover the happier past, are now divorced. She finds out, as Dick says, that "life kills love, as surely as death," though Mollie corrects him, saying "only life kills love--never death."[60] It is a wise servant, Marceline, who understands suffering and must explain what has happened between Mollie and Dick to a woman who has not ceased to love the husband taken from her the day of the wedding. Finally, Mariedel is able to reunite her friends, though she remains despondent and returns to Europe. The title derives from her awkward English, including the habit of placing verbs at the end of phrases.

Outcast, made for Emanuel Cohen's Major Productions, was the only film Florey ever directed on loan-out. A high-quality picture in every respect, it was shot in six weeks during the last quarter of 1936. Although it marked the fourth time he had directed a medical drama, Outcast was his only true social consciousness movie--considering that on Monsieur Verdoux his function was primarily as a collaborator. While many of his other films had dealt with topical themes, this was usually done within the format of the thriller, something Outcast decidedly was not.

1932-1939: Long-Term Contract Director   201

The issue <u>Outcast</u> sought to expose was lynching, but unfortunately the film came in the midst of a spate of similar pictures and, like most, avoided the racial dimension. Because the story was a personal one, with Florey's orientation not aimed at controversy, <u>Outcast</u> seemed a weak follow-up to many of its more strident contemporaries. Had this not been the case, <u>Outcast</u> would undoubtedly have received more attention, but it was overshadowed and neglected in its time, a tendency recent critics have failed to correct.

The excellent screenplay by Doris Malloy and Dore Schary was uncontrived and completely believable, telling of a doctor, played by Warren William, who is persecuted because one of his patients committed suicide. Despite being "one of the greatest surgeons in America," he finds no hospital will have him, and his expertise is wasted--a fact powerfully visualized when he passes an unending line of patients waiting for help he can no longer give. William seeks refuge and resumes his practice in a small town, but his identity is found out and he is threatened with a lynching.

<u>Outcast</u> offered one of the most beautiful examples of Florey's style. The scenes of the gathering mob, lyrically and poetically photographed by Rudolph Maté amid the wintry snows of Nevada, are particularly effective (and give an idea how the similar portions of <u>Frankenstein</u> would have looked, had Florey been allowed to direct them). The location shots are excellently matched with those taken in the studio and do much to enhance the authentic atmosphere--and diminish the inevitable staginess--of the lynching sequence. Producer Cohen arranged for the use of the General Service Studios rather than working on the Paramount lot.

<u>Outcast</u> was an exceptional movie in every regard, one Florey could be proud of and on which Cohen complimented him.[61] <u>Daily Variety</u> described the movie as "a powerful, convincing drama, told with simple eloquence and haunting impression," of "grim and uncompromising intensity."[62] Most unusual was the gruelingly slow operation on little Jackie Moran and his sudden, accidental murder by his mother--a scene that is shocking and unforgettable, even by today's no-holds-barred standards. In this respect, <u>Outcast</u>, with its naturalistic style, was a portent of Florey's shift toward realism in the forties.

<u>Outcast</u> also gave clear evidence of the superior

The lynching sequence in <u>Outcast</u>, one of Florey's first films in a naturalistic style, with Karen Morley, Warren William, Matthew Betz, and Lewis Stone.

performances Florey could draw from his cast when given a good script and capable players. Most impressive was Lewis Stone, in "one of his finest performances,"[63] whose characterization of a country lawyer contributed greatly to the emotional power of the lynching sequence. Another standout was Esther Dale portraying with complete conviction the malevolent mother of Moran, taking on all the qualities of cruel, thoughtless prejudice, as well as the penalty for its consequences. Warren William and Karen Morley were equally capable, and every supporting player was of a high caliber, with not one off-key performance in the picture.

King of Gamblers (also called Czar of the Slot-Machines) inaugurated a long series of middle-to-low budget gangster thrillers that came increasingly to dominate the assignments Paramount gave Florey in the next few years. It was certainly an auspicious beginning. Shot in March 1937, King of Gamblers was planned as only routine product but turned out to be near showcase quality. The film was singled out from among the run of untrumpeted movies by critics for the high quality of its script, direction, and acting. "An unpretentious picture that tops in interest and appeal those which arrive on Broadway with benefit of ballyhoo,"[64] is how one critic described this programmer.

"With a big name cast," speculated The Hollywood Reporter, "the picture would soar."[65] Nonetheless, in King of Gamblers Florey had the best-known and most capable trio of performers he was ever to work with at Paramount. Lloyd Nolan was the scrappy hero and Akim Tamiroff the suave gangster competing for singer Claire Trevor. "The acting is as fine as can be found in any current picture. The cast is magnetic, the acting compelling...."[66]

The players managed to infuse their characters with a sense of realism and sympathy that went far beyond their stereotyped roles, giving them sufficient validity to be regarded as life-like and realistic figures. Particularly impressive is Tamiroff's multi-faceted gangster, at one moment murdering a rival with ease, at the next executing an associate for the cold-blooded killing of innocent children. (Tamiroff habitually puts his finger between his collar and neck when nervous, as if feeling the ever-tightening noose of fate.) Yet he remains almost pathetic in his love for Trevor, sincere and patient but at the same time hopeless while he in turn is forced to cause the death of her girl friend. On the other hand, the pleasant romance between Nolan and Trevor is believable, providing welcome relief and balance that keeps the movie from becoming too grim.

The screenplay, one of the best Florey was ever given, was based on a story by crime novelist Tiffany Thayer. The rather complex tale moves at breakneck speed, allowing no time for pause. While not especially original in outline or conception, the plot was "a little more sophisticated than usual," said Daily Variety, having "kept to a realistic groove that may shock some customers, but which is nonetheless an accurate picture of urban underworld life."[67]

To the intriguing script, fully-rounded characterizations and quality acting, Florey added superb direction, a steady but whirlwind pace, and perfect timing, which came together to make a film of terrific excitement. His imaginative touches enlightened the photography and atmosphere of King of Gamblers, traits that developed into typical hallmarks of his later thrillers at Paramount. A number of interesting angles are used, particularly in Evelyn Brent's waterfront dive, shot with heavily oblique compositions and using Nolan's movement into an overhead shot and concealment behind shadowy curtains to reveal the danger he is in. Nolan's scenes in Tamiroff's office near the conclusion also reveal Florey experimenting with brief subjective viewpoints, along with unusual angles and compositions in the fight scene that follows.

Suspense builds throughout King of Gamblers, and the final reels are almost unbearably exciting and action-filled. Although it lacks the serious possibilities for drama and character development inherent in Florey's three preceding pictures, King of Gamblers is at least the technical equal of any of them in the virtuosity of its plot, pacing, photography, and performances. By the end of the year, Florey would direct a virtual remake, Dangerous to Know, with the emphasis on character rather than mystery, accenting the tragic elements of the story.

Unfortunately, the successful release of King of Gamblers would soon encourage Paramount to hand Florey more and more crime melodramas until he became typecast. His stylistic expertise was used to redeem mediocre scripts, leading in a few months to virtual exile in Paramount's "B" unit--ironically because of his abilities, not due to any inadequacies.

Mountain Music came to Florey in the manner which made him so often frustrated in his position as a contract director. "I became immune from surprise," he would say.[68] Receiving a call from William LeBaron, the new Paramount studio boss, he was instructed to begin the next day on a musical-comedy set in the backwoods of Arkansas. "But I'm a Frenchman--I don't know anything about hillbillies!"

Florey protested to no avail.[69] However, as it turned out, he rather enjoyed the production and in future years would remember it fondly.

Mountain Music, made in March and April, was a broad, zany comedy, full of slapstick, often not making much sense. These were all elements of Florey's own unsophisticated comedic style and they were in extreme evidence here; The Hollywood Reporter called his direction "dashing and riotously unrestrained."[70] While Mountain Music may seem today to be very much of its own era, when hillbillies were a source of more humor, the picture was a huge success on its release. For three months during the summer of 1937 Mountain Music was Paramount's top box-office attraction, pulling in $2 million in receipts.[71] The movie Florey felt so unqualified to make became, along with The Cocoanuts, the most popular comedy of his career.

This Way Please, another high-budgeted musical comedy, followed Mountain Music in May and June. Neither were very typical of Florey's work except for a few unusual camera angles. This Way Please was considerably more refined, tending to rely on witty dialogue instead of silliness for amusement. Further, it had an interesting gallery of "guest" players and was faster paced, better written, and generally superior to its predecessor. A well-constructed, amusing and enjoyable movie, This Way Please was of a quality equivalent to many of the pleasant (if not memorable) musicals so typical of the 1930s. Florey's success with these two light efforts, and especially the staggering popularity of Mountain Music, prompted Paramount to give him a pay raise and deluge him with offers of similar scripts, which he was hard pressed to turn down.

In the summer of 1937 Florey made a return trip to the Orient. His companion this time was Nick Grinde, a friend and director at Warner Bros. They went to collect backgrounds for some films that would never be made, and though both men enjoyed the journey immensely, it did not turn out as they had expected, for they stepped straight into a war.

The first stop was Japan. There they spent several weeks visiting the local studios and attending many Noh and Kabuki plays, which fascinated Florey. Despite talk of an impending conflict, the pair departed for Korea and Manchuria.

Within days, a train they had been barred from boarding was
blown up, and the Sino-Japanese war broke out. Traveling
towards Harbin, Florey was arrested but soon released after
trying to make some scenes of troop movements with a hand-
held 16mm camera. Next they headed for Shanghai by boat
but were caught in a typhoon. This delay in turn saved
them from being trapped in a city rapidly turning into a
battlefield. After so many narrow escapes during only a few
weeks on the mainland, they had had enough and returned
home.

Daughter of Shanghai presented Florey with the challenge of revitalizing the career of Anna May Wong, who had
been absent from the screen for two years and with whom he
had previously been associated on A Study in Scarlet in
1932. Florey relates, "George Archainbaud was supposed to
direct it, but it was switched to me by ["B" unit production
chief Harold] Hurley over a weekend and I had but a couple
of days to get it ready." Although the story "was not one
of the best," the film was completed in about twenty days
in October 1937.[72]

Daughter of Shanghai was a quickly-paced topical ex-
ploitation thriller dealing with the always timely subject of
illegal immigration. Nearly every phase of the smuggling of
aliens into the United States is explored as the narrative unfolds. The plight of those who fall into the grip of immigration racketeers is made shockingly vivid in the opening sequence. A plane is spotted by a government patrol aircraft,
and the gangsters at the controls get rid of the incriminating
evidence by simply opening bomb bay-style doors, dumping
their illegal human cargo thousands of feet into the ocean.

Wong portrays the daughter of a Chinatown art dealer
who is killed when he refused to employ illegals in his business. Vowing to destroy those who murdered her father,
she brushes the police aside and sets out to uncover the
smuggling ring herself. Trampling on expectations and
stereotypes, she proves herself intrepid and courageous.
Wong finds her way to the criminal hideout, a mysterious
island called Port O'Juan. Securing the confidence of the
villains, she discovers the necessary evidence to convict
them--all the while staying several steps ahead of F.B.I.
men on the same trail. One of these was portrayed by
Philip Ahn, possibly the only time an Oriental has played

an F.B.I. agent, according to Carlos Clarens.73 Thus, Daughter of Shanghai is especially interesting for showing an immigration racket exposed by members of the very race it exploits.

The direction, set design, and photography are well above the "B" level and the perils-of-Anna type plot. The movie was made with a knowing sense of humor that glosses over the unlikelihood of many of the twists in plot, the players imbuing some of their more unfortunate lines with a subtly amusing tongue-in-cheek quality. The photography is extremely dark, as if taking place entirely at night, with only a few interiors well illuminated. This produces a sense of menace and uncertainty in every scene. The limited lighting allows for very creative effects; for example, the action of a fight is seen only as shadows crossing a close-up of Wong's face. Many clever camera angles enhance the mystery and punctuate moments of high suspense, particularly in the cafe sequences. The decor and design of the sets contribute to the sense of semi-realism which the story relies upon for dramatic effect, while at the same time effectively capturing Wong's Oriental allure.

Another quality distinguishing Daughter of Shanghai is the sense of mood and atmosphere evoked in Florey's direction, both in the Chinatown setting and particularly in Port O'Juan. This is an exotic, tropical island somewhere off the coast of the Americas, a haven for outcasts and lawlessness. Here, in a setting reminiscent of von Sternberg,74 the aliens gather to be transported to the United States. On the island is a steamy cafe where Virginia Dabney and later Wong perform their mesmerizing dances to the leers of a disreputable-looking audience, including a pet monkey. Florey did so well with his star that he was assigned to direct her next vehicle, Dangerous to Know, and was for a time scheduled to guide her through King of Chinatown--which, however, eventually went to his friend Nick Grinde.

Dangerous to Know can be regarded in some ways as a virtual remake of Florey's King of Gamblers, made only three films and nine months before. Most obviously, both movies feature the same two male leads in similar roles--Akim Tamiroff as the gangster and Lloyd Nolan as the representative of justice (in King of Gamblers he plays an investigative journalist and in <u>Dangerous to Know</u> he is a police inspector), with Harvey Stephens, Porter Hall, and Barlowe Borland again in supporting parts. In neither case is Nolan responsible for Tamiroff's undoing, which is brought about by the gangster's love for a woman he cannot have: in the first version, Claire Trevor; and in the second, Gail Patrick. That desire in <u>Dangerous to Know</u> is complicated by the presence of his mistress, Anna May Wong. As had been the case in Tamiroff's effort to win the love of Trevor, his attempt to force a marriage with Patrick causes him to follow a course of action that leads to the exposure of his criminal activities.

But while the two pictures use some of the same performers, situations, and themes, and while both have elements of suspense and human drama, <u>Dangerous to Know</u> is primarily a character study, almost a love story--while <u>King of Gamblers</u> was a thriller. Florey was frustrated in his career by the shallow scripts he was often assigned; not satisfied by the quality he was able to bring to his thrillers, he still wished to direct stories of more substance. <u>Dangerous to Know</u>, telling of the unraveling of a gangster as he attempts to maneuver into respectable society, offered Florey the kind of drama he preferred, combining emotional power with an exciting, fast-paced plot.

<u>Dangerous to Know</u> had an excellent script, adapted from the play and novel <u>On the Spot</u> (1931) by Edgar Wallace. This was one of the latter's best and most popular pieces, put on paper in four days and inspired by Al Capone. Wallace's biographer Margaret Lane has called <u>On the Spot</u> perhaps "the finest melodrama of our time."

> It differs from all his other crime plays in its complete lack of mystery.... The identity of the villain is not concealed from the audience ... we are a witness to his crimes of murder and cruelty, and his extravagant pretensions, his lust, greed and ruthlessness are displayed as openly as the malevolence of Iago. In such a character his weaknesses and superficial attractions become almost as terrifying as his vices ... seated at the organ [he] is a conception of convincing villainy in the grand manner ... a polished and appalling figure of criminality.[75]

1932-1939: Long-Term Contract Director

Among Florey's frequent collaborators at Paramount were screenwriter Horace McCoy, cameraman Theodor Sparkhul, and performers Anna May Wong and Akim Tamiroff, seen here on the set of Dangerous to Know, the masterpiece on which they were all involved.

One of the strongest sources of any of Florey's pictures, this helped to give the tale a literary depth and complexity that set it apart from the other gangster dramas Florey directed at Paramount. And yet in the screenplay the characters were made even more three-dimensional than they had been in Wallace's conception. The dialogue was filled with subtleties and nuances, as individuals seldom approach their subject except in a roundabout way, keeping their true intentions masked. Indeed, the greatness of Dangerous to Know is not surprising considering the combination of talent involved: from author Wallace and scriptwriter Horace McCoy, to cameramen Theodor Sparkhul and Karl Struss, to director Florey and the memorable pairing of stars Tamiroff and Wong.

Despite being shot--in December 1937--on only a

moderate budget, Dangerous to Know had all the polish and gloss of a more leisurely-made picture. The careful, deliberate direction, the uniformly superlative range of compositions, images, and sequences, all of a very high standard, were a testament to Florey's ability to quickly make a first-rate film on a short schedule, especially when he had a good script and capable players. There was none of the feeling of work being done under the pressure of a deadline that had marred his previous Wong vehicle, Daughter of Shanghai.

The two principal players, Tamiroff and Wong, had an interesting collaboration with Florey. Their obvious foreign descent and the quality of the exotic and unexpected which they are able to bring to their performances blend and harmonize perfectly with Florey's European visual style and emphasis on the close-up. Both give sympathetic and touching interpretations of their roles; for Wong, it was a familiar one--she had played the same part on stage. (Tamiroff's role had been originated in the London theater by Charles Laughton.) Wong's glamor and allure are captured in many effective portrait shots, which, with the new and striking costumes she wore in contrast to Patrick's plain black in nearly every scene, emphasize her Oriental background and its cultural connotations, laying the groundwork for her final climactic scene.

Tamiroff's gangster is presented as a twentieth-century Napoleon of the metropolis, a comparison made only briefly in the dialogue but repeated constantly through the decor of his home. This set was personally decorated by Florey with innumerable items from his own Napoleonic collection and even some of his furniture brought from the Orient. These objects are accented in the composition of the shots so that, for example, Tamiroff leans on a statue of Napoleon as he discusses how well he governs the city; he also faces policeman Nolan from behind a small bust of Napoleon. Highlighting the comparison between the Emperor and the mobster in this way was doubtless Florey's idea and is most effective in the subtly suggestive and chiefly visual manner in which he presents it, avoiding any such cliche as forthrightly labeling Tamiroff a "Napoleon of crime."

One of the first sequences of Dangerous to Know features a birthday party held for Tamiroff in his mansion. This is a beautiful and spacious home, bathed in white and

light with circular stained-glass windows and organ music
playing in the background, lending to the residence a
cathedral-like feeling. The guests are visited in individual
long-take vignettes with various camera movements going
from one group to another and quick cutting coming only
in the dialogue and reaction shots. The conflict is immediately stated when Tamiroff explains to his mistress (Wong)
that all the guests are people he has bought on his path to
dominate the city; now, no longer satisfied, he wants to
conquer the elite of society who still snub him. When he
spots socialite Patrick crashing his party, he begins to woo
her as part of his new campaign. Seeing this, "hostess"
Wong, already treated with studied rudeness by the other
guests, drops her teacup, which smashes on the floor.
Patrick is impressed with this gangster who "talks like a
poet," but quickly loses her fascination for a man she realizes is of another world and eventually grows to hate him.
Tamiroff's moods are expressed in his organ-playing; both
he and his mistress will communicate their innermost emotions through music, which becomes a motif in the movie.

A very Floreyesque touch occurs with the clever use
of the camera in a scene where Tamiroff confronts an associate (Edward Pawley) with the knowledge that he has betrayed a trust, and a phony suicide is staged. Tamiroff
approaches Pawley's apartment in a tall building; his shadow
first moves up to the door before his back enters the scene.
Tamiroff presses the doorbell, turns with his side to the
camera, and glances into the lens as the camera moves in on
the door, eliminating him from sight. At this point the view
becomes entirely subjective: Pawley opens the door, and
the camera begins to look directly into his fearful face as he
sees Tamiroff--although the spectator does not. Stammering,
confessing, he steps back into and across the room, finally
moving out of view to get a drink; the camera then cuts
back to show Tamiroff standing just where Pawley would
have left him. All this is accomplished without a jolt or
any unnatural feeling as the camera gradually moves into
and out of subjective perspective.

As Tamiroff is preparing for the forced marriage with
Patrick, he is surprised to find Wong pouring herself a
drink--a practice of which he, a bootlegger, disapproves.
At this point Florey handles their farewell scene in a manner quite different from what one would expect. Instead of

a traditional emotion-charged, perhaps hysterical, performance, the parting of the gangster and his discarded mistress is portrayed in a quiet, dignified way. Rather than speak directly, Wong turns on a phonograph, playing a few bars of a song, and her eyes look at Tamiroff endearingly, her tears speaking far more eloquently than words. (She plays "Thanks for the Memories," which Florey had suggested; it was the first time this tune had been used in a motion picture.) Both characters have used music as their chief mode of expressing emotion, he on the organ and she with the record. Tamiroff realizes he may be foolish in seeking Patrick, but it is too late for him to change his mind. Unlike Wong, however, he fails to sense that this is the end for him.

Wong's fatalism has made Tamiroff realize that in his hour of success he is not happy. He walks over to the organ and begins to play as Nolan watches through the window. Wong produces a small, curved knife from her purse and follows to where Tamiroff is moodily absorbed in his music. The next sequence occurs in a series of close-ups and contrasting, unusual angles. She gazes at him lovingly and smiles, choking back tears. Tamiroff stares upward with his back to her, his fingers playing without pause, appearing unknowing and uncertain. Ever so slowly she reaches out her hand to his shoulder--a gesture he fails to notice and which he had rejected several reels earlier. A cold, embittered expression comes over her face; she can endure every assault on her pride except his. She joins him in looking up, as if in supplication. Holding the knife, she plunges it down into herself, out of camera range. Tamiroff's eyes remain stationary as he fails to realize that anything has happened. She staggers and falls behind him. He looks aside, notices she is gone, calls her, and stops playing. He is shocked to find her lying on the floor. Not realizing that she is dead, he asks her what she has done and picks up the knife. Nolan, having seen all, marches in, arrests Tamiroff, and tells him that he will at last be punished for the faked suicide of Pawley and his other murders--ironically, he will die for a crime he did not commit: the murder of his mistress.

King of Alcatraz, made in July 1938, is the best of Florey's action-oriented "B" thrillers from the Paramount years (King of Gamblers had been at the programmer level).

1932-1939: Long-Term Contract Director   213

By virtue of an exciting story, good performances, and whirlwind direction, the film overcame its modest origins and nominal budget to become a classic of its type.

All of the right ingredients seem to come together here. King of Alcatraz was an ideal script for Florey because of its essentially visual nature and sparse dialogue. The narrative, of escaped gangsters who highjack an unsuspecting freighter (the movie was titled Modern Pirates in France), is extremely well constructed, with a number of surprising twists in the plot which made it seem quite original at the time. The situations--even a more than usually convincing romance-- are absorbing and believable, presented in a tough, realistic manner. The suspense is enhanced by the alternation of scenes between heroes and villains, especially in the sequence of a medical operation conducted across the ocean via instructions transmitted by wireless. Added interest is provided by a fascinating cast, including such veterans as Harry Carey, Gustav von Seyffertitz, and Tom Tyler, along with rising talents Robert Preston (in his debut), Dennis Morgan, and Anthony Quinn. However, contract players Lloyd Nolan, Gail Patrick, and J. Carrol Naish were hardly outshone.

Above all, it was the perfect pacing of King of Alcatraz that made it so successful. From the rip-roaring waterfront fights of the radio operators to the capture of the criminals, seldom has a movie been better in this regard. Florey's style retained a measure of functional expressionism, although his approach was basically straightforward. "Told with exceptional directorial skill," as one reviewer commented, it "is a kind of picture which makes meaningless the classification of A and B...."[76] Today, King of Alcatraz retains all its value as sheer escapist entertainment, a flawless example of the low-budget thriller at its simplest, unpretentious best.

Disbarred, made in September, was another smooth, fast-paced "B" thriller that had a moderately unusual plot. It tells of a brilliant woman lawyer, Gail Patrick, who unknowingly becomes the tool of a gang of criminals. Today Disbarred--the title refers to a supporting character, not Miss Patrick--is most interesting from a sociological point of view. Patrick repeatedly rejects the suggestions of relatives and beaus that she undertake a role more traditional for her sex. Her enjoyment and competence in her work are stressed, while her romantic interests, Otto Kruger and Robert Preston, are strictly secondary. Both men respect and admire her as a professional and discover that she views love and a career as not incompatible. After overcoming his initial resentment of her attitude, Preston convinces her to leave the racketeers for a position alongside him in the District Attorney's office, and their marriage soon follows. Thus, a low-budget picture made a deviation from the Hollywood norm, revealing a more progressive outlook than many "A" movies of the same period--although Disbarred could hardly be regarded as making a feminist statement.

Hotel Imperial was a remake of a classic silent film directed by Mauritz Stiller and starring Pola Negri. Ernst Lubitsch, on becoming head of production at Paramount in 1935, pushed for a new version, to be titled I Loved a Soldier, and assigned the direction to Henry Hathaway with Marlene Dietrich in the lead role. But the picture was plagued by frequent rewrites, causing production to fall rapidly behind schedule. Dietrich, thought to be "box-office poison," was replaced by Margaret Sullavan, and shortly thereafter the project was shelved. Lubitsch himself then fell from power, to a large degree because of the expensive fiasco.

Three years later, Hotel Imperial started production once again, but this time it was planned with a much less spectacular budget, shooting taking place on a two-month schedule in November and December of 1938. Robert Thoeren abbreviated the original script to fit the revised plans, and one of Europe's favorite actresses, the Italian Isa Miranda, was imported for the lead with the hope she might become a new Dietrich. Finally, a director was selected with a reputation for finishing productions on time and within cost limitations--Robert Florey. His reaction to all this was to say, "The package fell in my lap."77

Hotel Imperial shared many similarities with Till We Meet Again: it is set in Europe during World War I, and the plot contains romance and mystery with some fighting also thrown in. But either in the original script handed Hathaway or in the revision Florey was given things were amiss. The narrative is confused and unsatisfying, lacking the dramatic force and convincing characterization that had distinguished Till We Meet Again. Unlike that movie, the romance--by now the leads were Miranda and a colorless Ray Milland--is never adequately motivated or explained. Their serious but unconvincing acting was rather in conflict with the tongue-in-cheek performances of supporting players Gene Lockhart and Curt Bois, while Reginald Owen added the sort of broad humor Florey enjoyed. On the other hand, J. Carrol Naish seems an odd choice to play a "lady-killer." Hotel Imperial suffered from the "A" syndrome of trying to be all things--a mystery, a romance, a war story, and satire-- and failing to do any of them truly well.

Faced with weak plot and central characterizations, Florey chose to emphasize the suspense and comedy elements, trying to unify a confused narrative through the only means available to him, visual technique. The photographic style was self-conscious, stunning, and often artistic. He embellished scenes by adding many personal touches, with a special abundance of subjective shots and bizarre, disorienting camera angles. These aspects gave tension to a number of the sequences, raising them above the standard reached by the film as a whole. The first half of the movie achieved greater success, the satirical tone prevailing, but the remainder, with the ascendance of straight romantic drama, was only of an ordinary quality. Florey was not too pleased with the result of his efforts; it would be his last picture for a number of years to utilize a distinctly European style. Indeed, Hotel Imperial was far more popular on the continent; in France it became Paramount's leading release of the season. For domestic audiences, however, all the expense and time the studio had put into the project seemed to little avail, and Hotel Imperial did only moderate business.

The Magnificent Fraud was the last major film Florey made at Paramount and one of his favorites. Shot on a six-week schedule in February and March of 1939, it had one of the most imaginative and original scenarios Florey was ever to direct. Excellently cast, the leads were two veterans of his previous films, Lloyd Nolan and Akim Tamiroff. The latter, in the starring position, had a dual role that offered him the opportunity for a bravura performance.

The Magnificent Fraud tells a Ruritanian story of impersonation, romance, and political intrigue in a mythical South American republic. While remaining almost always surprising,

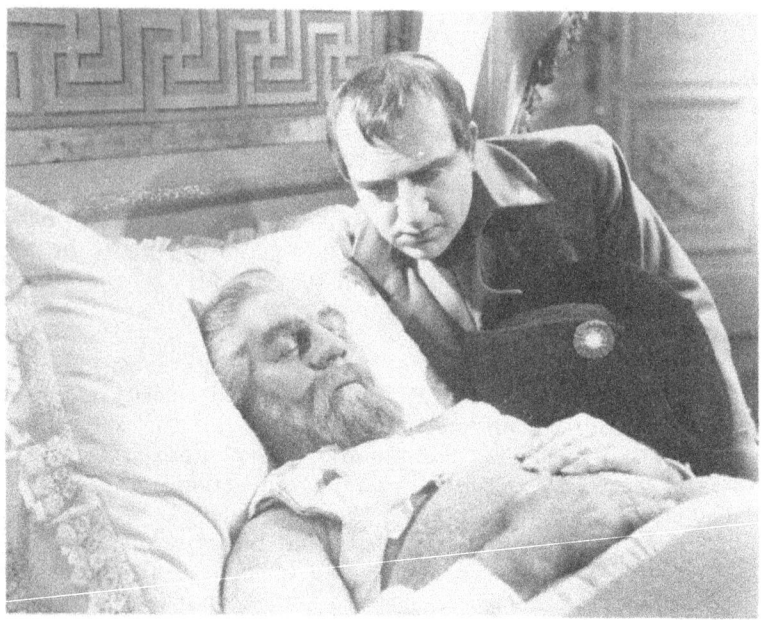

Akim Tamiroff in his dual role in The Magnificent Fraud, as the dying President Alvarado and the theatrical impersonator Jules LeCroix.

the film never ventures beyond the bounds of believability for that turbulent region. However, despite the strength of the script's basic idea, the tale dwells too long on a trite love triangle which interrupts and slows the main story, throwing the whole narrative somewhat off balance.

    This flaw is made more noticeable by Florey's rather relaxed pace (he also supervised the editing). Following an exciting and amusing opening, one expects the tempo to remain at an equivalent speed; instead, events begin to drag a bit as the plot thins and romance displaces the intrigue. The Magnificent Fraud turns reflective, becoming almost a character study, and concentrates on the swirl of life surrounding the main characters under unusual circumstances in an exotic environment. Not until the conclusion does the action element return to the fore. The story is told in a straightforward manner, avoiding many unusual camera effects, which contributes to the believability of the events portrayed. The result is a film more memorable for its basic idea than for its realization.

Benefitting from Florey's frequent travels to Central and South America--he had long wanted to make a film set in that area--and an "A" class budget allowing location shooting in San Diego and Mexico, The Magnificent Fraud was enriched by a sure sense of atmosphere. By his choice of camera angles, decor, and lighting, Florey successfully summoned the almost dreamy quality and sense of listlessness of an elusive resort, creating an aura both realistic and legendary. Seldom if ever has a Latin locale been made more tangible. The Magnificent Fraud pictured sympathetically and without prejudice the conflicts in a South American country, reflecting the effects of President Roosevelt's Good Neighbor Policy on popular attitudes as well as Paramount's effort to capture a larger share of the Latin market. The movie remains contemporary thanks to its depiction of the region's political instability, the threat of military dictators, and the continuing difficulties entailed by foreign loans.

In sum, The Magnificent Fraud is a good movie that missed the possibility of greatness. The chief fault lay in the scenarist's attempt to interject a dull and over-written romance; the studio was then trying to launch Nolan as a new Clark Gable. But the picture has compensating values in the fine performances and pervasive feeling for atmosphere. Avoiding genre conventions, the original story idea was unlike the standard Hollywood product. It offered a presentation of life and political machinations in South America that was one of the best, least stereotyped portraits of that area ever to come from an American studio.

Destination Unknown, a six-page scenario Florey wrote and copyrighted in May 1939, marked the only occasion he proposed a project that openly confronted a contemporary political issue: Outcast had been an assignment, and The Desert Song and Rogues' Regiment, both of which he also authored, were cloaked in the guise of adventure thrillers. Whereas he usually avoided mixing politics with his films, now he was moved by the events of the day--he had just returned from a six-week vacation in Europe--to write a grim drama of Jews who escape from Czechoslovakia and hire a freighter to take them to Palestine.

On arriving and attempting to land, they are attacked by both the Arabs and the British, who force them back to sea. Subsequently, the narrative takes place amost entirely aboard the ship and has a minimum of melodrama, emphasizing the suffering of the passengers. In an aimless voyage--hence the title--the ship is refused entry or the right to buy supplies at every Mediterranean port. Soon the boatload of 400 refugees is reduced by disease and starvation to a mere two dozen. Drifting, the survivors are at last found by a British cruiser, whose crew, moved by their plight, takes pity and arranges for them to immigrate legally to Palestine.

Not surprisingly, Florey got nowhere with his idea, despite the fact that he believed it would not be necessary to mention the words "Jews" or "Nazis" on the screen. The story was applicable to any persecuted group but also had unmistakable connotations for the time; moreover, in a preface Florey indicated, without being specific, that it was based on fact.[78] In truth, Destination Unknown was an exposure of not only anti-Semitism but also the international refusal to take responsibility that made the Holocaust possible--a significant proposal for a movie in the context of 1939 or indeed any time afterwards.

Florey continued to have hope for the idea even as the years went by and entrusted the scenario to Robert Buckner, a producer and scenarist at Warner Bros. But Hal Wallis and Jack Warner "thought it too aggressively pro-Jewish for the general public, although of course they didn't put it quite so bluntly" to Buckner.[79] However, after the war Buckner did manage to write and produce a picture of his own (Sword in the Desert, 1949) dealing with the British-Zionist-Arab conflict.

The Broken Heart Cafe, based on a one-page outline by A.L. Jarrett, was turned into a seventy-eight page screenplay by Florey in June 1939. The script, which was never produced, was kept short by leaving some dialogue to be filled in later; and Florey's camera directions were more spare than usual, though an abundance of close-ups as well as some subjective and depth compositions were indicated. Writing against a deadline, he transformed a story of extraordinary coincidences that place a man on death row into a surreal tale of malevolent fate that prefigures the somber mood of film noir.

The central character, Reese Bigelow, is pursued by an unrelenting doom that causes him to be fired from his job; framed by gangsters and arrested for a murder he didn't commit; forced by brutal police to sign a confession while only semi-conscious; abandoned by his family, friends, fiancée, and two lawyers, who all believe him guilty; and tormented by an insane prison warden. Bigelow is even approached by a wealthy man with a blind relative who wants to purchase Bigelow's eyes for a transplant after his execution. Virtually all the people Bigelow encounters seek to do him harm whether he knows them or not. His only ally is a prostitute with whom he has a platonic relationship (though they are romantically united by the conclusion), but even she is blackmailed into withholding testimony in his favor. All of this might seem to go beyond credibility, but in Florey's hands The Broken Heart Cafe is believable because of its nightmarish quality. The unlikeliness of the narrative gives it a sense of the bizarre, of a world gone mad with the aim of persecuting one sane, innocent individual.

The Broken Heart Cafe would clearly have been a "B" crime thriller, but it went beyond the conventions of the genre to explore spatial dislocation (similar though different locales and recurring characters inhabiting them) and aberrant human behavior, and to justify paranoia as an understandable emotion. It reflected the irrational underside of Florey's canon, rarely seen except in the context of the horror movie. But when this aspect of his directorial personality burst forth, as in The Florentine Dagger, The Beast with Five Fingers, and Alcoa Theatre: The Clock Struck Twelve, it invariably did so with breathtaking force. It seems safe to say that had The Broken Heart Cafe been made in 1939, it would unquestionably have marked the beginning of film noir, being conceived well before such progenitors as Citizen Kane and The Maltese Falcon.

Death of a Champion, shot in five weeks in the early summer, was one of Florey's minor assignments at Paramount. An overly-complicated whodunit, the picture was an attempt to start a new series based on the adventures of a "human encyclopedia," Lynne Overman, and his annoyingly comical sidekick, teenager Donald O'Connor. But the combination was not to Florey's taste, while the setting of a dog show--and Florey a confirmed cat-lover!--was not conducive to his ability to create suspense from atmosphere. The result was a mediocre film, appealing chiefly to connoisseurs of the then popular animal exhibitions, an audience Paramount hoped to reach with this effort.

Parole Fixer was the first of a pair of "B" gangster movies Florey would direct between August and October, along with Women Without Names. While both were from the writing team of William Lipman and Horace McCoy (who also adapted Dangerous to Know) and dealt with the subject of law and order, the screenplays offered diametrically opposed ideologies. (Florey was also anxious to film McCoy's novel, They Shoot Horses, Don't They?, only to be told the idea was "crazy and that such a picture could never be made.")[80]

Parole Fixer was the third in a series of four "B's" Paramount made from J. Edgar Hoover's book, Persons in Hiding. This installment tells how racketeers corrupt the parole system by launching public crusades for the release of "men who never had a decent chance"--but are in fact unrepentant criminals. The theme of the story makes it a virtual social consciousness movie, but one with a conservative tinge as it denounces thoughtless liberalism and exalts the efforts and sacrifices of the F.B.I. and its agents.

Although perhaps unoriginal, the narrative was convincing, well written, and compelling in its simplicity. The tension was enhanced by the style of dramatic realism with which Florey directed, so that Parole Fixer, despite a cast devoid of big-name performers, became in many ways more satisfying than a confused big-budget feature like Hotel Imperial. Made in only eighteen days, Parole Fixer is a fast-paced, slick production. With a running time of only fifty-seven minutes, it closely resembles television crime shows in length, structure, and tone. Experience in such motion pictures doubtless helped prepare Florey for the new medium nearly two decades later.

Women Without Names told another crime story, one with an entirely different theme from Parole Fixer. This time the forces of the law have run amuck, committing a miscarriage of justice that sends two innocent people to prison. However, despite the opportunity for social commentary, Florey refused to explore the wider implications of the narrative, instead observing its effect on a few individuals as he had in Outcast.

1932-1939: Long-Term Contract Director

Though lacking the tight construction and exciting plot of Parole Fixer, Women Without Names does have more emotional depth. It provided Florey with an opportunity to prove his talent for directing a large cast of little-known performers in a variety of roles. Particularly in evidence was his skill for quickly delineating character through revealing and expressive close-ups. Stylistically, he kept Women Without Names darkly lit, befitting its somber mood, and used an abundance of high angle shots--even a few directly overhead--to emphasize the feeling of claustrophobia experienced by the inmates.

Following completion of Women Without Names in October 1939, Florey's contract at Paramount came up for renewal. Y. Frank Freeman had just replaced William LeBaron as production chief, and in the first few weeks of the new regime nearly all the studio's directors were forced out of their jobs. Coinciding with this corporate turnover was the start of World War II in Europe. Anxious over the possible loss of revenue from overseas distribution, Paramount only invited Florey to stay on if he would take a fifty-percent cut in salary. Insulted at this response to his exhausting schedule of seventeen features successfully completed over the last four years, Florey refused the offer, leaving Paramount for the last time.

On October 25, 1939, Florey married Virginia Dabney, an actress who had appeared in a number of his films. (His first marriage, to Aileen Dee, a Canadian, had ended in divorce in 1936 after eight years.) Miss Dabney was a native of Atlanta who had come to California in the mid-1920s. Her dancing skill during her movie debut in Forty-Second Street (1933) won her a contract from Warner Bros. as a "Busby Berkeley girl," and soon she had moved up to bit parts, freelancing for a number of companies. While Dabney made brief appearances in Smarty, The Woman in Red, and The Pay-Off, it was not until the spring of 1937 that she and Florey actually met. Paramount had signed her for Mountain Music and This Way Please, and friendship quickly blossomed into romance. From then on, she appeared in most of his pictures--Disbarred, Hotel Imperial, The Magnificent Fraud--with her most important roles coming in Daughter of Shanghai, King of Alcatraz, and Women Without Names. Dabney was often miscast as a nonchalant gangster's moll or as a fundamentally good-hearted girl who associates with the wrong types, although her blond hair and soft Southern accent suited her best for lighter fare. Indeed, she had never planned to be an actress: happening onto employment at the studios, she was more than satisifed at having a well-paying job as support for herself and her mother during the Depression. Once married, she had no ambition to continue her career and retired from the screen. The couple lived a quiet, private life, although remaining active for a time in the French colony--especially during the war years.

 The period 1932-39 was an incredibly prolific one for Florey, who directed thirty films in eight years, averaging one every three months or less. While working at such a pace was always hard, it was especially grueling at Warner Bros. Florey was surprised to discover, while making <u>Girl Missing</u>, that conditions at Warners were no easier than at some of the smaller independent companies. "I had to work just as fast, if not faster, in a big studio as I had done making films for Bischoff earlier in the year at K.B.S.," he said.[81] However, all but the most prestigious Warners products during 1932-34 were made in three or four weeks; this was standard policy on shooting schedules, and Florey's record was little different from other studio directors during the same years. Production chief Hal Wallis summed up the company philosophy when he remarked (discussing <u>Don't Bet on Blondes</u>), "We want to make this production fast and ... we want to make it cheap."[82] Florey, more diplomatic, later said his task was "to make good films with little money."[83]

 The most difficult part of laboring at Warners was the interference that was a regular part of Hal Wallis' management. Despite acknowledgment that Florey was "supposed to be a damn good camerman himself,"[84] Wallis frequently went so far as to dictate in memos what type of shots and angles to use, along with business for the actors in scenes. For instance, on <u>Smarty</u> he ordered Florey to avoid close-ups in favor of two-shots, while on <u>Registered Nurse</u> he found fault with whatever Florey was doing, whether it was close-ups, two-shots, medium shots, or long shots.

 Even more frustrating was the manner in which Florey was discouraged from trying to contribute to a picture before shooting would begin. He was regularly given inadequate time--sometimes only a weekend--to prepare his continuities. Suggestions for improvements were apt to receive, as in this example (relating to Smarty), a curt rebuff from Wallis:

> I don't know why it is necessary to go through this procedure with you every time you make a picture but it seems to be a ritual that is necessary so we will go through it just once more and have it over with.... After you get this note will you please settle down to work with the cast that you have and with the script that you have and make the picture and don't let me hear any more "squawks" as I am getting sick and tired of them.[85]

And yet at the same time Florey was liable to be blamed for any deficiencies the system caused. He once defended himself this way on Bedside:

> Regarding all the sets, I am not consulted about their construction. I am using what is given to me, mostly sets already standing up from other pictures. I did not choose any actor or bits in the picture, the casting director saying that he was in charge of casting and that I could not interfere with him.[86]

Florey was probably least discontented with the studio system during his term at Paramount in the late 1930s, where the conditions were quite different. The working atmosphere was more tolerant, without the excessive managerial interference that had marred the Warner years. Marguerite Roberts, co-author of Hollywood Boulevard, remembered that "Florey was a highly respected director around Paramount, and I was lucky to get a chance to work with him."[87] The producers at Paramount were generally easier to get along with, and Florey particularly liked Harold Hurley, head of the "B" unit. Florey would have been content to continue with him, since Hurley (also a victim of the Freeman purge) allowed him more leisurely schedules and bigger budgets than he had received at Warners. As one might expect, with Paramount's large European contingent Florey had many friends at the studio and was able to collaborate on more than one occasion with favorite cameramen like Harry Fischbeck, Theodor Sparkhul, and Karl Struss.

While the Paramount years afforded Florey more satisfaction than those at Warner Bros., his position as a long-term contract director for a single company meant he was still at the mercy of whatever project the studio might choose to hand him. He could receive an assignment, or it could be changed, on a day's notice. His opinion of the script and whether it suited his talents mattered little. Much of his time was spent making various tests, trick shots, replacing colleagues temporarily absent, as well as doing second unit chores and shooting retakes and added scenes for movies done by others. These conditions never changed, regardless of which studio he was at, as long as he was on a long-term contract.

The types of films given Florey at Warner Bros. and Paramount were, however, strikingly different. Warners gave him a variety of genres to work with, predominantly vehicles for leading actresses: Bette Davis (Ex-Lady), Kay Francis (The House on 56th Street), Bebe Daniels (Registered Nurse), Joan Blondell (Smarty), Mary Astor (I Am a Thief), Barbara Stanwyck (The Woman in Red). On all of these he acquitted himself well. On the other hand, Paramount took advantage almost exclusively of his skill with the thriller. Neither company gave him the historical biographies he was most eager to do, although the plans and ideas he submitted for these are often as interesting as some of the second-string projects he actually did direct, more accurately reflecting his real interests and goals. In later years, when asked which of this period he most fondly recalled, he would usually mention The House on 56th Street, Smarty, The Woman in Red, The Preview Murder Mystery, Till We Meet Again, and Mountain Music.

Florey was often kept in the medium- to low-budget realm, despite the fact that he was known as reliable, seldom going over and often finishing under schedule and budget. While he received his share of "A" films, the failure to more generally promote him to better tasks is especially odd given the exceptional commercial success of his major projects such as The House on 56th Street, Smarty, The Woman in Red, and Mountain Music. In the case of Paramount, home of the most talented directors in the business, this was probably the result of the fierce competition for the best projects, a corollary to working at a prestige studio that offered better pay and more artistic freedom. As well, during this time the company was emerging from a long period of financial turmoil.

The result was that at Paramount Florey was given many mediocre scripts which he had to attempt to brighten with an imaginative visual style and fast pacing. The company noticed his skill in improving small films, beginning with King of Gamblers, and proceeded to inundate him with such assignments, exploiting his talent mercilessly. In some cases he succeeded in making a minor picture shine, but with others the situation was hopeless. Florey grew discouraged during the latter half of his tenure at Paramount, vexed over his virtual exile to the "B" unit. But his abilities were not always wasted on such movies, because they provided him with an opportunity to experiment with the uses of European techniques in the American feature. By the end of these years, however, his style became more naturalistic, less Germanic, and better adapted to American sensibilities; his approach had evolved and matured with experience as a long-term contract director.

NOTES

1. Daryl F. Zanuck, letter to Robert Florey, December 10, 1932, Florey collection.
2. W.B. Dover to Roy Obringer, inter-office communication, September 22, 1932, Robert Florey legal file, Warner Bros. collection, University of Southern California Special Collections Library.
3. Robert Florey, letter to Carlos Clarens, December 13, 1976.
4. Ted Sennett, Warner Bros. Presents (New York: Arlington House, 1970), p. 127.
5. "'Ex-Lady' Is Plenty Hot--Director Robert Florey Pulls a 'Lubitsch' with Some of the Situations," unidentified magazine clipping (n.d.), scrapbook 1931-39, Florey collection.
6. Robert Florey to Jack Warner, inter-office communication, June 19, 1933, Napoleon file, Warner Bros. collection.
7. Robert Florey, interview with the author, January 30, 1979.
8. Robert Florey, Joan of Arc, treatment, draft from Paramount envelope dated March 8, 1940, pp. 2-3, Florey collection.

9. Jack Spears, letter to the author, November 15, 1982.
10. The Hollywood Reporter, October 17, 1933.
11. Robert Florey, Hollywood D'Hier et D'Aujourd'Hui (Paris: Editions Prisma, 1948), p. 170.
12. John S. Cohen, Jr., New York Sun, December 1, 1933.
13. Hal Wallis to Robert Florey, inter-office communication, August 11, 1933, The House on 56th Street file 1958, Warner Bros. collection.
14. New York News, December 1, 1933.
15. "Brilliant Opening Sequence for House on 56th Street," Hollywood Spectator (n.d.), scrapbook 1931-39, Florey collection.
16. Robert Florey, letter to Carlos Clarens, November 13, 1976.
17. The Hollywood Reporter, October 17, 1933.
18. Ibid.
19. Florey, Hollywood D'Hier et D'Aujourd'Hui, p. 172.
20. Lillie Hayward and Rian James, Bedside, Final script, September 19, 1933, p. 115, Warner Bros. collection.
21. Eric H. Rideout, The American Film (London: Mitre Press, 1937), p. 59.
22. Florey, Hollywood D'Hier et D'Aujourd'Hui, p. 173.
23. Ibid., pp. 173, 184.
24. Motion Picture Herald, July 21, 1934.
25. Irving Rapper, interview with the author, March 7, 1985.
26. Florey, Hollywood D'Hier et D'Aujourd'Hui, p. 179.
27. Hal Wallis to Robert Florey, inter-office communication, August 29, 1934, I Am a Thief file 1995, Warner Bros. collection.
28. Jack Warner, letter to Robert Florey, January 14, 1935, Florey collection.
29. F.S.N., "At the Roxy," The New York Times, March 23, 1935.
30. Motion Picture Herald, March 23, 1935.
31. Harry Joe Brown to Hal Wallis, inter-office communication, December 8, 1934, The Florentine Dagger file 1998, Warner Bros. collection.
32. Robert Florey, letter to Ray Cabana, January 16, 1979, Florey collection.
33. W.B. Dover to Roy Obringer, inter-office communication, December 28, 1932, Robert Florey legal file, Warner Bros. collection.
34. Daily Variety, September 9, 1935.
35. Robert Florey, photo album II: 1931-40, Florey collection.

36. Florey, Hollywood D'Hier et D'Aujourd'Hui, p. 186.
37. Daily Variety, October 19, 1935.
38. James R. Parish and Michael R. Pitts with Gregory William Mank, Hollywood on Hollywood (Metuchen, N.J.: Scarecrow Press, 1978), p. 295.
39. Variety, March 25, 1936.
40. Daily Variety, February 6, 1936.
41. "Interesting Murder Mystery," Hollywood Spectator, February 15, 1936.
42. The Hollywood Reporter, quoted in Till We Meet Again advertising brochure, Florey pressbook collection.
43. Jack Spears, Hollywood: The Golden Era (New York: A.S. Barnes, 1971), p. 352.
44. René Clair, Cinema Yesterday and Today (New York: Dover, 1972), p. 193.
45. All were written in French and published in Europe. Florey always felt more comfortable composing in his native language; unfortunately, not one of his books has been translated into English. See Appendix A.
46. Among the authors who have acknowledged the usefulness of Florey's books in their own writings are Charles Ford, Hollywood Story ([Paris]: La Jeune Parque, 1968); Theodore Huff, Charlie Chaplin (New York: Henry Schuman, 1951); Pierre Leprohon, Le cinema cette aventure (Paris: Editions Andre Bonne, 1970); Georges Sadoul, Histoire du cinema mondial (Paris: Flammarion, 1949); Herman G. Weinberg, The Lubitsch Touch (New York: Dover, 1968).
47. John Baxter, The Hollywood Exiles (New York: A.S. Barnes, 1974), p. 140.
48. John Russell Taylor, Strangers in Paradise (New York: Holt, Rinehart and Winston, 1983), p. 174.
49. Leonard Maltin, "Directors on TV--Robert Florey," Film Fan Monthly, No. 126 (December 1971):25.
50. Robert Florey, letter to Anthony Slide, October 20, 1978.
51. Ibid.
52. Anthony Slide, "'Hollywood Boulevard'" in Frank Magill, ed., Magill's Survey of Cinema, second series (Englewood Cliffs, N.J.: Salem Press, 1981), pp. 1041-1042.
53. Parish, et al., Hollywood on Hollywood, p. 163.
54. Welford Beaton, Hollywood Spectator, reprinted on Paramount advertisement, Florey collection.
55. Ibid.

56. Parish, et al., Hollywood on Hollywood, p. 163.
57. Variety, September 23, 1936.
58. "Memoir: 'Hollywood Boulevard,' Candid-Camera Tale, Revives Ex-Stars," Newsweek, 8 (September 26, 1936):27.
59. Beaton, Hollywood Spectator.
60. Robert Florey, Times So Unsettled Are, Incomplete continuity, September 15, 1936, p. G-23, Florey collection.
61. Emanuel Cohen, letter to Robert Florey, January 7, 1937, Florey collection.
62. Daily Variety, January 27, 1937, p. 3ff.
63. Ibid.
64. Robert Lusk, "Unheralded Film Lauded by Broadway," unidentified newspaper clipping, July 10, 1937, scrapbook 1931-39, Florey collection.
65. Hollywood Reporter, April 13, 1937, p. 3ff.
66. Lusk, "Unheralded Film...."
67. Daily Variety (n.d.), scrapbook 1931-39, Florey collection.
68. Florey, letter to Ray Cabana.
69. Florey interview.
70. The Hollywood Reporter, June 9, 1937.
71. Variety, July 14, 1937; Florey, Hollywood D'Hier et D'Aujourd'Hui, p. 195; Florey interview.
72. Robert Florey, letter to Carlos Clarens, December 13, 1976.
73. Carlos Clarens, letter to Robert Florey, December 2, 1976.
74. Charles Higham, "Visitors to Sydney," Sight and Sound, 31 (Summer 1962):120.
75. Margaret Lane, Edgar Wallace: The Biography of a Phenomenon (London: Hamish Hamilton, 1964), p. 271.
76. Bert Harlen, "Excellent Entertainment ...," unidentified magazine clipping (n.d.), scrapbook 1931-39, Florey collection.
77. Robert Florey, letter to Carlos Clarens, January 31, 1977.
78. Robert Florey, Destination Unknown, scenario, May 31, 1939, p. 1, Florey collection. Destination Unknown was written prior to the events on which the book and film Voyage of the Damned were based.
79. Robert Buckner, letter to the author, July 19, 1984.
80. Florey, letter to Carlos Clarens, December 13, 1976.

81. Ibid.
82. Hal Wallis to William Koenig, inter-office communication, April 29, 1935, Robert Florey legal file, Warner Bros. collection.
83. Florey, Hollywood D'Hier et D'Aujourd'Hui, p. 186.
84. Hal Wallis to Sam Bischoff, inter-office communication, December 22, 1933, Registered Nurse file 2062, Warner Bros. collection.
85. Hal Wallis to Robert Florey, inter-office communication, January 11, 1934, Smarty file 1962, Warner Bros. collection.
86. Robert Florey to Hal Wallis, inter-office communication, October 7, 1933, Bedside file, Warner Bros. collection.
87. Marguerite Roberts, letter to the author, March 18, 1986,

Chapter V

1940-1950: SHORT-TERM CONTRACTS
AND INDEPENDENT

Unlike the previous seven years, the 1940s were for Florey a time of instability. No longer so prolific, he now averaged only two films a year. He began the decade with a series of short-term contracts, never staying with a studio for longer than two years or more than three movies; after World War II, he would turn independent.

Nick Carter, the fictional American detective whose exploits have been recounted in hundreds of dime novels, was one of Florey's childhood heroes. In April 1940, after a few months of unemployment, he wrote two brief outlines for films based on Carter's investigations, perhaps because M-G-M was starting a series based on the character (directed by Florey's friend Jacques Tourneur). Though neither of Florey's stories were produced, they do reveal how he could invest a formulaic genre with original plot elements.

Nick Carter in China demonstrated a knowledge of the Orient that would enhance some later projects. The setting is actually Tibet, and the outline used the curious political and religious systems of that country as a background for an espionage tale that sets two rival factions of lamas against each other.

Nick Carter in Paris, also called Nick Carter vs. Arsene Lupin, was planned out in considerably more detail. It was inspired by a Saturday Evening Post article[1] that previously served as the basis for an unproduced screenplay, Beware of Imitations, on which Florey had collaborated at

1940-1950: Short-Term Contracts

Warner Bros. in 1934. The Post piece explained thefts from the Louvre as part of an elaborate scheme by duplicitous art forgers to swindle crooked collectors. From this premise Florey developed a new tale that presaged film noir, with everyone becoming tainted by deception and a detective, tempted toward villainy, who only remains on the right side of law at the last minute.

COLUMBIA, 1940-41

With studio production slowed because of the war in Europe, Florey had a difficult time finding a new position after he left Paramount. Following months of idleness, his agent finally convinced him to take a job offered by one of the minors, Columbia. Because of his dislike for studio boss Harry Cohn, Florey had not worked at Columbia since The Romantic Age, a silent he directed fourteen years earlier. While hardly enthusiastic about returning, Florey signed in September 1940, preferring to keep busy rather than adopt the posture of the aloof but unemployed artist. The deal called for three so-called "action pictures," movies made on low budgets in twelve days. The first two, The Face Behind the Mask and Meet Boston Blackie, took two months including preparation time and were shot back-to-back; the third, Two in a Taxi, was done in the spring of the following year.

These hasty schedules were especially difficult on the initial two efforts, since each required extensive use of location exteriors. The cameraman was Franz F. Planer, lately arrived from Germany; unfortunately, despite his great talent, he was still unaccustomed to working at the American pace. "I had to sacrifice many shots," Florey said, "to catch up on the time lost in lighting."[2] But even with these problems, their collaboration on The Face Behind the Mask and Meet Boston Blackie resulted in some of the best films of Florey's career.

The Face Behind the Mask was the first film under the Columbia contract, and to judge by the superlative result, Florey's return to directing released a burst of pent-up talent. The movie is widely acknowledged to be among Hollywood's greatest "B" pictures[3] and is unquestionably one of Florey's masterpieces, perhaps even his greatest film. He

Florey and cameraman Franz Planer (seated) filming the initial meeting of Peter Lorre and George E. Stone by an atmospheric dockside in The Face Behind the Mask.

had the opportunity to revise the script and write the continuity; by the time he was through, it was little short of brilliant. The story, while containing elements of several genres--horror, gangster, love and revenge--transcended all of them and was perfectly suited to Florey's skills. Strangely, it marked the fourth time he had dealt with an unusual theme, the effect of facial mutilation on men's lives and characters. Although his earlier films, Face Value, The Florentine Dagger, and The Preview Murder Mystery (and later Alfred Hitchcock Presents: Where Beauty Lies), dealt with the same subject, it cannot be said to have affected Florey deeply despite having appeared more often in his movies than could be expected.

The Face Behind the Mask was chiefly though by no

means a pure horror film. The story is of an immigrant, played by Peter Lorre, who arrives in New York full of hope, only to be trapped in a hotel fire and have his face hideously scarred. Florey handles a potentially repulsive tale in a tasteful, non-gruesome manner. He knew that horror withheld can be much more real and effective than a bloody shock-effect. There is only one full glimpse of the burned face, seen in a mirror in a brief medium shot just after the bandages have been removed. Florey went so far as to suggest to the studio that Lorre's character should be used as a sort of "walking camera, hardly ever seeing" his face.[4] As usual, Florey was several years ahead of his time, proposing innovations later brought to fruition by others.

Through most of the movie, Lorre's character is supposed to be wearing a lifelike rubber mask that approximates his original appearance. This so-called mask, while achieving a highly unsettling effect, was actually nothing more than white powder and two pieces of tape. Fortunately Lorre was an actor skillful enough to manipulate his face to simulate a mask where there was none. The eeriness of the unnatural face is redoubled by Lorre's costume, which was--characteristically for Florey--both simple and effective, consisting of a long black coat with turned-up collar and dark scarf, concealing Lorre's neck and revealing only his "mask"; the hands and face appear strangely white and unreal in contrast to the darkness that covers the rest of his body.

Although he is still able to work despite the accident, Lorre is refused employment because of his disfigurement. Only one man is kind to him (George E. Stone), a small-time crook. To keep himself and his newfound but seriously ill friend alive, Lorre begins a life of crime, though only as a thief; he is never guilty of murder. Florey typically portrays the film's gangsters in an unglamorous and unromanticized manner.

Florey deliberately de-emphasized the horror elements of <u>The Face Behind the Mask</u>, giving it none of the stylization that accompanied such pure horror pictures as <u>Murders in the Rue Morgue</u> and <u>The Beast with Five Fingers</u>. Instead, <u>Face Behind the Mask</u> is told in an almost realistic manner, dwelling on Lorre's misery and the development of his character after the accident.

Florey was especially fond of overhead camera angles, as exemplified by this frame from The Face Behind the Mask.

These human qualities make the romantic interlude believable and touching. Lorre meets a lonely blind girl, Evelyn Keyes, who truly "sees" with her soul, recognizing intuitively the kindliness and gentleness of the man everyone else finds repulsive. Their affection, symbolized by the natural happiness of a little dog, grows quickly; Lorre quits the gang and the lovers are about to be married when the criminals, suspicious of his actions, arrange her death.

In a remarkable sequence, Stone escapes to telephone Lorre of their plans. Just before Lorre receives the call, Keyes goes with the dog to turn on the car radio, her only other companion. Warned, Lorre runs out of the house in a long tilted overhead shot, yelling for her, only to see the garage containing the car go up in a huge explosion. Lorre vows revenge and in a startling climax flies the gangsters to the middle of the desert, where he crashes their

1940-1950: Short-Term Contracts   235

The meeting of the scarred Peter Lorre (concealed behind mask, scarf and dark coat) and the blind girl, Evelyn Keyes, which initiates their romance in The Face Behind the Mask.

plane. Although he must die along with the criminals, he is able to watch their torment as they kill one another or expire of thirst.

The Face Behind the Mask was a story dependent on a strong and capable actor in the lead role, and fortunately Lorre was perfect for the part. It required not only the portrayal of a man disintegrating under a horrible fate, but also an incredible amount of physical control over his facial muscles to give the effect of the mask, allowing him to express emotion only through his eyes in close-ups. His performance was brilliant, making it truly "his picture"; Florey wrote, "Lorre in this film did one of his best creations since the unforgettable M."[5] This was all the more remarkable as Lorre didn't enjoy being rushed, a fact complicated by his drinking habits which included a straight Pernod for breakfast. Florey had to try and take all the star's scenes in the morning--this was not always possible--since by the afternoon he had become undirectable. Despite this problem the two became good friends and acquired a great respect for each other; they could laugh together over their involvements in many a ghoulish film. In important supporting roles, Keyes and Stone were excellent, and capable character actors filled the remaining parts The film was an amazing demonstration of the possibilities for fine acting even under the tremendous pressures of a two-week schedule.

The Face Behind the Mask offered Florey an ideal opportunity to exercise his skills with a European visual style. Lorre's social milieu is treated realistically, but moments of high tension are appropriately punctuated by Florey's typical angled shots, as when Lorre first sees his scarred face or while he tries to rescue Keyes. A memorable sequence is the interrogation of Stone by the gangsters after Lorre has left them, shot through a fireplace with a camera on the inside. Flames flicker threateningly in the lower part of the foreground as the mobsters push Stone toward the fire. Lorre's costume--the black coat in contrast to the white face and hands--and the unnatural acting style required by the "mask" were in themselves rather expressionistic devices. To help the costume stand out and to keep it from blending into the background, shadows were less frequent than was usual with Florey, with the major exception of the waterfront scene where Lorre and Stone first meet.

The Face Behind the Mask was the most deeply felt of Florey's movies since his depictions of Hollywood's forgotten players. It displayed a characteristic sympathy and compassion not only for the handicapped, but for all of life's downtrodden and underdogs--a frequent motif in Florey's films. Florey was known as a sensitive, generous man; it was this human understanding and compassion he brought to his direction of Face Behind the Mask that made it a great movie. The extraordinary story required an emotional sympathy, which Florey had for the character and his plight.

A truly unusual picture in both content and treatment, The Face Behind the Mask was completely outside the ordinary Hollywood tradition. While not precisely socially conscious, it did offer an uncompromising view of human anguish; unexpectedly, it won a small following in its time. One of the few "B" films to be repeatedly re-issued (as late as 1955), Face Behind the Mask has grown in popularity over the years and is recognized as one of the few genuine classics of low-budget filmmaking during the studio era.

Meet Boston Blackie, while having none of the profundity or depth of The Face Behind the Mask, was still a worthy successor in its own right. In terms of pace, construction, and suspense, Meet Boston Blackie was the best of Florey's "B" action thrillers since King of Alcatraz (although not quite as sprightly and even as the latter). Meet Boston Blackie is an espionage thriller with a plot in many ways reminiscent of The 39 Steps (1935): the hero becomes briefly involved with a girl who is promptly killed, leaving behind only a clue about spies who are using a theatrical front. Faced with a murder charge, he goes on an extended chase, acquiring a female companion (Rochelle Hudson) as he tries to solve the case and uncover the villains before capture by the police.

While not as rich as The 39 Steps, Meet Boston Blackie is no less well executed, especially considering the constraints of budget and shooting schedule under which it was made. Blackie had the advantage of an inventive, nimble script by Jay Dratler, with some amusing dialogue. The story itself unfolds at too rapid a rate to reveal any gaps that may have existed in the narrative, and there was none of the piling on of obvious improbabilities that were so often typical of the "B" film (as was the case in Women Without Names and Lady Gangster). A number of clever motifs gave the movie unity and a consistent flavor, such as Chester Morris (as Blackie) escaping handcuffs and his messages on mirrors--always anticipated with interest. The characterizations were good, especially those of the leads, perfectly embodied by Morris and Hudson, although the support was admittedly a bit stereotyped (not having the vitality found throughout King of Alcatraz, for instance). In the case of the title role, Morris maintained an intriguing sense of ambiguity as to the extent of his criminal past that was not revealed until the last moment, although his charm engenders abundant sympathy.

Meet Boston Blackie has only a bare-bones plot, providing the minimum of necessary information with very little explication; however, nothing essential is left out. The picture was directed and edited at a lightning pace, proceeding relentlessly, while never too rapidly--once again, Florey's sense of timing was impeccable. Combined with the constant pursuit of Morris, this tends to give the film an almost surreal tone. For instance, trapped in a railroad car, Morris comments to Hudson that he doesn't even know the beginning of this adventure, "and for all I know we may both be corpses on the next page." The spectator is kept in a similar state of suspense throughout.

Meet Boston Blackie is set primarily in a Coney Island amusement park, a perfect milieu for Florey and his skills. There are the barkers and trios of exotic dancers from the Murders in the Rue Morgue carnival and the food concessionaire who would later appear in The Crooked Way. As in Rue Morgue and the television films, The David Niven Show: Lifeline and Twilight Zone: Perchance to Dream, this locale is one full of the lure of danger, menace, and secrets of the unknown and mysterious. The "Tunnel of Horror" in particular seems to offer refuge and concealment before turning into a place of actual terror; the papier-mâché ghouls only appear after the presence of the villains has provided a very real source of peril.

These settings naturally provide an opportunity for many of Florey's typical compositions and lighting schemes. The choice of angles is uniformly effective: for example, a surprising overhead leading to Morris' discovery of a corpse, or the eerie feeling as he and Hudson are concealed under a dock listening to the plans of the spies. Florey obviously enjoyed photographing an amusing confrontation between Morris and the police as the latter are trapped in an elevator shaft, each looking at the other not only through extreme angles but separating foreground grillworks as well. While this scene recalled King of Gamblers, the insertion of several switching stop-and-go signs brings back memories of the same mechanism used as a framing device in Hollywood Boulevard.

Meet Boston Blackie was, and is, a nearly perfect "B" movie. Not only was it made in twelve days like the programmer The Face Behind the Mask, but it had an even lower budget. Nevertheless, Columbia was hoping to revive with Morris a series that had been dormant since 1927. Thus it was a project of some importance (even if cheaply made) that was placed in Florey's hands, and he acquitted himself well. Meet Boston Blackie was popular with audiences and launched a series that was to last fourteen pictures and nine years. However, while the inaugural film was not well received by critics, who condemned anything that threatened yet another multi-feature detective saga, Meet Boston Blackie has achieved a growing reputation over the years as a classic of "B" suspense. It is certainly regarded as one, if not the best, of the "Blackie" group: "Ensuing members of the series had their moments, but none came up to the entertainment standards set by the opener."[6]

"Lone Wolf," a contemporary Columbia mystery series starring Florey's friend Warren William, was a likely outlet for Florey's talents, and he developed an untitled seven-page proposal for an entry. The narrative was designed to be produced as a "B," for instance seeming to promise a trip to the Orient which never takes place--a device already used in Daughter of Shanghai. This was not the only influence, however; even more apparent is the affect of The Face Behind the Mask on Florey's imagination. The "Lone Wolf" plot hinged on two of his favorite themes and interests, the Far East and disguises. Both are combined in a mystery about a set of Oriental masks which together provide the key to a centuries-old treasure in Thailand. Unfortunately, the plot turns mediocre with an overly-complex, dialogue-ridden ending that fails to fulfill the potential of the story's premise, reminding one of the limits the low-budget requirement can place on the filmmaker.

Two in a Taxi was an unfortunate little film, distorted almost beyond recognition from the original intent. The idea was conceived in 1940 by Malvin Wald, after watching a performance of Clifford Odets' stage play, Waiting for Lefty. Wald knew that this piece was much too militantly pro-union to be brought directly to the screen, but hoped that a story of the hardships and struggles of New York cabbies might eventually be adapted into movie material. Thanks to his sympathy for their cause, he obtained the assistance of the drivers' organization and was in the process of collecting true-to-life facts and anecdotes when he met newspaperman Morton Thompson, who became his collaborator. Together they developed a story, entitled One-Way Street, a sort of "urban Grapes of Wrath for the cab-drivers."[7]

Submitted to all the major studios, only Columbia responded, but there production chief Sam Briskin was enthusiastic about its possibilities. However, none of his top producers shared this reaction, so of necessity he handed it to his brother Irving, head of the Columbia "B" unit. Wald and Thompson were then hired to transform the property into screenplay form. They turned in a socially conscious, feature-length script, envisaging such stars as John Garfield and Sylvia Sidney. But Irving Briskin, "a man of poor taste and no discrimination," decided he preferred to make the idea amusing, assigning Howard J. Green to author a rewrite.[8] Green deleted many scenes, replacing them with various worn-out gags and transforming the project into low-budget material.

Nonetheless, some of the dramatic underpinnings remained in the story, lending it almost a dual quality. But Florey was unaware of the origins of Two in a Taxi, since it was presented to him on short notice merely as a silly, low-life comedy--although he would probably not have been a good choice to direct had it remained in the socially conscious form. As it was, Two in a Taxi had only lightweight performers and ran just over an hour; the result, to judge from reviews, was a generally mediocre picture that did average business. Some discerning critics, however, did recognize the film's serious undertones; William K. Everson, for example, believes Two in a Taxi to be much underrated. Florey's attitude was harsher, disliking the assignment from the first and regarding it as perhaps his most minor effort. He was thus especially pleased when Bryan Foy invited him

1940-1950: Short-Term Contracts 241

to leave Columbia and return to Warner Bros. a few months later.

WARNER BROS. (MIDDLE PERIOD), 1941-1942

Dangerously They Live returned Florey to Warners on August 20, 1941, after an absence of six years. He soon found that he had to rewrite the script and prepare the continuity before the commencement of shooting September 8, "and it's obvious he added much," claimed Variety.9 Designed as a medium-budget thriller, the film was shot in twenty-six days (five over schedule) on a budget of $300,000. But the immediacy of the subject matter--Nazi "fifth column" spy activities in the United States--caused Dangerously They Live to be given "A" treatment when it was put into distribution in 1942.

Despite a rather ordinary scenario containing some inconsistencies and improbable dialogue, Dangerously They Live had a number of distinguishing elements in a generally engrossing plot line. Florey built up the propaganda angle, as intern John Garfield discovers that a patient, Nancy Coleman--who claims she is a British agent sought by the Germans--is not, as he had supposed, suffering from delusions. Garfield is made aware of the peril of domestic subversion in a persuasive, allegorical manner indicative of the movie having been made before America entered the war. Back in June 1941, Florey had volunteered his services freely to government filmmakers (an offer never taken up), and his eagerness to call attention to the need for American involvement in the burgeoning conflict made Dangerously They Live one of his favorite Warners pictures.

Florey creates an intriguing sense of confusion in the audience during the first third of the film, forcing viewers to share Garfield's sense of uncertainty regarding Coleman's claims. Three separate points of view are utilized, those of Garfield, Coleman, and the chief Nazi, Raymond Massey; each is unsure what the others actually know. This approach, combined with other incidents such as amnesia, paranoia, and the abuse of psychiatry (by Massey)--all motifs of film noir--tend to align Dangerously They Live with this incipient movement.10 For instance, when Garfield has discovered the conspiracy, Massey places him in an asylum; in this way, Garfield discovers the other side of insanity as an inmate rather than analyst.

Stylistically, Dangerously They Live contains little evidence of expressionism, but there are abundant novel camera angles, appropriately placed and modulated so as to contribute effectively to the mood of the story. After a slow beginning, the pace builds steadily to an exciting climax. All of these assets, added to some quality acting and Florey's vigorous direction, lift Dangerously They Live above the average of its type.

Lady Gangster was Florey's last true "B," a twelve-day quickie made in February 1942, just as Warner's low-budget entries were going into a precipitous decline that would last for the remainder of the war.[11] He frankly regarded this as his worst film and, in a half-facetious attempt to conceal his involvement, decided to work under a pseudonym for the only time in his career. His wife suggested reversing his name, and Warners proved amenable to the idea, giving directorial credit to "Florian Roberts."

But his association with Lady Gangster has not been forgotten and, suprisingly, the movie has been mentioned rather frequently in recent years--although it is hard to comprehend why. Arguably, Florey was correct in his severe estimation of Lady Gangster: the character's motivations stretch credibility, and the story seems often contrived, full of rambling cliches that hardly create much suspense. A vehicle for Faye Emerson's debut in a lead role, her performance as a "lady gangster" is confusing. But she can hardly be blamed: Emerson must attempt to build a heroine out of a criminal by choice who steals from her henchmen and arranges for the death of an innocent man who has crossed her. In a narrative with such reversals, the support is scarcely of much assistance; one of the few to act believably was Julie Bishop, hired the very day shooting began.

However, Lady Gangster does contain some redeeming features that have points of similarity with previous Florey efforts. Like Women Without Names, much of the action is set in a women's prison, but here that setting is rendered in a far more brutal, and probably realistic, fashion. In

1940-1950: Short-Term Contracts

the activity room containing inmates knitting, dancing, or ironing as a loud radio plays incessantly, the jail more closely resembles an asylum filled with unforgettably degenerative faces. Most remarkable is Dorothy Adams as the strange "Deaf Annie," whose ability to lip-read allows her to supply information to her only friend, Ruth Ford, the prison informer. The special power given by the handicap is cleverly captured in several shots using composition in depth as Adams observes conversations, taking place in the foreground, from a distance or with mirrors. Florey compassionately portrays her condition, as he had with Peter Lorre in The Face Behind the Mask, by showing the depth of the maelstrom in which she is trapped, with its cruelty, mobsters, and corrupt prison wardens.

The Desert Song, a major commercial and artistic triumph for Florey, was also one of the most difficult films of his career. This despite the fact that the long-awaited remake of an early talkie had one of his biggest budgets, it was his first (and only) movie in color, and he co-authored the screenplay with producer Robert Buckner. Although these advantages must have been satisfying, the production was taxing because of management interference, grueling location work, and the censorship to which the completed picture was eventually subjected.

On February 26, 1942, Florey signed a contract specifically to direct The Desert Song and began four months of preparations the same day. The task of overcoming the creaky, cliche-ridden nature of the stage property had stumped Warner's stable of writers throughout the 1930s. But Florey and Buckner seized upon the idea of completely revamping the old operetta "in a singularly clever fashion."[12] The mythical setting of the original was modernized into a very timely drama of rebellion in French West Africa just prior to the outbreak of World War II. Buckner and Florey also overhauled the humor by adding, for comic relief, an American reporter whose "scoops" are constantly censored by an effeminate French government official--a sly dig at the Hays office but also an ironic foreshadowing of the film's fate at the hands of censors. Strangely, despite the collaboration on the new screenplay, studio publicity during production attributed sole authorship to Florey, while the final release credits made no mention at all of the scriptwriters. Only the authors of the stage play from which it was adapted were listed.

Eavesdropping on the eavesdropper: a humorous scene in The Desert Song as the local French censor (extreme left) keeps an eye on the American reporter (Lynne Overman, bottom center) overhearing the report of a Riff attack told to the villainous Caid, Victor Francen--also heard by the French military officer Bruce Cabot. With such compositions as these, Florey kept the plot progressing during the performance of the interior musical numbers.

The updated story, based on fact, told of Nazi manipulation of the French colonial office into assisting with the construction of a trans-Saharan railway. French troops were used to force Arab tribesmen to labor at gunpoint with only meager rations despite the intolerable heat of the desert--all to build a rail line secretly financed by Germans for the future military goals of the Third Reich. Within this context, the almost fairy-tale story from the operetta of the oppression of native peoples took on a political significance that was wholly lacking before. Florey (whose views on colonialism were clear, while Buckner's were uncertain) intentionally imbued the plot with a

Scenes of French cruelties to the Arabs were disapproved of by the wartime censors and the Free French, with this particular shot eliminated from the final domestic print of The Desert Song.

condemnation of French imperialism. This was done by showing how easily the Germans used the French for their own ends and by depicting the cruelties deliberately inflicted by both nationalities on the Arabs. As the hero, Dennis Morgan, says to French singer Irene Manning, "The only cultural benefit they've [the Arabs] had from our civilization is a kick in the face, a hundred years of slaughter and slavery."

Production lasted seventy-two days (eight over schedule), from June to September. Familiar with North Africa from a 1923 visit to Algiers, Florey sought to reproduce the North African desert locales with the utmost realism to add to the authenticity of the topical story. The war naturally made it necessary to select a filming location within the continental United States; finally, an Indian reservation near Gallup, New Mexico, was chosen as most resembling the Sahara. Twenty-four days were spent in location photography, with the sandstorms and 110° heat of the desert in June making work for cast, crew, and equipment extremely difficult. It was the last such elaborate location jaunt before wartime restrictions went into effect, and cost $107,000, nearly twice the amount budgeted. Back at the studio, Florey found to his dismay that Warners had decided to accent the musical numbers, whereas all of his efforts had been toward an adventure drama. Most of the songs and dances were handled by a separate unit under LeRoy Prinz, Florey's friend and frequent collaborator. After assisting on the preliminary editing of <u>The Desert Song</u>, Florey left Warners at the expiration of his contract, September 22, 1942, less than satisfied.

However, his attention to detailed recreations noticeably added to the movie's persuasive sense of accuracy. The location footage was photographed and utilized most effectively, contributing not only to the political subtext but also capturing and conveying the lure of the desert setting. Such visual motifs as composition in depth, shooting through Moorish gates and windows, or framing shots in other ways added to the atmosphere. The settings created in the studio, from the elaborate costumes to the narrow city streets--even when panned from overhead during Morgan's chase by gendarmes--were equally good. Once again Florey actively participated in the set design, including many items from his collection to enhance the decor. Especially noteworthy

1940-1950: Short-Term Contracts 247

Photographing through Arabic doorways and windows served as a visual motif in <u>The Desert Song</u> and aided in summoning an authentic atmosphere. (Bruce Cabot and Dennis Morgan in center.)

were the scenes in the dense, smoky cafe of Gene Lockhart as "Père FanFan," an old legionnaire who has gone native and caters to the Arab taste. The Europeans and their feelings of cultural superiority intrude palpably here, amid the incessant, sultry din of the music and dancing girls, while the Americans adapt readily to foreign customs. Ironically, FanFan's seems a much more vital place, of true comradeship, as opposed to the music hall where Manning sings, a staid outpost of European tradition that seems misplaced--and whose most eager customer is the corrupt Caid, played by Victor Francen.

Perhaps most surprising, considering the budgetary and generic constraints the studio had so long imposed on Florey, was the mastery he exhibited for the adventure picture in his first attempt at the type. The spectacular elements, like the stirring, large-scale action sequences, the desert vistas and battles, were handled magnificently, showing a true flair for the genre. Despite the encumbrance of the musical interludes and a hero who could not be shown indulging in any remotely violent acts, The Desert Song is kept within the appropriate and necessary bounds of adventure, not succumbing to the artificiality on which other musicals of this type (The Pirate, Camelot) have foundered.

Morgan's "El Khobar" belongs to the school of adventurers dedicated to a political objective: fighting and overcoming oppression. However, this invocation of generic conventions tends gradually to reduce the "message" on the nature of colonialism. By the end of the narrative, the chief villain has proven to be the Arab chieftain, Francen, a tool of the Nazis who has betrayed his own people. Bruce Cabot, the French commander bribed by Francen, is rather suddenly appalled to find out the treasonous effect of his Vichy-style policies when Morgan exposes them. The Arabs in turn lay down their arms for the promise of justice and fair treatment from a democratic France, although audiences of World War II knew that this would hardly remain the case. Thus, at the time of the release of The Desert Song, Newsweek could fairly comment, "You will have to be prepared for political ramifications which make for a little contemporary significance and considerably more contemporary confusion."[13]

As a musical, The Desert Song is every bit as distinguished as in other respects. Florey and Buckner (who had just written <u>Yankee Doodle Dandy</u>) did their best to integrate the music and singing into the narrative in a functional manner, succeeding more often than they failed, with results far superior to either the 1929 or 1953 versions. The credits and opening reels prudently just permit the melodies, allowing the music to become established as an underlying element before introducing the lyrics and songs. Most appropriate was the use of the music as background for the action scenes, shown effectively by a lone rider summoning the rebel forces for the initial attack on the French railroad to free the Riff prisoners.

Manning's character was conveniently and wisely converted into a singer by profession in the Buckner-Florey script, rather than simply a love-struck girl who breaks into song opportunely. Although during her opening number at the music hall the plot pauses at a virtual standstill in the traditional manner of musicals, in most other instances Florey managed to keep events progressing during the songs' performances. Examples of the latter include "You and I," when several desert vistas unfold before our eyes in a nonseamless effort to depict Manning's subjective imagination, and during the patriotic dance ("Let the Bugle Blow") which helps to convince Bruce Cabot that honor demands he investigate Morgan's allegations against Victor Francen. Another example of the tendency to use the music to further the plot was in the adaptation of "The Riff Song" into an ostensibly idle piano keyboard piece that secretly tells the captured Arabs of the presence of their leader, unknown to the French. As had previously been the case in Florey's <u>Till We Meet Again</u>, music serves a practical purpose in <u>The Desert Song</u>.

> Each song has a ritual meaning to the Riffs, and, in turn, they dictate a prearranged course of action.... In this fashion, many of the songs from the original operetta are retained.... The Romberg melodies become coded forms of communication in this new libretto.[14]

In such ways, Florey tried to obtain probable transitions into, and motivations for, the music and songs. Although there was a separate musical director (LeRoy Prinz) and unit, Florey insisted on directing the connecting passages between dialogue and song. He was not content with the typical method of allowing the musical numbers to be mounted in a detachable manner from the rest of the film. Some songs from the play, difficult to adapt in this way, were dropped entirely, while others were treated as preexisting entities, appearing in the course of the drama with an apparent lack of self-consciousness--rather than as spontaneously-created expressions of heightened emotion. Even the full singing of the title medley was only hinted at throughout and withheld until the very end, when it fit the celebratory mood of a victorious climax and did not seem overly operatic in nature. Thus, through the use of the music as motifs to underline action and emotional states and in his attempts to justify the introduction of the songs, Florey made a material contribution with The Desert Song toward the goal of a fully integrated movie musical.

Warner Bros. had originally planned to have The Desert Song in release by the beginning of 1943, but by then it had become thoroughly enmeshed in complications of wartime censorship. The film had been written and production was underway before all the various wartime guidelines had been fully codified. As early as December 21, 1942, an analysis by viewers of the Office of War Information's Bureau of Motion Pictures condemned it for an unsympathetic presentation of the French, recommending either a complete revision or shelving for the duration of the conflict.[15] The movie was held up through the spring on the basis of its portrayal of French imperialism and cooperation with the Germans. A scene of Dennis Morgan's dialogue was re-shot to tone down his denunciation of French governance of Morocco, although Buckner managed to prevent a diminution of the ambiguity over Bruce Cabot's collaborationist role.[16] But apparently the real reason for the delay was a semi-official indication that the State Department did not appreciate anything that might undermine an effort at rapprochement with the French by depicting them in an unfavorable light.[17] November 1942 had seen the Allied invasion of North Africa, and the acceptance of surrender from Vichy leader Admiral Jean-François Darlan was widely deplored. Idealists were outraged by this pragmatism on the part of the Roosevelt administration, and a film which so forcefully denounced the Vichy French could only have fueled the controversy.

Despite receiving permission in April 1943 to export The Desert Song to most English-speaking countries and Latin America, Warner Bros. decided to wait until December of that year before premiering the picture. By this time Darlan was dead and the episode was displaced by more recent news. Even then the movie ran into political trouble as the Free French pressed Warners to eliminate certain scenes bearing on colonialism.[18] Not until August 1944 was The Desert Song granted a general export license, and only with a provision precluding the film going to countries with substantial Moslem or Arab populations,[19] presumably because of the glorification of a native revolt. The picture was finally exhibited in France after the war, in mid-1946.

After all the difficulties, however, the effort put into The Desert Song proved worthwhile. Going into general domestic release early in 1944, fifteen months after its completion, it was a box-office champion for February and ran up the best hold-over record of any movie that season.[20] Critical reaction was generally favorable as well, although few took notice or understood the film's political implications. This commercial success would convince Warners to put Florey back under contract, by which time he had already completed two pictures at other studios.

In spite of co-authoring and directing a movie meritorious in so many respects, Florey has received virtually no recognition over the years for his achievements in The Desert Song--probably because it has been out of circulation since the remake of 1953. This has been a loss both for audiences and Florey's reputation. Admittedly, in his version the straightforward melding of a serious story with the operetta form is at times discomforting and is certainly least convincing in trying to reconcile the two key contradictory ingredients (singer and adventurer) of Morgan's character. However, to accept the hopeless silliness of the original property is infintely worse, as the remake proved. Buckner and Florey devised a distinctive approach, jettisoning its antiquated encumbrances and taking the story seriously by placing the accent on the adventure, rather than leaving it as a backdrop. This sets their version apart from the others, and it was considerably more successful as a result. Their Desert Song marked the only time the property has been treated with ingenuity and a sense of what is appropriately filmic. In total, Florey handled a difficult task admirably, creating a movie that hardly dates despite its timely nature, with many scenes that still capture the imagination.

TWENTIETH CENTURY-FOX, 1942-1943

Following completion of The Desert Song, Warner Bros. waited to release the picture and gauge public response before determining whether to take up the option on Florey's contract. In the interim he was allowed to take his services elsewhere. Executive Bryan Foy, who had moved to Twentieth Century-Fox, immediately offered Florey employment, and he signed a writer-director contract on September 28, 1942. During the fall he spent a couple of months collaborating on an unproduced screenplay, based on the contemporary war autobiography, I Escaped from Hong Kong. Then for several weeks he directed scenes of aerial combat shot in the studio with miniatures and rear projection. This film, Bomber's Moon, also contained sequences directed by Edward Ludwig and Harold Schuster, and these various contributions were listed under the collective pseudonym of Charles Fuhr.

Roger Touhy--Gangster, also known as Roger Touhy--Last of the Gangsters, was a film based on actual events, a forerunner of the semi-documentary movement in postwar Hollywood cinema. Touhy, member of a large Chicago gangland family, had been convicted of kidnapping in 1936 and was given a ninety-nine-year sentence to be served at Stateville Prison, Joliet, Illinois. But on October 9, 1942, he and some cohorts staged an amazing daytime jailbreak, and for the next two months the story of the manhunt for Touhy, the most intensive of the war years, was headline news. Finally, on December 29, the Chicago hide-out of Touhy and his gang was located; surrounded by police and F.B.I. agents, Touhy and most of his followers surrendered.

A topical motion picture exploiting the sensational prison break of the Touhy gang was set into motion at Twentieth Century-Fox by Foy as soon as the news of the capture was heard, and Florey was quickly transferred to the new project. On January 23, 1943, he went to Chicago with a camera crew to photograph the actual locations of the Touhy band's surrender. When Florey left Hollywood, not even a first draft screenplay had been submitted, so he had the unique opportunity to base his camera work on the known facts of the case rather than on a script.

"The shooting at 1254-56 Leland Avenue had taken

place just a few days before," recalled Florey, "and the place was a mess."[21]

> The bloody stairway had remained exactly in the state it had been in several days previous at the time of the end of the bandits. From the height of a floor the bullets of the machine guns had cut the ramp in half; the bullets had been buried in the plaster of the walls. Here and there were spots of blood which had become dried.[22]

"We photographed all ... of Touhy's hideouts ... in order to duplicate them at the studio."[23] In quest of authenticity, Florey joined police detectives for a week,

> visiting the spots made famous by the criminal annals of the time of Prohibition.... I visited dives and palaces, tribunals of districts, morgues and prisons, hide-outs in the suburbs and places where the stars of banditry had been found at the end of "rides" concluding their abduction by their enemies.[24]

The company spent several weeks in Illinois, including ten days at Stateville Prison, shooting backgrounds and "plates" that would later have the stars added in the foreground, and re-enacting the escape in long shots. Florey said:

> We worked and lived surrounded by 5,000 of the most dangerous criminals in the United States, and the director of the prison authorized us to use the "trustees" to do the little jobs or to stand-in for certain actors of the film. For the first time in the history of prisons, I filmed an escape of a prisoner on the spot....[25]

The outdoor work was done in temperatures seven degrees below zero, with "a polar wind which blew in our faces all day long."[26] Snow covered the ground, adding to the forbidding look of the prison in the picture, described by Manny Farber as "grim and chilling."[27] Florey was even able to interview Touhy and members of his gang then at Joliet. "It was the first time that such a thorough location shooting had taken place."[28] Two months elapsed before completion of the

The first on-location re-creation of a prison escape was photographed at Illinois's Joliet Prison in January 1943 for Roger Touhy--Gangster, with trustees doubling in this long shot for the performers who would portray the actual criminals in the film.

final script, which incorporated the location footage already shot. The movie was completed in thirty-three days at the studio in April and May on a $200,000 budget (less than the sum allotted).

On July 12, 1943, Fox gave Roger Touhy--Gangster "one of the most unique previews staged in film history"[29] --in the prison assembly hall of Touhy's own Stateville Penitentiary. In attendance were hundreds of state and federal officials, including Governor Dwight H. Green, along with 1,600 inmates of Stateville. Embarrassment mounted as the motion picture began without sound: someone had sabotaged amplifiers between the afternoon trial run and the evening performance. As the equipment was repaired, the audience waited, sweltering: a valve had been opened, sending steam into the radiators of the hall. In spite of the trouble, the scheduled preview managed to take place, an hour and a half late.

The threat of censorship hung over the Touhy story from the writing stage through the final editing. The authors used only the actual names of Touhy and his chief lieutenant "Owl" Banghart, substituting pseudonyms for the rest of the real-life characters. The fact that Touhy was alive required that "a certain amount of compulsory tact [be] used in the presentation of his life."[30] This did not deter Touhy from suing Fox for a million dollars, claiming his privacy and constitutional rights had been violated. Although he won a temporary court order on August 3, 1943, barring exhibition of the picture, he eventually lost the case.

Though the filmmakers had secured the cooperation of state and local officials in making the picture, there had been no assistance from the F.B.I. The Federal agency now complained that their work on Touhy's capture was shown mistakenly to be the responsibility of local authorities, and the movie was withdrawn for retakes, additional footage, and re-editing. The Bureau insisted on a disclaimer at the beginning stating that the portrayal of F.B.I. agents in the film implied no endorsement or approval of the picture by the agency.

The next hurdle was the approval of the Hays office, which was difficult to obtain with tightened wartime censorship restrictions. Florey commented,

> I don't know if the fact of having filmed on location had been the cause of the violence which erupted from each frame when we saw the picture for the first time in the private projection room of Foy, but nevertheless we realized immediately that we were in trouble with Mr. Hays and the censorship! We were not mistaken.[31]

The Hays Office demanded that the studio cut more than one reel of the picture, claiming the crimes had been depicted in too brutal a fashion. "Bad for the general public," Florey was told.[32] "Its presentation was authorized only on the formal condition that it never be shown outside the United States!"[33] Caught between lawsuits and censorship, Fox considered shelving the film, then waited a year before releasing it (still as an "A" movie), a delay that ruined the movie's topical value. Amazingly, in the release version the narrative flows smoothly without any breaks to indicate where the cuts were made.

With Roger Touhy--Gangster, Florey moved decisively away from the European artistic influence which had affected his style so much, in favor of stark realism and a semi-documentary manner. Florey found the direction of Roger Touhy--Gangster a challenge:

> From the directing point of view, it had been much more interesting for me to recreate this gangsterism atmosphere, as in the form of the "March of Time" of crime, in preference to stories of love and adventure artificially composed by our scenarists.[34]

The use of authentic location footage taken at Stateville Prison added a sense of realism to Roger Touhy--Gangster, as in this scene with George E. Stone (left) and Preston Foster (right, in the title role).

1940-1950: Short-Term Contracts

Although this was his only movie so completely dominated by the nonfiction method, realism would exert a growing influence on his features with a factual basis.

Several sequences show the contrasts in Florey's style and how successfully they were combined in Roger Touhy--Gangster. The location footage shot at Stateville Prison is extensively and creatively used, combined almost imperceptibly with studio shots, and lends the strongest aura of authenticity to the picture. The combination is most effective in the prison escape sequence, with long shots and window scenes from the prison footage mixed with medium shots and close-ups from the studio shooting. The result "is cool and distanced, as if shot by a newsreel crew"[35]--yet it is also highly dramatic.

There are a number of other devices used to attain the feel of a documentary. The story is enclosed in plain, chiseled-in-granite credits. The plot is propelled by the frequent use of newspaper headlines, in place of titles or a narrator, that give the factual validity of documentation. For a similar purpose, one scene places the gang in a movie theater where they happen to see a newsreel discussing the manhunt for themselves. At one point the plot builds to an expected confrontation between Preston Foster (as Touhy) and a former associate who turned state's evidence--only to have that man killed without explanation by another inmate, an incident too improbable to be used except in a factual context. The movie does not end in a bloody final shootout as one expects in a gangster film, but in the meek surrender of an outsmarted Foster, a resolution that makes the plot seem less contrived.

Alternatively, Florey's brand of expressionism comes through only in a few scenes, as during the opening montage of prohibition gunfire from racing cars. The gang's capture in a miserable waterfront apartment gave Florey a chance to insert some of his characteristic atmospheric elements, working with darkness, fog, and shadow to create the film's only mysterious sequence. Views of the F.B.I. surrounding the tenement and the band's capture beneath blinding searchlights also owed much of their effectiveness to Florey's old style.

Roger Touhy--Gangster represents the criminal as neither hero nor victim; indeed there is no one in the picture

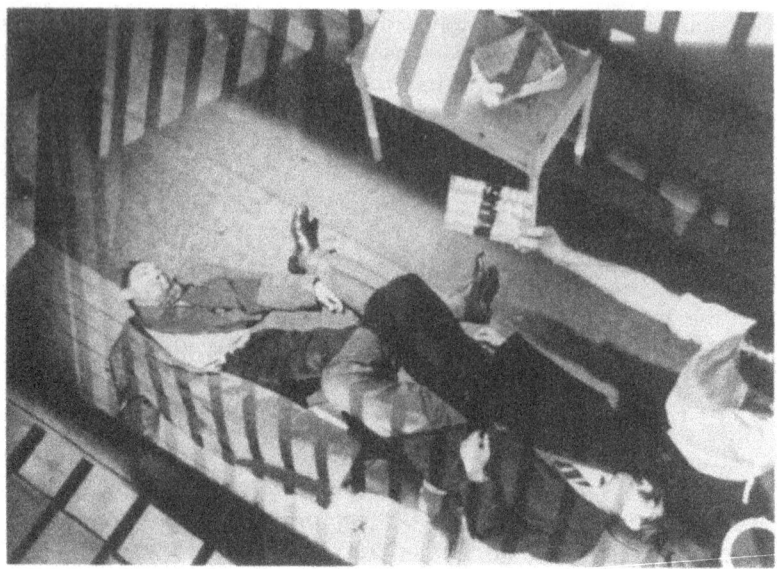

The combination of expressionism and realism in <u>Roger Touhy--Gangster</u> is revealed by the use of shadows and camera angle in this frame.

to admire or feel sympathy for. "There is no romance, no sentiment, no kindliness in this picture," wrote one critic.[36] Foster is cruel and sadistic, as shown by his treatment of a kidnapped victim and in his savage beating of two henchmen who have become drunk, a scene "as brutal (and effective) as anything one will ever see."[37] His own lieutenant, Victor McLaglen as Banghart, delivers Foster's epitaph when, on their capture, McLaglen tells Foster he will request to be transferred to Alcatraz to get away from the "cheap thieves and gunmen" of Stateville.

Neither are the law enforcement officials portrayed heroically. This is not a "G-men" picture, perhaps one reason the F.B.I. disliked it. The gang is not caught by adroit police but rather by the gangster's lack of draft cards and ignorance of wartime conditions. Foster and his hoods are merely stupid and ignorant, their leader characterized by his belief in astrology as an "exact science" and mocked by McLaglen constantly correcting his grammar.

Roger Touhy--Gangster features an impressive gallery of veteran gangland supporting players who give performances of a high quality, particularly Foster as the violent Touhy. Most interesting is McLaglen, playing a role far different from his usual genial drunken Irishman: under Florey's direction, McLaglen was transformed into a cruel but well-educated menace. When the gang asks why he associates with them, McLaglen replies, "Because the lower vertebrates have always fascinated me"--a comment Foster and his cohorts fail to comprehend.

Roger Touhy--Gangster is historically important both as the first motion picture to violate the Hays office injunction against making biographies of gangsters (Monogram's Dillinger, made two years later, has often been incorrectly credited with initially breaking this rule), and as the first Hollywood movie to realistically portray gangland activity. As film historian Carlos Clarens has pointed out, Touhy, although

> disowned by the [Federal Bureau of Investigation], pioneered the quasi-documentary techniques that two years later would become the trademark of the semi-factual exposés endorsed by the F.B.I., such as location photography, precise identification of characters and locale, and a concluding on-camera speech by an official [deleted from some prints].[38]

Released at a time--June 1944--when gangster movies were no longer common, Roger Touhy--Gangster was "'novelty' entertainment,"[39] according to The Hollywood Reporter, and became popular. Time dubbed Touhy

> a double helping of nostalgia for cinemaddicts who remember some of the most exciting U.S. movies ever made--such gangster films as Underworld, Drag Net, Public Enemy, Little Caesar.[40]

Daily Variety commented that Roger Touhy--Gangster "has audience values in its very lack of theatrical license."[41] The film's semi-documentary methods won wide praise, especially as it made possible an unglamorized, realistic study of a gangster on the screen without any loss of suspense or interest. One critic summed it up this way:

The picture gives the impression of sticking to the
facts, thus building up an atmosphere of authenticity more exciting than the cheap fiction of most
prison thrillers.[42]

REPUBLIC, 1943-1944

Man from Frisco took Florey to Republic studios for the only
time in his career. Moving into the field of big-budget
films, Republic engaged Florey in late 1943 to direct one of
their major productions of the season, a film supposedly
loosely based on the life and ideas of shipbuilder Henry
Kaiser. However, this was hardly a biographical drama.
Instead, Man from Frisco presented "a badly fictionalized
amalgam of the real life roles of Kaiser and his yard boss,
Clay P. Bedford." Enormous liberties were taken with the
facts, such as having the lead, played by Michael O'Shea,
in conflict with the community surrounding his factory; as
well, O'Shea was a young man, whereas Kaiser was sixty-
two at this time. Indeed, a character portrayed by Robert
Warwick, who has only a few lines, more closely resembles
Kaiser.[43]

Man from Frisco was another picture made in the realist style, with six weeks spent at the Kaiser shipyards in
Oakland and Richmond photographing backgrounds for which
the movie received praise. This location trip gave Florey
the chance to meet Kaiser, and he enjoyed directing the
homefront hero in a short made in December. Shooting on
Man from Frisco took place from October 1943 through February 1944. While Florey disliked the melodramatic script from
which he had to work, he was pleased with his treatment at
Republic.

WARNER BROS. (FINAL PERIOD),
1944-1946

After his year-and-a-half hiatus at Twentieth Century-Fox
and Republic, Florey returned to Warner Bros. in early 1944.
Despite several other tempting offers, he was prompted to
sign on January 27 when Jack Warner promised that the
prestigious God Is My Co-Pilot would be his first assignment
under the new contract. Florey reported to work as soon

1940-1950: Short-Term Contracts 261

as he had finished Man from Frisco, on February 28. While he began preparations for his new film immediately, several other matters were to occupy portions of his time. These included two unproduced scripts he had been preparing on his own for several years, in which he tried to interest Warners, as well as a brief time out in June for eight days shooting on the confused and trouble-plagued production of Escape in the Desert, to which three other directors--Byron Haskin, William McGann, and Edward Blatt (only the third received credit)--also contributed.

Carnival--La Vie Parisienne, subtitled "A Romanced Biography of Jacques Offenbach," was a thirty-six-page unproduced treatment written in September 1943. Florey had long wanted to make a biography of a great musician or artist and had suggested as subjects Nijinsky, Toulouse-Lautrec, Vincent Van Gogh, and The Moon and Sixpence; he also spent nearly a month with Robert Buckner reviewing the possibilities for a new version of Trilby. All of these suggestions were rebuffed; the studios regarded Florey as an impractical dreamer, telling him such projects were commercially unfeasible.

In subsequent years he would be gratified to see most of his ideas filmed and become popular, although it was frustrating not to be responsible for any of them. However, in 1953 he was able to make two television shows with Loretta Young portraying Charlotte Brontë and Clara Schumann; the latter centered on the intensity and torment of the creative process, especially its effect on the composer's family. The critical acclaim for these shows--the Schumann episode won an Emmy nomination--indicated Florey's talent for handling the subject matter.

In the case of Carnival, a number of studios were interested in the story. After rejoining Warners, Florey found producer Robert Buckner very enthusiastic about the idea; he envisioned it as a light musical comedy, a French version of Yankee Doodle Dandy (which he had written in 1941). Buckner convinced Jack Warner and Hal Wallis to share his view, but legal problems with the Offenbach estate caused the project to be abandoned.

Carnival contained elements of many of Florey's foremost interests. It was a historical biography set in France (primarily his beloved Paris) in the world of music, art, and literature at the time of the Napoleons, and involved a love story. Florey had a special fondness for the era, which he had previously created for <u>Murders in the Rue Morgue</u> and as technical advisor for <u>La Boheme</u>, a movie he would have given his soul to direct.

<u>Carnival</u> is rich in descriptions of the setting and atmosphere of Paris, reveling in the French customs of the period, meticulously observed with the delight of a historian and a native recreating his homeland. Florey took care to see that nearly every prominent French person of the time (roughly 1840-1870, though he wanted to avoid intrusive dates) appears, from Henri Murger to Nadar to Napoleon III. Offenbach forms an intense desire to meet the nation's leader, out of which grows an ironic dénouement.

Florey set up a fundamental conflict early in the narrative between the success Offenbach finds as his public career develops and the failures he experiences in his private life as he constantly falls in love with women above his social position, even after marriage. Offenbach's most unfortunate affair is with the temperamental star of his theater, whom he must constantly flatter into staying on the stage rather than becoming the mistress of one of many wealthy men from around the world. She forces him to call on her the evening of the debut of his new operetta, but on arriving he discovers that the man preparing a drink in her kitchen is none other than the Emperor, Napoleon III. Florey handled this final humiliation of Offenbach, and his other similar frustrations, with frankness and continental sophistication.

Naturally, Florey was interested in more than presenting Offenbach's life and times. He also wanted to provide an opportunity for the enjoyment of some of the composer's music. The long span of years covered allowed Florey to examine the evolution of Offenbach's style, from its earliest inspirations to his mature masterpieces. The innovations Offenbach brought to lively musical comedies were pointed out, and Florey carefully devised ingenious and unusual ways to justify the performance of compositions in the course of the narrative. The music is integrated during opportune moments, such as rehearsals, a Bohemian Christmas party, under the difficult star's balcony to entice her into singing the roles written for her, or cutting back and forth between Offenbach's new cancan premiering on stage and the composer running back to his theater, flustered after his indiscreet encounter with Napoleon.

The Wormwood Scrubs Murder Cases was based on the novel L'Assassin Habite au 21 (Paris: Librarie des Champs-Elysees, 1939), by the Belgian author S.A. Steeman. Florey completed the adaptation into a seventy-page screenplay in April 1944. The screenplay was short because only some portions had been broken down into continuity form, with many of the scenes and especially the dialogue simply described in brief, to be filled in at a later date had the film ever been made. Florey had been working intermittently on the project for five years and had even written the author, who much admired his Hotel Imperial, but the effort was abandoned upon learning that H.G. Cluzot had made a comedic version in occupied France.

Florey's Wormwood Scrubs Murder Cases was to have been a typically British mystery and had much in common with A Study in Scarlet. The setting is London in 1900; most of the crucial action takes place in lonely, fog-bound streets. Included are an intriguing variety of suspects, each carefully delineated with curious character traits. The plot is complex, full of times, dates, and alibis, with an ingenious solution. In two murder sequences, Florey added his touch by indicating that although a victim was to be in conversation with the killer, suspense would be maintained by not allowing the killer's face to appear.

God Is My Co-Pilot was one of Florey's most important assignments to date, and he approached it with an immense amount of enthusiasm. He had wanted to make an aviation film for at least a dozen years, but his only experience in the genre had been with the second unit biplanes of The Cohens and the Kellys in Paris seventeen years earlier and on Bomber's Moon, which had been shot inside the Twentieth Century-Fox studios. For God Is My Co-Pilot, however, with the assistance of Colonel Robert Lee Scott, Jr. on whose best-selling autobiography it was based (and who served as technical advisor on the production), Warners had obtained the cooperation of the Army Air Corps. With a fleet of P-40s and their crews at Warners' disposal, "it was possible for us to film actual aerial combat [shot by Charles Marshall] and really sensational exteriors" which contributed materially to the picture's sense of authenticity and epic quality.44 Much of this footage, however, was edited out by Jack Warner.

God Is My Co-Pilot is the story of Scott's exploits as an ace in the Flying Tigers during the year following the Japanese attack on Pearl Harbor (and is vastly superior to the run-of-the-mill heroics of Republic's The Flying Tigers, 1942). Scott's book was adapted by Peter Milne, with the final screenplay written primarily by producer Robert Buckner in consultation with Florey and Scott himself. After meticulous preparation, production lasted sixty-five days (five over schedule), from July to October 1944. Commented Buckner, "Florey greatly improved on the book, and the script, in the excellent way he directed it."45 Florey's knowledge of the Chinese setting enhanced the movie's atmosphere considerably. The harmonious performances by the cast of Warners regulars, particularly Raymond Massey as General Chennault, were effective; Dennis Morgan's work as Colonel Scott won high praise, placing him in the front ranks of the season's dramatic stars.

God Is My Co-Pilot was filmed in a straightforward manner, with minimal thrills and heroics, serving as a further indication of Florey's shift toward realism in the 1940s. There was no effort to glamorize the elements; instead, he allowed the events to speak eloquently for themselves. The movie "bears the unmistakable stamp of truth," wrote Newsweek.46 Box Office Digest added, "the direction of Robert Florey retains the touch of biographical honesty while moving steadily at good motion picture pace...."47

God Is My Co-Pilot belongs to the tradition of war films that would later find their fullest expression in Twelve O'Clock High (1950), although Florey's had a spiritual rather than a pacifist or psychological theme. It dwells introspectively on the personal stress on ordinary men under war conditions as they try to find and preserve the beliefs they are fighting for. Combat-derived tension is kept to a minimum in favor of an exploration of Morgan's troubled conscience as he tries to reconcile the killing he is part of with the humanitarian goals of the Allied side. The story is frankly but richly sentimental, appealing directly to the emotions of a war-weary public with an uplifting assurance that there is a God who knows the fighting men and wants them

1940-1950: Short-Term Contracts 265

Florey's style became steadily more subtle through the
1940s, as typified by his use of depth, foreground window
and camera angle in this shot of Raymond Massey and Dennis
Morgan in God Is My Co-Pilot.

to live. This message is delivered simply and directly as
Morgan undergoes a religious conversion that enables him to
believe in the movie's title. (This scene is very understated,
and the lack of credibility some find in it may be due to the
casting of Alan Hale as the missionary, a strong contrast to
so many of his previous comic characterizations.[48]) Morgan's
faith is of the secular and patriotic variety, appropriate to a
man of action and unencumbered by dogma.

    God Is My Co-Pilot turned out to be probably the most
popular picture Florey ever made and one of his personal
favorites. The movie was a box office champion and brought
in the largest grosses of any Warners release that season.
Photoplay named it one of the ten best films of 1945, based
on a survey of audience preferences. More meaningful,

however, was a survey published by the Army Signal Corps that showed God Is My Co-Pilot to have been the favorite motion picture exhibited to the GI's between 1942-45.[49]

Why this phenomenal popularity, especially among servicemen? By the last year of the war, audiences, all too familiar with the miseries the war brought about, were satiated with simple reproductions of the conflict, and movies about the war were becoming steadily less popular. God Is My Co-Pilot sensitively examined the emotions and feelings of the soldier, acknowledging the burden fighting placed on his conscience. It captured in a moving and understanding way the mood of the time, giving reassurance that the sacrifices of the war were worthwhile. It offered a consolation in a deity present at the side of the soldier, Who cared whether he lived or died, on Whose side and in Whose name the war was being conducted. But while modern critics tend to cringe at such old-fashioned notions, preferring the blood-and-thunder epics of the same period, it was precisely this message that made God Is My Co-Pilot so popular in its day. This was indeed the goal of the filmmakers, summed up by Buckner in a production memo.

> This religious-spiritual theme, deftly-handled and not over-stressed, will ... give more stature and humane warmth to this picture.... We have all the action any picture could wish, and more; but this simple, rugged philosophy of the combat pilot can lift this picture by its heels as something you'll long remember.[50]

The Adventures of Don Juan was handed to Florey in October 1944, even as he was still directing God Is My Co-Pilot. This new film was to be shot in color, star Errol Flynn, and use the same exteriors in Balboa Park, San Diego, that had served so well as the Latin setting in The Magnificent Fraud. Florey's delight at finally having the historical drama he had always wanted was so great that he launched straight into a tremendous research effort on the period without even taking a pause after his rigorous directorial labors. At the same time, with the encouragement of producer Jerry Wald, Florey worked on overhauling the script with writer Herbert Dalmas. Florey would invent characters (including the King's intrepid dwarf and Juan's sidekick) and situations, typing them into continuity form with Dalmas inserting dialogue.

1940-1950: Short-Term Contracts

Finally, in December, after two months, they had a 167-page final script ready, of which Florey claimed about half was his creation. As usual, his continuity was detailed, with staging and camera placement planned more carefully than was typical for an ordinary director; several of his characteristic stylistic touches were also in evidence. A few weeks later, however, Florey was abruptly taken off The Adventures of Don Juan and transferred to a far less prestigious assignment, Danger Signal, not at all the kind he had hoped for after the popularity of God Is My Co-Pilot. Raoul Walsh replaced him on Don Juan, but with a strike at the studio a few months later the project was postponed for two years, after which it was taken over by Vincent Sherman. Naturally, Florey was angry at being shoved aside, having made all the preparations to direct--even planning the sets with a technical adviser. And although Dalmas later received story credit for his contributions when the film was finally released in 1948 (George Oppenheimer and Harry Kurnitz were listed for the screenplay), Florey was ignored. But by then he would be too busy at Universal-International with Rogues' Regiment to seek arbitration in the matter.

Had Florey directed Don Juan, it would likely have confirmed him in the adventure genre, a move he already had begun with The Desert Song and would later recapture with Outpost in Morocco. The script he wrote with Dalmas reflects the influence of Douglas Fairbanks--for whom Florey had worked during the production of Robin Hood--in such scenes as Juan's elaborate escape down a bell-tolling rope. Also apparent is a concern for period recreation and detail: the script moves considerably more slowly and with a degree of complexity less than in the final movie, with Juan serving in not quite so pivotal a role so as to place greater emphasis on the historical characters surrounding him. Florey had switched the historical setting both to assure greater accuracy and to take advantage of a huge costume inventory already on hand at Warners. By and large, the essentials of the Dalmas-Florey script underwent relatively little change over the interval prior to eventual filming and, although the conclusion was considerably revised and improved, the plan for the final duel and even much of the dialogue were retained.

The Adventures of Don Juan was not Florey's only

attempt at composing a swashbuckler. In April 1952 he
authored a six-page unproduced treatment entitled, <u>Henri
John Morgan the Pirate</u>, cleverly constructing a story around
the limitation of only using already existing sets, for what
would apparently have been a low-budget production.
(Whether he was writing for a movie or a telefilm is unclear;
in the more doubtful case of the latter, it would have been
at least an hour show and quite possibly a pilot.) While
opening in a light-hearted, fast-paced fashion similar to
Henry King's <u>The Black Swan</u> (1942), Florey's narrative
soon became more serious, centering on the mercy Morgan
shows a brother and sister--with whom he falls in love--and
their reciprocity when the Spaniards capture him. Although
at the end safe and reunited with his bride-to-be, and promoted to the social status of a gentleman by Britain, Morgan
announces he will never reveal the whereabouts of all his
hidden loot. In sum, <u>Henri John Morgan the Pirate</u> was an
entertaining tale, despite its modest nature and lack of originality.

    <u>Danger Signal</u> had been suggested for Florey as early
as November 30, 1944, by producer William Jacobs, who hoped
the film could be shot in a minimum of time and thought
Florey best qualified for the project. Although Jacobs was
personally liked by Florey, he did not enjoy any of the three
movies they worked on together--the others being <u>Lady Gang-
ster</u> and <u>The Beast with Five Fingers</u>. <u>Danger Signal</u> already had a long history, with the Hays Office at one time
rejecting the entire story as morally unacceptable; twenty-
one writers and five years were needed to adapt Phyllis
Bottome's 1939 novel to the screen. The final result was a
modest production tailored for two young contract players,
Faye Emerson (who had recently become the wife of Elliot
Roosevelt) and Zachary Scott.

    <u>Danger Signal</u> has received some attention in recent
years for its noir ingredients, although, visually speaking,
these are relatively insignificant. Its only true appearance
is in the opening sequence with Scott escaping into a dark
alley (over which the credits had been superimposed), followed by his fruitless search for shelter--due to the wartime
housing shortage--shot from various bizarre angles. Otherwise, the style is quite ordinary, relying mostly on high-
key lighting and often using very natural outdoor settings.
Thematically, <u>Danger Signal</u> has more in common with noir,

and it is interesting to note that one of the important uncredited screenwriters was Vera Caspary (<u>Laura</u>), who contributed the details of Scott's sordid romance with Emerson.

The psychoanalytic tone of Bottome's book was diluted in the final script to emphasize the progression of a modern-day Don Juan with homicidal tendencies--Scott. In the opening scene he flees a murder, steals a service medal, and passes off an injury acquired in his escape as a war wound. Finding refuge as a boarder, he charms his way into the homes and hearts of a plain, hard-working stenographer (Emerson) and her mother. But after practicing his attractions on the former, Scott shifts his attention to her younger sister when he learns that she stands to gain a sizeable inheritance upon her marriage, making jealous rivals of the two women.

Until this point, the fast pace of <u>Danger Signal</u> conceals the weaknesses in the plot and the stereotyped characters. But in the final third of the picture these faults are exposed as the story becomes steadily more unmotivated and predictable, the dialogue more filled with cliches. The climax --as Emerson tries to poison Scott--was betrayed by the production code's strict policy regarding the motive of revenge. This impasse was resolved through her unlikely failure of nerve combined with the convenient sudden arrival of the police, frightening Scott into falling off a cliff as he attempts escape. The dissatisfaction aroused by this improbable turn of events is compounded by a dreadfully long, happily-ever-after tacked-on ending, as the two sisters return to old beaus. While the weakness of the conclusion was readily acknowledged, <u>Danger Signal</u> was received surprisingly well by critics; there may have been a preference among audiences, as well as censors, to avoid stigmatizing Emerson as a murderer.

Even as he invested <u>Danger Signal</u> with a convincing build-up of tension, Florey, whose heart was never in the project, could not overcome the film's limitations. Many of the supporting players are especially weak, notably Rosemary De Camp's female psychiatrist, a part both poorly written and performed. There were many other frustrations in the movie's production, including delays and interruptions that would cause the shooting to run forty days (nine over schedule), during March, April, and May of 1945. However,

Florey managed to keep the picture within its $400,000 budget. Despite its pretensions, Danger Signal is ultimately a shallow film, one without any depth or insight; whatever possibilities the property may originally have had were diluted by the Hays Office. In the end, only a slick and efficient production redeems Danger Signal from utter mediocrity.

During the 1940s Florey was employed more often at Warner Bros. than any other company, and generally he was glad to be there--with certain reservations. He had great respect for his collaborators and the various technicians; the only drawback was that Jack Warner's influence made one feel "they all learned their trade at the same school." Warner personally edited and re-cut many of the studio's films, following methods he had inherited from former production chief Daryl Zanuck. Florey remarked:

> J.L. Warner insisted on maintaining the action pacing. One evening at his home, while watching an actor who had been shot by a villain and was taking his time--perhaps two or three seconds--before dying, J.L.W. said: "Die you S.O.B. Die faster." Then, turning to the editor and myself, added: "As soon as that guy is shot, don't let him agonize forever--cut to the heavy, hold his close-up for a few frames, then cut back to the other guy, already dead."

Directors knew they were expected to obtain complete coverage "from all possible angles" in order to permit Warner to re-cut his movies in this way; he would demand retakes to obtain additional angles or a change in a performance or costume even if a schedule had to be pushed back. He "had dictated notes that were delivered at the studio gate to the directors as they arrived early in the morning," Florey recalled. "Some were unexpected, for instance: 'Retake sequence, scenes 142 to 159, the leading man wore a lousy looking necktie not acceptable in a Warner film.'" Thus there was little room for a director's creativity, and many would cater to Warner's fondness for "forceful low wide angles, foreground pieces, originality of composition in the [house] style." While Warner would listen to the suggestions of the director in editing, there was no guarantee that he would abide by them; "J.L.W. didn't always keep his word nor fulfill his promises."[51]

J. Carrol Naish paying his respects to the dead pianist (Victor Francen) in one of the low wide-angle foreground compositions so admired by Jack Warner, in a frame deleted from The Beast with Five Fingers.

The Beast with Five Fingers was the last movie Florey would make on a studio contract and was one of his worst experiences working in that capacity, exhibiting many of the traditional difficulties he had with the selection of a project and the final fate of the picture after it has passed through his hands. Beast was an assignment he strenuously resisted, taking a three-month suspension rather than accept it. But when he returned, he found the script to Beast still on his desk and reluctantly went ahead with it. To his own surprise, he began to enjoy the challenge the horror tale presented; between November 1945 and February 1946, shooting lasted ten weeks (seven days over schedule) on a budget of $750,000.

The real star of The Beast with Five Fingers was a disembodied hand, a subject about which some unintended

amusement arose. The special effects department received the following instructions:

> Glove Hand with stump, ready for photographic test Tuesday, December 11, 1945.
> Mechanical Hand to crawl on floor, etc., ready for photographic test Wednesday December 12th 1945.
> Mechanical Hand to claw at face and throat ready for photographic test Thursday December 13th 1945.[52]

There was even some disagreement over the aesthetic properties the hand should possess:

> Mr. Trilling saw the test and objected to the length of the wrist on the present hand, and there was some mention of using a longer, scrawnier hand.
> If we use the present hand, it can be cut down and made irregular at the wrist....[53]

All of this brought out Florey's sometimes macabre sense of humor, and so he decided to have as much fun with it as possible. Tests and shots were made of the hands of everyone involved, an idea that was later transformed into a promotional gimmick (match the star with his hand). One scene, where the "beast" emerges from a box, its fingers wriggling like the tentacles of an octopus, was played by Florey with his own hand as he crouched under a table.

The photography of The Beast with Five Fingers is possibly the most ingenious and effective of all Florey's films. For once he had an adequate schedule, and the difference in style this allowed is evident in the prevalence of longer takes and mobile camerawork, with fewer brief shots except for inserts of an artistic nature. Although the film is filled with odd angles, shadows, and unusual compositions, not one of these devices was ever superfluous or overdone, each so perfectly integrated into the action and appropriate to the scene that it is virtually unnoticeable. The camera is almost constantly on the move, changing position and alternating between subjective and objective viewpoints to

---

[Opposite:] Florey directing the hand as it plays the piano in The Beast with Five Fingers.

reveal new perspectives and shifting perceptions. As well, these devices serve to govern the pace of the movie. Thus, Florey brilliantly obtains an extremely sophisticated control over the spectator that becomes increasingly complex and subtle as the story progresses.

<u>The Beast with Five Fingers</u> marks a return to Florey's early roots in German expressionism and the avant-garde, away from his 1940s style of realism. He superbly uses many stylistic effects, as he had in <u>Murders in the Rue Morgue</u> and <u>The Florentine Dagger</u>, adapting them into the horror genre so as to be palatable to the American audience. However, <u>The Beast with Five Fingers</u> is far more complex in its plot than <u>Rue Morgue</u>, demanding a greater participation on the part of the viewer since the story deals with discerning the obsessions of a lunatic and how they cause his mental disintegration. Such a theme related <u>Beast</u> by content as well as by visual style with the silent German cinema, so concerned with death, insanity, and souls tormented by dark forces. This kinship was immediately recognized when the picture came out; <u>Variety</u> reported that <u>Beast</u> was "reminiscent in mood of <u>The Cabinet of Dr. Caligari</u>,"[54] though perhaps <u>The Hands of Orlac</u> (Germany, 1924) was a more direct influence.

<u>The Beast with Five Fingers</u> features a number of scenes superbly staged and shot amid ornate settings that create a strong mood of horror. The main characters are introduced in a particularly unsettling sequence. The camera zooms in on a sparsely decorated chamber with a huge piano in the center. At the keyboard Victor Francen plays with only his left hand, a look of unnatural, almost fanatical concentration on his face. Robert Alda steps behind the piano to wheel Francen to the next room, revealing that the pianist is partially paralyzed; as Francen says, "All my will is concentrated in these fingers." At dinner, he demands to know of his guests--his secretary (Peter Lorre), his nurse (Andrea King), and Alda--whether they think he is sane or not. Their hesitant answers reveal them to be self-seeking pragmatists. All but King are interested in living off the invalid's wealth, and therefore it is in her favor that Francen then makes his will. Returning to the piano, Francen begins to play the same musical theme, his guests looking on glumly, as the camera pulls out of the scene in an inverse of the opening--a cinematic curtain on the first act of the drama.

1940-1950: Short-Term Contracts

That night Francen awakes in an almost supernatural dream. A violent storm has wrenched one of his windows open, and he crawls out of bed into his wheelchair to call nurse King. Going down the hall, he sees all the rooms around him begin to take on a swimming motion, as if photographed through water. This is clearly recognized as his subjective vision, because reverse shots including Francen appear normal. His sensations increase, going back and forth between subjective and objective views, until the old man loses balance and falls down a staircase. His death restores the camera to its customary perspective of reality.

The scenes and acting of Peter Lorre as Francen's deranged secretary are the most powerful in the movie, while not quite of the unforgettable tour de force caliber of the previous Florey-Lorre collaboration, The Face Behind the Mask. Lorre's strangeness is captured from his introduction, shot through the skeletal crossbars of a globe as he reads a book on astrology. He often moves in a sort of sleepy delirium, like a somnambulist. His lisping voice and facial contortions are accentuated, while his dark brows and globulous eyes are constantly in movement, seen in frequent close-ups. His divided psyche is characterized by his white face at odds with completely dark clothing, a contrast recalling The Face Behind the Mask. Lorre clearly has a streak of insanity apparent from his first scene, but only later does it grow into homicidal mania. Unfortunately, many of the supporting players, particularly the bland Alda and mediocre King as an unconvincing romantic couple, cannot match the strength Lorre achieved in his scenes. His only rivals are the excellent Victor Francen who, however, dies early in the story, and J. Carrol Naish, who adds humor and suspense throughout.

Doubtless the most memorable sequence of The Beast with Five Fingers are those of Francen's disembodied hand coming to life and committing mayhem. These scenes were also the most difficult to film, and they required all of Florey's imagination and resourcefulness. The terror these scenes create is a monument to his abilities. By their very nature, these scenes were visualized primarily in the mind of the director; indeed, he rewrote some of the action of the hand in the script himself.[55] (In this he may have been influenced by the memory of the trick films of Georges Méliès, where limbs often became separated from bodies via apparent magic.)[56] Florey also suggested some of the eerie sound

Mesmerized by the dead pianist's ring, Peter Lorre falls into the trance during which he will be subject to hallucinations of a malevolent hand in The Beast with Five Fingers.

effects, such as the reversal of a fire crackling and rooster crowing foreshadowing the hand's appearance, and air pressure escaping from an echo chamber to announce its presence --"each grotesque movement synchronized with a shrill, jarring sound."[57] The hand emerges from a box, behind a bookshelf, and out of a fireplace, frequently photographed so that it occupies the foreground as the players watch it, looking into the camera from the background. The unusual nature of this horror led to a number of censorship difficulties which Florey surmounted with skill, such as the scene where Lorre nails the hand to a board. Faced with a demand that this be shown off-screen, Florey heightened its effectiveness by shooting from a low angle, the hammer blows seeming to strike directly at the spectator with unnatural loudness.

Following Francen's death, a murder occurs, and when his crypt is discovered disturbed and his missing hand apparently self-amputated, people begin to believe it may have a malevolent life of its own. Events gradually indicate that the only one who actually sees the hand moving is Lorre, the victim of growing insanity. This becomes evident when he begins to menace King but is suddenly diverted by seeing and hearing the hand playing the piano.[58] The camera cuts back and forth between the hand playing and a barren, silent keyboard, intermingled with five pans across the faces of Lorre and King, making the audience gradually realize that while King sees and hears nothing, Lorre imagines the hand playing. Just as Francen had before his death, Lorre becomes obsessed with the piano, the victim of delusions. Finally Lorre throws the hand into a fireplace, but it reemerges from the flames to strangle him; on his death the hand vanishes before our eyes. (The original ending called for Alda and King to discover the charred remains of the hand still in the fireplace, indicating that Lorre had imagined the attack; but this scene was deleted from the final cut.)

"The camera technicians' trick photography makes these hallucinations shockingly plausible,"[59] and much of the story has been "projected through Lorre's eyes, without any explanation of the switches from straight narration to scenes registered by Lorre's deranged mind."[60] This central fault in the picture is the result of extensive editing made on The Beast with Five Fingers between its completion, in

February 1946, after which Florey left Warners, and its December opening. He had tried to eliminate this inconsistency between the actually severed but lifeless hand seen by several characters and the final image of the hand disappearing after having strangled Lorre by emphasizing the psychological dimension of the tale. Florey wanted the audience to realize, by interpreting on its own the visual style, that the "living" hand they saw was the result of having shared Lorre's understanding of events. Florey suggested shooting the story as seen through the consciousness of Lorre's character, an approach the director later used successfully in television shows such as A Letter to Loretta: The Mirror and Alcoa Theater: The Clock Struck Twelve. "The sets would have to be designed and photographed in an expressionist style and edited accordingly," he said.[61] For instance, Florey wanted to alter the scene where Lorre nails the menacing hand to one where he stabs his own hand, demonstrating unmistakably that a self-destructive hallucination has taken over his mind. In this way, much of the ambiguity, and even confusion, that exists in the movie in its present state would have been avoided.

He discussed the notion with the performer who would have to interpret such a difficult role, and "Peter, interested by the idea, accompanied me to the producer's office who, of course, dismissed it as commercially unthinkable."[62] Concern was also expressed over the possibility that such a scene would be censored. Thus, Florey could only create expressionistic effects with lighting and camera positioning --which he did masterfully--without recourse to the bizarre set design that had contributed to The Hole in the Wall and Murders in the Rue Morgue. Only in the sequences of Lorre alone in the library, pursued and terrified by the hand, was Florey's basic intention essentially preserved.

Instead, a long-winded whodunit-like explanation is necessary to account for the various phenomenon presented. Naish, a policeman, discovers a number of mechanical devices Lorre had used to propagate the legend of a murderous, ambulatory hand and assumes that a mental breakdown on Lorre's part had made him come to believe in the illusion himself. But the explanation was too quick and pat to be wholly satisfying for "the audience that knows more and has seen more than the policeman."[63] In the edited release version, the

1940-1950: Short-Term Contracts 279

spectator is suddenly told that what has been seen and accepted for most of the picture as objective reality is instead wholly a figment of someone's imagination--a difficult switch to bring off, although it works surprisingly well. However, not tying together all the clues convincingly gives The Beast with Five Fingers a more modern, surrealist tone, lauded by continental critics.

As he had done with Frankenstein and Murders in the Rue Morgue, Florey, over the objections of screenwriter Curt Siodmak, sought to relieve the tensions and heaviness of the horror with humor. He deliberately spread some levity so that, occasionally, The Beast with Five Fingers "seems to be kidding this type of film, and, yet, at other times, to be deadly serious."[64] Florey saves the best trick for the end: just when Naish has explained away the hand, it reappears-- only to turn out to be a mislaid glove. As Naish, looking at the audience in close-up, mutters that no one could believe in a hand walking around, a hand moves toward his throat-- his own. "How do you like that? My own hand!" Naish says to us, in Florey's final laugh at the whole idea of Beast.

The Beast with Five Fingers went into general release in early 1947, meeting good reviews and better business than expected in a time when horror pictures were extremely scarce. It became popular in Europe and is today one of the mainstays of Florey's reputation as a director. It is also interesting to note that it marked the first time one of his films had music composed by a Hollywood great, Max Steiner; seldom did Florey's work have a score to speak of (and how many famous directors would have the same reputation had they labored under this handicap?). But Florey was not pleased with the final release cut of Beast with Five Fingers and practically disowned it, telling friends it was a poor film and not to see it. Certainly he was far too harsh a judge of his own work, for Beast is regarded as a classic horror movie, innovative and influential in its day and still effective and successful with modern audiences.

INDEPENDENT, 1946-1950

Monsieur Verdoux was based on a true incident, the case of Landru, who killed over a dozen women in post-World War I

France. His trial was a sensation in its day, and the story had been the subject of films in France and Germany. In the early 1940s Orson Welles conceived of an American screen version of Landru's life and managed to intrigue Charlie Chaplin with the idea. At first the two planned to collaborate, but their approaches to the story differed considerably; Welles conceived it as a tragedy and Chaplin as a comedy. Welles soon withdrew from the venture, selling his rights to Chaplin for a few thousand dollars. Chaplin spent the next four years working on the script, and by early 1946 was preparing to put the movie into production.

Robert Florey had known Chaplin personally for more than twenty-five years, and his admiration for the comedian extended back to childhood, when he had drawn Chaplin caricatures at age fifteen. Florey first met "Charlot" (as the French called him) in 1921 while preparing an article on the comedian for Cinemagazine, and the two became fast friends; six years later Florey wrote a book on Chaplin published in France. They saw one another frequently over the ensuing years; Chaplin had taken an interest in Florey's experimental picture, The Life and Death of 9413--a Hollywood Extra, and Florey was consulted by Chaplin about some of the roles he contemplated playing. Now at liberty following the expiration of his Warner Bros.' contract, Florey went to visit Chaplin to wish him luck on his new production.

Upon seeing his old friend again, Florey received an invitation to join Chaplin for dinner. He recalled:

> Before, during and after the meal, Charlie Chaplin narrated to me the episodes of his story and performed a few scenes for me; he also had me listen to the musical accompaniment of certain sequences, which were already formulating in his mind; I also asked him to let me become familiar with his scenario, and promised to return the next day to tell him what I thought of it.... I worked very late to summarize my notes in about twenty pages, some of which bore upon certain weak points which the critics have recently found fault with ... and especially with errors regarding French judicial customs, and the atmosphere of the film. A few days later, as I was explaining to him the idea of a "gag" which had occurred to me ... Charlie said to me suddenly: "You should be the director of my film."[65]

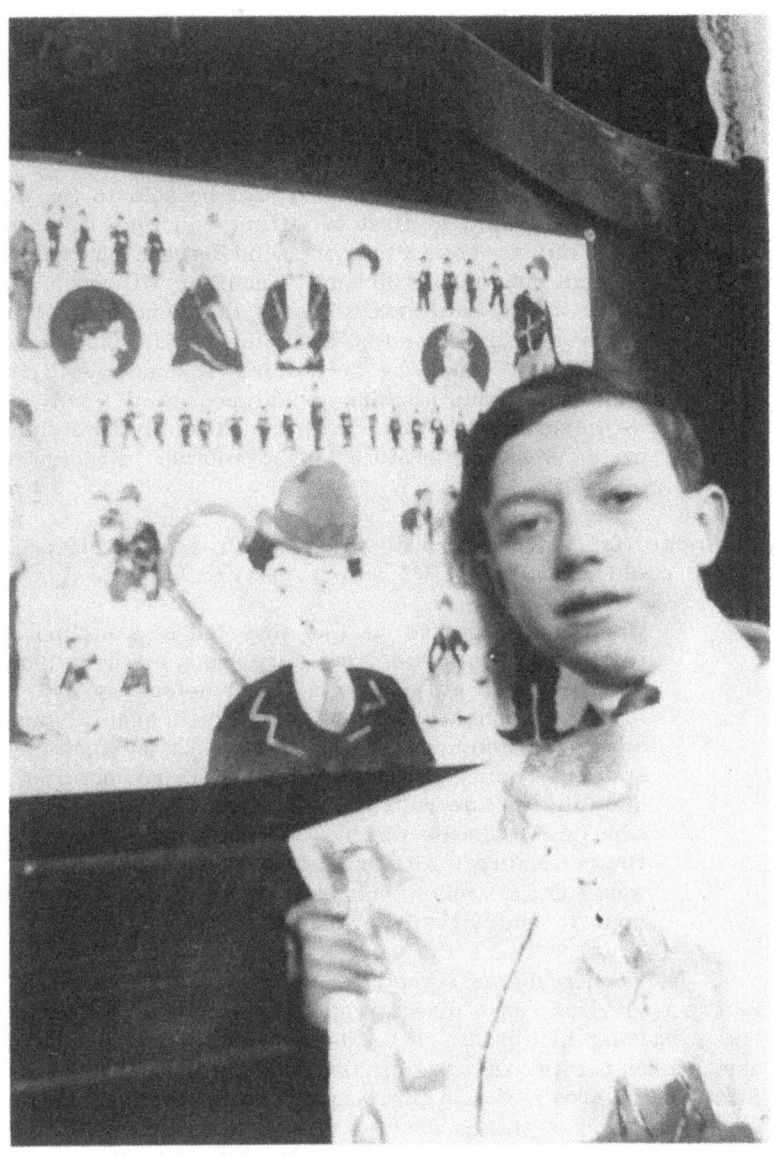

Florey had idolized Charlie Chaplin from the time he was a teen-ager, drawing caricatures of the comedian in Switzerland in 1916.

The two men enjoyed one another's company, and
Florey was free from contractual obligations; these factors,
combined with their long friendship and Chaplin's need for
assistance, caused the comedian to seek Florey's talents for
use in his picture.

> The following week ... he asked me to collaborate
> in the direction and in the production of his film
> as associate director.
> "You understand, don't you," he said to me.
> "I had thought at first of letting you take full con-
> trol, but my conception of each of these characters
> is such that we would surely conflict with each
> other if you had another one. However, I can't
> do everything myself, I am in nearly all the scenes,
> and I can't supervise everything at once. And then,
> there is all this machine technique. And finally,
> we have to work fast; it is important that we finish
> in ten weeks; therefore I need another 'director' to
> assist me."[66]

The opportunity to collaborate with Chaplin was an offer
Florey could not refuse.

> When Charlie asked me like that, all of a sudden,
> to be his collaborator, my surprise was such that I
> accepted with enthusiasm. I had before my eyes a
> sort of "flashback," and I saw myself again, young,
> at the beginning of the other war ... my feet in the
> snow, a twenty-sous coin clutched in my hand and
> standing in line with the other kids to "go see
> Charlie." Charlie was now offering me the oppor-
> tunity to direct with him; for several months, I
> was going to follow his preparatory efforts, from
> hour to hour, then work at his side.[67]

The contract was signed on April 24, 1946, engaging
Florey's services "as a director and/or associate director"
and promising him credit as the latter on a separate title
card on all prints, advertising, and publicity in the United
States and abroad.[68] Chaplin commemorated the partnership
by naming one of the characters Floray--which proved
ironic, since this was one of Chaplin's victims in the movie.
Florey was at that time in the front ranks of Hollywood directors, following the phenomenal popularity of <u>The Desert</u>

Song and God Is My Co-Pilot.69 For the first and only time Chaplin chose to work with an established filmmaker of reputation and importance; all his former and future associations were with individuals moving up the ladder of success, whose fame would come after their work with him. (These included Monta Bell, Harry d'Abbadie d'Arrast, A. Edward Sutherland and Jean de Limur on A Woman of Paris in 1923, and Robert Aldrich on Limelight in 1952.) The employment of Florey was indicative of an unspoken need for guidance, according to Jack Spears:

> Significantly, Chaplin's dependence upon capable assistants was greatest during his ventures into drama--A Woman of Paris, Monsieur Verdoux, and Limelight--a realm in which his talent was uncertain.70

For the next month, Florey worked with Chaplin on the final drafts of the script. Florey did not care for the story's political implications, his humorous style tending toward slapstick rather than black comedy. He wrote,

> The mood of the text sometimes seemed to me much too macabre; besides, there was much repetition, and the exposé of his theories was rather confused. Many little things which could have been shown on the screen were explained at length in sometimes awkward dialogue.

Florey, who from the outset was never under any misapprehension that Monsieur Verdoux would have the popularity of Chaplin's previous efforts, thought the story too solemn and sought to lighten it. But Florey noticed that Chaplin,

> during brief instants ... gives me the impression sometimes that "his heart is no longer in it," and that he forces himself to make people laugh. All this is felt in the cynical and disillusioned character of M. Verdoux.71

Florey made a number of alterations in the script, including the reappearing dressmaker's dummy and the last glass of rum, and succeeded in eliminating some of the more grisly murders. He was able to convince Chaplin to reduce his speeches and suggested the idea of the reporter's interview in prison in order to divide the final address into segments.

Florey wrote the continuity of Monsieur Verdoux himself. Concerned with obtaining the proper background,

> I did my best with what I had on hand to try to "Frenchify" the ghetto of The Great Dictator and to create a likely, or probable, French atmosphere. But these details didn't particularly interest Charlie....72

Aside from choosing Martha Raye and the performers for the roles of the girl, the detective, and Verdoux's real family, Chaplin left the entire casting of the picture to Florey. Not having made a movie in seven years, Chaplin was unfamiliar with Hollywood's character players, while Florey had worked with many of them, directing eleven features in the interval since the comedian's last screen effort. Florey also engaged Curt Courant from Warner Bros. for "artistic supervision."

Production began in May with Florey filming exteriors at Big Bear and Lake Arrowhead. Shooting lasted only twelve weeks, running through the early part of September; for Chaplin, this was record time. Florey, accustomed to much tighter schedules, doubtless helped push things along. The budget ended up at about $2 million, far in excess of what Florey was used to; he was constantly displeased with Chaplin's wasteful methods.

As soon as shooting with the star began, Florey found that Chaplin was "impossible to work with."73 "After more than a half-century in filmmaking, he is still unlettered in the mechanics of putting a motion picture together," wrote Spears.74 Florey's attempts to correct Chaplin's technical deficiencies were repulsed. "He would become angry that we could even have a doubt about his infallibility of judgment"; nonetheless, a few days later, Chaplin would order a retake, using the suggestions he had originally rejected, without ever admitting he had been wrong.

> Thus, "honor" was satisfied, and after all, as they say in English, "The King can do no wrong." It was a matter of "planting" the idea in the head of our "enfant terrible" and of letting it germinate in

1940-1950: Short-Term Contracts

him, until he could at last adopt it and bring it out as his own.[75]

Chaplin soon grew to resent his associate and any proposal he made. Being overruled by a studio was no new experience for Florey, but he found that having the same happen at the hands of a friend was a profoundly disillusioning experience.

While Florey was noted for running a jovial set, Chaplin was moody, giving constant instructions, many of which conflicted or made little sense. Detesting the filmmaking apparatus, Chaplin's methods were erratic; he would begin with the scenes of most interest to him, jumping from set to set, shooting out of continuity within the scenes.

> We film the scene once, ten times, thirty times.... After the thirty-fifth take Charlie says to me:

Chaplin with his associate director, Robert Florey, on the set of Monsieur Verdoux.

> "Robert, just once more, to be sure." We are
> "sure" around the fiftieth take. "Sure" at least
> for that day, but tomorrow after the showing, if
> Charlie isn't completely satisfied, we will start over
> again.

Chaplin would often rudely leave the set after his scenes were finished, leaving Florey and the other players to film the responses and reaction shots alone. Sometimes he would disappear for days or go to Catalina without advance notice.

> Often, Charlie gets into great rages which last only
> a few moments. Everything then took on exagger-
> ated proportions. If, at the showing, an insignifi-
> cant detail didn't satisfy him, he was off on his
> high horse. He fulminates. His film is ruined, de-
> stroyed, it's a real conspiracy. He has to do it all
> over, that's going to cost him an arm and a leg--
> all because a corner of the set seemed a little dark.
> And then the storm passes, he films a scene that
> pleases him, everything is better, he smiles, he is
> content, he is gracious, charming, enchanting, and
> what an enchanter. The suppliers whom he has
> abundantly bawled out are ready to forget every-
> thing, he is so amiable, so nice that you can't hold
> a grudge against him; and then, probably to obtain
> complete forgiveness, he begins to play for us one
> of his pantomimes, and everybody splits their sides
> laughing--everybody says "Dear old Charlie!"--
> and still later we return to the projection, Charlie
> is now in a good mood and the "dark corner of the
> set" doesn't seem to bad to him, after all, we won't
> have to do it over, everyone is pleased, at least
> until the next thunderbolt which will strike in five
> minutes or three days depending on the mood of the
> Master.[76]

In <u>Monsieur Verdoux</u> Chaplin's ignorance of sound techniques and cinematic values became painfully apparent. Florey commented:

> At times, I thought myself back again in the wonder-
> ful days of Keystone.... Chaplin knows what he's
> trying to obtain without however knowing how to ex-
> press it; he doesn't see with a photographic eye....

> Charlie despises technology, apparatus, cameras, sound effects, machines in general, and lights.... Charlie is the irreconcilable enemy of all that is photographic composition, daring camera angle shots.... All that is not immobile in long shot showing him from head to feet is for him "Hollywood 'chi-chi'...." "I am the unusual, I do not need unusual camera angles...."[77]

The result of Chaplin's preferred technique was to give Verdoux the old-fashioned visual appearance of an early talkie, filled with many uninterrupted long takes favoring Chaplin, who still believed "my feet speak as loudly as my face."[78] Close-ups were a particular problem; Chaplin would have them shot of himself but deny reaction shots to the other performers. His attitude toward technicians was a condescending one.

> "You will have a shadow on your face when you stop near the door," murmurs Curt Courant. "I laugh at your shadow," answers Charlie, "it's natural to have some shadow, after all. Let's go, let's start. Hurry! Hurry!" But he has changed his movement and now the silhouette of the microphone stands out clearly for several seconds on the wall of the background. It is pointed out to him. "It doesn't matter to me," he says. "They will think that it's a bird; let's go, hurry up, film!" And confusion reigns because Courant is changing one of the "spots" to avoid the shadow of the microphone. "Why are you changing again?" he asks, more and more nervous. "You annoy me with all your technical tricks. Come on, hurry up!"[79]

While his primitive style may have been tolerable for his silent work, Monsieur Verdoux, as a dialogue comedy of the late 1940s, required the application of more sophisticated, modern techniques, and Chaplin's stubbornness in clinging to outmoded ways did damage to the movie.

Despite Chaplin's determination to rebuke his assistants, Florey undoubtedly made some contributions to the filming of Monsieur Verdoux.[80] While the movie contains little of Chaplin's usual pathos, Florey's characteristic sensitivity is present. He turned the picture in a more realistic direction; he successfully argued against a fantasy epilogue showing Verdoux in heaven. The meeting of Chaplin and the girl, Marilyn Nash, dressed in typical private-eye garb, has a vague film noir ambiance that may reflect Florey's influence. Florey shot alone many sequences that did not contain Chaplin, as well as the pick-ups and location shots. While Chaplin was on Catalina for several days, Florey directed scenes of crowds and riots to indicate depression and unrest in Europe. His flair for composition and angles jarred with Chaplin's style, however, and most of the sequence was dropped in favor of awkward newsreels. One shot with a typical Florey touch does remain--an overhead angle zooming in on a businessman putting a gun to his head.

The second assistant director on Monsieur Verdoux had been Wheeler Dryden, who was generally despised by Chaplin. The child of one of his mother's dubious early marriages, Chaplin allowed Dryden to eke out a living over the years as a handyman or errand boy at his studio. According to Maurice Bessy, Chaplin especially enjoyed doling out bit parts to Dryden that required him to receive "kicks in the pants."[81] Although Dryden's tasks were too menial to have contributed to Verdoux or any other picture, Chaplin finally found a substantive use for him, one that startled Florey.

> I didn't suspect the little trick that our star-author-producer was preparing for me. It wasn't, in fact, until the presentation of Monsieur Verdoux at the Academy Award Theatre on Melrose, in Hollywood, that I saw on the credits my title of "associate director" preceded by another title granting a title identical to mine to Wheeler Dryden! Naturally, the fact of being "sandwiched" between Dryden and Chaplin minimized the importance of my functions.[82]

In fact, Chaplin had also tried, unsuccessfully, to convince the Directors Guild to allow him to place Dryden's name on the same card with Florey's.[83] For the French advertising, Chaplin utterly violated the agreement, listing Florey as only assistant director with Dryden. Chaplin further ordered that no publicity be given to Florey's work on the picture. Although many friends urged Florey to sue Chaplin to correct the billing, he preferred not to. The two never saw or spoke to one another after the last day of shooting in early September.

Monsieur Verdoux did very poorly at the box office and contributed to Chaplin's declining popularity. None of this affected Florey's career, however. He wrote in detail of his experiences working on Verdoux in his book, Hollywood D'Hier et D'Aujourd'Hui (in a chapter entitled, "Working with Charlot"), published in Paris in 1948. Four years later, he co-authored Monsieur Chaplin ou le rire dans le nuit ("Mr. Chaplin or the Laugh in the Night"), with Maurice Bessy. As Florey realized, "Chaplin has had enough of Charlie, whom he doesn't resemble anymore!"[84]

Tarzan and the Mermaids brought Florey under contract, after some months of idleness, to Sol Lesser to direct the sixth in that producer's series of Tarzan pictures. One of the most elaborate of Lesser's entries--and the last to star Johnny Weissmuller--Tarzan and the Mermaids offered Florey his first chance since 1930 to shoot a film entirely outside of the United States. However, this project was probably one of the low points of his career as far as the caliber of the movie is concerned, although it was more challenging than such low-grade "B" films as Lady Gangster or Two in a Taxi, with their twelve-day schedules. In its day, Tarzan and the Mermaids aroused special curiosity for featuring Linda Christian in a lead role; by the time of release, gossip columns were abuzz with rumors of her romance with Tyrone Power, who had been simultaneously filming Captain from Castile on a nearby location.

Tarzan and the Mermaids at various stages combines musical, fantasy, and adventure elements, with the accent on the latter. Perhaps the best moments come in the fantasy portions, especially in the opening reel as a strange aura is created with shots emphasizing skyward angles and a clanging, host-of-angels score by Dimitri Tiomkin. From there, however, the narrative deteriorates rapidly; Florey regarded the story as frivolous, to say the least. The acting is satisfactory (at best); only George Zucco seems entirely comfortable as an evil high priest. Indeed, the best performance is perhaps delivered by Cheetah, whose grimaces provide an appropriate commentary on the unfolding plot. Overall, Tarzan and the Mermaids is a mediocre picture, but the action and aquatic scenes are effective, winding up to an exciting climax that probably satisfied its audience, serving as passable juvenile fare.

The worst drawback of Tarzan and the Mermaids was

undoubtedly the introduction, for the first time in the series, of abundant music and singing. Unfortunately, the inane character played by the Mexican idol John Laurenz provides dreadful interludes of hokum made all the more unbearable by his infantile warbling. (The producer insisted on this role, even though the cast has visible difficulty concealing their embarrassment at Laurenz' performance.) On the other hand, Tiomkin tries to dominate the movie with an overpowering, other-worldly score that only tends to emphasize the story's weaknesses, drawing into sharp relief what too often should have been left underplayed.

Lesser decided on another first by sending the entire Tarzan crew to film entirely on location in Mexico. One month was spent selecting the locales to be utilized, finally settling chiefly on the Guerreo coast near Apaculco and the Aztec Pyramid of Teotihuacan, with interiors shot at the Churubusco studios of Mexico City. Because of the fantasy overtones of the story (still placed in Africa), these exteriors provide some added interest to Weissmuller's exploits; little attempt is made to conceal the Latin atmosphere. Florey was most proud of the interesting compositions he obtained for the diving sequence, perfectly timed and choreographed in a ballet-like performance. Variety wrote that Tarzan and the Mermaids had "some spectacular camera work, probably the best on any Tarzan film."[85] While at times all of the varying backgrounds contrast too much, occasionally failing to edit well, gradually one becomes accustomed to this effect; it even improves some scenes, such as the isolated confrontation between Zucco and Weissmuller and the latter's chase of Linda Christian's captors to the seacoast.

Familiar with Mexico from his travels in the 1930s, Florey was able to infuse Tarzan and the Mermaids with the best possible production values during the shooting in July and August of 1947. There were numerous aggravations, like the artistic notions of cameraman Gabriel Figueroa, who "made me wait four hours to get a close-up of Cheeta because he wanted three white clouds to lay exactly above each other in the background above the Pacific!"[86] These many months of location work proved exausting, especially to Florey, a diabetic; reduced to eating nothing but fruit, he lost thirty-one pounds. As he explained afterwards,

> The trouble ... is that a real jungle doesn't look

1940-1950: Short-Term Contracts

like a Hollywood jungle. It's all matted growth and mud, with malaria, mosquitos, scorpions, crocodiles and little tigers that jump at you. When we'd get back from location every day, even a big guy like Johnny Weissmuller was buckling at the knees.[87]

Rogues' Regiment returned Florey to Universal for one picture, sixteen years after the chaos of Frankenstein. This class-A production turned out to be the last feature both written and directed by Florey. Rogues' Regiment, a spy tale with elements of adventure mixed in, was grounded in fact: the disappearance of Martin Bormann in the last days of World War II and the worldwide search to apprehend the only member of Hitler's inner circle not found and tried for war crimes. The movie offered speculation on where Bormann might have gone, presenting a convincing portrayal of the actions and paranoia of a man fleeing the justice of the entire civilized globe. The plot marked a return to the topical thriller, a genre in which Florey had distinguished himself, although he had not directed a film of this type since Roger Touhy--Gangster.

Rogues' Regiment was Florey's last association with writer-producer Robert Buckner, with whom he had made The Desert Song and God Is My Co-Pilot at Warner Bros. The two had worked well as a team: Buckner operated smoothly within the studio and was a good writer of dialogue, while Florey contributed his talents as a visualist and originator of unusual scenarios. Buckner described their relationship this way:

> We struck it off from the start.... We overlapped in many ways, a pleasant meld of ideas, and I think our individual shares were almost inseparable in the final scripts: not always in the final film, of course, which is largely and rightly the director's. We never argued, except constructively, and we worked very fast. It was an ideal collaboration and I never experienced it as happily with anyone else.[88]

In 1947 Buckner left Warners to join Universal-International as part of their effort to become an "A" studio. In early November, he read a short article in Life magazine about the infiltration of the ranks of the post-war French Foreign Legion by former Nazis. Buckner believed that this offered a promising idea;[89] within days he had a story outline, which was approved on November 16, and he collaborated with Florey on the treatment, completed December 11. Buckner, aware of Florey's vast knowledge of French history and enthusiasm for Foreign Legion lore, correctly believed he would be of tremendous assistance in developing the plot.[90] Before the end of the month Florey was retained by Universal not only to complete the script (with Buckner), but to direct as well. Perhaps the studio was influenced by an argument Buckner had also put forward at Warners, that "we proved on Desert Song this combining of writer-producer-director from the ground up is the fastest, most satisfactory and efficient working plan that is possible."[91]

Unlike The Desert Song, where neither Buckner or Florey had received credit for their adaptation, the authors of Rogues' Regiment were credited, with Buckner also listed as producer and Florey as director. However--as was seemingly Universal's habit when employing Florey as a writer-director--his contributions to the script were minimized.[92] The final credits, which came out in May, listed Florey and Buckner as collaborating on the "original story," for which Florey had received no compensation; Buckner was listed as sole author of the script, although he believed Florey deserved equal credit with him.[93] Florey was distressed at this misrepresentation of their respective shares in the writing, but he went ahead with the project anyway. Shot on a forty-day schedule in April and May of 1948, the production was finished only a few days behind time and the cost did not exceed the $1.13 million budget.

Rogues' Regiment is a tale of muted heroism almost devoid of glamor. Ironically, the audience comes to know and understand the character modeled on Bormann, played by Stephen McNally, and those around him--Marta Toren, Vincent Price and Philip Ahn--better than the "star." Ostensibly the hero, Dick Powell is placed in an ambiguous position since he must join the very force in which the villain has found refuge. None of the characters is what he or she appears to be: everyone has adopted a mask or disguise of some sort, just as the Foreign Legion itself is made up of men with unknown pasts and assumed names. Powell, an American agent searching for McNally, has taken the role of a disillusioned soldier joining the Legion. Toren, a

1940-1950: Short-Term Contracts

French spy, masquerades as a singer in a nightclub. Price, a German and gunrunner from the Communists to the Vietnamese rebels, fronts as a Dutch antiques merchant. McNally pretends to be a former German private who, like Powell, knowing no other life than soldiering, joins the Legion. Ahn impersonates just another Vietnamese rebel, rather than their leader. All of this helps to allow for rather more complex characterizations than are typical for an espionage picture; for example, Price's real affection for Toren makes him a much more human individual than he would otherwise be. The cast etches their roles with flavor and conviction, although unfortunately Powell makes too much of his caustic, hard-boiled stereotype and is in rather a different key from the others.

Rogues' Regiment seeks to demythologize the legendary French Foreign Legion by presenting the facts of the contemporary Legion and its operations in French Indochina. Here are none of the beautiful uniforms or the despotic commanders of Beau Geste, nor are the Legionnaires fighting an obscure enemy of marauding Arabs, but rather Vietnamese--whom the audience come to know in the progress of the film--united in rebellion against French colonization. The men joining the Legion are not seeking honor; instead, they simply are ignorant of anything but fighting.

The Legion is desperate for enlistments because of the high toll of the Indochinese war. "If they can walk, sign them up," is the new motto of the movie's French colonel. The result is that the Saigon outpost has become a haven for German soldiers who either don't want--or are afraid--to return home. So many ex-Nazis have joined that this contingent of the Foreign Legion has become known as the "Fourth Reich" or "Rogues' Regiment." In portraying this situation, Florey once again showed his ability to devise a story from the news headlines (as he had done previously with Buckner on The Desert Song), for such was the true state of affairs in the Legion at the time. "The Legion's strength numbers upward of 25,000 men, more than 60 per cent of whom, according to the best estimates, are Germans." Two fifths of this fighting force was based in French Indochina. Perhaps Florey had heard the "grim joke that 'der Führer' and Martin Bormann themselves are sweating it out as buck privates in the anonymous ranks of the Legion."[94]

Rogues' Regiment is most interesting today as "one of the first films dealing with Vietnam," examining conditions as the Vietnamese faced France in 1948 (and, similarly, the United States two decades later).[95] The war is presented as a pointless one, Vietnamese and French ambushing one another, taking prisoners, and then being captured themselves in a cyclical struggle that drags on endlessly. The underlying story deals with the question of self-rule for the native people and the inevitable decline of colonial power within the country. A basic neutrality toward the Indochinese conflict is maintained in the narrative, with no attempt to resolve the clash between French and Vietnamese-- unlike the Arabs' final submission to colonial authority at the end of The Desert Song. However, there is generally more sympathy for the Vietnamese. For instance, the French are caricatured by a stuffy colonel who naively sees a world divided only between "The Internationale" and "La Marseillaise," refusing to understand the indigenous desire for independence.

In handling such a background, Florey faced many of the same problems he had met while writing and directing The Desert Song five years earlier. He was convinced that his native France was wrong to try to keep control of an empire, and he sympathized with the movements attempting to overthrow foreign domination. At the same time, he knew that in the Hollywood of 1947-48 no studio would produce a movie denouncing colonialism. Buckner was unconcerned with the issue, and Florey wisely kept to himself the fact that he had "a message."[96] He had to obscure this aspect of the story by making it an integral element of an otherwise traditional plot. The same principal had been tried in Desert Song: Florey had enveloped its viewpoint in a romantic musical adventure, yet still it had run into censorship. So for Rogues' Regiment Florey placed the colonial conflict firmly in the background, keeping it secondary to the main plot of spies and Nazi-hunting.

As in Desert Song, he aligned the forces of colonialism alongside those of Fascism, showing the Foreign Legion in Vietnam accepting former German soldiers into their ranks. Many of these new recruits are guilty of war crimes and are running away from the executions and imprisonments they would have merited from the Nuremberg tribunals. None of the soldiers of any nationality in the Legion desire to fight the Vietnamese in the film; they are mere mercenaries obeying orders. The only ones eager to fight are the French officers, who represent the outmoded thinking of a bygone age.

Thus, when the Legionnaires and the Vietnamese come to battle, Florey cleverly places the viewer in a situation where he cannot customarily root for the side he feels most akin to, for it includes the Nazis. Making them the opponents of the Vietnamese casts the latter in a new and more positive light. Powell is carefully kept from reflecting on the Vietnamese or swinging the audience's sympathy toward the Legion; he is a transitory member, enlisting only in his attempt to uncover McNally. Powell's goal is to uncover Nazis, not to aid France's colonial aims. When his job is done, he leaves Vietnam to return to the United States; Toren is seen with him, intimating that both French and Americans would do well to follow their example.

In fact, next to Powell, the most admirable character in Rogues' Regiment is the leader of the Vietnamese rebels, played by Philip Ahn (an actor Florey admired and whose services he utilized on every possible occasion). Ahn's concern is purely for his fellow countrymen and their cause; he lives by his own code, outwits the French, and leads his people to victory. He also avoids a bloodbath confrontation with the French by working to make Vietnam seem unworthy of their efforts and hoping for a negotiated settlement. Ironically, liberals apparently did not appreciate this subtext, presumably because it was placed in the context of an action thriller rather than an openly political film. The New Republic wrote condescendingly of Rogues' Regiment: "For a two-fisted melodrama, which is all it is, it is overloaded with historical allusion and political significance."[97]

Florey also resisted the temptation to link the rebels with Communist influence. Ahn, while accepting Price's aid pragmatically, refuses to follow the strategy that is suggested along with it. The Vietnamese are portrayed as willing to use whatever partners will help them win independence, while taking orders from no one. Although the fact of Communist presence is explicitly mentioned, it is in such a way as to be minimized in significance. The attitude taken toward this angle by the studio was the same. A publicity man suggested that Hedda Hopper might devote a full column to Rogues'

Philip Ahn (center) as the leader of the Vietnamese rebels, and Vincent Price, a communist gun-runner, in Rogues' Regiment.

Regiment if producer Buckner gave her an interview asserting that the movie illustrates Communist influence behind the uprisings in French Indochina. Beside the proposal, handwritten, was the comment of studio executive Al Horwitz: "Good to stay away from."98 Apparently there was no pressure to turn Rogues' Regiment into an anti-Communist statement.

The Oriental setting of Rogues' Regiment gave Florey a chance to apply some of what he had seen and learned during his visits to Asia. As usual, he managed to create a very authentic and fascinating atmosphere, adding substantially to the visual interest of the picture. The art director was Florey's long time friend and associate, Gabriel Scognamillo. Florey's feeling for the Orient is especially evident in the home of Price, covered with a mass of lush vines and creepers, and in the carefully created and com-

1940-1950: Short-Term Contracts

pletely convincing set-up of the ambush of the Legionnaires by the Vietnamese, shot in the swamps of Baldwin Lake.

The visual style of Rogues' Regiment owed something both to Florey's conversion to realism and his expressionist background. The movie begins in a documentary-like fashion, recreating the cremation of Hitler and Eva Braun. It goes on to a recapitulation of the Nuremberg trials, complete with newsreel footage and narrator, before leading into the ongoing search for McNally. While the camera is used in a generally functional manner, it is at the same time creative and effective. The first scenes of McNally's entry into Saigon, his meeting with Price and the tattoo artist, are photographed almost entirely in dark medium shots or close-ups, with few long shots. This gives the effect of confined, oppressive space, conveying the mood of the escaped Nazi's desperation. Not until McNally's emergence into the bar where Toren sings does the tension subside, with the space becoming light and opening up into frequent long shots.

Florey's skill with mood and atmosphere is revealed in this shot of Dick Powell and Philip Ahn in Rogues' Regiment, with the narrow backstreets of Saigon creating a feeling of enclosed space and danger for the Legionnaire.

But during the battle in the jungle, the foliage and shadows bring back the feeling of confinement, leading up to McNally's murder of his old comrade, Henry Rowland, another ex-Nazi in the Legion.

    The heavy darkness resumes again in the final scenes in Price's house, prior to his murder. There are several well-photographed chases through the dank, eerie streets of Saigon. The final fist fight between McNally and Powell has some of the ambiance customarily associated with film noir (such as dark lighting and enclosed spaces), overtones of which have appeared throughout. The fight exposes the physical clumsiness of both men, removing any aura of heroism from Powell's character; he is simply a tough-guy who happens to be on the right side. It is only luck, not superior brains or brawn, that enables Powell to capture McNally so he can be taken to Nuremberg for trial.

    Rogues' Regiment is not only an exciting picture of its genre, but one that grows in fascination due to its multifaceted plot. Florey was satisfied with his efforts; after seven months on the project, he felt it had come out well. The film demonstrates the type of story and style he preferred when he had adequate production time and was not interfered with or assigned a script. The movie opened in November 1948 to ordinary business, due largely to the generally negative reaction to films reminiscent of World War II. Also, Powell refused to give publicity of Rogues' Regiment because two of his other pictures were in release at the same time, and he believed his efforts would only mean competing with himself. Robert Buckner remembered that the movie's profit-making potential was also harmed when Rogues' Regiment was "banned in France and in all French possessions because they thought their Foreign Legion was not respectfully presented."[99] Apparently the French perceived the statement Florey was making on colonialism, a realization that seemed to pass by most American audiences.

    Rogues' Regiment had effects on Florey's future that he could never have guessed. His knowledge of the Foreign Legion caused him to be asked to direct Outpost in Morocco later the same year. More importantly, the acquaintance with Dick Powell and Powell's admiration for Florey's work would lead to a new period in the director's career. Four years later, when Florey was just starting in television,

1940-1950: Short-Term Contracts

Powell, Charles Boyer, and David Niven were putting together Four Star Playhouse and hired Florey as their first director.

Outpost in Morocco was another Foreign Legion film, but of a wholly different nature from Rogues' Regiment. Instead of a realistic view of the contemporary Legion, Outpost in Morocco offers a romanticized period tale, although not quite as mythical in its overtones as Beau Geste. Outpost in Morocco is an archetypal adventure film, a satisfactory reworking of the formula, if neither memorable or distinctive. Many of the plot elements lack originality, and the script, while maintaining interest, is marred by some unlikely incidents, lapses in causality, and several underdeveloped supporting characters. However, these disadvantages are overcome by excellent pacing as the plot steadily mounts in tension and is enhanced by an effective musical score (which perhaps asserts itself too continuously).

Most impressive was the constant intercutting of footage shot in Morocco by Phil Rosen, using the actual Foreign Legion. These "account for some spectacle values that are rarely achieved these days in Hollywood because of enormous production costs."[100] Owing to the authentic desert locations used as background and the impressive long shots, Outpost in Morocco acquires a vastness in scope, almost an epic dimension. Aware of the potential perils of the final editing smoothly cutting together exterior scenes shot in Morocco with those taken in Southern California and the studio, Florey and cameraman Lucien Andriot managed to keep the differences minimized. This may have constrained Florey's stylistic freedom, although his habit of continuity planning was probably essential in this case. Such a method of assembling a movie was not new to co-author and producer Joseph Ermolieff, who in Europe during the mid 1930s shot battle scenes for a motion picture of Jules Verne's novel Michael Strogoff and then, between 1937-43, produced German, French, American, and Mexican versions; each utilized the same original footage but had new dialogue sequences shot separately with various casts in the different countries.

Florey directed all of the cast scenes and process shots for Outpost in Morocco in thirty-six days during August and September 1948. Although this was another "A" production, some of the set decorations were disappointingly

Florey's collection of French military artifacts proved useful in adding to the decor of Outpost in Morocco, with John Litel, George Raft, and Akim Tamiroff.

plain, especially those not noticeably enhanced by military items from Florey's collection. In a number of respects, Outpost in Morocco had much in common with his previous films, particularly The Desert Song and Till We Meet Again. The Legionnaires are not the tough stoics of Rogues' Regiment but vulnerable, humanized individuals--most notably Akim Tamiroff in a vivid supporting characterization. The story's two key ingredients are action and romance, pairing two ill-fated lovers, Legion officer George Raft and Marie Windsor, who is convincing as the daughter of a local Emir. Unfortunately, theirs is also a less than credible match, due to the dialogue and situations they were given. Windsor is trapped between affection for Raft and her own heritage (her ambitious and ruthless father leads an uprising against the French). She is killed while attempting to stop the attack by an order Raft must give under fire to save his own men. Again, war seems useless at the end; the call to patriotism has only torn apart the two lovers and, in this instance, doomed them, souring the military victory.

After wanting to make a movie of this type for so long, Florey was well satisfied with the final product, and it was one of his personal favorites. Outpost in Morocco was an independent venture sponsored by two of his old friends: Sam Bischoff, the executive producer, and Ermolieff, whom Florey had known since 1921 when serving him on Tempête in France. The product of a one-time company, Moroccan Pictures, Outpost in Morocco was released by United Artists in 1949 to brisk business at the box office.

The Crooked Way forcefully etches the post-World War II confusion, cynicism and discouragement that were the hallmarks of film noir. John Payne is cast as a sympathetic, anonymous veteran, the victim of a shrapnel-induced head wound that has resulted in complete and permanent amnesia--lending a certain nightmarish quality to the series of terrifying experiences he will undergo. The movie opens as he departs a mental hospital to search for his background and adjust to civilian life on his own. Once again Florey was dealing with the type of psychological melodrama of human disintegration he had handled so brilliantly in The Florentine Dagger, Dangerous to Know, The Face Behind the Mask, and even in the script of Frankenstein.

Arriving in Los Angeles, Payne is accosted by police and gangsters alike; apparently everyone knows who he is-- or was--but himself. Naturally, his loss of memory is disbelieved, so Payne goes along with all he encounters in an effort to find out what has caused his insidious reputation. Discovering that he was a wife-beater and mobster-turned-state's evidence, he meets the vengeful partner he betrayed, Sonny Tufts. He also encounters his ex-wife, Ellen Drew, now the head of a gambling ring. Unlike Payne's complex, shifting persona, both of these characters are rather stereotypical, with Drew particularly ambiguous as she begins to believe in his reformation but is intimidated by the criminals around her.

The Crooked Way is at its most vivid in the utterly convincing depiction of a cold-blooded underworld. The picture was remarkable at the time for its brutality, with such violent beatings and gunfights that it still remains grueling today. Indeed, there was more overall viciousness evident in this movie and its characters--especially Tufts' portrait of a cruel gangster without any redeeming features--than in any previous Florey effort. Not since Roger Touhy --Gangster had he handled a story of mobsters, and a number of critics complained that The Crooked Way went too far.

Violence was hardly the main weakness of the picture: despite the absorbing premise, its originality was not sustained, with the plot relying more on cliches as it progressed toward a conclusion. "While containing plenty of action, it fails to generate the necessary suspense...."[101] Another factor making this more noticeable was the movie's difference from many of Florey's program thrillers. Although not quite a prestige picture, and made in less than a month (in December 1948), The Crooked Way was meticulously done in the "A" style. It was palpably more involved than the usual genre piece, often loosening its deliberate pace to indulge in details and character vignettes, including such traits as habits and gestures. The cast was a rather large one, allowing each individual to develop and reveal carefully delineated personal quirks--and usually be gunned down as the drama drew to a close.

Probably the most remarkable aspect of The Crooked Way was its combination of realism and expressionism into a compatible style, a tendency already exhibited in Rogues' Regiment. Now, with an urban story, Florey relied heavily on location photography in and around Los Angeles. Much of this was shot at night, resulting in a new stylization that emphasized the disorienting confusion of such a milieu, with its myriad of bright signs flashing against the black night. These contrasts of light and shade were maintained in the interiors as well, relying on low-key expressionist photography and generally avoiding the bizarre angles that had appeared in so much of Florey's other thriller work. But the compositions were always beautifully and artistically lit, with the shadows conveying the dark, uncertain areas of Payne's mind and the cruelties of the world he is thrust into.

The Crooked Way is nevertheless not an entirely

1940-1950: Short-Term Contracts

Location photography at night created the effect of noir realism for The Crooked Way, with John Payne.

satisfactory movie and seems to have failed to fulfill some of its potential. While the photography, atmosphere, and often the acting, are exceptional throughout, there are disturbing gaps in the storyline. The motivations of Payne and especially Drew are not always clear, with little attempt to clarify them, and the plot eventually boils down to a standard "cops and robbers" confrontation.[102] This is doubly disappointing since The Crooked Way is the sort of character study of disturbed personalities that Florey often did so well; it should have offered an even greater opportunity for the exercise of his unique talents. Curiously, despite his many innovative years laboring with an expressionistic style in the thriller form, this is his only completely noir feature, at least during the height of the cycle; most of his similar work was in 1930s "B" movies or 1950s television.

Johnny One-Eye followed The Crooked Way as the second film Florey directed while under contract to Benedict Bogeaus, an independent producer embarking on his most ambitious movies to date and releasing through United Artists.

Both films were medium-budget variations on the gangster formula, with scripts authored by Richard H. Landau. Florey had no desire to return to genre pictures, but with production rapidly waning, he had little choice other than to accept what was offered, particularly since he was not affiliated with any studio.

Johnny One-Eye was, however, more conventional than its predecessor; based on a Damon Runyon story, it tells of a little girl, her dog (the title character), and the aging mobster (Pat O'Brien) who makes a redemptive sacrifice for them. It was shot in July and August 1949 and, like The Crooked Way, included extensive location work, this time in New York City. The location cameraman was William Miller, while Lucien Andriot handled the studio photography.

The Vicious Years (retitled The Gangster We Made for its release in Great Britain) was the last movie Robert Florey directed, an independent production for Anson Bond's Emerald Films. It was shot in November 1949 in twelve days on a budget of about $150,000. But despite the speed and cast of unknowns with which it was made, the film earned excellent reviews and much acclaim. Set in post-war Italy, The Vicious Years was favorably compared with the neorealist films coming from that country. "If you did not know it was filmed on a Hollywood sound stage, you might think it came from a Rossellini or a De Sica, so superb is its shock realism."[103] Unfortunately, shortly after its premier, the distributor, Film Classics, folded, and the production reverted to Bond. He had trouble finding a company to release a picture with such uncertain commercial prospects and eventually settled for only limited distribution through Monogram. One result of The Vicious Years was that, despite its warm critical reception, most of the offers Florey subsequently received were from small independents.

Adventures of Captain Fabian was the last theatrical movie Florey worked on, one which kept him employed-- if often frustrated--through much of 1950. The project was the result of a short-lived association between Errol Flynn, star and author of the script, and producer William Marshall, a sometime singer, actor, promoter, and husband of co-star Micheline Presle. An aspiring director with no previous experience, Marshall engaged Florey initially as

1940-1950: Short-Term Contracts

co-director, then as full director of a separate French version, with Marshall to handle the subsequent English adaptation. However, there were difficulties with the French government and film guilds in obtaining permission for American citizens, such as Florey and the principal performers, to work in France. These were followed by protracted contractual difficulties between the financiers on both sides of the Atlantic, causing long delays through the late spring and early summer. Finally, it was decided to make just one picture, in English, and Marshall at the very last moment managed to supersede Florey and take the directorial reins for himself.

Nonetheless, because of Marshall's lack of experience (in subsequent years he directed only two other pictures), Florey was kept on as an uncredited directorial consultant. This position enabled Marshall to take advantage of Florey's expertise, or ignore him. Florey accepted this arrangement with equanimity, a reaction easier to understand considering that he was already in France, the original contract having included an expenses-paid trip for himself and his wife. That had been the main factor in convincing him to take the job; he never had any illusions about the potboiler nature of the script.

Despite the role he was given, Florey made some contributions to Adventures of Captain Fabian. Old friends, like actors Victor Francen and Jim Gerald and set designer Eugéne Lourié, were brought into the production. Errol Flynn's dissipated behavior was an occasional problem for Florey, although the actor took a liking to him; it was fifteen years since Florey had directed Flynn in his first American speaking role in Don't Bet on Blondes. At one time the actor even asked Florey to be best man at his forthcoming wedding to Patrice Wymore, an invitation Florey managed to evade. Florey was on the set every day during production, from August to October, on location at the Villefrance harbor in Nice and at La Victorine, Billancourt, and Boulogne studios. A few shots typical of Florey's style are recognizable here and there, and he was allowed to direct most of the final reel of the dockside melee.

Upon its release the following year by Republic Pictures, Adventures of Captain Fabian received mediocre reviews; one problem was that Flynn's presence and the title led to expectations of an adventure film, when in truth the movie was a "woman's" melodrama, although Micheline Presle did not have the stature and skill to make it her vehicle. Florey summed it up as "an unfortunate undertaking for all --I wasted six months on this project."[104]

The decade of the 1940s had more twists and surprises and the fewest precedents of any period in Florey's career. At last he was able to work on the films for which he was best suited. After Two in a Taxi, all of his stories were dramatic ones. Most were still thrillers, whether of the gangster, spy, or horror variety. But there were new types as well: a social-realist drama (The Vicious Years); war movies, as the times might lead one to expect; and most surprising, some modern adventure films (The Desert Song, Tarzan and the Mermaids, Rogues' Regiment, Outpost in Morocco--along with work on the script of The Adventures of Don Juan), a genre he had never handled before.

It is hard to overestimate the impact of World War II on Florey's career. The loss of continental markets meant a decline in Hollywood production; opportunities for employment became scarce and led to a series of short-term contracts from cautious studios. His personal concern over events in Europe impelled him to assist artists who had fled fascism, helping them to settle and find a place in the American movie industry. The world situation manifested itself in his films early, especially since his sentiments had been actively interventionist at least as early as 1939. It was then he wrote the unproduced scenarios for Destination Unknown, with Nick Carter in China following a year later. But these stories were not fashionable at the time, and instead Florey had to be content with fifth column spy tales such as Meet Boston Blackie and Dangerously They Live. In between making these, he had volunteered for film-related military service (on June 13, 1941), an offer that was declined. His primary contribution to the war effort would come through The Desert Song, Man from Frisco, and especially God Is My Co-Pilot. But even with the end of the conflict, he did not lose interest in its aftereffects, warning of lingering fascism (Rogues' Regiment) and the dangers facing an orphan generation growing up in the rubble of postwar Italy (The Vicious Years). Florey was pleased to make these pictures relating to the war and regarded several as among his best work.

1940-1950: Short-Term Contracts

The 1940s undoubtedly marked the peak of Florey's commercial success. The biggest and most prestigious productions he made were the trilogy with Robert Buckner as producer--<u>The Desert Song</u>, <u>God Is My Co-Pilot</u>, and <u>Rogues' Regiment</u>--the first and last of which they co-authored. <u>Desert Song</u> was the most popular film Florey had written since <u>Frankenstein</u>. While the first two with Buckner were his top-grossing movies of the decade, just as artistic, if not more so, was the pair with Peter Lorre: <u>The Face Behind the Mask</u> and <u>The Beast with Five Fingers</u>.

Although Florey had begun the 1940s by directing some of the best of all his "B" pictures, two years later he graduated at last to the rank of "A" class productions, leaving low budgets for good. But despite having predominantly top-budget projects, he continued to be plagued by bad luck; the delays in releasing <u>The Desert Song</u> and <u>Roger Touhy--Gangster</u> (neither of which was his fault) probably cost him long-term contracts. When Florey returned to Warner Bros., the studio did not keep him on prestigious assignments, despite the twin successes of <u>The Desert Song</u> and <u>God Is My Co-Pilot</u>. Instead he was handed oddities like <u>Danger Signal</u> and <u>The Beast with Five Fingers</u>, which he might have enjoyed in his youth but failed to appreciate now.

With larger budgets, Florey's style became more impersonal, less unusual and noticeable. He became more interested in quality acting than cinematic experimentation. This tendency was compounded by his developing interest in techniques of realism, shown in <u>Roger Touhy--Gangster</u> and also to varying degrees in several subsequent motion pictures. Expressionism could still be discerned in his thrillers, though in a much smoother, less ostentatious, more sophisticated form, as exemplified by <u>The Beast with Five Fingers</u>. He had become a director capable of a variety of styles, able to choose and utilize the one most appropriate; gone were the days when content seemed to be of less significance than technique, as occasionally was the case in his 1930s films directed on long-term contracts.

Coincident with the peak of Florey's box-office success, the seeds of his commercial decline were already becoming apparent. This could be seen in his tendency to wander from studio to studio, from Columbia to Warners to Twentieth

Century-Fox to Republic and back to Warners. After five contracts for eleven pictures in six years, he unfortunately severed his relations with the big studios in 1946. The latter half of the decade was spent as an independent, working on eight movies for seven different producers. The simultaneous collapse of the studio system made the downward spiral of Florey's own career inevitable. This is not to say his talents diminished, only the number of opportunities to exercise them. However, this independence did allow for the collaboration on Monsieur Verdoux which, along with Florey's authorship of Frankenstein, has won him the most fame.

NOTES

1. Karl Decker, "Why and How the Mona Lisa Was Stolen," Saturday Evening Post, June 25, 1932, pp. 14-15, 89-92.
2. Robert Florey, letter to James Curtis, September 28, 1975.
3. Calvin Thomas Beck, Heroes of the Horrors (New York: Macmillan, 1975), pp. 204-207; Doug McClelland, The Golden Age of "B" Movies (Nashville: Charter House, 1978), pp. 93-95; Don Miller, "The American 'B' Film," Focus on Film, No. 5 (September-October 1970), pp. 31-32.
4. "Notes," in I. Von Cube, The Face Behind the Mask, Third Draft Continuity, September 20, 1940, Florey collection.
5. Robert Florey, Hollywood D'Hier et D'Aujourd'Hui (Paris: Editions Prisma, 1948), p. 198.
6. Don Miller, "B" Movies (New York: Curtis, 1973), p. 177.
7. Malvin Wald, interview with the author, June 27, 1985.
8. Ibid.
9. Variety, April 15, 1942.
10. George Morris, John Garfield (New York: Jove, 1977), pp. 81-82.
11. Miller, "B" Movies, p. 267.
12. Allen L. Woll. The Hollywood Musical Goes to War (Chicago: Nelson-Hall, 1983), p. 76.
13. "Air-Conditioned Desert," Newsweek, 22 (December 27, 1943):82.
14. Woll, p. 77.
15. Dorothy Jones and Larry Williams, Office of War

Information Bureau of Motion Pictures, Hollywood Office, Film Analysis Section Feature Viewing, December 21, 1942, MPD Overseas Branch, Box 3515, RG 208, National Archives.
16. Robert Buckner, letter to Nelson Poynter (Bureau of Motion Pictures), March 3, 1943, Office of War Information file, Jack Warner collection, University of Southern California Special Collections Library.
17. Ulric Bell to Nelson Poynter, Office of War Information Memorandum, March 5, 1943; Ulric Bell, memo to Watterson Rothacker (Overseas Branch, Motion Picture Bureau), March 5, 1943. Office of War Information, MPD Overseas Branch, Box 3515, RG 208, National Archives.
18. Robert Schless to J.L. Warner, Vitagraph inter-office communication, February 7, 1944; unsigned reply (presumably from Jack Warner), letter to Robert Schless, February 10, 1944. Desert Song (1943) Story File, Box D-13 #3, Warner Bros. collection, University of Southern California Special Collections Library.
19. Watterson Rothacker (Office of Censorship, Los Angeles Board of Review), letter to Steve Trilling, August 12, 1944, Desert Song (1943) story file, Box D-13 #3, Warner Bros. collection.
20. Motion Picture Herald, March 25, 1944, p. 49; "'Song' Hits High," The Hollywood Reporter, November 24, 1944.
21. Robert Florey in Carlos Clarens, Crime Movies (New York: W.W. Norton, 1980), p. 181.
22. Florey, Hollywood D'Hier et D'Aujourd'Hui, p. 201.
23. Robert Florey, letter to Carlos Clarens, November 13, 1976.
24. Florey, Hollywood D'Hier et D'Aujourd'Hui, p. 201.
25. Ibid.
26. Ibid., p. 202.
27. Manny Farber, "Three New Ones," New Republic, 8 (July 3, 1944):16.
28. Clarens, p. 181.
29. "Anyway, Roger Touhy [Film Version] Again Gets a Sensational Press," unidentified newspaper clipping, July 14, 1943, Florey collection.
30. Otis L. Guernsey, Jr., New York Herald-Tribune, June 5, 1944.
31. Florey, Hollywood D'Hier et D'Aujourd'Hui, p. 202.

32. Clarens, p. 181.
33. Florey, Hollywood D'Hier et D'Aujourd'Hui, p. 202.
34. Ibid.
35. Clarens, p. 183.
36. Alton Cook, New York World Telegram, June 3, 1944.
37. Variety, May 21, 1944, p. 10.
38. Clarens, p. 183.
39. "'Touhy--Gangster' Welcome Return to Action Drama," Hollywood Reporter (n.d.), loose clipping, Florey collection.
40. Time, 43 (June 19, 1944):96.
41. Daily Variety (n.d.), loose clipping, Florey collection.
42. Eileen Creelman, "The New Movie," New York Sun, June 5, 1944, p. 22.
43. Mark S. Foster, letters to the author, February 25, 1985 and July 8, 1985. Dr. Foster is at work on a forthcoming biography of Henry Kaiser.
44. Florey, Hollywood D'Hier et D'Aujourd'Hui, p. 204.
45. Robert Buckner, letter to the author, July 19, 1984.
46. "And Warner Bros., Navigator," Newsweek, 25 (April 2, 1945):78.
47. "'God Is My Co-Pilot' ... Powerful Air-War Pic," Box Office Digest, 16 (February 28, 1945).
48. "And Warner Bros., Navigator," p. 78.
49. Motion Picture Herald (n.d.), loose clipping, Florey collection; The Hollywood Reporter, June 6, 1945; "The Year's Ten Most Popular Motion Pictures," Photoplay Certificate Award Program, 1945; "17 War Films Among the Top 60 Shown in 1942-45 to GIs," Variety (n.d.), loose clipping, Florey collection; Jack Spears, Hollywood: The Golden Era (New York: A.S. Barnes, 1971), p. 355.
50. Robert Buckner to J.L. Warner, inter-office communication, April 8, 1944, Robert Buckner 1944 file in Steve Trilling files, Box 3, Jack Warner collection.
51. Robert Florey, letter to Ray Cabana, February 16, 1979, Florey collection.
52. T.C. Wright to Hansen, Luecker and William Jacobs, inter-office communication, December 11, 1945, The Beast with Five Fingers file, Warner Bros. collection.
53. Bill McGann to T.C. Wright, inter-office communication, January 3, 1946, The Beast with Five Fingers file, Warner Bros. collection.
54. Variety, December 25, 1946.
55. Contrary to the claims of Luis Buñuel and some of his

partisans, the Spanish director made no contributions of any sort to The Beast with Five Fingers. Although it is true that he was employed for a time in the Warner Bros. dubbing department (July 8, 1944, to November 10, 1945), Buñuel had left the studio by the time shooting on Beast began. The Warner archives at the University of Southern California, Special Collections Library, indicate what Buñuel's activities were--and working on Beast was not among them--as well as the absence of his name from among those associated with Beast. The movie was intended for Florey from the beginning; no other director was ever considered.

Buñuel's statement in his autobiography (Buñuel, My Last Sigh, translated by Abigail Israel [New York: Alfred A. Knopf, 1983], p. 189), "At [Florey's] suggestion, I thought up a scene that shows the beast, a living hand, moving through a library," is belied in every stage by the facts. First, Florey had only met Buñuel once, briefly, many years earlier and was hardly impressed with his films. Second, Buñuel worked only as a dubbing producer and was never in the scenario department. Third, the scene Buñuel described was not original with him or even the screenwriter of Beast, Curt Siodmak, but was already included in William Fryer Harvey's short story on which the picture was based. Indeed, the early outline for the visualization of Harvey's ideas for the "beast's" movements in the movie was written by Florey, as his hand-typed drafts attests; these can still be found in his own and the Warner Bros. collection. Florey's long involvement with expressionism and previous handling of surrealistic imagery--from his avant-garde films through his efforts in The Florentine Dagger and the horror genre to such scripts of his own as Frankenstein, Monsieur de Paris, and The Broken Heart Cafe--indicate that he was hardly in need of assistance in conjuring and handling the bizarre elements of The Beast with Five Fingers.

56. Paul Hammond, Marvelous Méliès (New York: St. Martin's, 1975), p. 101.
57. Stephen D. Youngkin, James Bigwood, and Raymond G. Cabana, Jr., The Films of Peter Lorre (Secaucus, N.J.: Citadel, 1982), p. 190.

58. Part of this scene was deleted from the release version of The Beast with Five Fingers. On January 14, 1946, a number of shots were added to page 120 of the script which have a similarity to some of the trick photography used in Florey's avant-garde films, particularly The Loves of Zero, as well as a scene in the Astoria short, Lillian Roth and Her Piano Boys. First, there were to be double and triple exposures of the piano keyboard over Peter Lorre's face, with an enormous hand filling the screen. Second, the camera was to be used as if it were the keyboard, a huge silhouetted hand playing over the lens. Third, from a side distorted angle, the hand and keyboard were to change proportion drastically, one enlarging while the other became minuscule and then vice-versa. Fourth, zooming in to a large close-up of Lorre, the hand was to seem to continue playing in a double exposure over his face, trying to strangle him. Fifth, the piano was to seem to rise toward the balcony on which Lorre stood, filling the screen, before returning to normal size.
59. Time, 49 (January 13, 1947):100.
60. Variety, December 25, 1946.
61. Robert Florey, letter to Al Taylor (n.d.), Florey collection.
62. Ibid.
63. Film Daily (n.d.), loose clipping, The Beast with Five Fingers file, Warner Bros. collection.
64. George H. Jackson, Los Angeles Herald-Express, February 20, 1947.
65. Florey, Hollywood D'Hier et D'Aujourd'Hui, pp. 336-337.
66. Ibid., p. 337.
67. Ibid., pp. 337-338.
68. Contract between Robert Florey and Chaplin Studios Inc., April 24, 1946, p. 1, Florey collection. Reprinted in "En attendant Verdoux," Ecran, July 1972, p. 14.
69. Box Office Digest (n.d.), p. 13, Florey collection.
70. Spears, p. 226.
71. Florey, Hollywood D'Hier et D'Aujourd'Hui, p. 349, 343.
72. Ibid., p. 349.
73. Robert Florey, interview with the author, January 30, 1979.
74. Spears, p. 227.
75. Florey, Hollywood D'Hier et D'Aujourd'Hui, p. 347.

1940-1950: Short-Term Contracts

76. Ibid., pp. 345, 347.
77. Ibid., pp. 339, 343, 346.
78. Florey interview.
79. Florey, Hollywood D'Hier et D'Aujourd'Hui, pp. 356-357.
80. Spears, p. 248. The presence of Martha Raye, whom Florey had directed nine years earlier in one of her first hit pictures, Mountain Music, gave him an ally in the effort to lighten Monsieur Verdoux. The most amusing scenes in the movie come as Verdoux begins to lose control, with Raye frustrating all his attempts to murder her. Although Chaplin had written her role in Monsieur Verdoux with Raye in mind, he would later downplay her importance, commenting that "her performance was in a different key from the rest of the film." (Charles Chaplin, My Life in Pictures [New York: Grosset and Dunlap, 1975], p. 290.)
81. Maurice Bessy, Les Passagers du souvenir (Paris: Editions Albin Michel, 1977), p. 273.
82. Florey, Hollywood D'Hier et D'Aujourd'Hui, p. 338.
83. Directors Guild, inter-office correspondence with Robert Florey, October 19, 1946, Florey collection.
84. Florey, Hollywood D'Hier et D'Aujourd'Hui, p. 357.
85. Variety, March 24, 1948.
86. Robert Florey, letter to Jack Spears, August 28, 1968.
87. Robert Florey in unidentified newspaper clipping (n.d.), Florey collection.
88. Buckner, letter to the author, July 19, 1984.
89. Robert Sherrod, "Foreign Legion," Life, 23 (November 10, 1947):8-14.
90. Robert Buckner, letter to the author, August 28, 1984.
91. Robert Buckner to Steve Trilling, inter-office communication, March 3, 1944, Robert Buckner 1944 file in Steve Trilling files, Box 3, Jack Warner collection.
92. For details on the peculiar ratio of payments Florey and Buckner received for their work on the script, see Rogues' Regiment file 06494 (Production Budget), Universal collection, University of Southern California Special Collections Library.
93. Buckner, letter to the author, July 19, 1984.
94. Fred Sparks and Edward P. Morgan, "The French Foreign Legion Goes German," Saturday Evening Post, 221 (March 26, 1949):19.
95. "Services Today for Robert Florey, 79, Film Director," Los Angeles Times, May 18, 1979, Part IV, p. 20.

96. Buckner, letter to the author, August 28, 1984.
97. Robert Hatch, "Cinema: Fresnay and Powell," New Republic, 120 (January 3, 1949):29. For a contrasting view, see Philip G. Hartung, "Put Out More Flags," Commonweal, 49 (December 17, 1948):259-260.
98. Rogues' Regiment file 21915 (Publicity Campaign Key--Notes), Universal collection.
99. Buckner, letter to the author, July 19, 1984.
100. The Hollywood Reporter, May 21, 1949.
101. Variety, April 27, 1949.
102. Daily Variety, April 26, 1949.
103. Reed Porter, Los Angeles Mirror, reprinted in Daily Variety, May 17, 1950, p. 5.
104. Florey interview.

Chapter VI

1951-1963: TELEVISION PIONEER

By spring 1951, employment on features was becoming steadily more difficult to find. Florey's experiences the previous year on <u>Adventures of Captain Fabian</u> had proven the hazardous circumstances independent directors worked under. This made Florey willing to try a suggestion he had received over a year earlier--working in television, although he would only consider the filmed, not "live," variety. Filmed television was starting to demand the experience of those with a background in the movies rather than radio or theater, and producers were looking for new talent who would not regard the small screen as beneath them. (However, Florey's exclusive activity in filmed over "live" drama, and lack of socially-conscious elements in his shows, has caused many media historians--with their bias for the latter forms--to largely overlook his career in television.)

    Making this transition was a daring move at the time, since motion picture studios were still fighting the new medium by exiling from features any personnel who attempted the switch. In spite of the risk, Florey decided to jump ship and cast his lot with a newly developing form; as it turned out, he secured a place in the ground floor of filmed television anthologies. He was ready for something new and different, having no objection to making quality short films under the right circumstances, as his avant-garde movies and fondness for <u>Night Club</u>, <u>The Pusher-in-the-Face</u>, and <u>Bonjour, New York!</u> demonstrated. With the beginning of the rise of filmed television, Florey's last reservations about the new medium were satisfied, and he was ready to make the transition. As he commented,

1951-1963: Television Pioneer

> The time came when movie production slowed way down. The only offers came from small independents, the movie houses were closing. Television! Unless working at his craft, there is nothing much for a director in Hollywood, and after several months of idleness I decided to take "le taureau par les cornes" [the bull by the horns] and directed a first TV show in ideal conditions....[1]

This initial attempt was accomplished with ease on May 15 and 16 at the Walt Disney studio. NBC had suggested that Disney make a ten-minute segment for <u>Ford Festival</u> to tout their forthcoming release of <u>Alice in Wonderland</u>. The experiment proved a success, and five months later, when Disney needed a director to film an hour-long special to be broadcast Christmas afternoon, Florey was again his choice. The budget ($200,000) and schedule (several weeks) were lavish for this production, more so than many of Florey's "B" films. He remarked, "Walt spoils his directors, time and money for productions, just like in the good old movie days."[2] Florey was especially pleased when he was able to convince his friend Victor Francen to allow his ten-year-old daughter Leno to star in the show.

But the decision to enter television almost certainly meant giving up any hope of returning to theatrical motion pictures. Florey would have to make his own way; Disney, to whom he was very grateful for the chance to make such a prestigious debut in the new medium, would not be able to use Florey again until 1954, when commencing the regular weekly series <u>Disneyland</u>. Florey was then hired as a "live action" director, shooting new shows as well as narration, introductory, and connecting material to present preexisting films for broadcast. In this capacity, he helped guide Disney to the personal popularity that won him an Emmy nomination as Most Outstanding New Personality of 1954; the show received the Best Variety Series award the same year.

However, in late 1951 such success as an established

[Opposite:] Florey undertook his first television shows in 1951 for Walt Disney.

television director was still in the future. In November of 1951, Florey, at the urging of his old friend cameraman Paul Ivano, filmed the first of his dramatic shows for television. He undertook a pair of independently-produced half-hour thrillers starring Akim Tamiroff: <u>Trouble on Pier 12</u> (originally titled <u>The Ship From Macabao</u> and broadcast the next year on the <u>Schlitz Playhouse of Stars</u> series) and <u>Detective of French Sûreté</u>. In April 1952, Florey joined the short-lived National Repertory Theater to direct another thirty-minute film, <u>The Victim</u>. Starring Arthur Kennedy, it won critical praise in special showings but was not aired commercially until 1956 (on <u>Ethel Barrymore Theater</u>). Although jobs seemed disappointingly sporadic at this time, word began to spread of the ease with which Florey adjusted his techniques to the new medium and his success in finishing his television projects on schedule. Then, in July, he directed two <u>Favorite Story</u> fantasies with Adolphe Menjou (about whom he had co-authored a book in 1927). Menjou, delighted with the quality of Florey's work, recommended him to Charles Boyer, who was about to form his own television production company with Dick Powell. Both already knew Florey, Boyer through Hollywood's French colony and Powell as star of <u>Rogues' Regiment</u>. Joined shortly thereafter by David Niven, they decided to give Florey the "break" that would launch him onto a long career as one of the leading directors in television.

He was asked to helm the new series, <u>Four Star Playhouse</u>, in which the three performers were to be regulars along with a periodic guest such as Ronald Colman or Merle Oberon. This anthology had a number of features that made it unique. Each star was empowered not only to choose the scripts that best suited his skills, but also to function as producer of his segments. Collectively, they searched through plays and short stories that could be adapted into effective half-hour vehicles for one another. The standard of these films was very high, the result of fine talent in nearly every department: the writing by Blake Edwards, John and Gwen Bagni, and others, the elaborate settings of art director Duncan Cramer, and the elegant photography by George Diskant, not to mention fine performances from the principals and their supporting casts. All of these elements would be honored during the four-year lifetime of the series.

In its initial season, 1952-53, <u>Four Star Playhouse</u>

1951-1963: Television Pioneer

Florey and his collaborators on Four Star Playhouse, David Niven, Charles Boyer, and Dick Powell, receive the news that their show has been named Best Dramatic TV Film Program by Billboard in 1953. Besides Four Star Playhouse, Florey later also directed Niven and Boyer in Alcoa/Goodyear Theater--A Turn of Fate, and Powell in Zane Grey Theater and The June Allyson Show.

appeared biweekly, and Florey directed all but two of the nineteen segments. "Those were the days!" he said, "We had good stories, good little dramas."[3] He had a favorable contract, calling for a minimum of thirty weeks of exclusive employment during which he was to direct no more than twenty shows; there was even a stipulation that he would assist in the preparation and editing. For the first time in his career, he found his opinions consistently listened to, and he was able to labor without the interference that had so plagued his years with the movie studios. "I realized that on TV I had my chance to direct as I pleased for the first time."[4] Boyer was especially willing to trust Florey's judgment and allowed him wide latitude to experiment. Under these conditions, Florey found that he preferred directing television to features, calling the new medium "a director's dream come true."

> It's immensely satisfying to see the finished picture the way I shot it. In theatrical pictures, on the other hand, by the time the producers, cutters, and so on, get through with the film, I don't recognize it.
>
> You can do your best work in TV because there isn't any interference. In a major theatrical studio, the picture is out of your hands. I find TV satisfying, refreshing, and a real challenge. You rise--or fall--by what is on the screen, on your own, untampered work.
>
> It's a tough grind, shooting a picture in two or three days, but I like it. In motion pictures a director is forced to do things whether he wants to or not.[5]

The series was sold on the basis of a pair of pilots made in the summer of 1952. The first, My Wife Geraldine, was an off-beat, sentimental little love story. Boyer portrays an aging bachelor who, finding that employers want only married men, surrounds himself with relics of an imagined wife, convincing others and almost himself that he is really married. The second pilot starred Dick Powell in one of his many roles as a private investigator; Dante's Inferno inspired further exploits of the same character and, years later, a series of its own. Both of these demonstrated Florey's talent with imaginative treatment of widely divergent material.

Another of the season's episodes with Boyer, The Last Voyage, won Florey the first award for television directing given by the Directors Guild (of which he had been a founding member), an honor he would be nominated for five additional times. In fact, because of a last minute change in Boyer's schedule, The Last Voyage, a wartime thriller, had to be shot in a mere two-and-a-half days, proving once again that the pressure of limitations often brought out the best of Florey's talent. One of Niven's episodes, a story of an orphan entitled No Identity, was named Best Dramatic Show of 1953 by Billboard, which named the entire series their choice for Best Filmed Dramas.

However, Florey's favorite shows were three done with guest star Ronald Colman (in his television debut), with whom Florey had previously worked as assistant director twenty-five years earlier on The Magic Flame. Written by Milton Merlin, Colman starred in The Lost Silk Hat, The Man Who Walked Out on Himself, and The Ladies on His Mind. Each of these was rather experimental in nature, the first being an adaptation of a one-set play by Lord Dunsany, the second a surrealist one-man show, and the third a whimsical look at a psychiatrist's fantasies about his female patients.

The last of these took five days to shoot, an example of the willingness of Four Star Playhouse, especially in its early years, to extend the schedule if an exceptional script required it. Typically, a segment began with two days of rehearsals, with actors running through the lines the first day, then practicing on the set before spending three days shooting. Such careful preparation, more than was usually accorded series of the period, doubtless helped account for the high quality achieved. Another result was a trait notable in much of Florey's work for the small screen: a resemblance to cinematic forms, allowing setting and mood to unfold slowly, at a deliberate pace--unlike the frenetic rhythm usually associated with television.

After eight months with Four Star Playhouse, Florey was lured away by the promise of a ten percent share of the profits, in addition to his regular salary and residuals, to direct all the episodes of Loretta Young's new series. Like Florey, she had also decided to abandon features, and her series (originally titled A Letter to Loretta, later changed to The Loretta Young Show) was constructed around her star presence with a variety of vehicles chosen according to her range of talents and personal values. She was determined to distinguish her anthology from the competition by demanding the most from her collaborators and striving for a high degree of excellence, with segments budgeted at close to $30,000 apiece. The dominant influence was Young's, not that of her director, who had to conform his style to the needs of the series.

However, she respected Florey's opinions and he was involved in preparing and selecting scripts and co-stars. A number of episodes reflect his personal concerns, such as the historical biographies of Charlotte Brontë (called close to "the high level of the legitimate theater at its best"[6]) and

The Loretta Young Show: The Clara Schumann Story won Florey nominations for Emmy and Directors Guild awards. Loretta Young (right) portrayed the wife and George Nader (second from left) the composer, who has just lost his mind after attempting suicide.

Clara Schumann, which won him Directors Guild and Emmy nominations for Best Direction. Young's series was widely popular and received critical praise including Emmy nominations for Best New Program and for Young as Best Actress in both 1953 and 1954. But the schedule was a hard one--thirty-six episodes--and Florey did not feel equal to another strenuous season. Nonetheless, the series had been launched on an eight-year run, Young had made a successful transition to television, and Florey had proven himself a master of intimate domestic drama--all worthy achievements.

Loretta Young's husband and manager, Tom Lewis, executive producer of the series, thanked Florey:

> Your skill as a director was a great factor in our success for the year. Your ability to discuss and to weigh ideas and values and to reject some and embrace others--without regard to their authorship --was a great value to us and the series.
> Your encouragement to Loretta anent the various characterizations required of her in so many pictures was of enormous help to her--and it sprang from your patience and sympathy as a man, as much as from your art as a director. In short, you initiated us into the tense demanding business of television, generously giving us of an experience we did not have, and we are deeply grateful to you.[7]

After the year with Loretta Young, Florey returned to Four Star Playhouse for two more seasons. Now a weekly series, Tay Garnett, Roy Kellino, and Florey helmed over half of the segments. He was informed by Dick Powell, the series' business manager, that their sponsors were pressing for more commercial, less artistic fare. However, Four Star Playhouse continued to be of high quality, and one segment, 1955's The Executioner, a tale of intrigue behind the iron curtain, won Florey his third nomination for the Directors Guild award. Two more, Magic Night and Something Very Special, along with stock footage, were shot entirely on location and at the St. Maurice Studio in France. All three of these starred Charles Boyer.

The thirty-eight segments of Four Star Playhouse Florey directed between 1952-56 were no doubt the best of his television work; indeed, he thought them the high point of his entire career. Although this particular series lasted only four years, the corporation behind it, Four Star Television, endured, and he continued to direct for it often.

Beginning simultaneously with the last two seasons of Four Star Playhouse, Florey also contributed thirty-two anthology dramas for Schlitz Playhouse of Stars between 1954-57. They were made first at Meridian Pictures, then at Universal, and had an intelligent and understanding producer in William Self. Commented Florey: "He had an excellent story department, a fine cameraman, George Clemens, and a great Art Director, Serge Krizman. We all worked together in great harmony and enjoyed our work. We made our films fast and for little money."[8]

By 1956, the second, less distinguished part of Florey's television career was beginning. His output remained of a high caliber, but never again would he have the degree of luxury and freedom accorded to him in his initial years. The days when he preferred directing television films to theatrical movies were numbered. But he never attempted a comeback to the big screen, preferring the steady employment of television to the uncertainties of independent feature production.

The next company he signed to direct with was Universal-Revue. In the first of several stints there, he directed for only their five leading series (as stipulated in his contract), most notably a half-dozen segments of Joseph Cotten's On Trial--which Florey especially enjoyed--and two of Wagon Train. One from each series--The De Santre Affair (with Joan Fontaine) and The Ruth Owens Story (with Shelley Winters), respectively--won him his fourth and fifth nominations from the Directors Guild.

Despite this success, Florey was not happy at Universal, where directors did not command the respect they had at Four Star and the making of television films was done on a mass-production basis. A typical encounter came with a producer who went so far as to deny him an office at the studio. Florey responded, not with angry words, but by setting up a desk outside the main building, using rocks to hold down his papers--a reaction that won him proper space.[9]

Universal forced him to turn out half-hour shows on two-day schedules, more than twice the speed he had worked on even the cheapest motion pictures. He wrote:

> No rehearsals. A day perhaps of "preparation." No time for several takes, not even for two takes, everything has to be staged on the spot and instantly, the director must average ten scenes an hour, often more if the story takes place in many different sets and exteriors ... one has to think extremely fast and always be on the go to bring to the screen in two days what used to take two weeks or more in the good old movie days....[10]

His complaints that this pace was too fast to allow for quality work were futile.

In late 1957 Florey returned to Four Star to direct seventeen segments of their new anthology series, Alcoa/ Goodyear Theater--A Turn of Fate. Most of these were suspense dramas of a very high caliber. The scripts were ingenious, often witty; George Diskant contributed the excellent photography; and the atmosphere and pacing were far superior to other shows of the type. Once more there was a rotating team of stars, including Jack Lemmon, Robert Ryan, Jane Powell, and, again, Charles Boyer and David Niven. The latter two turned in especially distinguished performances, as did many of the supporting players. A few segments, such as Night Caller and My Wife's Next Husband, were of a quality equal to many of Florey's 1930's "B" movies.

Perhaps the most intriguing of these, and one of his television masterpieces, is The Clock Struck Twelve. This is a complex, intricate tale of a doctor descending into schizophrenia after committing a murder. Vaguely noir in flavor, it provided a perfect opportunity for Florey to put on one of his greatest displays of expressionism, in the style of The Life and Death of 9413--a Hollywood Extra and The Florentine Dagger. Most of The Clock Struck Twelve was apparently shot silent, concentrating on the intensity of Charles Boyer's acting through close-ups and voice-overs to achieve an interior monologue. A mood of fear mounting to hysteria is created by the visual motif of clocks and the constant verbal enumeration of a countdown to midnight; atmosphere is evoked by Boyer's continual fleeing through dark, rain-soaked streets whose only illumination comes from lonely street lamps. Seldom, if ever, has Florey's talent for exploring a tortured soul in a surrealistic manner been better exhibited. Together with other shows, like A Letter to Loretta: The Mirror, it revealed Florey's skill with themes of insanity, especially in gradually conveying to the audience, without recourse to dialogue explication, the madness of a character. Such shows make credible his assertion that he hoped to handle The Beast with Five Fingers in just such a way.

In subsequent years Florey freelanced, directing primarily for Four Star and Universal, but also at Desilu, Twentieth Century-Fox, Ziv, M-G-M and the Hal Roach studios. He was called upon to direct many "pilot" shows; among the most lauded were The David Niven Show: Lifeline

(1959), Michael Shayne, Detective (1960) and The Restless Gun (1957), which was originally broadcast as a Schlitz Playhouse segment. One of his pilots, Carolyn, starring Celeste Holm and independently made for NBC in 1953, was the only television film he both produced and directed. More than in his motion picture years, he was offered scripts whose elements intrigued him--tales of romance, history, fantasy, or suspense--and his services were usually in such demand that he was able to choose from among them.

For instance, he signed with Roach, not out of the need to stay employed, but to do pilots he enjoyed and unusual, high-quality historical pieces--Telephone Time: Chico and the Archbishop and Crime Classics: The Crime of Bathsheba Spooner. (These programs were hardly low-cost items--the former was budgeted at $41,000--and each was shot during three days, with one of rehearsals, in 1956.) Such shows, along with others set in various periods of the past, like Fedar and On Leave, made for Schlitz Playhouse of Stars in 1955, offered Florey the opportunity to work with a genre he had always enjoyed. These, along with an occasional prestige adaptation such as Judith Anderson in a W. Somerset Maugham tale, The Star and the Story: The Creative Impulse (1954), were among the key reasons Florey preferred television to motion pictures for a time.

But by the end of the 1950s, episodic series with predictable regular weekly characters were increasingly replacing anthologies, and Florey's output came to be increasingly dominated by two genres: detective stories and westerns. There were numerous episodes of Markham and Michael Shayne, formulaic private-eye series that must have reminded him of his lesser "B" films. Most of the westerns were for Desilu's popular saga, The Texan, and Florey frankly took them only for income during a slow season. They held little interest for him, and he was no longer strong enough to enjoy the rigorous location work, which often called for shooting four episodes back-to-back in ten days. His friend Lloyd Nolan recalled, "When Bob's health began to fail in his later years, one after another it would be a western, and that means fighting the sun and long hours and long drives into the Calabasas or further. It just wore him down. He began to hate television."[11] Florey's prior westerns were chiefly for Four Star's Zane Grey Theater, done as a favor to Dick Powell, while the

1951-1963: Television Pioneer 327

Wagon Train segments, because of their hour length, were a different matter entirely. One of Florey's associates explained:

> None of the things we did were a great piece of art or anything like that, they were just entertainment. I know on the thrillers he used to take them quite seriously, because that was in his genre, that he liked. Other shows, more run-of-the-mill things, he wouldn't take too seriously; he couldn't. He was competent, and would get it out on time and on budget. The Wagon Trains he took pretty seriously, because he was interested in all types of history, and he would get the most that he could out of those.[12]

According to contemporary critics, Florey was an "ex-film innovator turned champ TV director,"[13] whose work on the small screen demonstrated that he "is best with suspense. He pays attention to detail, and gets first-class camerawork into his films."[14] These evaluations are validated by the testimony of Willard Sheldon, who collaborated many times with Florey at Universal-Revue, first as assistant director and later as production manager. Florey planned each shot in advance, often filling his television scripts with diagrams and notations, just as he did on his movies. Said Sheldon:

> He knew exactly what he was doing, always. He had prepared and had done his homework before he came in; there was never any hesitation or groping. He knew his sets: he'd work out the groundplan very carefully, and he'd always come in a few days before we started and go over the sets. Some directors were very flippant and careless, but Bob was never that way. Bob was always very proud of his work, and tried to do the best that he could; he wouldn't just fluff stuff off.[15]

Florey's long experience with fast production techniques was of considerable assistance in adapting to the whirlwind demands of television schedules. Even by comparison to a quickie or "action picture" made in twelve days, an hour-long television show (actually closer to forty-five minutes with commercials and credits discounted) was a rush job in five or six days. Often, especially when two or more shows were to be made back-to-back, weekends were spent writing out the shooting continuities as Florey planned by memory how to use old standing sets and exteriors as background. When hired for a half-hour show, it would usually be for a week, with preparations and shooting taking two or three days apiece, while an hour segment would be for ten days. The first day would be spent becoming familiar with the script, often at home or in a producer's antechamber. "The second day," said Florey, "the director will walk around the stages with the art director, picking up old sets to see how they can be adjusted to the story. The third day he'll go out looking for locations...."[16] On quality shows with major stars, such as those for Four Star and Loretta Young, he seldom had less than three shooting days and one of rehearsals for a half-hour segment. But once photography was completed, the director was off the payroll or at work on his next project, giving him no opportunity to affect the editing. His salary usually ranged between $750-$1,250 for a thirty-minute show, and around $2,500 for an hour, not including residuals; he had typically averaged $1,000 a week when directing motion pictures.

Even such detailed planning as Florey undertook could not always fend off the difficulties attendant on the hectic labor of television, but he was able to adapt himself calmly to any troubles that arose. Within the framework of the time available in the shooting schedule, he "was meticulous. Bob was prone to be a perfectionist in many ways, and that was something you just couldn't do, but he always turned out a good job of work."[17]

Although assigned a crew and with little say over his cast, Florey always managed to make his personality felt while utilizing their talents. His television casts were usually every bit as competent as those in his movies, and many had more famous names than he had dealt with in motion pictures. He frequently directed such individuals as Charles Boyer, David Niven, Ronald Colman, Merle Oberon, Jack Lemmon, Robert Ryan, Loretta Young, Joseph Cotten, and Gene Kelly, as well as others like Barbara Stanwyck and Ray Milland, who had starred in some of Florey's movies. His "French charm worked wonders on the egos of the big screen who were forced to accept that their lustre was now lacking."[18] As Robert Morley wrote to Florey (after <u>The Dick Powell Show: The Big Day</u>, 1962), "I did so enjoy doing our little film and thank you again for making everything so relaxed and painless. Would there were more directors like you."[19] Even in the later years of television, with more hurried schedules, Florey still managed to elicit striking performances; for example, note <u>Alfred Hitchcock Presents: A Jury of Her Peers</u> (1961), a sensitive suspense drama of conscience (photographed in two days) in which Ann Harding suppresses evidence that could convict a friend of murder.

When handed a script, Florey could usually make changes in it, frequently adding or deleting dialogue, sometimes rewriting entire sequences. The speed of production, and the lack of interference in the early days of television, made it possible for him to make the sort of wholesale revisions that were often not possible on his movies. As long as he had a compatible producer, he could adjust any problems that he foresaw in the script; this was especially true at Four Star. "Bob was able to handle things well and pretty much got stories the way he wanted them."[20] Generally speaking, he managed to have at least as much--if not more--impact on his television scripts than he had on his theatrical pictures.

In 1953, Powell and Boyer asked Florey to suggest ideas for a historical series to star Arthur Kennedy, Edward Arnold and Diana Lynn, to be filmed in Europe if the original locales survived. Florey responded with suggestions for stories concerning such figures as François Villon, Leonardo da Vinci and Mona Lisa, Van Gogh, Louis Pasteur, and--naturally--a trilogy on Napoleon. There were also to be tales of the Bohemians, the Statue of Liberty, the voyages of Columbus, Louis XIII and Cardinal Richelieu, and the French and American Revolutions. None of these were ever realized.

Apparently, on only two occasions did Florey have an actual role in the writing of his television scripts. Soon after signing his first contract with Universal-Revue, he submitted a four-page outline for a dramatization of the trial, imprisonment, and execution of Mata Hari. It was based almost entirely on fact and supplied extensive historical background material; he suggested it for <u>On Trial</u>, a series reenacting authentic courtroom cases. A few months later it was developed into a half-hour teleplay by Gabrielle Upton and Larry Marcus, with Florey directing and Merle Oberon playing the lead. The final title of the film was I Will Not Die, and it was broadcast in the General Electric Theater anthology. Daily Variety wrote, "Florey wisely explores new fields for screen treatments of Mata Hari, by dwelling on the results of her activities, rather than her undoubted glamor. Miss Oberon turns in a well conceived portrayal of the spy's growing terror, while not concealing Mata Hari's attractions."[21] The same year, 1957, Florey also co-authored the script of The Les Rand Story, a Wagon Train drama with Sterling Hayden.

By the 1960s, as Florey approached the end of his fifth decade in the film industry, he was becoming steadily more depressed at the declining quality of television. According to Jack Spears, he

> complained many times about the rushed production in TV, the presence of an assistant director who did not assist but was present to prod the director to keep to schedule.... I think he found making TV films not much fun in his last days. He complained about cheap budgets, the necessity of making do with inappropriate sets.[22]

Executives unschooled in filmmaking began to impose themselves on the creative process, and directors lost their independence. Gone were the ecstatic days when Florey had preferred television to movies.

Nevertheless, his reputation was such that he continued to attract witty, offbeat scripts (such as Alcoa Premiere: It Takes a Thief, 1962), with most of his shows coming out well. He was prominently associated with such prestigious series as Barbara Stanwyck Theater, Alfred Hitchcock Presents, and Going My Way. Twentieth Century-Fox hired Florey for nine episodes of Adventures in Paradise and sent him on a cruise to the South Pacific to do extensive location photography for another dozen in 1961. He turned more and more to one-hour shows, filming over thirty of this length, most of which, especially the early ones, were well received.

In 1959, he was awarded his sixth nomination for the Directors Guild award for Westinghouse-Desilu Playhouse:

The Innocent Assassin, an hour-length drama of Irish rebels and one of his favorites. Florey's television work was always more appreciated in France than in his adopted country, just as his features had been. His first sixty-minute drama, Wire Service: The Johnny Rath Story, made in 1955 for Desilu, had been given one of only five mentions out of 125 television films from around the world entered at the 1958 Cannes Film and Television Festival. Florey's Wagon Train: The Ruth Owens Story and Westinghouse-Desilu Playhouse: The Innocent Assassin were also honored abroad. After viewing these, André Bazin commented, "I find them better made than those of Hitchcock...."[23]

Among Florey's most distinctive films for the small screen were a number dealing with the supernatural, such as his Favorite Story segments; The Man On the Train, The Man Who Walked Out on Himself and The Devil to Pay for Four Star Playhouse; Schlitz Playhouse of Stars: Step Right Up and Die (1956); and Zane Grey Theater: Sundown at Bitter Creek (1958), a ghostly western. Two of his most widely seen horror shows were for the series The Twilight Zone (budgeted at between $28,000-$34,000 apiece). Made in 1959, these were The Fever, a gambling fantasy, and Perchance to Dream. The latter was the more interesting, investigating a man's frantic state when he cannot sleep, obsessed by a belief that a malevolant woman is pursuing him to his death. The tale involves a reenactment of his dream that resolves itself in an amusement park, a locale Florey suffuses with expressionism, odd angles, and a mood of paranoia. He deliberately chose to create the story in this surreal manner: "I told the producer that I could do much better on an empty big stage at M-G-M with some light effects and double exposures ... I spoke to the art director and the set dresser, telling them about the few props I would require, and how I intended to create the atmosphere of Luna Park, and the kind of angles I was going to shoot. They all accepted my ideas; the film was made in a little less than three days."[24]

During his last four years of television directing, Florey did a number of shows combining fantasy and horror with science fiction. His skill with the bizarre was appropriate to all these types, and his reliance on camerawork and artificial decor for mood, rather than effects, prevented the exigencies of television from being a hindrance. Steeped in the Georges Méliès-Jules Verne tradition, together with his talent for suspense, Florey demonstrated once more his skill with the genre he had done so much to create with Frankenstein. Two of these shows were, in fact, a partial reworking of ideas and themes from his original script and were made at Universal. Thriller: The Incredible Doktor Markesan (1962) ironically united Florey with Boris Karloff, reversing his most famous role to portraying a mad scientist who resuscitates the dead. Florey enjoyed creating all the ghoulish effects, and the result was one of the most popular and memorable hours he filmed. Alfred Hitchcock Presents: The Changing Heart (1960) tells of an old clockmaker who saves a dying girl by converting her into a ticking automaton. Credited to a script by Robert Bloch, the story is also an updated version of Jules Verne's classic, "Master Zacharius, or the Watch's Soul," with which Florey was familiar from his childhood.

The last shows he directed before retirement were a pair of "space" stories, Outer Limits: Moonstone and Twilight Zone: The Long Morrow. The latter was one of the finest of Florey's television films. Using the situation of an astronaut sent on a forty-year mission into the far reaches of space, it delicately explores how this prospect humanizes him, especially as he first encounters romance. The cruel twist of fate that awaits the lovers' reunion is sensitively acted, and the entire plot is invested with a strong feeling for devotion and sentiment. Most effective in the otherwise subdued visuals is the elegy of intercutting and fading between the astronaut's flashbacks and longings, meditating as he lies frozen in a glass casket (shades of The Cabinet of Dr. Caligari and Johann the Coffin Maker?) on his spaceship as the years pass slowly, bringing no relief from the loneliness and memories.

During the early 1960s, declining health forced Florey to direct fewer and fewer shows until he did only three in 1963. After a dozen years of television, his constitution was no longer equal to the grueling demands of days lasting twelve or more hours. In early 1966 he remarked, "Having made about [250 shows] I became quite ill and am now obliged to take a long rest."[25] That rest eventually became a permanent retirement. Nonetheless, the studios hoped he would resume directing, and he continued to receive offers for a few years until it was clear he could not return.

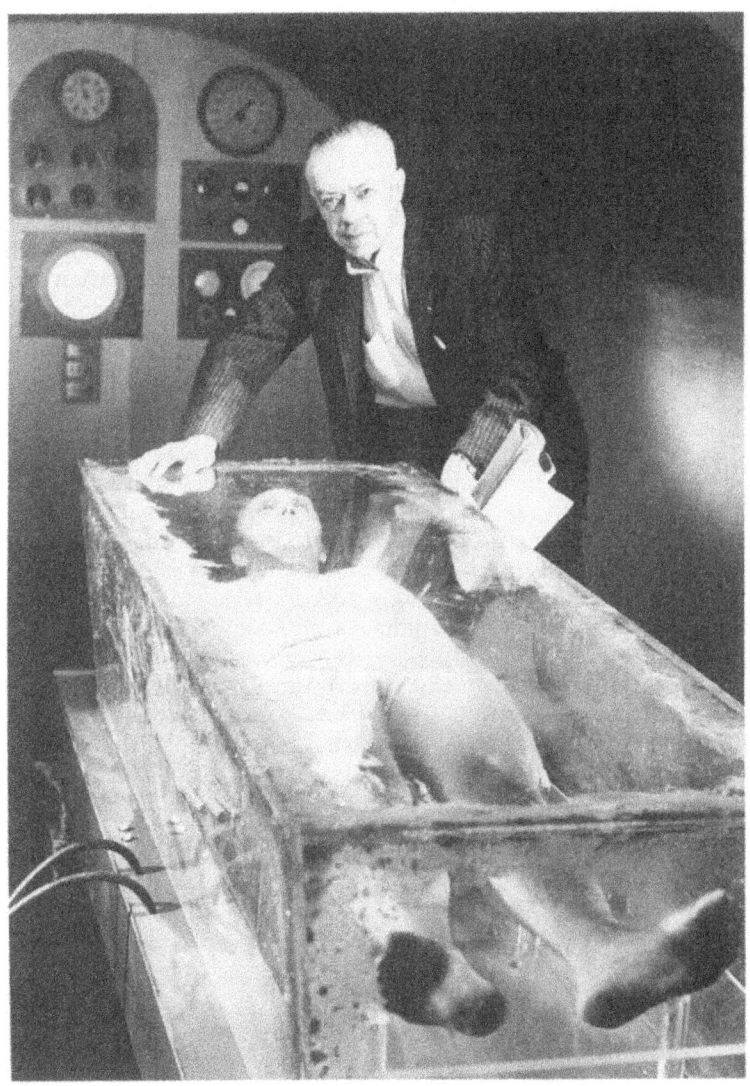

Florey's last film, the television show Twilight Zone: The Long Morrow, with Robert Lansing, had overtones from The Cabinet of Dr. Caligari and Johann the Coffin Maker.

"They liked him, kept him on, doing different things; finally he was the one who decided he didn't want to do any more, not the studios."[26]

Thus, Florey was one of the first major commercial directors to enter television, helping to secure respectability for the new medium and leading other directors to follow the same path. He once again proved his adaptability and talent as an innovator by the ease with which he adjusted to the demand of small screen, thirty-minute dramas (hour-long shows were closer to the format he had known in "B" films). His many awards reveal the high estimation in which he was held at this time, particularly by his colleagues. "You are still leading the way," said Irving Rapper, his assistant from Astoria days.[27]

"A list of series for which Florey directed reads like a list of every major series in television," wrote Leonard Maltin.[28] At its best, much of Florey's work on the small screen, especially at Four Star in the 1950s, was of a quality equal, and sometimes superior, to many of his motion pictures. "My first television years brought me the artistic freedom I didn't have making sixty-five [feature] films," Florey commented before sponsors and supervisors began their interference.[29] While in later years he would be frustrated by failing health and deteriorating standards of television drama, he continued to demonstrate an inventiveness and skill, undiminished even at the end of his long career.

NOTES

1. Robert Florey, letter to Henry Hart, June 12, 1959.
2. Ibid.
3. Leonard Maltin, "Directors on TV--Robert Florey," Film Fan Monthly, No. 126 (December 1971):23.
4. Ibid., p. 22.
5. "SDG Award Winner Prefers Megging TV to Theatrical Pix," Daily Variety, January 26, 1954.
6. Donald Kirkley, "Look and Listen with Donald Kirkley," Baltimore Sun (n.d.), p. 10. enlarged reprint, Florey collection.
7. Tom Lewis, letter to Robert Florey, May 25, 1954, Florey collection.
8. Maltin, p. 25.

9. Willard Sheldon, interview with the author, January 7, 1982.
10. Florey, letter to Henry Hart.
11. Lloyd Nolan, interview with the author, August 5, 1983.
12. Sheldon interview.
13. Herman G. Weinberg, "Coffee, Brandy and Cigars XXXIII," Film Culture, No. 21 (Summer 1960):89.
14. Don Miller, "Films on TV," Films in Review, 10 (June-July 1959):370.
15. Sheldon interview; Robert Florey television scripts collection, University of Southern California Special Collections Library.
16. Maltin, pp. 24-25.
17. Sheldon interview.
18. Christopher Wicking and Tise Vahimagi, The American Vein: Directors and Directions in Television (New York: E.P. Dutton, 1979), p. 124.
19. Robert Morley, letter to Robert Florey (n.d.), Florey collection.
20. Sheldon interview; Florey televison scripts collection.
21. Daily Variety, April 30, 1957.
22. Jack Spears, letter to the author, November 15, 1982.
23. André Bazin, "Festival du Telecinema," unidentified newspaper clipping (n.d.), Florey collection.
24. Maltin, p. 24.
25. Robert Florey, letter to Ray Cabana, March 11, 1966.
26. Sheldon interview.
27. Irving Rapper, letter to Robert Florey (n.d.), Florey collection.
28. Maltin, p. 24.
29. Robert Florey, unidentified correspondence, Florey collection; Cf. Robert Florey, La Lanterne magique (Lausanne: Cinémathèque suisse, 1966), pp. 186-193.

Chapter VII

1964-1979: RETIREMENT

Unlike so many other Hollywood figures ever-hopeful of returning to professional activity, Robert Florey had no difficulty in accepting retirement. He compassionately remarked of his friend and former mentor, Josef von Sternberg, "Joe, like many others, lived in the past and always hoped to direct 'a big one' again someday."[1] Florey, on the other hand, was a realist and quickly immersed himself in his many other interests, so that the remaining sixteen years of his life were busy and productive ones despite his frail health.

He shifted his attention once more to writing about the early years of the movies. Three more books were authored during his retirement years, La Lanterne magique (1966), Hollywood années zero (1972), and a profusely illustrated history of each of the Los Angeles studios, Hollywood Village (1986), published posthumously in France. These were his first volumes since Hollywood D'Hier et D'Aujourd'Hui (1948) and Monsieur Chaplin ou le rire dans la nuit (with Maurice Bessy, 1952), although Florey had continued to write innumerable articles for French film and television journals. His earliest books, published back in the 1920s, had become exceedingly scarce, high-valued collector's items; finally Deux ans dans les studios americains was reprinted in 1984.

Florey's initial works could be described as often journalistic in nature, but his later ones moved steadily away from a popular appeal toward specialized topics that called for immense research in the light of his experiences in Hollywood. Frequently he related knowledge that he had gained firsthand, or directly from famous individuals who had preceeded him; Florey was simultaneously both a witness to and a recorder of history. He was writing purely to preserve the past, not for any profit, and instead of royalties he requested extra copies to give to libraries, archives, and universities.

In style Florey could be a clever raconteur, enlightening by means of revealing stories that were not only amusing but served to illustrate a definite point. His mind was an incredible storehouse of facts, any one of which he could bring to bear on a problem at a moment's notice; the reach of his memory was so vast that he could recall any relevant details without needing to leaven them with fabrications. "Your own recitals of historical facts always have the devastating ring of truth to them," said Herman G. Weinberg.[2] Florey's memory was meticulous, with an innate sense of history that fortunately impelled him to write at length of what he had seen, often shortly after he had experienced it. "Such is the tone of Robert Florey, his care about detail, this precise and photographic memory of past events," wrote Maurice Bessy, "this love of the first ages of the cinema, which made of him an incomparable chronicler.... 'These are things which I saw and heard,' said Joinville. Florey recounts to us, he also, a tableau of which he is a living witness."[3]

These multiple talents allow diverse comments to be equally true of Florey's books: Anthony Slide's evaluation that all "are exemplary works of scholarship" and Weinberg's, "No one has written about Hollywood of the 'old days' with more buoyancy and charm than you."[4] The instincts of the historian were so strong in Florey that he seems to have taken more pride in his books than his films, believing the former more durable and regarding many of his celluloid efforts as rather ephemeral.[5] His dedication to his writing was shown when, only months prior to his death and at virtual peril to his life, he had his wife take him home from the hospital to choose stills from his collection desired by a publisher.

Florey helped perpetuate the lore of early Hollywood not only in his own writings, but through the assistance he rendered hundreds of other authors doing research. Weinberg was moved to say, "If I have been regarded in some quarters as a historian (film authority), it is <u>you</u> who are <u>my</u> historian."6 Kevin Brownlow wrote, "I regarded him as the Oracle of Delphi as far as film history was concerned."7 Jack Spears added, "Bob was such a kind man--never too busy to help me (and so many others) to ferret out information."8 So wide-ranging were Florey's contributions that dozens of books published years after his death still acknowledge his aid. He also generously gave, to many people, thousands of valuable stills from the vast collection he had accumulated during his years at the studios.

Yet Florey's most unique trait, for all his eagerness to assist others, was that none of it was self-promotional. In fact he avoided autobiography in his own books, preferring to talk of friends and associates he had known rather than of his own career. He refused to give taped interviews, thereby losing an opportunity to receive the greater recognition such recorded encounters engender. Apparently, having put so much time into his many books and articles, he preferred that scholars utilize them rather than oral histories.

Early in 1950, the French government had awarded Florey the order of Knight of the Legion of Honor in recognition of his contributions to motion pictures, his work on France's behalf in the United States, and his voluminous reporting on Hollywood over thirty years. He received four other honors from his native land over his lifetime: Officer of the Academy, the French Merit award, Chevalier des Arts et des Lettres, and the Palmes Academique.

Florey had a virtual fulltime job maintaining his vast room of French artifacts, primarily from the period of the Napoleons. Numbering many thousands of pieces, this collection filled every inch of a large room in his home--including walls, shelves, cupboards, and closets--and was the envy of many museums all over the world. In it, he said, one could find

> a piece of the bedroom chamber floor of Napoleon in Saint-Helena, a lock of hair of the Emperor, bonnets worn by the French revolutionaries on July 14th, 1789; armors, cuirasses, helmets and uniforms, letters of the Empresses Josephine and Marie-Louise, letters of the Marshals of France;

1964-1979: Retirement

Among those attending the reception when Florey received the Legion of Honor were Harry D'Arrast, Jacques Tourneur and Jean Benoit-Lèvy. Virginia Florey is in the center.

swords and pistols, ceramics, medals, and sabertaches; old Parisian shop signs, flag eagles, hats of generals, statuary and revolutionary posters and paintings.[9]

Even more amazing than this assemblage itself was the vast knowledge Florey had of each item. Although much beloved by him, he gave away many of these relics to friends and history buffs over the years. Following his death, most of this valuable collection--so extensive that it had its own book-length catalog[10]--was sold by Sotheby's at special auctions in Monte Carlo and later in London.

In his final years, Florey was steadily plagued by illness. As so many of the friends he had known over his lifetime died one by one, he felt himself isolated from the Hollywood where he had once been the companion and confidant of Valentino, Pickford, Fairbanks, Chaplin, and so many others. Increasingly, he enjoyed such simple pleasures as keeping up his home and tending to the garden. He and Mrs. Florey remained devoted to one another over their thirty-nine years of marriage, and her gentle care sustained him through the years of poor health.

In the spring of 1979, Florey entered the hospital for the last time. When faced with the prospect of being an invalid even in the event of recovery, he consciously determined that he would prefer not to live such a life. Though not a typically religious man, his Catholic upbringing reasserted itself in his last days. After receiving last rites, his wit was still in evidence: when the priest asked if there was anything further he could do, Florey replied, "No--is there anything I can do for you?"[11] Within hours, Robert Florey died, on May 16, 1979.

NOTES

1. Robert Florey, letter to Jack Spears, January 2, 1970.
2. Herman G. Weinberg, letter to Robert Florey, November 8, 19?, Florey correspondence.
3. Maurice Bessy, Les Passagers du souvenir (Paris: Editions Albin Michel, 1977), p. 83. Translation by Evelyn Copeland.
4. Anthony Slide in Christopher Lyon and Susan Doll, eds., International Dictionary of Films and Filmmakers, Volume 2 (Chicago: Macmillan, 1984), p. 191; Herman G. Weinberg, letter to Robert Florey, October 24, 1966 (?), Florey correspondence.
5. Virginia Florey, interviews with the author, 1980-1985.
6. Herman G. Weinberg, letter to Robert Florey, November 8, 19?.
7. Kevin Brownlow, letter to Virginia Florey, June 7, 1979.
8. Jack Spears, letter to the author, July 19, 1982.
9. Robert Florey, interview with the author, January 30, 1979.

10. Objets Militaires Provenant de la Collection de Robert Florey (Monte Carlo: Sotheby Parke Bernet Monaco S.A., 1980).
11. Virginia Florey, conversation with the author, May 1979.

CONCLUSION

Robert Florey has never achieved the fame his efforts have deserved for a number of reasons. His long association with the often-ignored "B" movie frequently left him without the resources to command consistent critical support. He was never able to link his talents and style to a rising star, nor was he compatible with the industry's drive for conformity.

One of the chief causes for the neglect of Florey over the ensuing years was his own lack of ego and self-promotion. The disdain in which he held many of his own masterpieces (such as The Beast with Five Fingers), his distaste for interviews and tendency to be eager to provide information on others but remain reticent about himself, doubtless discouraged some historians from investigating him.

There are other reasons Florey has been overlooked. One is the ingrained critical disinterest in the "B" film and programmer and an unwillingness to recognize its artistic potential. Another is the common misunderstanding of the position of contract directors in the 1930s and 1940s and the lack of autonomy they possessed. A third reason is the way Florey was typically deprived of proper on-screen credit for his scripts, causing his extensive work as a writer-director to be almost entirely overlooked to date. As well, many of his finest films, such as the last three avant-garde efforts or The Desert Song, have long been unavailable for study.

Too often historians have compounded the error of disregarding Florey by assuming that because of an absence of a large body of existing studies, he was unworthy of attention and had no style of his own. This has led them to mistakenly credit his achievements to others associated with him. For example, Slavko Vorkapich's spurious claims to The Life

Conclusion

and Death of 9413--a Hollywood Extra have been given credence without perceiving the movie's consistency with the remainder of Florey's ouevre; much the same has happened with Karl Freund and Murders in the Rue Morgue. Similarly, the determination of Universal and Charlie Chaplin to suppress Florey's involvement on Frankenstein and Monsieur Verdoux, respectively, have been largely perpetuated without question. Many of Florey's innovations in the photography of dance formations have been overlooked by historians who fail to discern more than the Marx Brothers' debut in The Cocoanuts. So too, Roger Touhy--Gangster has been virtually ignored despite its pioneering efforts in realism.

Florey was present and active in virtually every change to affect Hollywood. In the 1920s, it was the birth of the American avant-garde and the transition to sound in both America and Europe (where he also directed multilingual films). In the 1930s, he was a leader in double-bill features and the integration of artistic styles (such as expressionism and the avant-garde) into the American movie. He maintained this position during the following decade with the development of a style of realism and location shooting and with the rise of independent production; finally, he led the move of motion picture directors into filmed television in the early 1950s. As Robert Buckner wrote of Florey, "Few had more experience in the industry or over so many years, and he deserved a much greater reputation than he ever received.... He was a valuable part of cinema history, and few realize it."

While Florey was in the forefront of nearly all these movements, he tended to be more of an innovator than an inventor, to use a distinction made by Irving Rapper. The inspiration for much of Florey's technique came from the Europeans, but he was neither a mere imitator nor was he overshadowed by them. Instead, he created a unique style consisting of a wide variety of devices. In this respect, Florey is less of a "great" director (his movies were seldom labeled "best of the year") or a complete original, but rather one who made an important and influential contribution by applying new and experimental approaches to the feature. (Such pictures as The Cocoanuts, Murders in the Rue Morgue, Roger Touhy--Gangster, and his television anthology work fall into the latter category; The Life and Death of 9413--a Hollywood Extra and Frankenstein are the most famous among his classics.) Ironically, Florey's personal preference was for more prestigious, typically "A" films like The Magnificent Fraud, and yet he is--and deserves to be-- most vividly remembered for his quartet of psychological thrillers, The Florentine Dagger, Dangerous to Know, The Face Behind the Mask, and The Beast with Five Fingers, and superlative "B" films like King of Alcatraz.

    This comprehensive study of Robert Florey's life and films reveals that he was a gifted artist and determined experimenter whose work is marked by consistency as well as a constant leadership role in stylistic innovation. He is proof that it was possible for an independent spirit working in the major studios to turn out individualistic movies over a long career, despite the pressures for conformity. Whether in adopting expressionistic or avant-garde methods into American features or in developing styles of realism and filmed television drama, Florey was always in the forefront of those exploring new techniques. This quality made his pictures, as well as his contribution to cinema, unique.

BIBLIOGRAPHY

Ames, Leon. Interview with the author. Corona Del Mar, California, June 22, 1982.

Baxter, John. Hollywood in the Thirties. New York: A.S. Barnes, 1968, pp. 49, 77-79.

Bessy, Maurice. Les Passagers du souvenir. Paris: Editions Albin Michel, 1977, pp. 83-87.

Brosman, John. The Horror People. New York: St. Martin's, 1976, p. 270.

Buckner, Robert. Letters to the author. July 19, 1984; August 28, 1984; November 25, 1985.

Everson, William K. The Detective in Film. Secaucus, N.J.: Citadel, 1972, pp. 122-123, 128-129.

———. "The Influence of German Expressionism on the American Cinema." Film Review (1979-1980): 103-111.

Florey, Robert. "Foreign Atmosphere for the American Screen." Motion Picture Director (January 1926): 58-59. Reprinted in Richard Koszarski, ed., Hollywood Directors: 1914-1940. New York: Oxford University Press, 1976, pp. 118-122.

———. Hollywood D'Hier et D'Aujourd'Hui. Paris: Editions Prisma, 1948, pp. 8, 121-209, 267, 335-359.

———. Interview with the author. Los Angeles, California, January 30, 1979.

———. Private collection. Includes photo albums, scrapbooks, clippings, letters, contracts, scripts, stills, assorted advertising materials, and miscellaneous other items.

———. Television scripts collections. University of Southern California Special Collections Library; Columbia University.

Florey, Virginia. Interviews with the author. Los Angeles, California, 1980-85.

Folsey, George. Interview with the author. Los Angeles, California, February 8, 1983.

"Getting into Hollywood." The New York Times, December 16, 1928.

Hal Roach Studio collection. University of Southern California Special Collections Library. All files on the following television films:
Crime Classics
Telephone Time: Octaviano [Chico and the Archbishop]
White Collar Girl

Helmer, Adam. "Memoirs." Sight and Sound, 18 (December 1949): 29.

Higham, Charles. "Visitors to Sydney." Sight and Sound, 31 (Summer 1962): 120.

Huff, Theodore. "Book Reviews." Films in Review, 3 (April 1950): 31-32.

Ivano, Paul. Interview with the author. Van Nuys, California, November 13, 1981.

Jack Warner collection. University of Southern California Special Collections Library. The following files:
Buckner, Robert in Steve Trilling files
Jacobs, William in Steve Trilling files
Office of Censorship, 1942-43
Office of War Information, 1942-43

Jacobs, Lewis. The Rise of the American Film. 2nd edition. New York: Teachers College Press, 1965, pp. 333, 513, 524, 530, 547-549.

Katz, Ephraim. The Film Encyclopedia. New York: Perigee, 1979, pp. 427-428.

King, Henry. Interviews with the author. North Hollywood, California, March 30, 1979; July 28, 1981.

Koszarski, Richard. Hollywood Directors: 1914-1940. New York: Oxford University Press, 1976, p. 117.

Lacassin, Francis. "Robert Florey." Cinema 62, No. 67 (June 1962): 33-40.

Leopold, Marcel. "Robert Florey." Le Semaine a Geneva, No. 1042 (Mars 29-Avril 4, 1920).

Luft, Herbert G. "Robert Florey." Films in Review, 30 (August-September 1970): 444.

Maltin, Leonard. "Directors on TV--Robert Florey." Film Fan Monthly, No. 126 (December 1971): 22-27.

McCarthy, Todd. "Veteran Director Robert Florey Dies Here at 78." Daily Variety, May 18, 1979.

Miller, Don. "The American 'B' Film." Focus on Film, No. 5 (Winter 1979): 31-47.

_____. "B" Movies. New York: Curtis, 1973, pp. 43, 161-163, 267.

_____. "Films on TV." Films in Review, 10 (June-July 1959): 364, 370.

Nolan, Lloyd. Interview with the author. Los Angeles, California, August 5, 1983.

Noxon, Gerald F. "The European Influence on the Coming of Sound," in Evan William Cameron, ed., Sound and the Cinema. Pleasantville, N.Y.: Redgrave, 1980, pp. 148-150.

Objets Militaires Provenant de la Collection de Robert Florey. Monte Carlo: Sotheby Parke Bernet Monaco S.A., 1980.

Pearson, Joe. "Robert Florey." Hollywood Motion Picture Review, June 12, 1937, p. 8.

Quinlan, David. The Illustrated Guide to Film Directors. Totowa, N.J.: Barnes and Noble, 1983, pp. 96-97.

Rapper, Irving. Interview with the author. Los Angeles, California, March 7, 1985.

_____. Letter to the author. September 4, 1984.

Rideout, Eric H. The American Film. London: Mitre Press, 1937, p. 59.

Roberts, Marguerite. Letters to the author. March 18 & March 28, 1986.

Salmi, Markku. "Robert Florey." Film Dope, No. 16 (February 1979): 41-43.

Sheldon, Willard. Interview with the author. Los Angeles, California, January 7, 1982.

Siodmak, Curt. Letters to the author. August 23, 1984; September 19, 1984.

Slide, Anthony, in Christopher Lyon and Susan Doll, eds., International Dictionary of Films and Filmmakers, Volume 2. Chicago: Macmillan, 1984, pp. 190-191.

Smith, Ella. Starring Miss Barbara Stanwyck. New York: Crown, 1974, pp. 70, 73.

Spears, Jack. "Robert Florey." Films in Review, 11 (April 1960): 210-231.

_____. Hollywood: The Golden Era. New York: A.S. Barnes, 1971, pp. 226-254, 330-360, 400-403.

_____. Letters to the author. July 18, 1982; September 6, 1982; November 15, 1982; February 7, 1985; June 29, 1985.

"TV Door Open to New Directors." Daily Variety, 79 (June 1, 1953): 1.

Universal collection. University of Southern California Special Collections Library. All files and screenplays on the following films:
  Frankenstein
  Murders in the Rue Morgue
  Rogues' Regiment
  Sword in the Desert

Warner Bros. collection. University of Southern California Special Collections Library. All files on the following individuals, unproduced projects, and films:
  Buckner, Robert
  Buñuel, Luis
  Florey, Robert
  The Adventures of Don Juan (1948)
  The Beast with Five Fingers
  Bedside
  Beware of Imitations
  Danger Signal
  Dangerously They Live
  The Desert Song [all versions]
  Don't Bet on Blondes
  Escape in the Desert
  Ex-Lady
  The Florentine Dagger
  Girl Missing

Go into Your Dance
God Is My Co-Pilot
Going Highbrow
The House on 56th Street
I Am a Thief
I Sell Anything
I've Got Your Number
Lady Gangster
Lisbon Clipper
Napoleon
The Pay-Off
Registered Nurse
Smarty
Trilby
The Woman in Red

Wicking, Christopher, and Tise Vahimagi. The American Vein: Directors and Directions in Television. New York: E.P. Hutton, 1979, pp. 123-124.

Appendix A

BOOKS BY ROBERT FLOREY

All are profusely illustrated with photographs unless otherwise indicated.

Filmland--Los Angelès et Hollywood les capitales du cinèma. Paris: Editions de Cinemagazine, January 1923. 327 pages. Third edition, 1924.

Deux ans dans les studios amèricains. Prèface et illustre de 150 dessins de Joe Hämman. Paris: Jean Pascal, 1924. Paperback. 273 pages. Reprinted, Nice: Editions D'Aujourd'Hui, April 1984. Paperback.

Douglas Fairbanks, sa vie, ses films, ses aventures. Paris: Jean Pascal, 1926. Paperback. 63 pages.

*Pola Negri. Paris: Jean Pascal, December 1926. Paperback. 64 pages. (German language edition.) Leipzig: Librairie Nilsson, August 1927. Paperback. 64 pages.

*Charlie Chaplin. Prèface de Lucien Wahl. Paris: Jean Pascal, February 1927. Paperback. 64 pages.

*Andrè Tinchant et Robert Florey. Adolphe Menjou. Paris: Jean Pascal, June 1927. Paperback. 63 pages.

Hollywood D'Hier et D'Aujourd'Hui. Prèface de Renè Clair, (compliments of Charlie Chaplin), presentation de Maurice Bessy. Paris: Les Editions Prisma, June 4, 1948. Hardcover and paperback. 381 pages. Includes list of films written and directed by Florey.

Maurice Bessy et Robert Florey. Monsieur Chaplin ou le rire dans la nuit. Paris: Jacques Damase, January 25, 1952. Paperback. 228 pages.

---

*One of three volumes that appeared as part of the series "Les Grands artistes de l'ecran," in editions uniform with the book on Fairbanks.

La Lanterne magique. Prèface de Maurice Bessy, bio-biblio-
   filmographie ètablie par Francis Lacassin. Lausanne: La
   Cinèmatheque suisse, April 30, 1966. Paperback. 217 pages.

Renè Predal avec le concours de Robert Florey. Rudolf Valentino.
   No. 45 (paperback), collected in Volume 5 (hardcover), pages
   217-280, Anthologie du Cinema. Paris: L'Avant-Scene/C.I.B.,
   May 1969. 64 pages.

Hollywood années zéro. Paris: Editions Seghers, April 6, 1972.
   Paperback. 202 pages. Includes filmography of feature motion
   pictures directed by Florey.

Hollywood Village--Naissance des studios de Californie. Prèface de
   Maurice Bessy. Paris: Pymalion/Gèrard Watelet, May 1986.
   Hardcover. 208 pages.

Appendix B

FILMOGRAPHY

The following pages list the sixty-five feature films on which Robert Florey was either director or a principal co-author of the screenplay. His numerous shorts have not been included; all available information on them is indicated chronologically throughout the text. At the conclusion is a list of the movies on which he served as an uncredited replacement director or shot second-unit material, along with a complete list of the pictures for which he wrote screenplays. Usually he did not receive on-screen credit for his work in the latter capacity; such instances have been indicated with an asterisk (*) on each film's individual credits. The movies are listed in the order and with the date of their initial release. Florey was director on all unless otherwise indicated.

THAT MODEL FROM PARIS (Tiffany) 1926

Director: Louis J. Gasnier*
Scenario: Frederica Sagor,** from "The Right to Live" by
    Gouverneur Morris
Photography: Milton Moore, Mack Stengler

64 minutes (6,200 feet)

Cast: Marceline Day (Jane Miller), Bert Lytell (Robert Richmond), Eileen Percy (Mamie), Ward Crane (Morgan Grant), Miss Du Pont (Lila), Crauford Kent (Henry Marsh), Otto Lederer (Mr. Katz), Nellie Bly Baker (Masseuse).

ONE HOUR OF LOVE (Tiffany) 1927

Scenario: Sarah Y. Mason and Leete Renick Brown, from The
    Broken Gate by Emerson Hough

---
*Florey directed about half the film, without receiving credit, after Gasnier became ill.
**The actual writers were Florey and Houston "Bill" Branch.

Photography: Milton Moore, Mack Stengler
Art Director: Edwin B. Willis
Editor: James McKay

70 minutes (6,500 feet)

Cast: Jacqueline Logan ("Jerry" McKay), Robert Frazer (James Warren), Montagu Love (J.W. McKay), Taylor Holmes (Joe Monahan), Duane Thompson (Neely), Mildred Harris (Gwen), Hazel Keener (Vi), William Austin (Louis Carruthers), Henry Sedley (Tom Webb), Billy Bletcher ("Half Pint" Walker).

THE ROMANTIC AGE (Columbia) 1927

Supervisor: Harry Cohn
Story & Continuity: Dorothy Howell
Photography: Norbert Brodine

55 minutes (5,267 feet)

Cast: Eugene O'Brien (Stephen Winslow), Alberta Vaughn (Sally Sanborn), Stanley Taylor (Tom Winslow), Bert Woodruff (Butler).

FACE VALUE (Sterling) 1927

Producer: Joe Rock
Scenario: Frances Guihan, from her story
Photography: Herbert Kirkpatrick
Art Director: Charles D. Hall

4,393 feet

Cast: Fritzi Ridgeway (Muriel Stanley), Gene Gowing (Howard Crandall), Betty Baker (Clara), Paddy O'Flynn (Bert), Jack Mower (Arthur Wells), Edwards Davis (Crandall, Sr.), Joe Bonner (Butler).

THE HOLE IN THE WALL (Paramount--Famous-Lasky) 1929

Producer: Monta Bell
Dialogue Staged by: Irving Rapper
Adaptation & Dialogue: Pierre Collings, based on the play by Fred Jackson
Photography: George Folsey
Art Director: Ernst Fegté
Editor: Morton Blumenstock

73 minutes (5,850 feet; 7 reels)

Appendix B

Cast: Claudette Colbert (Jean Oliver), Edward G. Robinson (The Fox), David Newell (Gordon Grant), Nellie Savage (Madame Mystera), Donald Meek (Goofy), Alan Brooks (Jim), Louise Closser Hale (Mrs. Ramsey), Katherine Emmett (Mrs. Carslake), Marcia Kango (Marcia), Barry Macollum (Dogface), George MacQuarrie (Inspector), Helen Crane (Mrs. Lyons), Gamby-Hall Girls.

THE COCOANUTS (Paramount--Famous-Lasky) 1929

Producer: Monta Bell
Associate Producer: James R. Cowan
Directors: Joseph Santley and Robert Florey
Adaptation: Morris Ryskind, from the play by George Kaufman
Music & Lyrics: Irving Berlin
Photography: George Folsey
Art Director: Ernst Fegté

8,613 feet

Cast: Groucho Marx (Hammer), Harpo Marx (Harpo), Chico Marx (Chico), Zeppo Marx (Jamison), Mary Eaton (Polly), Oscar Shaw (Bob), Katherine Francis (Penelope), Margaret Dumont (Mrs. Potter), Cyril Ring (Yates), Basil Ruysdael (Hennessy), Sylvan Lee (Bell Captain), Gamby-Hall Girls and Allan K. Foster Girls (Dancers).

THE BATTLE OF PARIS (Paramount--Famous-Lasky) 1929

Story & Dialogue: Gene Markey
Music & Lyrics: Cole Porter
Photography: Bill Steiner

6,434 feet

Cast: Gertrude Lawrence (Georgie), Charles Ruggles (Zizi), Walter Petrie (Tony), Gladys Du Bois (Suzanne), Arthur Treacher (Harry), Joe King (Jack).

LA ROUTE EST BELLE (Braunberger-Richebé) 1929

Production Director: Roger Woog
Scenario & Dialogue: Pierre Wolff
Continuity: Robert Florey
Photography: Charles Rosher
Music: Andre Gailhard, Joseph Szulc, Philippe Pares, Georges Van Parys, Planchard and A. Bernard

73 minutes (8 reels)

Cast: Andre Bauge (Tony Landrin), Leon Bary (Comte Armand Hubert), Saturnin Fabré (Professeur Pique), Serge Freddy-Karl (Jacquot), Leon Belieres (Le Fripier), Mady Berry (Mme. Landrin), Tonia Navar, de la Comedie-Francaise (Mme. de la Carriere), Dorothy Dickson (herself), Laurette Fleury (Huguette Bouquet)

L'AMOUR CHANTE (Braunberger-Richebé) 1930

Production Director: Roger Woog
Scenario & Dialogue: Jacques Bousquet and Henri Falk
Adaptation: Jean-Charles Reynaud
Photography: Otto Kanturek and Edouard Hoesch
Decor: Julius von Borsody, Marc Allegret
Music: Jacques Bousquet and A. Bernard

105 minutes

Cast: Pierre Bertin, de la Comedie Francaise (Claude Merlerault), Louis Baron fils (M. Lherminois), Saturnin Fabre (M. Crespin), Fernand Gravey (Armand Petitjean), Yolande Laffon (Mme. Lherminois), Jeannine Merrey (Loulou Darling), Josseline Gael (Yvonne), Monthil (Mme. Couclier), Maryanne (Mère de Péléve).

EL PROFESOR DE MI SEÑORA (Cineas y Renacimiento Films) 1930

Photography: Otto Kanturek

Cast: Imperio Argentina, Valentin Parera, Alady, Crepin, Ortiz de Zarate, Lolo Frillo, Louis Torrecilla, Julia Lajos.

KOMM ZU MIR ZUM RENDEZ-VOUS (Harmonie Film G.M.B.H.) 1930

Producers: Gustav Schwab and Wilhelm Hubner, I. Rosenfeld Film G.M.B.H.
Director: Carl Boese
Continuity: Robert Florey and Carl Boese
Dialogue: Walter Hasenclever
Photography: Otto Kanturek and Eduard Hoesch
Art Director: Julius von Borsody
Music: Eduard Kunneke, Fritz Grothe, Arthur Guttmann

Cast: Ralph Arthur Roberts (Leon), Alexa Engstrom, (Antoinette), Walter Rilla (Armand), Szoke Szakall (Crepin), Lucie Englisch (Yvonne), Trude Lieske (Lulu), Fritz Schulz (Claude), Paul Morgan (Weber, Porfier), Margarete Kupfer (Frau Schild) The Plaza-Tiller-Girls.

Appendix B 357

LE BLANC ET LE NOIR (Braunberger-Richebé) 1931

Scenario & Dialogue: Sacha Guitry, from his play
Artistic Direction: Marc Allegret
Photography: Roger Hubert, Theodor Sparkuhl
Music: Philippe Pares, Georges Van Parys

107 minutes

Cast: Raimu (Marcel Desnoyers), Andre Alerme (Georges), Suzanne Dantes (Marguerite Desnoyers), Louis Baron fils (Grandfather Massicaut), Irene Wells (Peggy), Louis Kerly (Arthur), Charlotte Clasis (Mme. Massicaut), Fernandel (the groom), Pauline Carton (Mary), Monette Dinay (Josephine), Paul Pauley (Bureau chief), Charles Lamy (the doctor), the Jackson Girls.

FRANKENSTEIN (Universal) 1931

Producer: Carl Laemmle, Jr.
Associate Producer: E.M. Asher
Director: James Whale
Screenplay: Garrett Fort and Francis Edwards Faragoh [replaced by Robert Florey on French credits]; Based upon the composition by John L. Balderston; From the novel by Mary Shelley; Adapted from the play by Peggy Webling
Scenario Editor: Richard Schayer
Photography: Arthur Edeson
Art Director: Charles D. Hall
Editor: Clarence Kolster, Maurice Pivar (supervising)

70 minutes

Cast: Colin Clive (Henry Frankenstein), Mae Clarke (Elizabeth), John Boles (Victor Moritz), Boris Karloff (The Monster), Edward Van Sloan (Doctor Waldman), Frederick Kerr (Baron Frankenstein), Dwight Frye (Fritz), Lionel Belmore (Burgomaster), Marilyn Harris (Little Maria).

MURDERS IN THE RUE MORGUE (Universal) 1932

Producer: Carl Laemmle, Jr.
Associate Producer: E.M. Asher
Adaptation: Robert Florey, from the short story by Edgar Allan Poe
Screenplay: Tom Reed and Dale Van Every;* Additional Dialogue by John Huston

---

*Florey also collaborated on the screenplay, as well as being sole author of the adaptation.

Scenario Editor: Richard Schayer
Photography: Karl Freund
Art Director: Charles D. Hall
Editor: Milton Carruth, Maurice Pivar (supervising)

62 minutes

Cast: Sidney Fox (Camille L'Espanaye), Bela Lugosi (Dr. Mirakle), Leon Waycoff [Ames] (Pierre Dupin), Bert Roach (Paul), Brandon Hurst (Prefect of Police), Noble Johnson (Janos), D'Arcy Corrigan (Morgue Keeper), Betsy Ross Clarke (Mme. L'Espanaye), Arlene Francis (Woman of the Streets).

THE MAN CALLED BACK (KBS--Tiffany--World-Wide) 1932

Screenplay: Robert Presnell, from the novel Silent Thunder by Andrew Soutar*
Photography: Henry Sharp
Settings: Ralph DeLacy
Music: Val Burton
Editor: Rose Loewinger, Martin G. Cohn (Supervisor)

76 Minutes

Cast: Conrad Nagel (Dr. David Yorke), Doris Kenyon (Diana St. Claire), John Halliday (St. Claire), Juliette Compton (Vivian Lawrence), Reginald Owen (Dr. Atkins), Mona Maris (Lilaya), Alan Mowbray (King's Counsel), Gilbert Emery (Defense Counsel), Mae Busch (Rosie), John T. Murray (Corlis), Edgar Norton (Secretary), Lionel Belmore (Mr. Cartright), Clarissa Selwynne (Mrs. Cartright), Winter Hall (Judge), May Beatty (Mrs. Sanderson), George Pearce (Mr. Sanderson).

THOSE WE LOVE (KBS--Tiffany--World-Wide) 1932

Screenplay: F. Hugh Herbert, from a play by George Abbott and S.K. Lauren
Photography: Arthur Edeson
Settings: Ralph DeLacy
Music: Val Burton
Editor: Rose Loewinger, Martin G. Cohn (supervising)

77 minutes

Cast: Mary Astor (May), Kenneth MacKenna (Fred) Lilyan Tashman

---

*Florey (without receiving credit) collaborated equally with Presnell on the script.

Appendix B

(Valerie), Hale Hamilton (Blake), Tommy Conlon (Ricky), Earle Fox (Bert Parker), Forrester Harvey (Jake), Virginia Sale (Bertha), Pat O'Malley (Daley), Harvey Clark (Mr. Hart), Cecil Cunningham (Mrs. Henry Abbott), Edwin Maxwell (Marshall).

A STUDY IN SCARLET (Fox--World-Wide) 1933

Producers: Burt Kelly, Sam Bischoff and William Saal
Director: Edwin L. Marin
Screenplay: Robert Florey, from the novel by Sir Arthur Conan Doyle
Continuity & Dialogue: Reginald Owen
Photography: Arthur Edeson
Settings: Ralph DeLacy
Music: Val Burton
Editor: Rose Loewinger, Martin G. Cohn (supervising)

73 minutes

Cast: Reginald Owen (Sherlock Holmes), Anna May Wong (Mrs. Pyke), June Clyde (Eileen Forrester), Alan Dinehart (Merrydew), John Warburton (John Stanford), Warburton Gamble (Dr. Watson), J.M. Kerrigan (Jabez Wilson), Alan Mowbray (Lestrade), Doris Lloyd (Mrs. Murphy), Billy Bevan (Will Swallow), Leila Bennett (Dolly), Cecil Reynolds (Baker), Wyndham Standing (Capt. Pyke), Halliwell Hobbes (Dearing), Tetsu Komai (Ah Yet), Tempe Pigott (Mrs. Hudson).

GIRL MISSING (Warner Bros.--Vitaphone) 1933

Supervisor: Henry Blanke
Dialogue Director: Ben Markson
Screenplay: Carl Erickson and Don Mullaly, from their story
Photography: Arthur Todd
Art Director: Esdras Hartley
Editor: Ralph Dawson

69 minutes

Cast: Ben Lyon (Henry Gibson), Glenda Farrell (Kay Curtis), Mary Brian (June Dale), Peggy Shannon (Daisy), Lyle Talbot (Raymond Fox), Guy Kibbee (Kenneth Van Dusen), Harold Huber (Jim Hendricks), Edward Ellis (Inspector), Ferdinand Gottschalk (Alvin Bradford), Helen Ware (Mrs. Bradford), George Pat Collins (Crawford), Louise Beavers (Julie).

EX-LADY (Warner Bros.--Vitaphone) 1933

Supervisor: Lucien Hubbard

Dialogue Director: Stanley Logan
Screenplay: David Boehm, based on the play Illicit by Edith Fitzgerald and Robert Riskin
Photography: Tony Gaudio
Art Director: Bill Cannon
Editor: Harold McLennon

62 minutes

Cast: Bette Davis (Helen Bauer), Gene Raymond (Don Peterson), Frank McHugh (Hugo Van Hugh), Monroe Owsley (Nick Marvyn), Claire Dodd (Iris Van Hugh), Kay Strozzi (Peggy Smith), Ferdinand Gottschalk (Mr. Smith), Alphonse Ethier (The Father), Bodil Rosing (The Mother).

THE HOUSE ON 56th STREET (Warner Bros.--Vitaphone) 1933

Supervisor: James Seymour
Dialogue Director: William Keighley
Screenplay: Austin Parker and Sheridan Gibney, from the novel by Joseph Santley
Photography: Ernest Haller
Art Director: Esdras Hartley
Editor: Bud Bretherton

70 minutes

Cast: Kay Francis (Peggy), Ricardo Cortez (Blaine), Gene Raymond (Monte Van Tyle), John Halliday (Fiske), Margaret Lindsay (Eleanor), Frank McHugh (Hunt), Sheila Terry (Dolly), William Boyd (Bonelli), Hardie Albright (Henry), Philip Reed (Freddy), Phillip Faversham (Gordon), Henry O'Neill (Baxter), Walter Walker (Dr. Wyman), Nella Walker (Mrs. Van Tyle).

BEDSIDE (First National--Vitaphone--Warner Bros.) 1934

Supervisor: Sam Bischoff
Screenplay: Lillie Hayward and James Wharton; Additional Dialogue by Rian James; story by Manuel Seff and Harvey Thew
Photography: Sid Hickox
Art Director: Esdras Hartley
Editor: Harold McLennon

63 minutes

Cast: Warren William (Louis), Jean Muir (Caroline), Allen Jenkins (Sparks), David Landau (Smith), Kathryn Sergava (Maritza), Henry O'Neill (Dr. Chester), Donald Meek (Dr. Wiley), Renee Whitney (Varsova), Walter Walker (Dr. Michael), Philip Reed

Appendix B

(Interne), Philip Faversham (Interne), Louise Beavers (Pansy), Earle Foxe (Joe).

REGISTERED NURSE (First National--Vitaphone--Warner Bros.) 1934

Supervisor: Sam Bischoff
Dialogue Director: Arthur Greville Collins
Screenplay: Lillie Hayward and Peter Milne, from the play Miss Benton, R.N. by Florence Johns and Wilton Lackaye, Jr.
Photography: Sid Hickox
Art Director: Robert Haas
Editor: Jack Killifer

64 minutes

Cast: Bebe Daniels (Syvia Benton), Lyle Talbot (Dr. Connolly), John Halliday (Dr. Hedwig), Irene Franklin (Sadie), Sidney Toler (Sylvestrie), Gordon Westcott (Jim), Minna Gombell (Schloss), Beulah Bondi (McKenna), Vince Barnett (Jerry), Phillip Reed (Bill), Mayo Methot (Gloria), Renee Whitney (Ethel), Virginia Sale (Dixie), Ronnie Cosby (Dickie), Ed Gargan (Pat), Gordon Elliott (Male Nurse), George Humbert (Bonnelli).

SMARTY (Warner Bros.--Vitaphone) 1934

Supervisor: Robert Presnell
Dialogue Director: Frank McDonald
Screenplay: F. Hugh Herbert and Carl Erickson, from the play Hit Me Again by Herbert
Photography: George Barnes
Art Director: John Hughes
Editor: Howard Bretherton

64 minutes

Cast: Joan Blondell (Vicki), Warren William (Tony), Edward Everett Horton (Vernon), Frank McHugh (George), Claire Dodd (Anita), Joan Wheeler (Bonnie), Virginia Sale (Edna), Leonard Carey (Tilford).

I SELL ANYTHING (First National--Warner Bros.) 1935

Supervisor: Sam Bischoff
Screenplay: Brown Holmes and Sidney Sutherland; story by Albert J. Cohen and Robert T. Shannon
Photography: Sid Hickox

Art Director: Jack Holden
Editor: Terry Morse

70 minutes

Cast: Pat O'Brien (Spot Cash Cutler), Ann Dvorak (Barbara), Claire Dodd (Millicent Clark), Roscoe Carns (Monk), Hobart Cavanaugh (Stooge), Russell Hopton (Smiley Thompson), Robert Barrat (McPherson), Harry Tyler (Second Stooge), Gus Shy (Third Stooge), Leonard Carey (Pertwee), Ferdinand Gottschalk, (Barouche), Clay Clement (Peter Van Gruen).

I AM A THIEF (Warner Bros.) 1935

Supervisor: Henry Blanke
Dialogue Director: Frank McDonald
Screenplay: Ralph Block and Doris Malloy, from their story
Photography: Sid Hickox
Art Director: Jack Okey
Editor: Terry Morse

64 minutes

Cast: Mary Astor (Odette Mouclair), Ricardo Cortez (Pierre Londais), Dudley Digges (Colonel Jackson), Robert Barrat (Baron Van Kampf), Irving Pichel (Count Trentini), Hobart Cavanaugh (Daudet), Arthur Aylesworth (Francois), Ferdinand Gottschalk (M. Cassiet), Frank Reicher (Max Bolen), Florence Fair (Madame Cassiet), John Wray (Porricci), Oscar Apfel (Auctioneer).

THE WOMAN IN RED (First National--Warner Bros.) 1935

Supervisor: Harry Joe Brown
Dialogue Director: Stanley Logan
Screenplay: Mary McCall, Jr. and Peter Milne, from the novel North Shore by Wallace Irwin
Photography: Sol Polito
Art Director: Esdras Hartley
Editor: Terry Morse

68 minutes

Cast: Barbara Stanwyck (Shelby Barret), Gene Raymond (Johnny Wyatt), Genevieve Tobin (Nicho), John Eldredge (Eugene Fairchild), Phillip Reed (Dan), Dorothy Tree (Olga), Russell Hicks (Clayton), Nella Walker (Aunt Bettina), Claude Gillingwater (Grandfather Wyatt), Doris Lloyd (Mrs. Casserly), Hale Hamilton (Wyatt Furness), Arthur Treacher (Major Casserly), Ed Van Sloan (Foxall), Forrester Harvey (Mooney), Ann Shoemaker

Appendix B

(Cora), Gordon Elliott (Stuart Wyatt), Fred Vogeding (Nels Ericson), Eleanor Wesselhoft (Mrs. Agnew), Brandon Hurst (Uncle Emlen).

THE FLORENTINE DAGGER (Warner Bros.) 1935

Supervisor: Harry Joe Brown
Dialogue Director: Arthur Greville Collins
Screenplay: Tom Reed; Additional Dialogue by Brown Holmes; based on the novel by Ben Hecht
Photography: Arthur Todd
Art Directors: Anton Grot and Carl Jules Weyl
Editor: Thomas Pratt

70 minutes

Cast: Donald Woods (Cesare), Margaret Lindsay (Florence), C. Aubrey Smith (Dr. Lytton), Henry O'Neill (Victor Ballau), Robert Barrat (The Captain), Florence Fair (Teresa), Frank Reicher (Von Stein), Charles Judels (Salvatore), Rafaela Ottiano (Lili Salvatore), Paul Porcase (Antonio), Eily Malyon (Fredericka), Egon Brecher (Karl), Henry Kolker (Auctioneer), Herman Bing (The Baker).

GOING HIGHBROW (Warner Bros.) 1935

Supervisor: Sam Bischoff
Screenplay: Edward Kaufman and Sy Bartlett; Additional Dialogue, Ben Markson; based on the story "Social Pirates" by Ralph Spence
Photography: William Rees
Art Director: Esdras Hartley
Music & Lyrics: Louis Alter and John Scholl
Editor: Harold McLernon

68 minutes

Cast: Guy Kibbee (Matt Upshaw), ZaSu Pitts (Mrs. Upshaw), Edward Everett Horton (Augie), Ross Alexander (Harley Marsh), June Martel (Millicent), Gordon Westcott (Sam Long), Judy Canova (Annie).

DON'T BET ON BLONDES (Warner Bros.) 1935

Supervisor: Sam Bischoff
Dialogue Director: Arthur Greville Collins
Screenplay: Isabel Dawn and Boyce DeGaw, from their story
Photography: William Rees

Art Director: Esdras Hartley
Editor: Thomas Richards

62 minutes

Cast: Warren William ("Odds" Owen), Claire Dodd (Marilyn), Guy Kibbee (Colonel Youngblood), William Gargan ("Numbers"), Vince Barnett ("Brains"), Hobart Cavanaugh (Philbert O. Slemp), Clay Clement (T. Everett Markham), Errol Flynn (David Van Dusen), Spencer Charters (Doc), Walter Byron (Dwight Boardman), Eddie Shubert (Steve), Jack Norton (Slade), Mary Treen (Switchboard Operator), Maude Eburne (Ella Purdy), Herman Bing (Professor Gruber), Armando and Lita.

THE PAY-OFF (First National--Warner Bros.) 1935

Supervisor: Bryan Foy
Screenplay: George Bricker and Joel Sayre; story by Bricker
Photography: Arthur Todd
Art Director: Carl Weyl
Editor: Harold McLernon

68 minutes

Cast: James Dunn (Joe McCoy), Claire Dodd (Maxine), Patricia Ellis (Connie), Alan Dinehart (Marty Bleuler), Joseph Crehan (Harvey Morris), Frankie Darro (Jimmy Moore), Frank Sheridan (George Gorman), Eddie Shubert (Beetles Davis), Al Hill (Mike).

SHIP CAFE (Paramount) 1935

Producer: Harold Hurley
Supervisor: Lewis E. Gensler
Screenplay: Harlan Thompson and Herbert Fields, from their story
Photography: Theodor Sparkhul
Art Directors: Hans Dreier and Earl Hedrick
Music & Lyrics: Ray Noble, Harlan Thompson and Lewis E. Gensler
Songs: "I Won't Take No for an Answer," "Fatal Fascination," "Change Your Mind"
Dance Director: LeRoy Prinze
Editor: James Smith

74 minutes

Cast: Carl Brisson (Chris Anderson), Arline Judge (Ruby), Mady Christians (Countess Boranoff), William Frawley (Briney O'Brien), Eddie Davis (Himself), Inez Courtney (Molly), Grant Withers (Rocky Stone), Harry Woods (Donovan), Irving Bacon (Slim), Fred Warren (Harry), Jack Norton (Mr. Randall).

Appendix B 365

THE PREVIEW MURDER MYSTERY (Paramount) 1936

Producer: Harold Hurley
Screenplay: Brian Marlow and Robert Yost, from a story by Garnett Weston
Photography: Karl Struss
Art Directors: Hans Dreier and Earl Hedrick
Editor: James Smith

65 minutes

Cast: Reginald Denny (Johnny Morgan), Francis Drake (Peggy Madison), Gail Patrick (Claire Woodward), Rod LaRoque (Neil Dubeck), Ian Keith (E. Gordon Smith), George Barbier (Jerome Hewitt), Conway Tearle (Edwin Strange), Thomas Jackson (Lt. McKane), Jack Raymond (Tyson), Eddie Dunn (Tub Wilson), Bryant Washburn (Jennings), Lee Shumway (Chief of Police), Chester Conklin (Self), Jack Mulhall (Screen "Heavy"), Henry Kleinbach (Screen "Actor").

TILL WE MEET AGAIN (Paramount) 1936

Producer: Albert Lewis
Dialogue Director: William Russell
Adaptation: Morton Barteaux, from the play Reunion by Alfred Davis
Screenplay: Edwin Justus Mayer, Brian Marlow and Franklin Coen
Photography: Victor Milner
Art Directors: Hans Dreier and Roland Anderson

72 minutes

Cast: Herbert Marshall (Alan Barclay), Gertrude Michael (Elsa Duranyi), Lional Atwell (Ludwig), Rod LaRocque (Carl Schrottle), Guy Bates Post (Capt. Minton), Vallejo Gantner (Vogel), Torben Meyer (Kraus), Julia Faye (Nurse), Egon Brecher (Schultz).

HOLLYWOOD BOULEVARD (1936) Paramount

Producer: A.M. Botsford
Supervisor: Edward F. Cline
Screenplay: Marguerite Roberts;* story by Max Marcin and Faith Thomas

---

*Florey was the uncredited co-author of the story and screenplay.

Photography: Karl Struss
Art Directors: Hans Dreier and Earl Hedrick
Music: Gregory Stone
Editor: Harvey Johnston

75 minutes

Cast: John Halliday (John Blakeford), Marsha Hunt (Patricia Blakeford), Robert Cummings (Jay Wallace), C. Henry Gordon (Jordan Winslow), Frieda Inescort (Alice Winslow), Esther Ralston (Flora Moore), Esther Dale (Martha), Betty Compson (Betty), Albert Conti (Sanford), Richard Powell (Moran), Rita La Roy (Nella), Oscar Apfel (Dr. Inslow), Purnell Pratt (Mr. Steinman), Irving Bacon (Gus the Bartender), Lois Kent (Little Girl), Gregory Gay (Russian Writer), Eleanore Whitney (Herself), Tom Kennedy (Bouncer), Francis X. Bushman (Director of Desert Scene), Maurice Costello (Director), Charles Ray (Charlie Smith the Assistant Director), Mae Marsh (Carlotta Blakeford), Herbert Rawlinson (Manager of Grauman's Chinese Theatre), Jane Novak (Mrs. Steinman), Kathryn "Kitty" McHugh (Secretary), Bryant Washburn (Robert Martin), William Desmond (Guest), Bert Roach (Scenarist), Mabel Forrest (Mother), Roy D'Arcy (The Sheik), Jack Mulhall, Creighton Hale, and Gary Cooper (Men at Bar), Harry Myers and Frank Mayo (Themselves), Gertrude Simpson (Gossip), Jack Mower (Frank Stucky), Pat O'Malley (Dance Extra).

OUTCAST (Paramount--Major Productions) 1937

Producer: Emanuel Cohen
Screenplay: Doris Malloy and Dore Schary, from the novel Happiness Preferred by Frank R. Adams
Photography: Rudolph Maté
Art Director: Wiard Ihnen
Editor: Ray Curtis

73 minutes

Cast: Warren William (Dr. Philip Wendel Jones), Karen Morley (Margaret Stevens), Lewis Stone (Lawyer Abbott), Jackie Moran (Freddie), Christian Rub (Olaf), Esther Dale (Hattie Simmerson), Richard Carle (Mooney).

KING OF GAMBLERS (Paramount) 1937

Screenplay: Doris Anderson, from a story by Tiffany Thayer
Photography: Harry Fischbeck
Art Directors: Hans Dreier and Robert Odell
Songs: "Hate to Talk About Myself" by Ralph Rainger, Leo Robin

Appendix B

and Richard A. Whiting; "I'm Feelin' High" by Burton Lane and
Ralph Freed
Musical Direction: Boris Morros
Editor: Harvey Johnston

78 minutes

Cast: Claire Trevor (Dixie), Lloyd Nolan (Jim), Akim Tamiroff
(Steve Kalkas), Larry Crabbe (Eddie), Helen Burgess (Jackie
Nolan), Porter Hall (George Kramer), Harvey Stephens (J.G.
Temple), Barlowe Borland (Mr. Parker), Purnell Pratt (Strohm),
Colin Tapley (Joe), Paul Fix (Charlie), Cecil Cunningham (Big
Edna), Robert Gleckler (Ed Murkil), Nick Lukats (Taxi Driver),
Fay Holden (Nurse), John Patterson (Freddie), Evelyn Brent
(Cora), Estelle Etterre (Laura), Priscilla Lawson (Grace), Harry
Strang (Simeley), Richard Terry (Solly), Connie Tom (Tika),
Harry Worth (Chris), Louise Brooks (Joyce Beaton).

MOUNTAIN MUSIC (Paramount) 1937

Producer: Benjamin Glazer
Screenplay: John C. Moffitt, Duke Attebury, Russell Crouse and
Charles Lederer; based on a story by MacKinlay Kantor
Photography: Karl Struss
Art Direction: Hans Dreier and John Goodman
Words & Music: Sam Coslow
Songs: "If I Put My Heart in My Song," "Can't You Hear That
Mountain Music," "Thar She Comes," "Good Mornin'"
Dance Director: LeRoy Prinz
Editor: Eda Warren

76 minutes

Cast: Bob Burns (Bob Burnside), Martha Raye (Mary Beamish),
John Howard (Ardinger), Terry Walker (Lobelia), George Hayes
(Grandpappy), Jan Duggan (Ma), Fuzzy Knight (Amos), Rufe
Davis (Ham), Spencer Charters (Justice Sharody), Olin Howland
(Pappy), Charles Timblin (Shep), Wally Vernon (Odette Potts),
Georgia Simmons (Ma Shepardson), Arthur Hohl (Prosecuting
Attorney), Miranda Giles (Aunt Effie), William Burress (Mr.
Menafee), Buster Brodie (Snuffy), Rita LaRoy (Mrs. Lovelace),
Louis Natheaux (Mr. Lovelace), Goody Montgomery (Alice),
Virginia Dabney (Edna), Terry Ray (Helen).

THIS WAY PLEASE (Paramount) 1937

Producer: Mel Shauer
Screenplay: Grant Garrett, Seena Owen, and Howard J. Green;
based on a story by Maxwell Shane and Bill Thomas

Photography: Henry Sharp, Harry Fischbeck
Art Direction: Hans Dreier and Jack Otterson
Words & Music: "This Way Please," by Sam Coslow and Al Siegel; "Delighted to Meet You," by Coslow; "Is It Love or Infatuation," by Coslow and Frederick Hollander; "Voom Voom," by Coslow
Dance Director: LeRoy Prinz
Editor: Anne Bauchens

72 minutes

Cast: Charles "Buddy" Rogers (Brad Morgan), Betty Grable (Jane Morrow), Ned Sparks (Inky Wells), Jim and Marian Jordan (Fibber McGee and Molly), Porter Hall (S.J. Crawford), Lee Bowman (Stu Randall), Cecil Cunningham (Miss Eberhardt), Wally Vernon (Bumps), Romo Vincent (Trumps), Jerry Bergen (Mumps), Rufe Davis (Sound Effects Man), Mary Livingstone (Maxine Barry), Akim Tamiroff (Tartar Chieftain), John Patterson (Jim), Terry Walker (Miss Fairchild), Alma Ross (Janet), Virginia Dabney (Lee).

DAUGHTER OF SHANGHAI (Paramount) 1937

Screenplay: Gladys Unger and Garnett Weston, based on a story by Weston
Photography: Charles Schoenbaum
Art Directors: Hans Dreier and Robert Odell
Editor: Ellsworth Hoagland

67 minutes

Cast: Anna May Wong (Lan Ying Lin), Philip Ahn (Kim Lee), Charles Bickford (Otto Hartman), Larry Crabbe (Andrew Sleete), Cecil Cunningham (Mrs. Mary Hunt), J. Carrol Naish (Frank Barden), Evelyn Brent (Olga Derey), Anthony Quinn (Harry Morgan), Gino Corrado (Interpreter), John Patterson (James Lang), Fred Kohler (Cpatain Gulner), Frank Sully (Jake Kelly), Ching Wah Lee (Quan Lin), Maurice Liu (Ah Fong), Guy Bates Post (Lloyd Burkett), Virginia Dabney (Rita), Pierre Watkin (Mr. Yorkland), Archie Twitchell (Secretary), Mrs. Wong Wing (Amah), Ernest Whitman (Sam Blike), Mae Busch (Lill), Paul Fix (Miles), Charles Wilson (Schwartz).

DANGEROUS TO KNOW (Paramount) 1939

Producer: Edward T. Lowe
Screenplay: William R. Lipman and Horace McCoy, based on the play On the Spot by Edgar Wallace
Photography: Theodor Sparkuhl
Art Directors: Hans Dreier and John Goodman

Appendix B 369

Music: Boris Morros
Editor: Arthur Schmidt

70 minutes

Cast: Anna May Wong (Madam Lan Ying), Akim Tamiroff, (Stephen Recka), Gail Patrick (Margaret Van Kase), Lloyd Nolan (Inspector Brandon), Harvey Stephens (Philip Easton), Anthony Quinn (Nicholai Kusnoff), Roscoe Karns (Duncan), Porter Hall (Mayor Bradley), Barlowe Borland (Butler), Hedda Hopper (Mrs. Carson), Hugh Sothern (Harvey Greggson), Edward Pawley (John Rance).

KING OF ALCATRAZ (Paramount) 1938

Associate Producer: William C. Thomas
Screenplay: Irving Reis, from his story
Photography: Harry Fischbeck
Art Directors: Hans Dreier and Earl Hedrick
Editor: Eda Warren

56 minutes

Cast: Gail Patrick (Dale Borden), Lloyd Nolan (Raymond Grayson), Harry Carey (Captain Glennan), J. Carrol Naish (Steve Murkil), Robert Preston (Robert MacArthur), Anthony Quinn (Lou Gedney), Richard Stanley (First Mate Rogers), Virginia Dabney (Bonnie Larkin), Nora Cecil (Nora Kane), Emory Parnell (Olaf), Dorothy Howe (Dixie), John Hart (1st Radio Operator), Philip Warren (2nd Radio Operator), Porter Hall (Matthew Talbot), Richard Denning (Harry Vay), Tom Tyler (Gus Banshek), Konstantin Shayne (Murak).

DISBARRED (Paramount) 1939

Associate Producer: Stuart Walker
Screenplay: Lillie Hayward and Robert R. Presnell, based on a story by Harry Sauber
Photography: Harry Fischbeck
Art Directors: Hans Dreier and William Flannery
Editor: Arthur Schmidt

58 minutes

Cast: Gail Patrick (Joan Carroll), Robert Preston (Bradley Kent), Otto Kruger (Tyler Cradon), Sidney Toler (G.L. "Mardy" Mardeen), Helen MacKellar (Abbey Tennant), Virginia Dabney (Miss LaRue), Edward Marr (Harp Harrigan), Charles D. Brown (Jackson), Clay Clement (Attorney Roberts), Frank M. Thomas (G.H.

Blanchard, D.A.), John Hart (Reporter), Harry Worth (Reporter).

HOTEL IMPERIAL (Paramount) 1939

Screenplay: Gilbert Gabriel and Robert Thoeren, based on the play by Lajos Biro
Photography: William Mellor
Art Directors: Hans Dreier and Franz Bachelin
Music: Richard Hageman
Song: "There's Something Magic Saying Nitchevo," music and lyrics by Frederick Hollander and Ralph Freed
Editor: Chandler House

78 minutes

Cast: Isa Miranda (Anna), Ray Milland (Lieutenant Nemassy), Reginald Owen (General Videnko), Gene Lockhart (Elias), J. Carrol Naish (Kuprin), Curt Bois (Anton), Henry Victor (Sultanov), Albert Dekker (Sergeant), Don Cossack Chorus--Serge Jaroff, Conductor.

THE MAGNIFICENT FRAUD (Paramount) 1939

Producer: Harlan Thompson
Screenplay: Gilbert Gabriel and Walter Ferris, based on the story "Caviare for His Excellency" by Charles G. Booth
Photography: William Mellor
Art Directors: Hans Dreier and Ernst Fegté
Music: Phil Boutelje
Dances Staged by: LeRoy Prinz
Editor: James Smith

78 minutes

Cast: Akim Tamiroff (Jules LaCrois/President Don Miguel Esteban Alvarado), Lloyd Nolan (Sam Barr), Mary Boland (Aunt Jerry Genet), Patricia Morison (Claire Hill), George Zucco (Dr. Virgo), Steffi Duna (Carmelita), Robert Warwick (Gen. Hernandez), Frank Reicher (Senor Garcia Mendietta), Donald Gallaher (Dr. Diaz), Ernest Verebes (Castro), Robert Middlemass (Morales), Ernest Cossart (Duval), Ralph Forbes (Harrison Todd), Barbara Pepper (June), Abner Biberman (Lt. Ruiz), Alexander Woloshin (Santiago), Maude Eburne (Senora Moreno), Joseph Marievsky (Emilio).

DEATH OF A CHAMPION (Paramount) 1939

Screenplay: Stuart Palmer and Cortland Fitzsimmons, based on the

Appendix B 371

story "The Human Encyclopedia" by Frank Gruber
Photography: Stuart Thompson
Art Directors: Hans Dreier and Franz Bachelin
Editor: Archie Marshek

67 minutes

Cast: Lynne Overman (Oliver Quade), Virginia Dale (Patsy Doyle), Joseph Allen, Jr. (Richie Oakes), Donald O'Connor (Small Fry), Susan Paley (Lois Lanyard), Harry Davenport (Guy Lanyard), Robert Paige (Alec Temple), Mae Boley (Ma Sloane), Hal Brazeale (Gerald Lanyard), Frank M. Thomas (Chief Sanders), David Clyde (Angus McTavish), Walter Soderling (Hofnagel), Pierre Watkin (Albert Deacon), Bob McKenzie (Dr. Taylor).

PAROLE FIXER (Paramount) 1940

Associate Producer: Edward T. Lowe
Screenplay: William R. Lipman and Horace McCoy, based on the book Persons in Hiding by J. Edgar Hoover
Photography: Harry Fischbeck
Art Directors: Hans Dreier and John Goodman
Editor: Harvey Johnston

57 minutes

Cast: Robert Paige (Steve Eddson), William Henry (Scott Britton), Virginia Dale (Enid Casserly), Marjorie Gateson (Mrs. Thornton Casserly), Jack Carson (George Mattison), Anthony Quinn (Francis "Big Boy" Bradmore), Richard Denning (Bruce Eaton), Fay Helm (Rita Mattison), Lyle Talbot (Ross Waring), Harvey Stephens (Bartley Hanford), Wilfred Roberts (Frank Preston), Richard Carle (Gustav Kalkus), Paul McGrath (Tyler Craden), Gertrude Michael (Colette Menthe), Harry Shannon (Randall Porter), Louise Beavers (Aunt Lindy).

WOMEN WITHOUT NAMES (Paramount) 1940

Associate Producer: Eugene Zukor
Screenplay: William R. Lipman and Horace McCoy, based on a play by Ernest Booth
Photography: Charles Lang
Art Directors: Hans Dreier and William Flannery
Editor: Anne Bauchens

62 minutes

Cast: Ellen Drew (Joyce King), Robert Paige (Fred MacNeil), Judith Barrett (Peggy Athens), John Miljan (John Marlin), Fay Helm (Millie), John McGuire (Walter Ferris), Louise

Beavers (Ivory), James Seay (O'Grane), Esther Dale (Head Matron Inglis), Marjorie Main (Mrs. Lowry), Audrey Maynard (Maggie), Kitty Kelly (Countess), Virginia Dabney (Ruffles), Helen Lynch (Susie), Mae Busch (Rose), Frank M. Thomas (Warden Rynex).

THE FACE BEHIND THE MASK (Columbia) 1941

Producer: Wallace McDonald
Screenplay: Allen Vincent and Paul Jarrico; story by Arthur Levinson, based on a radio play by Thomas Edward O'Connell
Photography: Franz Planer
Art Director: Lionel Banks
Music: M.W. Stoloff
Editor: Charles Nelson

69 minutes

Cast: Peter Lorre (Janos Szaby), Evelyn Keyes (Helen Williams), Don Beddoe (Jim O'Hara), George E. Stone (Dinky), John Tyrrell (Watts), Stanley Brown (Harry), Al Seymour (Benson), James Seay (Jeff), Warren Ashe (Johnson), Charles Wilson (Chief O'Brien), George McKay (Terry Finnegan).

MEET BOSTON BLACKIE (Columbia) 1941

Producer: Ralph Cohn
Screenplay: Jay Dratler, based on the character created by Jack Boyle
Photography: Franz Planer
Art Director: Lionel Banks
Editor: James Sweeney

62 minutes

Cast: Chester Morris (Boston Blackie), Rochelle Hudson (Cecelia Bradley), Richard Lane (Inspector Faraday), Charles Wagenheim (The Runt), Constance Worth (Marilyn Howard), Jack O'Malley (Monk), George Magrill (Georgie), Michael Rand (Mechanical Man), Eddie Laughton (Freak Show Barker), John Tyrrell (Freak Show Doorman), Harry Anderson (Dart Game Barker), Byron Foulger (Blind Man), Schlitzie (Bird-Man).

TWO IN A TAXI (Columbia) 1941

Producer: Irving Briskin
Screenplay: Howard J. Green, Morton Thompson, Malvin Wald
Photography: George Mechan

Appendix B 373

Art Director: Lionel Banks
Music: M.W. Stoloff
Editor: Viola Lawrence

63 minutes

Cast: Anita Louise (Bonnie), Russell Hayden (Jimmy Owens), Noah Beery, Jr. (Sandy Connors), Dick Purcell (Bill Gratton), Chick Chandler (Sid), Fay Helm (Ethel), George Cleveland (Gas Station Proprietor), Frank Yaconelli (Tony Vitale), Ben Taggart (Sweeny), Paul Porcase (Herman), Henry Brandon (Professor), John Harmon (Benny), Ralph Peters (Zazu), James Seay (Christy Reardon).

DANGEROUSLY THEY LIVE (Warner Bros.) 1941

Associate Producer: Ben Stoloff
Screenplay: Marion Parsonnet
Dialogue Director: Hugh Cummings
Photography: L. William O'Connell
Art Director: Hugh Reticker
Editor: Harold McLernon

78 minutes

Cast: John Garfield (Dr. Michael Lewis), Nancy Coleman (Jane), Raymond Massey (Dr. Ingersoll), Lee Patrick (Nurse Johnson), Moroni Olsen (Mr. Goodwin), Esther Dale (Dawson), John Ridgely (John), Christian Rub (Steiner), Frank Reicher (Jarvis), Ben Welden (Eddie), Cliff Clark (John Dill), Roland Drew (Dr. Murdock), Arthur Aylsworth (Gate Keeper), John Harmon (George, Taxi Driver), Matthew Boulton (Capt. Hunter), Gavin Muir (Capt. Strong), Ilka Gruning (Mrs. Steiner), Frank M. Thomas (Ralph Bryan), James Seay (Carl).

LADY GANGSTER (Warner Bros.) 1942

Producer: William Jacobs
Director: Florian Roberts (pseudonym for Robert Florey)
Screenplay: Anthony Coldewey, based on a play by Dorothy Mackaye and Carlton Miles
Dialogue Director: Frank Fox
Photography: Arthur Todd
Art Director: Ted Smith
Editor: Harold McLernon

62 minutes

Cast: Faye Emerson (Dot Burton), Julie Bishop (Myrtle Reed),

Frank Wilcox (Kenneth Phillips), Roland Drew (Carey Wells), Jackie C. Gleason (Wilson), Ruth Ford (Lucy Fenton), Virginia Brissac (Mrs. Stoner), Dorothy Vaughn (Jenkins), Dorothy Adams (Deaf Annie), DeWolf Hopper (John), Vera Lewis (Ma Silsby), Herbert Rawlinsen (Lewis Sinten), Peggy Diggins (Mary), Charles Wilson (Detective), Bill Phillips (Stew), Frank Mayo (Walker), Leah Baird (Matron).

THE DESERT SONG (Warner Bros.) 1943

Producer: Robert Buckner
Screenplay: Based upon a play by Lawrence Schwab, Otto Harbach, Oscar Hammerstein II, Sigmund Romberg and Frank Mandel*
Dialogue Director: Harold Winston
Photography: Bert Glennon (Technicolor)
Art Director: Charles Novi
Music Adapted by: H. Roemheld
Additional Song: "Gay Parisienne" by Jack Scholl and Serge Walter
Dance Numbers Staged and Directed by: LeRoy Prinz
Editor: Frank Magee

96 minutes

Cast: Dennis Morgan (Paul Hudson), Irene Manning (Margot), Bruce Cabot (Fontaine), Lynne Overman (Johnny Walsh), Gene Lockhart (Père FanFan), Faye Emerson (Hajy), Victor Francen (Caid Youseff), Curt Bois (Francois), Jack LaRue (Lieutenant Bertin), Marcel Dalio (Tarbouch), Nestor Paiva (Benoit), Gerald Mohr (Hassan), Felix Basch (Heinzelman), Noble Johnson (Abdel Rahman), Wallis Clark (Pajot), Fritz Leiber (Ben Sidi), George Renavent (Radik), William Edmunds (Suliman), Egon Brecher (French Colonel), Duncan Renaldo (Captain of the Guards), Albert Morin (Muhammed).

ROGER TOUHY--GANGSTER (Twentieth Century-Fox), 1944

Producer: Lee Marcus
Screenplay: Crane Wilbur and Jerry Cady, story by Wilbur
Photography: Glen MacWilliams
Art Director: James Baseri, Lewis Creber
Music: Hugo W. Friedhofer
Editor: Harry Reynolds

65 minutes

---

*The new adaptation and screenplay was co-authored by Florey and producer Robert Buckner.

Appendix B 375

Cast: Preston Foster (Roger Touhy), Victor McLaglen (Owl Banghart), Lois Andrews (Daisy), Kent Taylor (Captain Steve Warren), Anthony Quinn (George Carroll), William Post, Jr. (Joe Sutton), Henry Morgan (Smoke Reardon), Matt Briggs (Cameron), Moroni Olsen (Riley), Reed Hadley (Drake), Trudy Marshall (Gloria), John Archer (Kerrigan), Frank Jenks (Troubles O'Connor), George E. Stone (Ice Box Hamilton).

MAN FROM FRISCO (Republic) 1944

Associate Producer: Albert J. Cohen
Screenplay: Ethel Hill, Arnold Manoff
Story & Adaptation: George Worthing Yates and George Carleton Brown
Photography: Jack Marta
Art Director: Russell Kimball
Music: Marlin Skiles
Editor: Ernest Nims

91 minutes

Cast: Michael O'Shea (Matt Braddock), Anne Shirley (Diana Kennedy), Gene Lockhart (Joel Kennedy), Anne Shoemaker (Martha Kennedy), Dan Duryea (Jim Benson), Stephanie Bachelor (Ruth Warnecke), Michael Barnitz (Baby Warnecke, Jr.), Tommy Bond (Russ Kennedy), Robert Warwick (Bruce McRae), Olin Howlin (Eben Whelock), Russell Simpson (Dr. Hershey), Stanley Andrews (Chief Campbell), Forbes Murray (Maritime Commissioner), Erville Alderson (Judge Mclain), Ray Walker (Johnny Rogers).

GOD IS MY CO-PILOT (Warner Bros.) 1945

Producer: Robert Buckner
Screenplay: Peter Milne and Abem Finkel, from the book by Colonel Robert Lee Scott, Jr.
Dialogue Director: Jack Gage
Photography: Sid Hickox
Art Director: John Hughes
Music: Franz Waxman
Editor: Folmer Blangsted

89 minutes

Cast: Dennis Morgan (Col. Robert L. Scott), Dane Clark (Johnny Petach), Raymond Massey (Gen. Chennault), Alan Hale (Big Mike), Andrea King (Catharine), John Ridgely (Tex Hill), Stanley Ridges (Col. Cooper), Craig Stevens (Rector), Warren Douglas (Bob Neal), Stephen Richards (Sgt. Baldridge), Charles Smith (Pvt. Motley), Minor Watson (Col. Haynes),

Richard Loo (Tokyo Joe), Murray Alper (Sgt. Aaltonen), Joel Allen (Lt. Sharp), Frank Tang (Chinese Captain), Paul Brook (Lt. Horner), John Miles (Lt. Wilson), Bernie Sell (John Allison), William Forrest (Dr. Reynolds), Danny Dowling (Frank Schiel), Philip Ahn (Jap Radio Announcer).

DANGER SIGNAL (Warner Bros.) 1945

Producer: William Jacobs
Screenplay: Adele Commandini and Graham Baker, from the novel by Phyllis Bottome
Dialogue Director: Jack Daniels
Photography: James Wong Howe
Art Director: Stanley Fleischer
Music: Adolph Deutsch
Editor: Frank Magee

80 minutes

Cast: Faye Emerson (Hilda Fenchurch), Zachary Scott (Ronnie Marsh), Dick Erdman (Bunkie Taylor), Rosemary DeCamp (Dr. Silla), Bruce Bennett (Dr. Andrew Lang), Mona Freeman (Anne Fenchurch), John Ridgely (Thomas Turner), Mary Servoss (Mrs. Fenchurch), Joyce Compton (Katie), Virginia Sale (Mrs. Crockett), Investigator (Addison Richards).

THE BEAST WITH FIVE FINGERS (Warner Bros.) 1946

Producer: William Jacobs
Screenplay: Curt Siodmak, from the short story by William Fryer Harvey
Dialogue Director: Jack Daniels
Photography: Wesley Anderson
Art Director: Stanley Fleischer
Music: Max Steiner
Editor: Frank Magee

90 minutes

Cast: Robert Alda (Bruce Conrad), Andrea King (Julie Holden), Peter Lorre (Hilary Cummins), Victor Francen (Francis Ingram), J. Carrol Naish (Ovidio Castanio), Charles Dingle (Raymond Arlington), John Alvin (Donald Arlington), David Hoffman (Duprex), Barbara Brown (Mrs. Miller), Patricia White (Clara), William Edmunds (Antonio), Belle Mitchell (Giovana), Ray Walker (Mr. Miller), Pedro de Cordoba (Horatio).

Appendix B 377

MONSIEUR VERDOUX (United Artists) 1947

Producer-Director: Charles Chaplin
Associate Directors: Robert Florey and Wheeler Dryden
Screenplay: Charles Chaplin, from his story
Artistic Supervision: Curtis Courant
Photography: Roland Totheroh
Art Direction: John Beckman
Music: Charles Chaplin
Editor: Willard Nico

123 minutes

Cast: Charles Chaplin (Henri Verdoux, alias Varnay, alias Bonheur, alias Floray), Mady Correll (Mona), Allison Roddan (Peter), Robert Lewis (Maurice Botello), Audrey Betz (Martha), Martha Raye (Annabella Bonheur), Ada-May (Annette), Isobel Elsom (Marie Grosnay), Marjorie Bennett (her maid), Helene Heigh (Yvonne), Margaret Hoffman (Lydia Floray), Marilyn Nash (the Girl), Irving Bacon (Pierre), Edwin Mills (Jean), Virginia Brissac (Carlotta), Almira Sessions (Lena), Eula Morgan (Phoebe), Bernard J. Nedell (Prefect of Police), Charles Evans (Detective Morrow), Arthur Hohl (Rental Agent), Vera Marshe (Vicki), John Harmon (Joe).

TARZAN AND THE MERMAIDS (RKO Radio Pictures) 1948

Producer: Sol Lesser
Screenplay: Carroll Young, from his story; based upon the characters created by Edgar Rice Burroughs
Photography: Jack Draper
Art Director: McClure Capps
Music: Dimitri Tiomkin
Editor: Merrill White (supervising), John Sheets (associate)

Associate Personnel--

Associate Producer: Joe Noriega
Associate Director: Miguel M. Delgado
Photography: Raul Martinez Solares, Gabriel Figueroa
Art Director: Gunther Gerzso

68 minutes

Cast: Johnny Weissmuller (Tarzan), Brenda Joyce (Jane), Linda Christian (Mara), John Laurenz (Benji), Fernando Wagner (Varga), Edward Ashley (Commissioner), Andrea Palma (Luana), George Zucco (Palanth), Gustavo Rojo (Tiko).

ROGUES' REGIMENT (Universal-International) 1948

Producer: Robert Buckner

Screenplay: Robert Buckner, story by Buckner and Robert Florey*
Photography: Maury Gertsman
Art Directors: Bernard Herzbrun, Gabriel Scognamillo
Music: Daniele Amfitheatrof
Songs: "Who Can Tell" and "Just for a While," music by Serge Walter, lyrics by Jack Brooks, German lyrics by Walter Jurmann
Dance Director: Billy Daniels
Editor: Ralph Dawson

86 minutes

Cast: Dick Powell (Whit Carbett), Marta Toren (Lili Maubert), Vincent Price (Mark Van Ratten), Stephen McNally (Carl Reicher), Edgar Barrier (Colonel Mauclaire), Henry Rowland (Erich Heindorf), Carol Thurston (Li-Ho-Kay), James Millican (Cobb), Philip Ahn (Tran Duy Gian), Richard Fraser (Rycroft), Otto Reichow (Stein), Kenny Washington (Sam Latch), Dennis Dengate (O'Hara), Frank Conroy (Colonel Lemercier), Martin Garralaga (Hazarat), James F. Nolan (American Colonel), Richard Loo (Kao Pang).

OUTPOST IN MOROCCO (United Artists--Moroccan Pictures) 1949

Executive Producer: Samuel Bischoff
Producer: Joseph N. Ermolieff
Screenplay: Charles Grayson and Paul de Sainte Colombo, story by Joseph N. Ermolieff
Photography: Lucien Andriot
Art Director: Arthur Lonergan
Music: Michel Michelet
Editor: George Arthur

92 minutes

Cast: George Raft (Captain Paul Gerard), Marie Windsor (Cara), Akim Tamiroff (Lieutenant Glysko), John Litel (Colonel Pascal), Eduard Franz (Emir of Bel Rashad), Crane Whitley (Caid Osman), Damien O'Flynn (Commandant Fronval).

THE CROOKED WAY (United Artists) 1949

Producer: Benedict Bogeaus
Screenplay: Richard H. Landau, based on the radio play "No Blade Too Sharp" by Robert Monroe

---

*Both the screenplay and the story were the product of collaborations between Florey and producer Robert Buckner.

Appendix B   379

Photography: John Alton
Production Designer: Van Nest Polglase
Music: Louis Forbes
Editor: Frank Sullivan

90 minutes

Cast: John Payne (Eddie Rice), Sonny Tufts (Vince Alexander), Ellen Drew (Nina), Rhys Williams (Lieutenant Williams), John Doucette (Sergeant Barrett), Charles Evans (Captain Anderson), John Harmon (Kelly), Percy Helton (Petey), Hal Fieberling (Coke), Harry Bronson (Danny), Greta Granstedt (Hazel), Crane Whitley (Dr. Kemble).

JOHNNY ONE-EYE (United Artists) 1950

Producer: Benedict Bogeaus
Screenplay: Richard H. Landau, from a short story by Damon Runyon
Photography: Lucien Andriot and William Miller
Production Designer: Van Nest Polglase
Music: Louis Forbes
Editor: Frank Sullivan

78 minutes

Cast: Pat O'Brien (Martin Martin), Wayne Morris (Dane Cory), Dolores Moran (Lily White), Gayle Reed (Elsie), Lawrence Cregar (Ambrose), Jack Averman (Lippy), Raymond Largay (Lawbooks), Donald Woods (Vet), Harry Bronson (Freddy).

THE VICIOUS YEARS (Emerald--Film Classics--Monogram) 1950

Producer: Anson Bond
Screenplay: N. Richard Nash, from his story
Photography: Henry Freulich
Art Director: Charles D. Hall
Music: Arthur Lange
Editor: Fred Allen

81 minutes

Cast: Tommy Cook (Mario), Sybil Merritt (Dina), Eduard Franz (Emilio), Gar Moore (Luca), Anthony Ross (Spezia), Marjorie Eaton (Zia Lola), Rusty Tamblyn (Tino), Eve Miller (Giulia), Lester Sharpe (Matteo), John Doucette (Giorgio), Crane Whitley (Leopoldi), Paul Gardini (Waiter), Carlo Tricoli (Doctor), James Lombardo (Schoolboy), Ida Smeraldo (Innkeeper), Nick Thompson (Fisherman).

* * *

Florey also directed portions of six films without receiving credit:

THAT MODEL FROM PARIS (Tiffany) 1926

Directed by Louis Gasnier

GO INTO YOUR DANCE (First National--Warner Bros.) 1935

Directed by Archie Mayo

ROSE OF THE RANCHO (Paramount) 1936

Directed by Marion Gering

BOMBER'S MOON (Twentieth Century-Fox) 1943

Directed by Charles Fuhr

ESCAPE IN THE DESERT (Warner Bros.) 1945

Directed by Edward A. Blatt

ADVENTURES OF CAPTAIN FABIAN (Republic--Silver Films) 1951

Directed by William Marshall

* * *

Florey directed uncredited second unit work on the following six films:

THE COHENS AND THE KELLYS IN PARIS (Universal--Super-Jewel) 1928

Directed by William Beaudine

GLORIFYING THE AMERICAN GIRL (Paramount--Famous-Lasky) 1929

Directed by Millard Webb

Appendix B   381

WITH BYRD AT THE SOUTH POLE (Paramount) 1930

[no director listed]

ANNA CHRISTIE (Metro-Goldwyn-Mayer) 1930

Directed by Clarence Brown (American version); Jacques Feyder (German and Swedish versions)

I'VE GOT YOUR NUMBER (Warner Bros.) 1934

Directed by Ray Enright

OIL FOR THE LAMPS OF CHINA (First National--Warner Bros.) 1935

Directed by Mervyn LeRoy

* * *

Florey was co-author of the following feature screenplays, generally without receiving credit; usually he also directed:

THAT MODEL FROM PARIS (1926)

KOMM' ZU MIR ZUM RENDEZ-VOUS (1930)

FRANKENSTEIN (1931)

MURDERS IN THE RUE MORGUE (1932)

THE MAN CALLED BACK (1932)

A STUDY IN SCARLET (1933)

HOLLYWOOD BOULEVARD (1936)

THE DESERT SONG (1943)

ROGUES' REGIMENT (1948)

* * *

He also made important uncredited contributions to the early development of the scripts of the following two features:

GOOD-BYE AGAIN (Warner Bros.) 1933

Screenplay by Ben Markson, from a play by George Haight and Alan Scott

THE ADVENTURES OF DON JUAN (Warner Bros.) 1948

Screenplay by George Oppenheimer and Harry Kurnitz, from a story by Herbert Dalmas

> Florey was involved to a less significant extent with many other screenplays without receiving credit. He also wrote scripts for many of the short films he directed, as indicated in the text.

Appendix C

TELEVISION FILMOGRAPHY

Each of the 225 television films listed below was directed by Robert Florey between 1951 and 1963. All were designed to fit into thirty-minute time periods except where otherwise indicated. Each series is arranged alphabetically under the season, with individual episodes listed chronologically by the date they were first aired. (Many, however, were filmed long before being shown, and frequently individual anthology segments would be repeated later in syndication under different series titles, such as Four Star Playhouse into Star Performance and also, with Schlitz Playhouse of Stars, into Suspense.

Series and Episode	Date of Original Broadcast
1950-51 Season	
FORD FESTIVAL	
[Alice in Wonderland segment]	6-13-51
1951-52 Season	
Detective of French Sûreté	?
The Walt Disney Christmas Show (60 min. special)	12-25-51
1952-53 Season	
FAVORITE STORY	
The Magician	1-18-53
The Gold Bug	1-25-53
FOUR STAR PLAYHOUSE	
My Wife Geraldine	9-25-52

Series and Episode	Date of Original Broadcast
Dante's Inferno	10-9-52
The Lost Silk Hat	10-23-52
Backstage	11-6-52
Welcome Home	11-20-52
The Island	12-4-52
Man on a Train	1-15-53
Trail's End	1-29-53
Sound Off, My Love	2-12-53
The Man in the Box	2-26-53
No Identity	3-12-53
The Man Who Walked Out on Himself	3-26-53
The Last Voyage	4-23-53
Night Ride	5-7-53
The Ladies on His Mind	5-21-53
Mr. Bingham	6-4-53
Shadowed	6-18-53

MY HERO--THE ROBERT CUMMINGS SHOW
    Lady Mortician   ?

SCHLITZ PLAYHOUSE OF STARS
    Trouble on Pier 12   10-10-52

White Collar Girl (pilot)   ?

1953-54 Season

FOUR STAR PLAYHOUSE
A Place of His Own	10-8-53
Love at Sea	10-15-53

A LETTER TO LORETTA
Trial Run	9-20-53
Turn of the Card	9-27-53
Prisoner at One O'Clock	10-4-53
Girl on a Flagpole	10-11-53
The Lady Killer	10-18-53
Earthquake	10-25-53
The One That Got Away	11-1-53
Kid Stuff	11-8-53
The Bronte Story	11-15-53
Thanksgiving at Beaver Run	11-22-53
This Is a Love Story	11-29-53
The Queen	12-6-53
The Faith of Chata	12-13-53
The Night My Father Came Home	12-20-53

Appendix C

Series and Episode	Date of Original Broadcast
Hotel Irritant	12-27-53
Inga	1-3-54
Secret Answer	1-17-54
The Mirror	1-24-54
The Hollywood Story	1-31-54
A Family Out of Us	2-7-54

THE LORETTA YOUNG SHOW
- Act of Faith — 2-14-54
- The Big Little Lie — 2-21-54
- The New York Story — 2-28-54
- Nobody's Boy — 3-7-54
- The Count of Ten — 3-14-54
- The Clara Schumann Story — 3-21-54
- Son, This Is Your Father — 3-28-54
- The First Man to Ask Her — 4-4-54
- Man's Estate — 4-11-54
- Forest Ranger — 4-18-54
- The Enchanted School Teacher — 4-25-54
- The Judgment — 5-2-54
- Ah, My Aching Heart — 5-9-54
- Dear Midge — 5-16-54
- Something Always Happens — 5-23-54
- Lady in Warpaint — 5-30-54

THE RANGE RIDER
- [episode title unknown] — ?

1954-55 Season

DISNEYLAND (60 mins.)
- The Disneyland Story — 10-27-54
- The Story of Donald Duck — 11-17-54
- A Story of Dogs — 12-1-54
- plus lead-ins, introductions, trailers, and narration for many other episodes

FOUR STAR PLAYHOUSE
- The Man in the Cellar — 9-30-54
- The Wallet — 10-21-54
- The Contest — 11-4-54
- My Own Dear Dragon — 11-18-54
- A Championship Affair — 12-16-54
- Stuffed Shirt — 1-13-55
- Fair Trial — 2-10-55
- Night at Lark Cottage — 3-24-55

Series and Episode	Date of Original Broadcast
The Executioner	6-9-55
SCHLITZ PLAYHOUSE OF STARS	
Mystery of Murder	11-26-54
Man Out of the Rain	1-14-55
Murder in Paradise	1-28-55
The Last Pilot Schooner	2-4-55
Fedar	3-4-55
Ride to the West	3-18-55
Tourists--Overnight	4-1-55
The Brute Next Door	4-29-55
Too Many Nelsons	5-13-55
Sentence of Death	5-20-55
Splendid with Swords	6-24-55
Visibility Zero	7-22-55
Too Late to Run	8-5-55
On Leave	8-12-55
The Quitter	9-23-55
THE STAR AND THE STORY	
The Norther	7-16-55

1955-56 Season

Carolyn [also produced by Florey] (pilot)	8-7-56
CRIME CLASSICS	
The Crime of Bathsheba Spooner (pilot)	?
FOUR STAR PLAYHOUSE	
The Firing Squad	10-6-55
The Devil to Pay	11-10-55
Something Very Special	12-1-55
Magic Night	1-12-56
The Command	2-23-56
Wall of Bamboo	4-19-56
Touch and Go	4-26-56
A Long Way from Texas	5-3-56
The Other Room	5-17-56
The Stacked Deck	6-28-56
SCHLITZ PLAYHOUSE OF STARS	
On the Nose	12-9-55
Foolproof	1-6-56

Appendix C   387

	Date of
Series and	Original
Episode	Broadcast

Dealer's Choice	1-13-56
Ordeal	2-24-56
Showdown at Painted Rock	3-2-56
Step Right Up and Die	4-27-56
Officer Needs Help	5-18-56
Witness to Condemn	6-22-56
Dara	7-27-56
Repercussion	8-10-56
Strange Defense	8-24-56
Midnight Kill	9-14-56
Top Secret	9-21-56

THE STAR AND THE STORY
   The Creative Impulse   12-3-55

1956-57 Season

ETHEL BARRYMORE THEATRE
   The Victim   9-21-56
   This Is Villa   10-12-56

GENERAL ELECTRIC THEATRE
   I Will Not Die [also original story by Florey]   4-28-57

JANE WYMAN THEATRE
   A Place in the Bay   12-25-56
   Killer's Pride   1-29-57

ON TRIAL--THE JOSEPH COTTEN SHOW
   The De Santre Affair   10-26-56
   The Case of the Girl on the Elsewhere   2-8-57
   The Case of the Panicky Man   3-8-57
   Alibi for Murder   4-26-57
   The Case of Sudden Death   5-10-57
   The Case of the Unmarked Grave   ?

SCHLITZ PLAYHOUSE
   The Trophy   10-12-56
   Terror in the Streets   1-18-57
   The Restless Gun (pilot)   3-29-57

STUDIO 57
   Mr. Cinderella   11-29-56

TELEPHONE TIME
   Chico and the Archbishop   11-18-56

Series and Episode	Date of Original Broadcast
WIRE SERVICE (60 mins.)	
The Johnny Rath Story	10-25-56
ZANE GREY THEATRE	
Vengeance Canyon	11-30-56

1957-58 Season

Charlie's Haunt (special)	?
THE FRANK SINATRA SHOW	
The Man on the Stairs	3-21-58
Ice House	?
M SQUAD	
The Watchdog	9-27-57
SCHLITZ PLAYHOUSE	
One Way Out	9-20-57
ALCOA/GOODYEAR THEATRE--A TURN OF FATE	
The Victim	1-6-58
In the Dark	1-13-58
Hidden Witness	1-27-58
Night Caller	2-10-58
The White Flag	2-17-58
Even a Thief Can Dream	3-10-58
The Seventh Letter	3-17-58
My Wife's Next Husband	4-21-58
The Giant Step	4-28-58
Most Likely to Succeed	5-5-58
The Lady Takes the Stand	5-12-58
Mr. Perfectionist	5-19-58
Decision by Terror	5-26-58
The Clock Struck Twelve	6-2-58
Disappearance	6-9-58
Three Dark Years	6-23-58
Decoy Duck	6-30-58
WAGON TRAIN (60 mins.)	
The John Cameron Story [credited to George Waggner; Florey directed "pick-up shots" only]	10-2-57
The Ruth Owens Story	10-9-57
The Les Rand Story [teleplay also co-authored by Florey]	10-16-57

Appendix C   389

	Date of
Series and	Original
Episode	Broadcast

ZANE GREY THEATRE
  The Open Cell   11-22-57
  Sundown at Bitter Creek   2-14-58

1958-59 Season

THE BLACK SADDLE
  Client: Robinson   2-21-59

DAVID NIVEN SHOW
  Lifeline   4-14-59

LOCK-UP
  Change of Heart   ?

MARKHAM
  The Sea Mark   6-6-59
  Vendetta in Venice   6-27-59

THE ROUGH RIDERS
  [episode title unknown; script #31B]   ?

THE TEXAN
  A Tree for Planting   11-10-58
  This Time of the Year   12-22-58
  No Love Wasted   3-9-59

WESTINGHOUSE-DESILU PLAYHOUSE (60 mins.)
  The Innocent Assassin   3-16-59

ZANE GREY THEATRE
  The Scaffold   10-9-58

1959-60 Season

THE JUNE ALLYSON SHOW
  The Doctor and the Redhead   4-25-60

MARKHAM
  Double Negative   9-26-59
  The Long Haul   10-10-59
  The Father   10-31-59
  Incident in Bel Air   11-7-59
  Round Trip to Mozambique   11-14-59

Series and Episode	Date of Original Broadcast
The Candy Story Jungle	1-9-60
The Victim	?
plus San Francisco location exteriors for various episodes	
Michael Shayne, Detective (60 mins.) (pilot)	4-1-60
THE TEXAN	
The Dishonest Posse	10-5-59
The Blue Norther	10-12-59
Thirty Hours to Kill	2-1-60
Twenty-Four Hours to Live	6-27-60
THE TWILIGHT ZONE	
Perchance to Dream	11-27-59
The Fever	1-29-60
THE UNTOUCHABLES (60 mins.)	
The Doreen Maney Story	3-31-60
ZANE GREY THEATRE	
The Set-Up	3-3-60
A Small Town That Died	3-10-60

1960-61 Season

ADVENTURES IN PARADISE (60 mins.)	
One Little Pearl	11-28-60
Treasure Hunt	1-9-61
The Angel of Death	3-6-61
A Penny a Day	4-24-61
The Hill of Ghosts	5-15-61
ALFRED HITCHCOCK PRESENTS	
The Changing Heart	1-3-61
BARBARA STANWYCK THEATRE	
Out of the Shadows	12-19-60
Shock	3-6-61
High Tension	3-27-61
CHECKMATE (60 mins.)	
Face in the Window	10-22-60
HONG KONG (60 mins.)	
Lady Godiva	2-8-61

Appendix C

Series and Episode	Date of Original Broadcast
MICHAEL SHAYNE (60 mins.)	
To Die Like a Dog	10-14-60
Call for Michael Shayne	11-4-60
plus Miami Beach location exteriors for numerous episodes	

1961-62 Season

ADVENTURES IN PARADISE (60 mins.)	
The Pretender	11-12-61
The Assassins	11-26-61
The Policeman's Holiday	1-28-62
plus Tahitian location exteriors for 12 segments	
ALCOA PREMIERE	
Tiger	3-20-62
It Takes a Thief	6-19-62
ALFRED HITCHCOCK PRESENTS	
A Jury of Her Peers	12-26-61
The Golden Opportunity	5-22-62
The Children of Alda Nuova	6-5-62
Where Beauty Lies	6-26-62
THRILLER (60 mins.)	
The Incredible Doktor Markesan	2-26-62

1962-63 Season

THE DICK POWELL SHOW (60 mins.)	
The Big Day	12-25-62
GOING MY WAY (60 mins.)	
Like My Own Brother	11-7-62
Ask Me No Question	12-5-62
Shoemaker's Child	1-30-63
Blessed Are the Meek	2-27-63

1963-64 Season

THE GREAT ADVENTURE (60 mins.)	
The Man Who Stole New York City	12-13-63

Series and Episode	Date of Original Broadcast
OUTER LIMITS (60 mins.)	
Moonstone	3-9-64
THE TWILIGHT ZONE	
The Long Morrow	1-10-64

Appendix D

CHARLES CHAPLIN'S TIRADE BETWEEN
TAKES OF MONSIEUR VERDOUX

The following item is reproduced in the exact manner of Florey's transcription.

> Soliloquy taken down between two takes
> of scene 480 Int.Greenhouse.Day.

Yes,yes- I see- So there is not a dead moment- he says: I'm not taking any chances- that's it- it will be cute- Make a note of this- no don't- what are you doing? The fresh air will do me good- no, no,please- what do I say? No don't tell me- however- then I say : Eh..wait..wait- watch me go through my girations- now we'll go right through- cramps- the worst attack...no,no,no..what is it?- I know- don't interrupt me- I am here, let me see- no - I am here- I dont need this. Dont rush this is quite a situation- yes yes- cramps and so forth and so on- I dont mind-we'll see- Keep it inside,old man, this is not a farce-slow- I want reality- drama- nO,no,however...yes yes..take this- What do I say? Now we'll try again very good...Oh, shut up- silence, I am trying to concentrate ...give me a chance...very good.This is very cute. I like to stay in the garden for a while- now I see- little bit stoopy- we'll take it now-are you ready? worst attack I have had in years...Are we ready? Worst attack...That's it we'll try one- how is the make up? You see what I mean? No do not pan..I do not care if you dont see him..Music and wedding bells and so forth and so on,it doesnt matter...They are all inside now,then you turn- you havent got your idea yet- now I am wandering- it is not right yet- rye- Worst attack...Are we ready? (loud belch) first,exactly-listen- then what's next? What's the speech? Don't tell me- put that down- make a note-yes,no. You see this man, you see...first of all...no for Christ sake...I pretend then I look and say: Eh? however that's it...Of course that's all the line he is not going to say it...Why? The worst attack I have had in..are we ready? That's what we had before...I dont care what you do, no no, yes and so forth...I...I ...I, be careful with my hair...Jesus...it's good enough before I get hot...I mean more that's the connotation,I mean yes, now..yes

God damn it man dont collapse here, thats what you mean, not here
...there stand there...not Bismo...Jesus..let's go- what are we
waiting for? Jesus you are concentrating on the bark and forgetting
the forest, I know, I know dont tell me, let's go, come on, on, now,
listen, the worst attack I have had..Yes, they are all in the house-
yes do that---will be very cute- you keep us more or less center-
I say...Wally- very good- I'll be up there- his line doesnt mean
anything- center me-no, listen (belch) Brrrrr...In...Brr Very
good idea- is my head in there? no, no, be very slow, especially for
that line- fine, no, you turn around, all right, yes? no- I am
sweating hurry up before I burn give me the comb- Tommy dear-
(one bar of Spanish song) lets go- will more or less, he he...
where are you coming- here we are...Rye...there- let me see the
set up...Exactly- suppose he comes here, give us our lighting
here- Curt give me a nice picture here- wait a moment- where is
my outside line- is that the extreme? How is my lighting? Dont pan
it doesnt matter cut him off- it doesnt mean anything- cut him more
or less- because it's a pity.O.K. Just one more rehearsal, so we
know. How do I look? Let it go then. I'll be fine there- watch -
hit me- so and so and so and so...rye.There is our position this
is very important, otherwise. The shadows are good- no more
lights.I dont think you need that, do you? so and so and so on
forth, fine, I see I see O.K. good lets go, the worst attack..
You dont want that then? why...so and so and what? the air will
do me good It doesnt matter- he says..Look...no no no, yet
somebody..however look... Yeah, yeah, Jesus let me see- God
damn so and so, that's it...We've got it! Immediately- start talking-
yeah, yeah, fine, are you ready? I'll go like this...no, Bismo isnt
there...Henderson that is...that's the connotation- I say- yes yes-
anything you like lets go, the worst cramps-push it for Christ sake,
very good, ah, ah, ready? When?I'll give him the last one-I wouldnt
so and so- first so and so...bla, bla, bla, what ever you say...rye.
Very nice, no we are not trying to match anything, It doesnt matter,
I'll have an insert there, I'll try to get in an advantageous light-
you crowd me here-back..exactly what I wanted- however- yes.
Those things DOESNT matter as long as they have sens-I say...
This light on me and so forth and so on-Good sure yes I see, now,
allright, wait a moment, I cannot think I am trying to think...that
helps...now then, out he goes, yeah, this is it this is the right
phsycology - possibly a cut here -sure- should be elongated more,
let me do this- when ever you are ready? Come on lets go, lets go
...What are we waiting for? The worst cramps I ever have had,
come on lets go, the worst cramps I ever have had, lets go...What
are you doing now? What is that flower pot hanging up there for?
What...Dark sky my ass...Take that crap out what are you trying
to do? Ruin me...I dont give a damn if it is dark for Christ sake...
All that Chichi and crap, I know what I am doing, you'll be hiding
the man...To Hell with the sky, take the god damn thing out...
Nuts...Now, do what I say, lets go, the worst cramps I ever...What
is it? No, get out..Dont bother me...Well are you ready? Come on,
lets get it more or less..Hurry..

Appendix D

(Scene is shot)

Wheeler says:" There was a slight pause,after the announcement.."

No,no,no shut up, you silly bastard, for Christ sake,we cut to Annabella,you dont understand anything about motion pictures, I know what I am doing, yeah, that's what I cut to, I have been in this business for 20...for 30 years, you dont think I am gaga? Oh, shut up...Syphilitic Christ...We cut to Annabella I know god damn well what I am doing...For Christ sake I have been cutting this scene in my mind for the past three years...I know exactly ...Yeah...then the music start...God Damn Stupid people....Oh, please,please,no,no,God.. Shut up...I cut the picture every minute that I am on the set, I know, it doesnt matter...To Hell with Bismo, get my face down there,then push and go up much faster...one two,push, Dont talk to me,are we ready,lets go, yes, yes lets get it more or less...compromise, go fast,are we ready? The worst cramps I ever have...Ready? Lets go, push it...Lets go...The worst cramps...

5 Minutes Later:

One more like that and we got it....

4 hours later:

O.K. the first one. N.G. the rest....

[Among those being addressed by Chaplin were William Frawley as Bismo, camera operator Wallace Chewing, cameraman Curtis Courant, and second assistant director Wheeler Dryden. During this scene the polygamous Verdoux is about to be re-married when he spots one of his wives, the indestructible Annabella (Martha Raye), among the wedding guests. Verdoux seeks to hide from her, feigning illness to best man Bismo.]

INDEX

Achron, E. 96
"action pictures" 231, 327
Adams, Dorothy 243, 374
Adorée, Renée 72
adventure genre 15, 18, 246, 248, 251, 267-268, 299, 305-306
Adventures in Paradise 330, 390-391
Adventures of Captain Fabian (1951) 24, 304-306, 315, 380
Adventures of Don Juan, The (1948) 18, 266-268, 306, 348, 381-382
Ahn, Philip 206-207, 295-297, 368, 376, 378
Alcoa Premiere: It Takes a Thief 29, 330, 391
Alcoa/Goodyear Theatre--A Turn of Fate 319, 325, 388
   Clock Struck Twelve, The 30, 36, 39, 42, 178, 219, 278, 325, 388
   My Wife's Next Husband 325, 388
   Night Caller 325, 388
Alda, Robert 275, 376
Aldrich, Robert 283
Alexander, Ross 183, 363
Alfred Hitchcock Presents 330, 390-391
   Changing Heart, The 29, 332, 390
   Golden Opportunity, The 22, 391
   Jury of Her Peers, A 22, 29, 329, 391
   Where Beauty Lies 232, 391
Alice Boulden 106
Alice in Wonderland (1951) 317, 383
Allegret, Marc 59, 123, 356-357
Allen, Lester 107
Ames, Leon xvii, 49-52, 137-139, 142-146, 345, 358
Amour Chante, L' 14, 59, 121-122, 356
And Then There Were None (Ten Little Indians) v, 152
Andriot, Lucien 71, 299, 304, 378-379
Animal Crackers (play) 113-114
Anna Christie (1930) 119, 380-381
Apache, L' 75
Applause (1929) 117
Archainbaud, George 206
Arnst, Bobbe 106
Assassin Habite au 21, L' (novel) 263
Astor, Gertrude 74

397

Astor, Mary   149, 175, 224, 358, 362
Astoria studios   52, 97, 104-120, 122, 156, 185, 312
atmosphere   26-28, 78, 217, 238, 246-248, 264, 284, 296-298, 331, 345
Atwill, Lionel   192, 365

"B" films   xi, xvi, 1-10, 22, 48-49, 52, 55-57, 60, 183, 203-204, 210, 212-213, 223-225, 231, 236-239, 242, 289, 307, 317, 325-327, 334, 342-344, 347
Back in Your Own Back Yard   105
Bad and the Beautiful, The (1953)   196
Bades, Jean   68
Bagni, John and Gwen   318
Balderston, John   158-159, 357
Banghart, "Owl"   255, 258, 375
Barbara Stanwyck Theatre   330, 390
Bardelys the Magnificent (1926)   76
Barnes, George   84, 361
Barrat, Robert   176, 180, 362-363
Barrymore, Ethel   105, 387
Barrymore, John   78
Battle of Paris, The (The Gay Lady)   14, 97, 118-119, 355
Baugé, André   120
Baumgarth, Victor   68
Bazin, André   331
Beast with Five Fingers, The   xv, 12-13, 19-20, 22, 28-32, 36, 39, 42-45, 49, 53, 91, 132, 178, 219, 233, 268, 271-279, 307, 310-312, 325, 342, 344, 348, 376
Beau Geste   293, 299
Beaudine, William   79, 380
Bedford, Clay P.   260
Bedside   7, 15, 23, 29, 169-172, 223, 348, 360-361
Bell, Monta   104-105, 108-109, 111-113, 118-119, 122, 283, 354-355
Bennett, Kathleen   74
Berkeley, Busby   43, 59, 117-118
Berlin--Symphony of a Great City (1927)   62
Bessy, Maurice   288-289, 336-337, 345, 351-352
Beware of Imitations   175, 230-231, 348
Big Parade, The (1925)   76
Billancourt studio   122-123, 305
Bing, Herman   138-139, 194, 363-364
Bird of Paradise (1932)   148
Birge, Humphrey   73-74
Bischoff, Sam   5, 147-148, 150-151, 222, 301, 359-361, 363, 378
Bishop, Julie   242, 373
Black Swan, The (1942)   268
Blanc et le Noir, Le   14, 59, 122-123, 357
Blanke, Henry   160, 359, 362
Blatt, Edward   261, 380
Blaydon, Richard   74

Index 399

Bloch, Robert 332
Blondell, Joan 170, 173-174, 224, 361
Blue Moon Murder Case, The see Girl Missing
Blues--A Rhapsody of Hollywood, The see The Life and Death of 9413--A Hollywood Extra
Boese, Carl 122, 356; see also The Golem
Bogeaus, Benedict 303, 378-379
Bohème, La (1926) 6, 76, 80, 82, 262, 329
Bois, Curt 215, 370, 374
Bomber's Moon (1943) 252, 263, 380
Bond, Anson 304, 379
Bonjour, New York! 14, 97-98, 109, 315
books by Florey 193-194, 227, 289, 336-338, 351-352
Borah Minnevitch and His Harmonica Rascals 105
Borgato, Agostino 92, 95, 96, 97
Borland, Barlowe 208, 367, 369
Bormann, Martin 291-292
Borzage, Frank 78, 92
Botsford, A.M. 195, 365
Bottome, Phyllis 268, 376
Boulogne studios 305
Boyd, William "Stage" 166, 360
Boyer, Charles 298-299, 318-320, 323, 325, 328
Branch, Houston Bill 77, 353
Braunberger, Pierre 100-101, 120-124, 155, 355-357
Bretherton, Howard 162, 361
Brice, Fannie 106
Bride of Frankenstein, The (1935) 130-132, 147
Briskin, Irving 240, 372
Briskin, Sam 240
British International Studios (Elstree) 121
Broadway Bill (1934) 183-184
Broadway Nights see Night Club
Broken Heart Cafe, The 28, 218-219, 311
Brontë, Charlotte see A Letter to Loretta: The Brontë Story
Brown, Harry Joe 178, 181, 362-363
Brush, Katherine 106
Buckner, Robert xvii, 5, 218, 243-244, 249-251, 261, 264, 266, 291-296, 298, 307, 313, 343, 345-346, 374-375, 377-378
Buñuel, Luis 310-311
Byrd, Richard E. 106

Cabanne, Christy 75-76
Cabinet of Dr. Caligari, The (1919) 13, 58, 80, 82, 89, 92, 100, 134, 141-143, 146, 190, 274, 332-333
Cabot, Bruce 244, 247, 374
Cagliostro 147
Camelot (1967) 248
camera angles 41-43, 62
cameramen 56-57

Cantor, Eddie 105-106
Capra, Frank 183-184
Captain from Castile (1948) 289
Carey, Harry 213, 369
Carillo, Mario 72
Carnival--La Vie Parisienne 28, 71, 261-263
Carolyn 326, 386
Carr, Jimmie, and his Silver Slipper Orchestra 106
Caspary, Vera 269
censorship 14, 173, 243-245, 250-251, 255-256, 268-270, 277, 346;
    see also Hays Office
Chapin, Marie Ann 199
Chaplin, Charlie 14, 19, 68, 72, 75, 78, 88, 99, 104, 114, 163,
    227, 280-289, 313, 340, 343, 351, 377, 393-395
Chaplin, Mildred Harris see Mildred Harris
Chevalier, Maurice 109, 118
Christian, Linda 289, 377
Christie, Agatha v, 152-153
Cinémagazine 71-72, 280, 351
Cirque de la Mort, Le (1918) 67
Citizen Kane (1940) 219
city symphony genre 98; see also Berlin--Symphony of a Great City
Clair, René 59, 70, 153, 193-194, 351
Claudine 69
Clemens, George 323
Cline, Eddie 195, 365
close-ups 43-44, 49, 173, 210, 212, 221, 287
"Clue Club" series 182
Cluzot, H.G. 263
Cocoanuts, The xv, 13-15, 20, 36, 41, 59, 91, 112-119, 134, 155-
    156, 167, 205, 343, 355
Coffin Maker, The see Johann the Coffin Maker
Cohen, Emanuel 200-201, 366
Cohens and the Kellys in Paris, The (1928) 79, 263, 380
Cohn, Harry 231, 354
Colbert, Claudette 111-112, 354
Collings, Pierre 107, 119, 185, 354
Colman, Ronald 318, 321, 328
colonialism 23-26, 244, 246, 248, 250-251, 294-296, 298
color 243, 266, 374
Columbia 78, 79, 231-241, 354, 372-373
comedy genre 13-14, 205, 283, 313
Conlon, Tommy 149, 359
Constant, Max 74
continuity 54-56, 223
Cooper, Gary 195, 366
Cortez, Ricardo 166, 175, 360, 362
Cotten, Joseph 324, 328, 387
Courant, Curtis 57, 284, 287, 377, 394-395
Cramer, Duncan 318
Creighton, Molly 69

Index

Crime Classics: The Crime of Bathsheba Spooner   326, 346, 386
Crooked Way, The   3, 11-12, 17, 22, 35, 178, 238, 301-304, 378-379
Cummings, Robert   198, 366, 384
Curtiz, Michael   162
Czar of the Slot Machines   see   King of Gamblers

D'Arrast, Harry d'Abbadie   283, 339
Dabney, Virginia   see   Virginia Florey
Dale, Esther   202, 366, 371-372
Dalmas, Herbert   266-267, 381-382
Dance Madness (1926)   76
Danchene, Frank   69
Danger Signal   7, 10, 11, 22, 267-270, 307, 348, 376
Dangerous to Know   ix, xiii, 7-8, 10-12, 17, 19-20, 22-23, 27-28, 37, 39, 44-45, 48-49, 52-53, 184, 204, 207-212, 220, 301, 344, 368-369
Dangerously They Live   2, 11, 15, 17, 23, 25, 36, 39, 42-44, 54, 241-242, 306, 348, 373
Daniels, Bebe   170-172, 224, 361
Dark, Christopher   53
Darlan, Jean-François   250-251
Daughter of Shanghai   10, 17, 20, 23, 27, 42, 44, 50, 106, 206-207, 221, 239, 368
David Niven Show: Lifeline, The   238, 325-326, 389
Davis, Bette   16, 162, 224, 360
de Rochefort, Charles   75
Death of a Champion   10, 219-220, 370-371
DeCamp, Rosemary   269, 376
DeCanonge, Maurice   73-74
Dee, Aileen   see   Aileen Dee Florey
DeGaulle, Charles   see   Gaulle, Charles de
Del Rio, Dolores   183
Del Ruth, Roy   175
Denny, Reginald   50, 188, 365
Desert Song, The (1943)   ix, 3, 5, 14-15, 20, 23, 25-27, 32, 36, 50, 54, 106, 217, 243-252, 267, 282-283, 291-294, 300, 306-307, 342, 348, 374, 381
Desert Song, The (1953)   251, 348
Desilu   325-326, 331
Destination Unknown   24, 28, 217-218, 306
detective genre   see   mystery genre
Detective of French Sûreté   318, 383
Deux ans dans les studios américains   74, 336, 351
dialogue   49-50
Dick Powell Show: The Big Day, The   328-329, 391
Dietrich, Marlene   214
Dillinger (1945)   259
Directors Guild   51, 194, 320, 322-324, 330
Disbarred   10-11, 17, 23, 213-214, 221, 369-370
Diskant, George   318, 325

Disney, Walt 5, 316-317, 383, 385
Disneyland 317, 385
Dodd, Claire 174, 183, 360-362, 364
Don Juan see The Adventures of Don Juan
Don't Bet on Blondes 2, 14, 56, 183, 222, 305, 348, 363-364
Douglas Fairbanks, sa vie, ses films, ses aventures 72, 351
Doyle, Sir Arthur Conan 150-153, 359
Dracula (1931) 59, 124-126, 137, 146
Drag Net, The (1928) 259
Dratler, Jay 237, 372
Dryden, Wheeler 288, 377, 395
Dunn, James 184, 364
Dunsany, Lord 321
Dupree, Minnie 106
Duvivier, Julien 194

Eddie Cantor 105
editing (including films personally edited by Florey) 45-49, 67, 167, 182, 213, 216, 238, 246, 319, 321, 328, 332
Edwards, Blake 318
Elter, Anielka 92, 94
Elter, Marco 92
Emerson, Faye 242, 268, 373-374, 376
Enright, Ray 170, 380-381
Ermolieff, Joseph 299-301, 378
Escape (1926) 75-76; see also The Exquisite Sinner
Escape in the Desert (1945) 261, 348, 380
Ethel Barrymore Theatre: The Victim 318, 387
Ex-Lady 16-17, 161-162, 224, 348, 359-360
Exquisite Sinner, The (1926) 76; see also Escape

F.B.I. (Federal Bureau of Investigation) 206-207, 255, 257-259
F.B.O. (Film Booking Office) 75, 88
Face Value 16, 19, 23, 78-79, 232, 354
Face Behind the Mask, The xv, 6, 8, 12-13, 19-23, 28, 39, 42-45, 52-54, 132, 184, 231-237, 239, 243, 275, 301, 307, 344, 372
Fairbanks, Douglas, Sr. 72, 75-76, 78, 83, 88, 99, 267, 340, 351
Famous Players-Lasky 73
fantasy genre 15, 28-30, 58, 289
Faragoh, Francis Edwards 128, 135, 357
Favorite Story 331, 383
    Gold Bug, The 29, 139, 383
    Magician, The 318, 383
Fegté, Ernst 111, 354-355
Feuillade, Louis 45, 54, 59, 70
Fifty-Fifty 73-74, 76
Figueroa, Gabriel 290, 377
Film Art Guild 95
Film Classics 304, 379

Index

film noir 11, 178, 218-219, 231, 241-242, 268-269, 288, 298, 301, 303, 325
Filmland 74, 351
First National see Warner Bros.
Fischbeck, Harry 223, 366, 368-369, 371
Fitzgerald, Edward 95
Fitzgerald, F. Scott 107
"Five Orange Pips, The" (short story) 151
Fleming, Victor 166
Florentine Dagger, The 10, 19, 22-23, 29-31, 36-39, 46, 111, 178-182, 219, 232, 274, 301, 311, 325, 344, 348, 363
Florey, Aileen Dee 221
Florey, Virginia (Dabney) v, xvii, 207, 221-222, 339-340, 346, 367-369, 372
Flying Tigers (1942) 264
Flynn, Emmett J. 71, 76, 78
Flynn, Errol 266, 304-306, 364
Folsey, George xvii, 105, 110, 115, 117, 119-120, 154, 346, 354-355
Ford Festival 317, 383
Forests of England see Trees of England
Fort, Garrett 125-126, 128-129, 135, 146-147, 357
Foster, Preston 105, 160, 259, 375
Four Star television 298-299, 318-319, 323-325, 329
Four Star Playhouse 298-299, 318-321, 323, 331, 383-386; also called Star Performance, Suspense
  [unproduced historical series episodes] 27, 329
  (Willie Dante episodes) 11; see also Dante's Inferno, A Long Way from Texas, The Stacked Deck
  Dante's Inferno 320, 384
  Devil to Pay, The 29, 331, 386
  Executioner, The 323, 386
  For Art's Sake (1953) 99
  Island, The 148, 384
  Ladies on His Mind, The 321, 384
  Last Voyage, The 320, 384
  Lost Silk Hat, The 321, 384
  Magic Night 323, 386
  Man on the Train, The 29, 331, 384
  Man Who Walked Out on Himself 29, 321, 331, 384
  My Wife Geraldine 320, 383
  No Identity 320, 384
  Something Very Special 323, 386
  Welcome Home 11, 384
Fox 71, 78, 154, 186, 359; see also Twentieth Century-Fox
Fox, Sidney 145, 162, 358
Foy, Bryan 240, 252, 364
Francen, Victor 194, 244, 271, 275, 305, 317, 374, 376
Francis, Anne 53
Francis, Kay 16, 166-169, 224, 355, 360
Frankenstein vi, xvi, 12-13, 22, 29, 54, 59-60, 91, 112, 124-137, 139-140, 146-147, 151, 154-156, 158-159, 161, 201, 279, 291,

301, 307-308, 311, 331-332, 343, 348, 357, 381
Freeman, Y. Frank   221, 223
French colony in Hollywood   72, 194, 222
French Foreign Legion   19, 291-295, 298-301
Freund, Karl   57, 60, 134, 144-146, 343, 358
Front Page, The (1931)   184
Frye, Dwight   126, 357
Fuhr, Charles   252, 380

Gambarelli, Maria   115, 156, 355
gangster genre   11-12, 16, 19, 22, 259
Gangster We Made, The   see   The Vicious Years
Garfield, John   240, 373
Garnett, Tay   323
Gasnier, Louis   75-77, 353, 380
Gaucho, The (1927)   83
Gaulle, Charles de   26
Gaumont studio (Nice)   70
Gay Deceiver, The (1926)   76
Gay Lady, The   see   The Battle of Paris
General Electric Theatre: I Will Not Die   18, 29, 329-330, 387
General Service Studios (Los Angeles)   201
George, Voya   86
Gerald, Jim   305
Gering, Marion   187, 220, 380
Gerrard, Douglas   72
Gershwin, George   80, 83, 86, 156
Geva, Tamara   106
Gfeller, Walter   68
Giersdorf sisters   156
Gilbert, John   77, 194
Girl Missing   10, 151, 160-161, 222, 348, 359
Gish, Lillian   80, 82
Glorifying the American Girl (1929)   106, 380
Glyn, Elinor   105, 108
Go into Your Dance (1935)   182, 349, 380
God Is My Co-Pilot   5, 7, 15, 20, 22, 25, 27, 32, 52-53, 174, 192, 260, 263-267, 282-283, 291, 306-307, 349, 375-376
Going Highbrow   14, 182-183, 349, 363
Going My Way   330, 391
Golem, The (1920)   127, 134
Good Earth, The (1937)   174
Good-bye Again (1933)   162, 381-382
Goulding, Edmund   76, 151
Grand Guignol plays   13, 67, 124, 159
Grand Hotel (1932)   195
Great Dictator, The (1940)   284
Green, Howard J.   240, 367, 372
"Grey Seal from Scotland Yard, The"   107; see also The Pusher-in-the-Face

Index 405

Grinde, Nick 50, 86, 205-207
Guitry, Sacha 14, 123, 357

Hal Roach studios 325-326, 346
Hale, Alan 265, 375
Hale, Chester 115
Hall, Charles D. ("Danny") 73, 132-133, 143-144, 354, 357-358, 379
Hall, Porter 208, 367-369
Halliday, John 53, 148, 166, 171, 197-198, 358, 360-361, 366
Hamilton, Hale 149, 359, 362
Hands of Orlac, The (1924) 274
Harmonie-Films 121-122
Harris, Mildred 194, 354
Harvey, William Fryer 311, 376
Haskin, Byron 261
Hathaway, Henry 214
Hays Office 179, 243, 255-256, 259, 268-270; see also censorship
Hecht, Ben 178, 363
Henri John Morgan the Pirate 267-268
Herbert, F. Hugh 148-149, 173, 358, 361
Heureuse Intervention, Une 69
historical genre 15, 17-18, 58, 166, 266-267, 299, 321-322, 326, 329-330
Hit Me Again see Smarty
Hitchcock, Alfred 59, 331, 390-391
Hitchcock, Raymond 107
Hole in the Wall, The ix, 12-13, 31, 58, 59, 91, 109-113, 155-156, 278, 354-355
Hollywood 19, 23, 80, 89-91, 193-199, 227; see also books by Florey
Hollywood années zero 336, 352
Hollywood Boulevard v, 16, 20, 22-23, 28, 36, 51, 53, 88, 91, 106, 193-199, 223, 239, 365-366, 381
Hollywood D'Hier et D'Aujourd'Hui 289, 336, 345-346, 351
Hollywood Extra 9413 see The Life and Death of 9413--A Hollywood Extra
Hollywood Village 336, 352
Hopper, Hedda xiii, 295-296, 369
horror genre 12-13, 19, 29-30, 60, 66, 67, 274, 279, 331-332, 345
Horton, Edward Everett 173, 182, 361, 363
Horwitz, Al 296
Hotel Imperial (1927) 214
Hotel Imperial (1939) 10, 17, 19-20, 25, 32, 41-42, 47, 91, 130, 192, 214-215, 220-221, 263, 370
House on 56th Street, The 7, 16-17, 23, 52-53, 166-169, 199, 224, 349, 360
Houseboat on the Styx, The (novel) 78
Hudson, Rochelle 237-238, 372
Hurley, Harold 5, 186, 206, 223, 364-365
Hurni, Arthur 92, 96
Huston, Walter 105
Hyman, Bernard 77

I Am a Thief 10, 175-177, 224, 349, 362
I Escaped from Hong Kong (book) 252
I Loved a Soldier 214
I Sell Anything 1, 11, 23, 174-175, 349, 361-362
Imperial Pictures 74
independent production 186, 230, 307-308, 315-316, 343
Invisible Man, The 124, 147
Isidore a la Deveine 68
Isidore Sur le Lac 69-70
Island of Dr. Moreau, The (novel) 140
Ivano, Paul xvii, 72, 73-74, 84, 88, 126-127, 318, 346
Ivanova, Nina 96
I've Got Your Number (1934) 170, 349, 380-381

Jackman, Fred 174
Jacobs, William 5, 268, 278, 346, 373, 376
Jarrett, A.L. 218
Jazz Singer, The (1927) 120
Jeanne d'Arc 17, 27, 165-166
Joan of Arc (1948) 165-166
Johann the Coffin Maker 29-30, 79, 91, 95-97, 99-101, 110, 332-333
Johnny One-Eye 12, 71, 303-304, 379
Joinville studios 156
Jolson, Al 182
journalism 67, 336-338
June Allyson Show: The Doctor and the Redhead, The 319, 389

K.B.S. 147-154, 222, 358-359
Kaiser, Henry 260, 310
Karloff, Boris 44, 124, 127, 129, 139, 147, 332, 357
Keeler, Ruby 182
Keighley, William 162, 360
Kellino, Roy 323
Kelly, Gene 328, 391
Kennedy, Arthur 318, 329
Keyes, Evelyn 235-236, 372
King, Andrea 275, 375-376
King, Henry xvii, 59, 76, 78, 79, 88, 268, 346
King of Alcatraz xii-xiii, 3, 7, 10-12, 17, 48, 184, 212-213, 221, 237-238, 344, 369
King of Chinatown (1939) 207
King of Gamblers (Czar of the Slot Machines) xi-xiii, 3, 7, 9-12, 17, 19-20, 23, 37, 39, 41, 45, 48, 184, 203-204, 207-208, 212, 239, 366-367
Komm Zu Mir Zum Rendez-vous 14, 122, 356, 381
Krainukov, George 174
Krizman, Serge 323

Lady Gangster 11, 237-238, 242-243, 268, 289, 349, 373-374

Index 407

Laemmle, Carl, Jr. 125, 127-128, 135, 357
Laemmle, Max 158
Landau, David 172, 360
Landau, Richard H. 304, 378-379
Landru 279-280
Lanterne magique, La 335-336, 352
Lanti, Stella de 74
Laura (1944) 268-269
Laurenz, John 290, 377
Lawrence, Gertrude 76, 118-119, 355
LeBaron, William 187, 204, 221
Lederman, Ross 183-184
Lemmon, Jack 325, 328
Leonard, Robert Z. 76
Lesser, Sol 289, 377
Letter, The (1929) 119
Letter to Loretta, A 16, 193, 198, 321-323, 384-385; see also The
    Loretta Young Show
    Brontë Story, The 29, 261, 384
    Hollywood Story, The 193, 198-199, 385
    Mirror, The 30, 278, 325, 385
    This Is a Love Story 193, 198-199, 384
Lewin, Albert 59-60
Lewis, Tom 322-323
Life and Death of 9413--A Hollywood Extra, The (The Blues--A
    Rhapsody of Hollywood, A Hollywood Extra, Hollywood Extra
    9413, Ninety-Seven Dollars [$97], Suicide of a Hollywood Extra) xv, 20, 22, 30, 36, 43, 79-93, 99-101, 104, 193, 196-
    199, 280, 325, 342-343
Life of Louis Pasteur, The (1935) see Pasteur, Lous
Lillian Roth and Her Band 105
Lillian Roth and Her Piano Boys 105, 312
Limelight (1952) 283
Limur, Jean de 72, 119, 283
Linder, Max 67, 71
Lindsay, Margaret 166, 180, 360, 363
Lipman, William 220, 368, 371
Little Caesar (1931) 259
Litvak, Anatole 194
Lloyd, Harold 195
location shooting 53, 73, 217, 231, 246, 252-254, 257, 260, 266,
    290-291, 296-297, 302-303, 323, 326, 328, 330, 343
Lockhart, Gene 215, 370, 374-375
Lone Wolf 10, 239
Loretta Young Show, The 16, 321-323, 385; see also A Letter to
    Loretta
    Clara Schumann Story, The 14, 261, 322, 385
Lorre, Peter 13, 44, 53, 132, 232-236, 275-276, 278, 307, 372, 376
Lourié, Eugène 194, 305
Loves of Zero, The 30-31, 58, 79, 91-95, 99-101, 312
Lubitsch, Ernst 59, 78, 162, 186, 214, 227
Ludwig, Edward 252

Ludwig, Emil 163
Lugosi, Bela 80, 124, 139-140, 142-143, 358

M (1931) 236
McCoy, Horace 209, 220, 368, 371
McGann, William 261
MacKenna, Kenneth 149, 358
McLaglen, Victor 259, 375
Mad Doctor, The 80-81, 141
Magic Flame, The (1927) 78, 96, 321
Magnificent Fraud, The xiii, 11, 17, 19-20, 23-25, 27-28, 46, 48, 52-53, 165, 215-217, 221, 266, 344, 370
Major Pictures 200, 366
Malloy, Doris 201, 362, 366
Maltese Falcon, The (1941) 219
Mamoulian, Rouben 59, 117
Man Called Back, The 16, 22, 148-149, 151, 153, 199, 358, 381
Man from Frisco 15, 23, 25, 32, 260-261, 306, 375
Man Without a Face, The see The Preview Murder Mystery
Marcus, Larry 329-330, 374
Marievsky, Joseph 91, 92, 94-95, 370
Marin, Edwin L. 60, 151-152, 154, 359
Markey, Gene 118, 355
Markham 326, 389-390
Markson, Ben 162, 359, 363, 381-382
Marsh, Adriane 86
Marsh, Mae 195, 366
Marshall, Charles 263-264
Marshall, Herbert 44, 53, 190, 192, 365
Marshall, William 304-305, 380
Martel, June 182, 363
Marx Brothers 113-118, 343, 355
Masked Bride, The (1925) 75
Massey, Raymond 264-265, 373, 375
"Master Zacharius, or the Watch's Soul" (short story) 332
Maté, Rudolph 57, 201, 366
Maupassant, Guy de 119
medical genre 15
Meehan, John 118
Meek, Donald 105, 355, 360
Meet Boston Blackie ix, 11, 16, 231, 237-239, 306, 372
Méliès, Georges 58, 65, 89, 275, 331-332
Menjou, Adolphe 75, 318, 351
Menzies, William Cameron 92-93, 95-96
Meridian Pictures 323
Merlin, Milton 321
Metro-Goldwyn-Mayer 1, 75-77, 119, 230, 325, 331, 381
Michael, Gertrude 192, 365, 371
Michael Shayne (series) 326, 391
Michael Shayne, Detective (pilot) 325-326, 390

Index

Michael Strogoff (novel)   299
Milland, Ray   47, 215, 328, 370
Miller, William   304, 379
Milne, Peter   264, 361, 375
Mir, David   96
Miranda, Isa   47, 214, 370
Modern Pirates   see   King of Alcatraz
Moguy, Leonide   194
Monogram   304, 379
Monsieur Chaplin ou le rire dans le nuit   289, 336, 351
Monsieur de Paris   12, 28-29, 160-161, 311
Monsieur Verdoux   vi, xv, 14-15, 19, 23, 53, 200, 279-289, 308, 313, 343, 377, 393-395
Monster Lives!, The   see   The New Adventures of Frankenstein--The Monster Lives!
Monte Carlo (1926)   76
Monte Cristo (1922)   71-72, 77
Moon and Sixpence, The (novel)   60, 261
Morgan, Dennis   213, 247, 264-265, 374-375
Morgan, Frank   151
Morgan, Helen   106
Morgan, Henri   see   Henri John Morgan the Pirate
Morley, Karen   202, 366
Morley, Robert   328-329
Moroccan Pictures   301, 378
Morris, Chester   237-238
Motion Picture Country Home   194
Mountain Music   13-14, 35-36, 56, 204-205, 221, 224, 313, 367
Murders in the Rue Morgue   xv, 12-13, 20, 30-31, 33, 37, 43, 49-51, 57-58, 60, 80, 91, 110, 124, 128, 133, 137-146, 155-156, 162, 233, 238, 262, 274, 278-279, 343, 348, 357-358, 381
Murnau, F.W.   59, 116, 134; see also Nosferatu
musical genre   14-15, 155, 205, 244, 246, 248-250, 262-263
mystery genre   10, 16, 58, 66, 263, 326

Nagel, Conrad   148, 358
Naish, J. Carrol   xii, 53, 213, 215, 271, 275, 368-370, 376
Napoleon Bonaparte   17, 162-165, 210, 329, 349
Napoleonic era   frontispiece, 58, 162-163, 261-262, 338-339, 347
National Repertory Theater   318
Nazimova, Alla   72, 75
Negri, Pola   75, 214, 351
New Adventures of Frankenstein--The Monster Lives!, The   29, 146-147
newspaper genre   184
Nick Carter   10, 28, 66, 230-231
Nick Carter in China   230, 306
Nick Carter in Paris (Nick Carter vs. Arsene Lupin)   230-231
Nick Carter vs. Arsene Lupin   see   Nick Carter in Paris
Night Club (Boradway Nights)   14, 106-107, 112, 315

Nijinsky 261
Ninety-Seven Dollars [$97]   see   The Life and Death of 9413--A Hollywood Extra
Niven, David   148, 298-299, 318-320, 325, 328
Nolan, Lloyd   xi-xiv, xvii, 6, 50, 52, 56-57, 203, 207-208, 213, 215, 217, 347, 367, 369-370
Nosferatu (1922)   59, 116

Oberon, Merle   318, 328-330
O'Brien, Pat   170, 175, 304, 362, 379
O'Connor, Donald   219, 371
Offenbach, Jacques   261-263
Oil for the Lamps of China (1935)   174, 380-381
On the Spot (novel and play)   208-209, 368
On Trial--The Joseph Cotten Show   324, 329, 387
   De Santre Affair, The   324, 387
One Hour of Love   77, 353-354
One Way Street   see   Two in a Taxi
Orient
   collection   181-182
   films   86-87, 174, 206, 230, 239, 296-297
   interests   58, 205, 230
   travels   86, 174, 205-206
Orpheline, L' (1921)   70
Outcast   15, 20, 23, 37, 52-53, 195, 200-202, 217, 220, 366
Outer Limits: Moonstone   29, 332. 392
Outpost in Morocco   18, 25-27, 71, 267, 298-301, 306, 378
Outward Bound (play)   119
Overman, Lynne   219, 244, 371, 374
Owen, Reginald   53, 107-108, 148, 150-154, 215, 358-359, 370

Paramount   xi, 1, 104-120, 122, 155, 186-225, 354-355, 364-372, 380-381
Paramount Famous Lasky   see   Paramount and Astoria studios
Paramount shorts   105-106
Paris (1926)   76
Parisian Nights (1925)   75
Parole Fixer   10-12, 23, 32, 220-221, 371
Pascal, Ernest   163
Pascal, Jean   71, 351
Pasteur, Louis   185-186, 329
Patrick, Gail   213, 365, 369
Pay-Off, The   2, 15, 22-23, 52-53, 183-186, 221, 349, 364
Payne, John   301, 303, 379
Pennington, Ann   106
performers and performances   49-53, 80, 89-90, 193-199, 236, 322-323, 328-329
Perinal, Georges   120
Persons in Hiding (book)   220, 371

Index 411

Phanton of the Opera, The 188
Pickford, Mary 72, 78, 121, 340
Pirate, The (1948) 248
Pitts, ZaSu 183, 363
Planer, Franz 57, 231-232, 372
Poe, Edgar Allan 128, 137-139, 357, 383
political exposés 22-23
political concerns and attitudes 22-26, 58, 201, 214, 217-218, 248, 293-296; see also social consciousness genre
Porter, Cole 119, 355
Powell, Dick 5, 293, 297-299, 318-320, 323, 326, 378
Powell, Jane 325
Presle, Micheline 304-306
Presnell, Robert 148, 358, 361, 369
prestige pictures 6, 17-18, 326
Preston, Robert xii-xiii, 213, 369
Preview see The Preview Murder Mystery
Preview Murder Mystery, The (Preview) 10, 19, 30, 37, 40, 43-44, 50, 91, 187-190, 193-199, 224, 232, 365
Price, Vincent 296, 378
Prinz, LeRoy 50-51, 246, 249, 364, 367-368, 370, 374
Private Life of Bel-Ami, The (novel) 60
production code see censorship, Hays Office
Profesor de mi Señora, El 14, 122, 356
programmer 2-3 (definition), 203-204, 210
"psychological" thriller see thriller genre
Public Enemy, The (1931) 259
Pusher-in-the-Face, The 14, 59, 106-108, 112-113, 315

"quickie" production 77
Quinn, Anthony xii, 213, 368-369, 371, 375
Quirk, James R. 156

R.U.R. (play) 119
Raft, George 300, 378
Rapper, Irving xvii, 3, 50, 52, 59, 104, 111-112, 155, 334, 343, 347, 354
Raucourt, Jules 84-85
Raye, Martha 53, 313, 367, 377
Raymond, Gene 166, 360, 362
realism 32-35, 61, 246, 252, 256-257, 259-260, 264, 287-288, 297, 302-303, 307, 343
Really, Caroline see Carolyn
"Red-Headed League, The" (short story) 151
Redeeming Sin, The (1925) 75
Reed, Carol 43
Reed, Tom 176, 357, 363
Rees, William 183, 363-364
Registered Nurse 15, 22-23, 52-53, 169-173, 222, 224, 349, 361

Renoir, Jean 39, 122-123, 194
Republic 2, 260, 264, 305, 307-308, 375, 380
Restless Gun, The see Schlitz Playhouse: The Restless Gun
Reunion see Till We Meet Again
"Rhapsody in Blue" 80, 83, 86, 88
Richebé, Roger 122-124, 355-357
Riesenfeld, Hugo 88
Roach, Bert 194, 358, 366
Roberts, Florian (pseudonym of Robert Florey) 242, 373
Roberts, Marguerite xvii, 51, 195, 223, 347, 365
Robin Hood (1922) 72, 267
Robinson, Edward G. 105, 111, 161, 163, 354
Rock, Joe 78, 354
Roger Touhy--Gangster (Roger Touhy--Last of the Gangsters) 11-12, 32, 61, 252-260, 291, 302, 307, 343, 374-375
Rogues' Regiment 5, 11-12, 15, 17, 19-20, 22-23, 25-28, 36-37, 54, 58, 174, 217, 267, 291-300, 302, 306-307, 313, 318, 348, 377-378, 381
Romantic Age, The 16, 78, 231, 354
Rooney, Pat, and Pat Rooney, Jr. 106
Rose, Jackson J. 119
Rose of the Rancho (1936) 187, 380
Rosen, Phil 76, 299
Rosher, Charles 121, 355
Rosita (1922) 59
Route est belle, La 14, 120-121, 123-124, 155, 355-356
Ruggles, Charles 118, 355
Ryan, Robert 325, 328

St. Maurice studio (Paris) 323
salaries 328
Salvation Hunters, The (1925) 99
Samuel Goldwyn Company 78
Santell, Al 75, 76
Santley, Joseph 106, 112, 115, 355, 360
Saturnin (1921) 70
Schary, Dore 201, 366
Schayer, Richard 124-125, 128, 137, 146, 357-358
Schenck, Joseph 88
Schlitz Playhouse: The Restless Gun 325-326, 387
Schlitz Playhouse of Stars 323, 384, 386-388; see also Schlitz Playhouse; also called Suspense
   Fedar 326, 386
   On Leave 326, 386
   Step Right Up and Die 331, 387
   Trouble on Pier 12 318, 384
Schultz, Franz 199
Schumann, Clara see The Loretta Young Show: The Clara Schumann Story
Schuster, Harold 252

Index

science finction genre 30, 331-333
Scognamillo, Gabriel 296, 378
Scott, Robert Lee, Jr. 263-264, 375
Scott, Zachary 268, 376
screenwriters 55
screenwriting by Florey 12, 54-56, 154-155, 224, 243, 252, 283-284, 291-292, 311, 313, 321, 329, 342, 353, 381-382
  unproduced original scripts by Florey see The Broken Heart Cafe, Carnival--La Vie Parisienne, Destination Unknown, Four Star Playhouse [unproduced historical series episodes], Henri John Morgan the Pirate, Jeanne d'Arc, Lone Wolf, Monsieur de Paris, The New Adventures of Frankenstein--The Monster Lives!, Nick Carter in China, Nick Carter in Paris, Times So Unsettled Are, The Wormwood Scrubs Murder Cases
  shorts written by Florey (alone or in collaboration) see Bonjour, New York!, Eddie Cantor, Fifty-Fifty, Une Heureuse Intervention, Isidore a la Deveine, Isidore Sur le Lac, Johann the Coffin Maker, The Life and Death of 9413--A Hollywood Extra, The Loves of Zero, The Mad Doctor, The Pusher-in-the-Face, Skyscraper Symphony
  television scripts co-authored by Florey see General Electric Theatre: I Will Not Die, Wagon Train: The Les Rand Story
  other contributions, suggestions, and interests see Beware of Imitations, The Bride of Frankenstein, Cagliostro, Charles de Gaulle, Four Star Playhouse: For Art's Sake, The Houseboat on the Styx, I Escaped from Hong Kong, The Invisible Man, Guy de Maupassant, The Moon and Sixpence, Napoleon Bonaparte, Nijinsky, Outward Bound, Louis Pasteur, The Private Life of Bel-Ami, R.U.R., The Suicide Club, Sword in the Desert, They Shoot Horses, Don't They?, Toulouse-Lautrec, Trilby, Vincent Van Gogh
Sea Gull, The (1926) 75
Self, William 5, 323
7th Heaven (1927) 78
Seyffertitz, Gustav von 213
Shavrova, Tamara 92
Sheik, The (1921) 72
Sheldon, Willard xvii, 49, 51, 56-57, 327, 348
Shelley, Mary 124, 135, 147, 357
Sherlock Holmes (1932) 150
Ship Cafe 14, 37, 186-187, 190, 364
Ship from Macabo, The see Schlitz Playhouse of Stars: Trouble on Pier 12
shorts directed by Florey see Alice Boulden, Back in Your Own Back Yard, Bonjour, New York!, Borah Minnevitch and His Harmonica Rascals, Eddie Cantor, Fifty-Fifty, Glorifying the American Girl, Une Heureuse Intervention, Isidore a la Deveine, Isidore Sur le Lac, Johann the Coffin Maker, The Life and Death of 9413--A Hollywood Extra, Lillian Roth and Her Band, Lillian Roth and Her Piano Boys, The Loves of Zero,

The Mad Doctor, Night Club, The Pusher-in-the-Face, Skyscraper Symphony, Songs and Dances of Lilliam Roth, Songs of Alice Boulden, Tito Schipa, Trees of England, Two Sketches with Elinor Glyn, What Is "It"?
Sidney, Sylvia 192, 240
Sign of Four, The (novel) 151
Silent Thunder (novel) 148, 358
Siodmak, Curt 279, 311, 348, 376
Skyscraper Symphony (Skyscrapers) 40, 62, 79, 97-101
Slessinger, Tess 199
Small, Edward 18
Smarty 1, 13-14, 173-174, 221-224, 349, 361
Smirnova, Tania 96
Smith, C. Aubrey 180-181, 363
Smith and Dale 156
social consciousness genre 15, 20-21, 23-24, 200-201, 217-218, 220-221, 237, 240, 306; see also political concerns and attitudes
Songs and Dances of Lillian Roth 105
Songs of Alice Boulden 105
sound 104-110, 112-115, 118, 155, 275-277, 343, 347
Soutar, Andrew 148, 358
Sparkhul, Theodor 57, 209, 223, 354, 357, 368
sports 67, 184
spy genre 10-11, 16, 293
Stahl, John M. 76
Stanwyck, Barbara 16, 176, 224, 328, 362, 390
Star and the Story: The Creative Impulse, The 326, 387
Star Performance 383; see also Four Star Playhouse
Steeman, S.A. 263
Stein, Nate 92
Steiner, Max 279, 376
Stephens, Harvey 208, 367, 369, 371
Sterling Pictures 78, 354
Sternberg, Josef von 8, 59, 75, 99, 207, 336
Stewart, Donald Ogden 106
Stone, Bennie 74
Stone, George E. 232, 236, 256, 372, 375
Stone, Lewis 202, 366
Straight from the Farm (1922) 72
Struss, Karl 57, 209, 223, 365-367
studio system 5-8, 53-56, 71, 155, 186, 190, 222-225, 271, 285, 307-308, 342, 344
Study in Scarlet, A v, 10, 17, 36, 39, 45, 54-55, 60, 150-154, 206, 263, 359, 381
subjective camera 45, 172-173, 204, 211, 233
Suicide Club, The (novelette) 147
Suicide of a Hollywood Extra see The Life and Death of 9413--A Hollywood Extra
Sunset Boulevard (1950) 196
Sunshine Comedies (Al St. John) 72
Suspense 383; see also Four Star Playhouse and Schlitz Playhouse

Index

of Stars
Sutherland, A. Edward 283
Swanson, Gloria 78
Swarthout, Gladys 187
swashbucklers see adventure genre
Switzerland 66-70, 281, 347
Sword in the Desert (1949) 218, 348

Talmadge, Norma 78
Tamiroff, Akim xii, 53, 163-165, 203, 207-210, 215-216, 300, 318, 367-369, 378
Tamoff, Serge 96
Tarzan and the Mermaids 15, 289-291, 306, 377
Tashman, Lilyan 149, 358-359
Taylor, Estelle 107
Telephone Time: Chico and the Archbishop 326, 346, 387
television 51, 53, 56, 61, 315-335, 343, 345, 347-349
television awards 51, 317-320, 322-324, 330-331
Tempête (1921) 301
Ten Little Indians see And Then There Were None
Texan, The 326, 389-390
"Thanks for the Memories" (song) 212
That Model from Paris 16, 76-77, 353, 381
Thayer, Tiffany 203-204, 366
theater 52, 67, 75, 182
Theatre du Casino de Geneva 67
They Shoot Horses, Don't They? (novel) 220
39 Steps, The (1935) 237
This Way Please 14, 48, 205, 221, 367-368
Thoeren, Robert 214, 370
Thompson, Morton 240, 372
Those We Love ix, 16, 49, 148-151, 358-359
Thriller: The Incredible Doktor Markesan 12, 29-30, 38, 44, 332, 391
thriller genre 9-10, 29-30, 48-49, 155, 203-204, 208, 224, 306, 327, 331-332, 345 (see also mystery, spy, gangster and horror genres); "psychological" thriller 21-22, 269, 278, 301, 331, 344
Tiffany 76-79, 353-354, 380; see also K.B.S.
Till We Meet Again (Reunion) 4, 10, 16-17, 19-20, 25, 27, 32, 44, 190-193, 199, 214-215, 224, 249, 300, 365
Time the Comedian (1925) 76
Times So Unsettled Are 16, 25, 199-200
Tiomkim, Dimitri 289, 377
Tito Schipa 106
Tobin, Genevieve 174, 362
Toland, Gregg 84-85
Tombet Films-Geneva 68-69
Tombet, Leon 67-69
Touhy, Roger 252-255, 259, 374-375; see also Roger Touhy--Gangster

Toulouse-Lautrec, Henri 261
Tourneur, Jacques 230, 339
Trees of England (Forests of England) 121
Trevor, Claire xii, 3, 204, 367
Trilby 261, 349
Trou dans le mur, Un (1931) 156
Tufts, Sonny 302, 379
Turn of Fate, A see Alcoa/Goodyear Theater--A Turn of Fate
Twelve O'Clock High (1950) 264
Twentieth Century-Fox 61, 252-260, 263, 307-308, 325, 374-375, 380
Twilight Zone, The 331, 390, 392
   Fever, The 22, 331, 390
   Long Morrow, The 29, 49, 332-333, 392
   Perchance to Dream 22, 43-44, 238, 331, 390
Two in a Taxi 14, 231, 240, 289, 306, 372-373
Two Sketches with Elinor Glyn 105
Tyler, Tom 213, 369

Ufa studios (Neubabelsberg) 75, 121-122
Underworld (1927) 259
United Artists 78, 88, 92, 301, 303, 377-379
Universal 56, 60, 73, 75, 78-79, 124-147, 267, 291-298, 323-325, 332, 343, 348, 357-358, 377-378, 380
Untouchables: The Doreen Maney Story, The 53, 390
Upton, Gabrielle 329-330

Valentino, Rudolf 72-73, 75, 340, 352
Van Gogh, Vincent 261, 329
Van Sloan, Edward 126-127, 357, 362
Verne, Jules 66, 299, 331-332
Vicious Years, The (The Gangster We Made) 3, 6, 15, 20, 23, 32, 304, 306, 379
Victim, The (1952) see Ethel Barrymore Theater: The Victim
Victor, Henry 82, 370
Victorine, La (studios) 305
Vidor, King 6, 76, 148
Visaroff, Michael 80-81
Vitaphone see Warner Bros.
Vorkapich, Slavko 84-88, 342-343
Voyage of the Damned 228

Wagon Train 324, 327, 388
   Les Rand Story, The 330, 388
   Ruth Owens Story, The 51, 324, 331, 388
Waiting for Lefty (play) 240
Wald, Jerry 266
Wald, Malvin xvii, 240, 372

Wallace, Edgar   208-209, 368
Wallis, Hal   166, 173-174, 176, 183, 185, 218, 222-223, 261
Walt Disney Christmas Show, The   317, 383
Wanger, Walter   113, 115, 118, 195
war genre   15, 19, 24-25, 191-192, 264, 266, 306
Warner, Jack   6, 46, 48, 177, 185, 218, 260-261, 264, 270-271
Warner Bros.   1, 7, 46, 48, 148, 151, 154, 160-186, 218, 222-225, 230-231, 240-252, 260-279, 291, 307-308, 346, 348-349, 359-364, 373-376, 380-382
Warner Bros. "house style"   270-271
Washington, G.D.   156
Waycoff, Leon   see   Ames, Leon
Webb, Millard   106, 380
Weinberg, Herman G.   227, 337
Weissmuller, Johnny   289, 291, 377
Welles, Orson   6, 39, 280; see also Citizen Kane
Wells, H.G.   140
western genre   66, 326-327
Westinghouse-Desilu Playhouse: The Innocent Assassin   330-331, 389
Wetzel, Al   109
Whale, James   13, 43, 60, 124, 127-134, 146, 357; see also The Invisible Man
What Is "It"?   105
Wheeler, Joan   174, 361
White Collar Girl   346, 384
William, Warren   3, 15, 172, 183, 202, 239, 360-361, 364, 366
Williams, Lewis   74
Windsor, Marie   300, 378
Wine (1924)   75
Winters, Shelley   51, 324
Wire Service: The Johnny Rath Story   32, 331, 388
With Byrd at the South Pole (1930)   106, 380-381
Woloshin, Alexander   96, 370
Woman Disputed, The (1928)   79-80, 92, 96
Woman in Red, The   4, 16-17, 39, 176-178, 221, 224, 349, 362-363
Woman of Paris, A (1923)   283
Women Without Names   10, 17, 20, 23, 220-221, 237-238, 242, 371-372
"women's" genre   15-17, 199, 305-306, 322, 332
Wong, Anna May   44, 53, 206-207, 209-210, 359, 368-369
Woods, Donald   178, 180, 363, 379
World War I   190, 200
World War II   24-25, 186, 221-222, 231, 241, 243-244, 246, 248, 250-251
   Florey's offer of service in U.S. government filmmaking   241, 266, 291
World-Wide   see   K.B.S.
Wormwood Scrubs Murder Cases, The   10, 153, 263

Yankee Doodle Dandy (1942)   248-249, 261

Young Loretta 16, 261, 321-323, 328, 384-385; see also A Letter to
    Loretta and The Loretta Young Show

Zane Grey Theatre 319, 326, 388-390
    Sundown at Bitter Creek 331, 389
Zanuck, Darryl F. 160-162, 270
Ziv 325
Zucco, George 289, 370, 377
Zukor, Adolph 190

The following articles and chapters in books are by the author of this volume, Brian Taves, and supplement the information in **Robert Florey, the French Expressionist.**

"Robert Florey and the Hollywood Avant Garde." In Bruce Posner, ed. **Unseen Cinema: Early American Avant-Garde Film 1893-1941.** New York: Anthology Film Archives, 2001. Pp. 103-108. Translated into French by Jean-Michel Bouhours, Bruce Posner, and Isabelle Ribadeau Dumas, ed. **En Marge de Hollywood La Premiere Avant-Garde Cinematographique Americaine 1893-1941.** Paris: Musee d=Art Americain Giverny/Editions du Centre Pompidou, 2003. Pp. 104-119.

"Rebels of the Twenties." In **Le Giornate del Cinema Muto 1999 Catalogo / 18th Pordenone Silent Film Festival Catalog.** Pordenone, Italy: 1999. Pp. 71-83.

"Studio Metamorphosis Columbia's Emergence From Poverty Row." In Robert Sklar and Vito Zaggario, eds., **Mr. Capra Goes to Columbia: Authorship and the Hollywood Studio System, A Case Study.** Philadelphia: Temple University Press, 1998. Pp. 222-254.

"Robert Florey and the Hollywood Avant Garde." In Jan Christopher Horak, ed., **Lovers of Cinema: The First American Film Avant Garde, 1919-45.** Madison: University of Wisconsin Press, 1995. Pp. 94-117.

"The 'B' Film: Hollywood's Other Half." In Tino Balio, Grand Design: **Hollywood as a Modern Business Enterprise, 1930-1939.** Volume 5 of the History of the American Cinema series. New York: Charles Scribners's Sons, 1993. Pp. 313-350, 431-433.

"On the Set of A STUDY IN SCARLET (1932)." **The Armchair Detective**, 22 (Spring 1989), 142-148.

"Robert Florey, Hollywood's Premier Director and Historian." **Southern California Quarterly**, 70 (Winter 1988), 427-429. Reprinted in a special pamphlet edition.

"Charlie Dearest." **Film Comment**, 24 (March April 1988), 63-69.

"Whose Hand? Correcting a Buñuel Myth." **Sight and Sound**, 56 (Summer 1987), 210-211.

"Gathering Filmland's Forgotten for HOLLYWOOD BOULEVARD." **Classic Images**, No. 143 (May 1987), 25-27, 63.

"Universal's Horror Tradition." **American Cinematographer**, 68 (April 1987), 36-48.

"Lloyd Nolan." **Classic Images**, No. 125 (November 1985), 40.

"Letter to the Editor [on THE LIFE AND DEATH OF 9413 -- A HOLLYWOOD EXTRA (1927)]." **Framework**, Nos. 26-27 (Spring 1985), 180-182.

"Paul Ivano: Cameraman for Hollywood's Greats." **Classic Images**, No. 111 (September 1984), 30-32.

Brian Taves (Ph.D., University of Southern California) is a film archivist with the Library of Congress, and is also the author of such books as **The Romance of Adventure: The Genre of Historical Adventure Movies**; **The Jules Verne Encyclopedia**; **Talbot Mundy, Philosopher of Adventure**; **P.G. Wodehouse and Hollywood: Screenwriting, Satires, and Adaptations**; and **Thomas Ince, Hollywood's Independent Pioneer**.

www.ingramcontent.com/pod-product-compliance
Lightning Source LLC
Chambersburg PA
CBHW050511170426
43201CB00013B/1920